A

Philip E. Lilienthal

BOOK

The publisher gratefully acknowledges the generous contribution to this book provided by the Asian Studies Endowment Fund of the University of California Press Foundation.

The Graves of Tarim

THE CALIFORNIA WORLD HISTORY LIBRARY

Edited by Edmund Burke III, Kenneth Pomeranz, and Patricia Seed

1. *The Unending Frontier: Environmental History of the Early Modern World,* by John F. Richards
2. *Maps of Time: An Introduction to Big History,* by David Christian
3. *The Graves of Tarim: Genealogy and Mobility across the Indian Ocean,* by Engseng Ho

The Graves of Tarim

Genealogy and Mobility across the Indian Ocean

Engseng Ho

UNIVERSITY OF CALIFORNIA PRESS
Berkeley / Los Angeles / London

University of California Press, one of the most distinguished university presses in the United States, enriches lives around the world by advancing scholarship in the humanities, social sciences, and natural sciences. Its activities are supported by the UC Press Foundation and by philanthropic contributions from individuals and institutions. For more information, visit www.ucpress.edu.

University of California Press
Berkeley and Los Angeles, California

University of California Press, Ltd.
London, England

Library of Congress Cataloging-in-Publication Data
Ho, Engseng.
The graves of Tarim : genealogy and mobility across the Indian Ocean / Engseng Ho.
p. cm.
Includes bibliographical references and index.
ISBN-13: 978-0-520-24453-5 (cloth : alk. paper), ISBN-10: 0-520-24453-2 (cloth : alk. paper)—ISBN-13: 978-0-520-24454-2 (pbk. : alk. paper), ISBN-10: 0-520-24454-0 (pbk. : alk. paper)
1. Hadramawt (Yemen : Province)—History. 2. Hadramawt (Yemen : Province)—Emigration and immigration—History. 3. Tarim (Yemen)—Antiquities. I. Title. II. Series.

DS247.7. H33 H615 2006
953.35—dc22 2005035585

Manufactured in the United States of America

15 14 13 12 11 10 09 08 07 06
10 9 8 7 6 5 4 3 2 1

The paper used in this publication meets the minimum requirements of ANSI/NISO Z39.48–1992 (R 1997) (*Permanence of Paper*).

Dedicated to the Muwalladīn,
wherever you may be

Contents

III. RETURNS

Illustrations

Figures

Maps

Tables

Acknowledgments

The argument of this book rests on a knowledge of names, persons whom the reader will get to know in the pages to follow. The book itself rests on the knowledge and kindness of persons I came to know in the course of its research and writing.

In Hadramawt, Shaykh ʿAlī Sālim Bukayr, Muḥammad ʿAbd al-Raḥmān al-Junayd, Abū Bakr bin Shihāb, and ʿAbd al-ʿAzīz bin ʿAqīl were unstinting with the fruits of their own studies, as were Shaykh ʿAbd Allāh al-Ḥaddād, Shaykh Faḍl Bā Faḍl, ʿAbd al-Majīd al-Tamīmī, ʿAbd al-Qādir ʿAbd al-Raḥmān al-Junayd, and Saqqāf ʿAlī al-Kāf. Fayṣal Mawlā al-Duwayla and family, ʿAbd al-Raḥmān ʿAlī Bilfaqīh and family, ʿAlī Bilfaqīh, ʿAwaḍ ʿUmar bin Yamānī and family, Anwār bin Yamānī, ʿUbayd bin Ḥamdūn and family, Sālim Bā Hādī and family, ʿAbd al-Qādir al-Ḥabshī, Amīn Bā Muʾmin and family, Muḥsin al-ʿAmrī, Ṣādiq ʿAlī al-Junayd, Aḥmad Mashhūr al-Junayd and family, Fayṣal bin Yamānī, ʿAbd Allāh bin Shamlān, Shafīq al-Tamīmī and family, "Dīk" bin Masʿūd and family, ʿAlī Bahbūḥ, and ʿAbd al-Raḥmān Shāmī shared knowledge unavailable in books, laced with warm hospitality and companionship. While the keepers of the Aḥqāf manuscript and printed-book libraries in Tarīm opened up the wealth of generations, their abundant humor and insights made the hours shorter: thanks are due Shaykh ʿAlī, ʿAbd Allāh al-ʿAydarūs, Ḥusayn al-Kāf, ʿAbd al-Qādir "Jīlānī" bin Shihāb, Sālim "Bū ʿAlwī" al-Mashhūr, ʿUmar bin Shihāb. At the Sayʾūn museum and archives, ʿAbd al-Qādir al-Ṣabbān, Muḥammad al-Ḥabshī, ʿAbd al-Raḥmān al-Saqqāf, and Muḥammad al-Ṣabbān were generous. In the Nusantara, Mohsen Alkaf, Abdul Kader al-Haddad, Sheikh "Habshee" Aljuneid, Abu Bakr Al-

Mashhoor, Sharifah Noor Alkaff, Ali bin Shihab, Samhari Baswedan, and Max Yusuf Alkadrie were equally so. Meilien Ho kept the work going while war was raging.

Staff and students at the Mukallā College of Education were always patient with an unusually slow student, especially Aḥmad bin Burayk, Sālim ʿUmar al-Khuḍar, Muḥammad Saʿīd Dāʾūd, Aḥmad ʿUbaydūn, ʿAbd al-Qādir Bā ʿĪsā, ʿAbd al-ʿAzīz al-Zuhayr, Aḥmad Shaybān, and ʿAbd Allāh Bā Shammākh. Ṣāliḥ Bā Ṣurra at Aden University made Mukallā possible. In Ṣanʿāʾ, Yūsuf ʿAbd Allāh, director of the General Organization for Antiquities, Manuscripts and Museums, provided generous sponsorship and advice. The Yemen Centre for Studies and Research furnished the necessary permissions, and Khālid al-Surayḥī made it all possible. McGuire Gibson showed up in the oddest places to pluck me out of the fire, whereas Manfred Wenner was the one who threw me in. David Warburton and Noha Sadek, resident directors of the American Institute for Yemeni Studies, and Frank Mermier of the Centre Francais opened the doors of their institutes and libraries. Iris Glosemeyer's loan of a crimson MZ added an unexpected dash, while Sheila Carapico, Anna Wuerth, Chuck Schmitz, Sylvaine Camelin, and Thomas Pritzkat always kept things exciting; Lisa Wedeen made it so again. Alexander Knysh was a shaykh in Ibn al-ʿArabī and all things Hadrami. Brinkley Messick's comments at important moments provided direction and impetus. Paul Dresch must wish he'd read fewer drafts, and better ones; his own writings show why. His eye for structure and sequence were indispensable in shaping the final text. Renaud Detalle was endlessly hospitable and a *marjaʿ*. Lucine Taminian was a bottomless *baḥr* of poetry and coffee. Michael Gilsenan, a guide on open waters, was willing to fill in the gaps with Conrad. Bernard Haykel, collaborator and counselor, I don't even know how to thank; an open hand comes with depth. Kathleen Donohue was as cogent and clear on two pages as on two hundred, allying a critical eye with a generous spirit. All typos are Sophie's.

Wadad Kadi opened up the world of manuscripts and directed me to Yūsuf ʿAbd Allāh. Fred Donner wore his learning lightly and passed it on easily. Farouk Mustapha was always forgiving. Raymond T. Smith led the way on long histories of strange families, as did G. William Skinner closer to home. Marshall Sahlins encouraged structures big and small; Valerio Valeri thought genealogies were everything. Nancy Munn's blend of aesthetics and theory proved seductive. Steve Caton and Michael Herzfeld commented insightfully on early and late drafts, and Stanley Tambiah, Ajantha Subramanian, and Vince Brown did so on oral ones. Tamara Neuman's reading helped with clarity, and Morgan Liu's exemplified it. Mary Steedly and Arthur Kleinman provided intellectual succor, and Woody Watson offered comparisons from China. Nur Yalman appreciated the finer points of cross-cultural kinship, while Randy Matory's diasporic religion provided it. Sugata Bose brought the Indian Ocean close, and the work and welcome of Sumit Mandal, Azyumardi Azra, Syed Farid Alatas, and William Roff drew me to its eastern shores. Andrew Shryock's summary, students, and seminar on Middle Eastern diasporas at the University of Michigan sharpened the closing arguments, and my own students in the mobility and Middle East seminars broadened the opening ones. Readers such as Noor O'Neill, Mana Kia, Anthony Shenoda, and Dadi Darmadi made it worth the while. Dadi Darmadi and Susan Farley made the final stretch short. At the University of California Press, Stan Holwitz's wise counsel leavened the experience and the text. The Harvard Academy for International and Area Studies provided an ideal setting for writing; I thank the chairs, Samuel Huntington and Jorge Dominguez, and guardian angels Jim Clem and Beth Baiter for making my visit possible and pleasurable. The American Institute of Yemeni Studies, the Social Science Research Council, the Ford Foundation, the American Council of Learned Societies, and FedEx made the journey a reality.

Note on Dates, Abbreviations, and Transliteration

All dates are Common Era unless otherwise noted.

The text contains the following abbreviations:

b.	bin or ibn, literally "son of" in Arab names
FO	Foreign Office
IORL	India Office Records Library, United Kingdom
PRO	Public Records Office, United Kingdom
SMA	Say'ūn Museum Archive, Yemen

Because this work seeks the recuperation of connectedness—histories and geographies, families and bibliographies—I use a standardized transliteration of Arabic words and names in most cases. I make exceptions for special nouns that have established renditions in the Latin script, including the names of public figures in Malay/Indonesian. The names properly transliterated here as Ḥaḍramawt (and its adjectival form, Ḥaḍramī) and Tarīm are also not transliterated due to their frequency in the text.

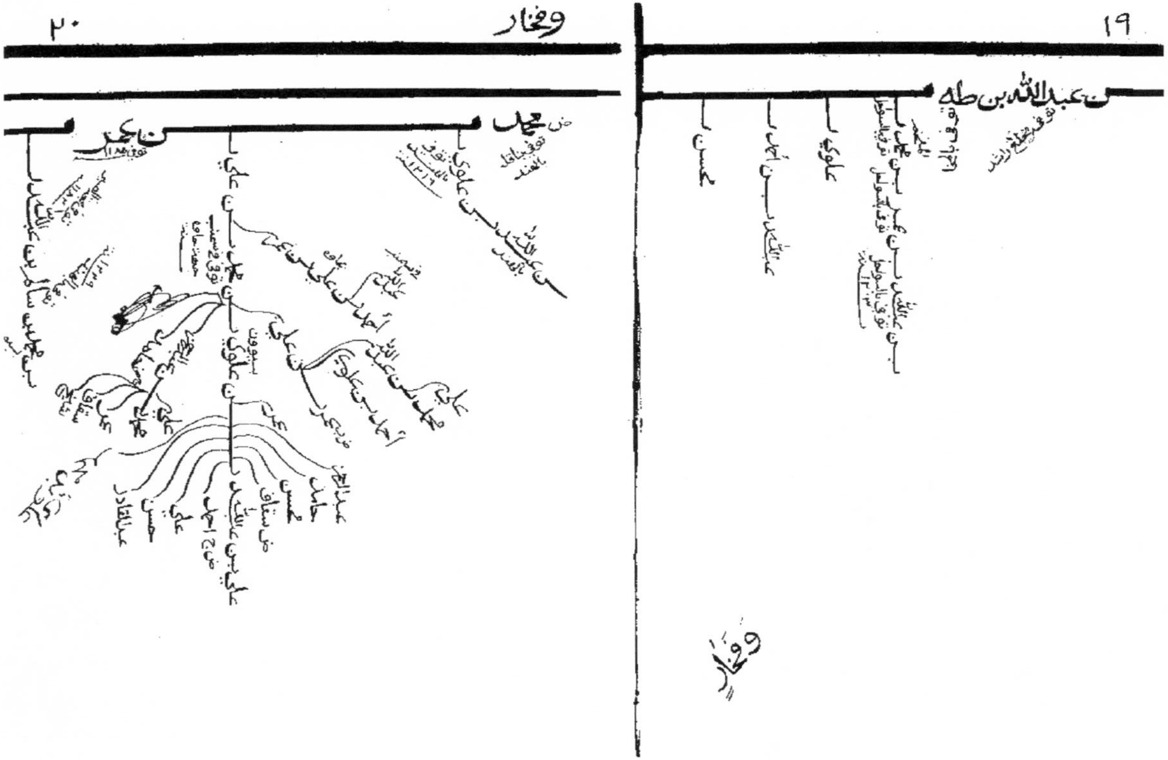

FIGURE 1. Diaspora in a genealogy, with location of places of death: India; Say'ūn; Java; Sumenep, Java; the Sawāḥil (East Africa), Mocha (Yemen).

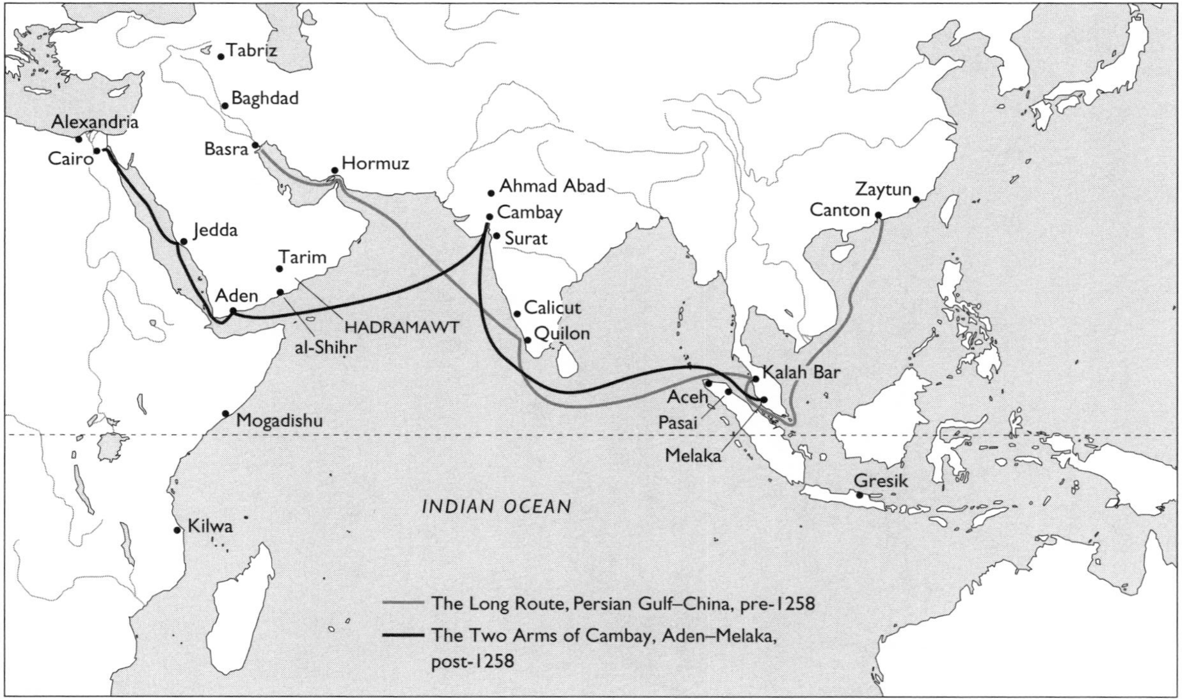

MAP 1. Trade routes across the Indian Ocean

Preface

Hadrami Society, an Old Diaspora

> And it is He who tamed the Sea, that from it you might feed on flesh tender and fresh, and pull fineries to costume yourselves with, and see the ships plying its waters. That you might desire His bounty. Perchance you would give thanks.
>
> The Holy Qur'an, The Bee (16:14).

This book tells a story of a society of persons dispersed (strewn, disseminated, scattered, settled, lost, found, drowned) around the Indian Ocean. The story is one of travel and mobility. We are emboldened in calling these persons a society, in the singular, only because they share stories about themselves and each other, many noble, but not all complimentary. We can give this society a name because many of its traveling stories begin in, and return to, a particular place. This place is the region of Ḥaḍramawt in present-day Yemen, near the South Arabian coast. Those who hail from Hadramawt call themselves Ḥaḍārima, or Ḥaḍramī in the singular. Hadramawt is a homeland for members of Hadrami society; it is intimate to some, mythical to others. Standing on its shore at the cartographic bottom of the Arabian Peninsula, one looks across the ocean seeking India and Java to the left and the coasts of East Africa, the *sawāḥil,* to the right. The Hadrami mariner Bā Ṭāyiʿ narrated a poem in each of these directions, stringing along ports like prayer beads, naming each for its patron saint: East Dīs, the wadi of ʿUmar (al-Muḥḍār al-Saqqāf); al-Mukallā, the bandar of Yaʿqūb; Burūm, the seaport of Mazāḥim; Aden, the bandar of al-ʿAydarūs; Mocha, the haven of ʿAlī (al-Shādhilī, master of coffee). Up the Red Sea coast, Jedda was named for Eve, the "grandmother" of all, thought to be buried there. As itinerary is chanted into liturgy, one learns to sail to the voice of a master as well, Bā Ṭāyiʿ's rhymes echoing between one's ears.

Places that make their living from the sea are ever aware of the capricious source of their sustenance. When the Venetians stole the remains of San Marco from Alexandria across the waters, then buried him in Venice and adorned a basilica to his glory as patron saint of their city, they proclaimed such awareness and honed that knowledge as a compass to steer their state of ships. The *Lion of San Marco,* his hind legs on the waves and his forepaws on the shore, stood as a reminder of the curious position of Venice, that improbable city perched on oak pilings, poised between land and sea, dwarf engrosser of giant empires. For Venice, the sea became a project of state, and the city joined the Doge's palace with San Marco's basilica. Venice's trading ships carried cannons, and its trading posts in the East doubled as diplomatic stations. As the partnership of flag and trade flowered in the "imperial age" of Venice during the Renaissance, Neptune and Mercury, the gods of navigation and commerce, joined San Marco in standing watch over the serenity of the maritime city-state.

Like Venice, Hadramawt is an improbable place, poised between the desert sands of the Empty Quarter and the copious waters of the Indian Ocean. Sending abroad generation upon generation of its offspring, Hadramawt too fed from the sea, costumed itself with foreign fineries, and perfumed its halls of prayer with exotic incense from points east. With a giant system of wadis irrigated by irregular rains, Hadramawt's domestic agriculture has been insufficient to feed the population in the past century, if not before. Gardens of date palms, gentleman farms forming suburbs around principal towns such as Tarim, Sayʾūn, and Shibām, are the province of those with merchant wealth from abroad. Indeed, nestled in the gardens and within earshot of the lazy thump-thumping of the old English Lister water pumps (ancient models now available new from India) are distinctly *faux* Palladian villas, mud-brick-and-plaster "wedding-cake" creations built in the early twentieth century after the fashion of colonial governments and millionaires in British India, Malaya, Singapore, and Dutch Java. Like the British and Dutch imperial seagoing economies, Hadramawt's economy echoed that of Venice and expressed its debt in the architecture of its gardens, nodding to Venice's hinterland retreat in the Veneto *terraferma*. In every case, investment in land provided new dimensions of enjoyment and status—as well as new resentments—to wealth from overseas.

Yet in a crucial respect, the Hadramis differed from their European counterparts in how they engaged the Indian Ocean. Their enterprises overseas were not backed by an equally mobile, armed state. The Portuguese, Dutch, and English in the Indian Ocean were strange new traders who brought their states with them. They created militarized trading-post empires in the Indian Ocean, following Venetian and Genoese precedents in the Mediterranean, and were wont to do business at the point of a gun. Hadramis and other non-Europeans—such as Gujaratis, Bohras, Chettiars, Buginese, and Malays—did not. Rather than elbow their way in, they comported themselves to local arrangements wherever they went. They settled and sojourned in towns big and small and entered into relations with locals that were more intimate, sticky, and prolonged than the Europeans could countenance. As well, Hadramis were drawn into dealings with the British and the Dutch, whose empires first followed their diaspora and then enveloped it. They were there before the Portuguese arrived and remained after the British left.

What did Hadramis do abroad in the five hundred years between the Portuguese and the British? Did they retain a sense of connection with the homeland or each other? Did they blend with locals abroad, turning native? Hadramis at home often viewed Hadrami society overseas with profound ambivalence. The outside, like the sea that sustains, is also a source of trouble, whence come powers that are hard to see and harder yet to contain. How can a society that engages so intensely with the outside world be so deeply distrustful of it at the same time? Such a condition is alien to many of today's societies, which are relatively new creations of liberal industrial empires of the past century and are keen to intensify the international bonds that have brought them forth. Nevertheless, one suspects that such ambivalence, a dose of cultural schizophrenia perhaps, may be common to societies that have long engaged with the outside world, whether on their own terms or not. Pluralism or paranoia? The pages that follow push at these two poles, exploring the extent of Hadramawt's engagement with the wider world as well as its distrust of that world. Within the large space created by this bifurcation of sentiments lies the experience of generations of an old diaspora, experience that may help us recognize the importance of mobility to society and think about its moral consequences. Perchance they would give thanks.

• • •

Over the past five hundred years, the many Hadramis who sailed to Bā Ṭāyiʿ's songs settled across the Indian Ocean, in coastal places like Kilwa, Lamu, Mogadishu, Aden, Mocha, Zabīd, Jedda, Cambay, Surat, Calicut, Aceh, Pattani, Melaka, Palembang, Riau, Banten, Pontianak, Makassar, and Timor. The many more Hadramis who traveled on British steamships in the past two centuries landed at the imperial ports of Dar es-Salaam, Zanzibar, Mombasa, Djibouti, Aden, Jedda, Bombay, Colombo, Penang, Singapore, Batavia, Surabaya. However these passengers traveled, most were men. Many took local wives, and their offspring became natives to these places of settlement, as well as members of the larger Hadrami society across the ocean. Hadrami society, then, is also a diaspora in the etymological sense of a scattering of seed. What matters is that the dispersed understand themselves to be linked by bonds, usually those of kinship. Such bonds exist and endure, rather than atrophy, only so long as people continue to speak, sing, recite, read, write, narrate, and otherwise represent them. Representations remind us of persons and places absent from sight; they make us mindful of them. Such representations do not always, or everywhere, last. How some people try to make them do so, why others seek to subvert them, is what we would like to know. As differences and disputes circle around how bonds of kinship are represented in diaspora, we need to study these representations. What do the traveling representations of a mobile people look like?

Of all the histories of peoples who traveled in the Indian Ocean, those of the Europeans are best known, largely because the bosses in Lisbon, London, and Amsterdam wanted to know what their motley crews were up to far away. The English East India Company called its employees "writers" and made them fill up detailed logs and journals in the heat of the tropics. The resulting writings now populate the archives of the British Library in London. With them, novelists such as Patrick O'Brian and historians such as K. N. Chaudhuri have spun vivid and compelling tales. One cannot say the same of the Gujaratis, Bohras, Banias, Chettiars, Shirazis, and Omanis who settled across the ocean. Neither can it be said of English "interlopers" who nibbled at the Honourable Company's monopoly and whose works are all the more valuable for being rare. Textual records of their experiences are not as forthcoming. The Cairo Geniza records made famous by Shlomo Dov Goitein thin out in the Indian Ocean, though they were picked up again in Amitav Ghosh's *In an An-*

tique Land and followed all the way to Malabar, ending in delicious ambiguity. In researching *The Glass Palace,* Ghosh subsequently searched through India and Southeast Asia to gather accounts of Indians who worked in and ran away from Burma as the Japanese chased out the British in the Second World War. The difference between the English and the Indians in leaving textual tracks has nothing to do with civilization or literacy. There were reasons for writing things down and for not doing so. As well, the gnawing criticism of termites played its part.

Like the English, the Hadramis wrote down many things. What they chose to write, and why, are questions this book asks. Genealogies were and remain a favorite. They are representations of kinship that command a special place in the Hadrami diaspora. Genealogy is very often a part of the stories people share in this diaspora, at times in the service of clarity and at others, of entanglement. In elemental form, as a series of linked names, a genealogy presents a linear aspect which may be pressed into service as a vehicle for narrative. The Hadrami diaspora possesses a rich literature that mobilizes genealogy toward many narrative ends. Genealogy combines with poetry, biography, history, law, novels, and prayers in the diaspora. How did such combinations come about? And why? As I pursued these questions, I was surprised to see them resolve into other questions: what, when, where—and who? As I studied the literature of the Hadrami diaspora, I began to see the formation of a canon of texts. The development of this canon seemed to draw energy from a process of hybridization, in which new genres kept combining with genealogical narratives in novel ways. Unlike some of the texts of classical Greece or modern anthropology, which progress by parricide, this canon was self-consciously accumulative, with successors acknowledging predecessors. The canon itself began to take on the appearance of a genealogy, and as its bibliography lengthened, the earlier texts seemed to rise in stature like ancestors, acquiring an aura of primordial generativity. Like genealogy, too, this movement became increasingly linear, with the many later texts pointing back to the fewer predecessors, as if to a diminishing point of perspective in a painting. The lines seemed to converge on the Hadrami town of Tarim, specifically on the graves of Tarim. Our story of the Hadrami diaspora begins there, with the first section of this book looking at the concept of burial. Burial is the act of combining a place, a person, a text, and a name at the gravestone. This simple act carries great creative, communicative potential. It gets things moving.

Linearity, of course, is the normal path of genealogy, and for linear paths to end in one place is common. Genealogy is often a narrative of origins, synthesizing arboreal metaphors that are as powerful as they are clichéd: tree, branches, roots, soil. The Hadrami lines of descent converge at the graves of Tarim and continue back to Muḥammad, the Prophet of Islam. The genealogy is thus made to bear a weighty narrative burden, becoming a vehicle for the onward movement of Islam. Anyone who finds himself or herself within this genealogy could be pressed into service. The texts that carry this message are themselves portable and travel, creating a world that expands and envelops persons within its ken.

But in travel, linearity is not everything. For just as these texts were hybrids, some of their authors turned out to be creoles, Hadramis born in the diaspora to foreign mothers. To take these texts and their authors seriously, one cannot focus solely on patrilineality, or Hadrami fathers from the homeland, as the genealogies seem to insist. The developed canon was not already contained in the ancestral texts, like an oak in an acorn. Rather, the hybrid texts by creole authors are understandable only through further exploration of their contents and the circumstances surrounding their composition. In other words, the canon incorporated contingency, the real-world blending of history, geography, and biography as people lived it abroad. In texts, patrilineality of the homeland and contingency of the diaspora overseas found ways of cohabiting. Yet while the tensions within that cohabitation are visible in the texts, they did not in themselves generate the movement of the canon, the change it underwent as it developed.

The textual canon of the Hadrami diaspora did not simply grow along internal lines, even if it came to resemble a genealogy. Instead, it acquired force and forward movement from local circumstances in the diaspora, from interchanges with foreign places and peoples. To trace the development of the canon through historical time thus requires us to explore the movement of the diaspora through geographical space. "Genealogical Travel," the middle section of this book, follows the diaspora as it moved outward, to Surat in India in the sixteenth and seventeenth centuries, to Mecca a little later, and then to the Malay Archipelago in the eighteenth to twentieth centuries. In these places, new societies were forming, and movement of Hadramis into them was part of the process. Participation gave Hadramis new diasporic experiences that shaped the texts they wrote. Indeed, their genealogies are not simply linear narratives that point back to origins; they appear to become transcultural languages within which translation is already taking place. We see accounts of strange customs, mothers' brothers, granny's delectable dishes: matrilateral relations, affinity, and alliance were other kinds of stories the genealogies told. While

Europeans who were mobile in the Indian Ocean brought only their genes, Hadramis carried along their genealogies as well. The consequences of this difference were profound and profoundly shaped the identifications, life chances, and experiences of Hadrami offspring. An examination of these experiences concludes the central section of the book and carries us to the third and final section, "Returns."

Burial is a place-making project that tends to bend diasporic journeys. Successful burials establish pilgrimage as an important form of travel. Pilgrimage becomes a highly developed genre in the Hadrami canon and shapes the diaspora with the idea of return. In the final section, we follow the creole offspring home to Hadramawt in a return movement. In the lives of repatriated creoles, the genealogies that traveled abroad were not only a transcultural language but a moral one. Hadrami migrations throughout the Indian Ocean were self-consciously linked with the propagation of Islam. This mission was written into the canonical texts, and the genealogies going back to the prophet Muḥammad ran through foundational figures, some of whom Bā Ṭāyiʿ invoked as patron saints of ports in his poems. Travel accounts by creoles who were born abroad often characterize journeys to Hadramawt as pilgrimages, so itineraries became means of moral cultivation. Movement within a genealogical text connects generations and creates obligations and exchanges between them. Beyond the text, returns and the exchanges they entail are part of broader journeys of pilgrimage. Like genealogy, pilgrimage is movement given moral meaning: the former gains meaning through time; the latter, across space.

This final section of the book looks at how the moralization of movement shapes the experiences and itineraries of returnees in Hadramawt. Because pilgrimage is a privileged arena that moralizes the movement of return, it provides a language for returns of other kinds as well. One may return from a career abroad or to a homeland one has never seen. One may return in triumph, in shame, or unnoticed. Returns may be from exile after a change in regime at home. Or they may *be* exile, after a change of regime abroad. Because return as pilgrimage is a language of morality, it provides a language for politics as well. The last chapters of the book document how various categories of people returned from the diaspora when political regimes changed in the homeland. The introduction of colonial rule in the 1930s was such a change, as was the demise of socialist government in the early 1990s. The moral language of pilgrimage has something to say about the politics of these returns. And in the process, the graves of Tarim, which stand as the object of pilgrimage *par excellence* for diasporic Hadramawt, have become caught up in a form of politics that seeks to revise the very language of morality itself.

As a place that brings together persons and texts, the grave has become the focus of an excess, the meeting point of many journeys traveled by mobile persons and mobile texts. We have said that travel changes textual traditions; it changes persons as well. At the graves of Tarim, where these changes meet, volatile forces gather, threatening to destroy the very gravestones that draw them in. Despite its storied place in the diaspora, the homeland is no longer a point where only lines of descent, wealth, and nostalgia converge, but also a place where incompatible projects and thoughts come together. Perhaps it always was that way.

PART ONE

Burial

CHAPTER I

The Society of the Absent

In a society of migrants, what is important is not where you were born, but where you die. This, if nothing else, makes a diaspora entirely different from a nation, both in concept and in sentiment. Persons belong to nations by virtue of being born into them. Individuals claim entitlement issuing from place of birth. The *nation* itself takes its name from the act of giving birth, *nasci*.

For migrants, by contrast, place of death is important because it often becomes the site of burial. Tombstones abroad acknowledge the shift in allegiance—from origins to destinations—that migrants take whole lifetimes or more to come to terms with. Where shall I be buried? Did the deceased leave instructions? In the old days, when migration was a journey to one's fate, that locational shift within individual consciousness marked the larger turn of the generations, from ancestors to descendants. Graves, while they are endpoints for migrants, are beginnings for their descendants, marking the truth of their presence in a land. For many diasporas, then, graves are significant places. Abroad, migrants who could no longer be close to their parents can be visited by their own children. Graves provide a ready point of return in a world where origins keep moving on.

A gravestone is a sign whose silent presence marks an absence. In this, the idea of a grave comprehends the many experiences of migration much better than that of "globalization," which loudly shouts its presence everywhere. Devices for speed allow persons to appear in many places at once: as voices in telephones, faces on the Internet, and bodies hurtling along in supersonic jets. In contrast to globalization's industrial instantaneity, diaspora is of long duration. Migration takes place over aeons.

Its time is reckoned in generations, with only four or five generations per century. How long do immigrants take to be assimilated? Some never are. Those who do, disappear. Absence, rather than presence, everywhere shapes diasporic experience.

While globalization denies absence by rushing around to cover it up, diasporas do the opposite. They acknowledge absence and chronically explore its meanings and its markings, such as at the grave. Is the absence of the dead forever? Will they come back, or will we join them? Is the absence of emigrants permanent? Will they come back, or will we join them? In old diasporas, questions of absence never go away; they continue to provoke responses each generation. Indeed, the sharing of such questions, and arguments over them, create and demarcate a society that one might call a diaspora. In this sense, a diaspora is not unlike a religion.[1]

For diasporas, as for religions, absence can be highly productive. Absence may make the heart grow fonder, but it also licenses new vices away from knowing eyes; teaches new skills; generates letters and poems; sends money, ideas, spouses, children, and novelties home; and plots triumphant returns. Death and departure cause obituaries and genealogies to be written, as they do tombstones. Etched on paper, names become mobile and acquire new lives, circulating beyond the grave. Like religions, diasporas act more slowly than globalization. But that may be because they expand the time and space of social life, rather than compress them. This is particularly true of diasporas of long standing.

The idea of time-space compression has been developed by David Harvey as a distinctive feature of capitalist postmodernity (Harvey 1989). Since the early 1990s, a revamped interest in diasporas has cast them in this hypermodern light, emphasizing an ease of mobility and omniscience approaching what used to be said of saints and gods. Such views of diaspora ride on the wave of a U.S.-dominated international order and technology regime that has been declared triumphant since the breakup of the Soviet Union. In this sense, the recent multiplication of diasporas, as

1. Judaism, the quintessential "religion of the book" is usually thought of as a diaspora as well, one founded specifically on exile. According to the *Oxford English Dictionary,* the term *Diaspora* was adopted into English in the late nineteenth century from the Greek of Deuteronomy (28:25), referring to the dispersal of the Jews after the Captivity. *Diaspora* in the sense of exile entered the English language in a moment of high nationalism and has been associated with its sentiments ever since. As exile, diaspora has been thought of as an abnormal condition. Nevertheless, a number of recent works argue for thinking of diaspora as a normal state of affairs in a Jewish tradition shaped by vital interchanges with others over millennia (Boyarin and Boyarin 2002; Ezrahi 2000; Gruen 2002).

registered in scholarship, should be seen not as the demise of the nation-state, but as a loosening of the post–World War II U.N. settlement, which sought to insert nations into a fixed configuration of mostly new, independent states polarized across the Yalta Line between the United States and the Soviet Union. Since the dismantling of the latter, scholars have studied diasporas as part of a larger, contemporary phenomenon called globalization, the economic *nom de guerre* of American triumphalism (Schivelbusch 2003: 291).[2] In this presentist mode, problems of absence often find solutions in the products of Microsoft and Boeing. As Ong's guerilla transnationalist overseas Chinese capitalist quips, "I can live anywhere in the world, but it must be near an airport" (Ong 1993: 41). Less optimistic observers see American-led neoliberalism as creating the problem by impoverishing nations (Johnson 2000; Stiglitz 2002), and emigration to America becomes one solution. Because America provides both the problem and its solution, aspiring nations seek America, and new diasporas thereby come into being.[3] The puzzle for theory becomes one of finding sources of autonomy, diasporic or otherwise, within the tight American embrace. In this compressed world, the dreamy aspirations of diasporic emigrés somehow mutate into nasty chauvinisms. The earnings of Indian millionaires in California's Silicon Valley and Irish working men in Roxbury, Massachusetts, fuel intractable ethnic conflicts back home. Recidivist long-distance nationalisms may travel far, but they hardly expand the time and space of social life (Anderson 1998; Schiller and Fouron 2001). In the global village, they narrow rather than expand the space for internal debate. In old diasporas, in contrast, the space for internal debate is often a large one, as the case below suggests.

A Case of Grave Destruction

In the early morning hours of 2 September 1994, some two thousand men armed with shovels, pickaxes, assault weapons, rocket-propelled grenades, and explosives descended on the grave complex of Abū Bakr al-ʿAydarūs in Aden. Al-ʿAydarūs is commonly held to be the patron saint *(walī)* of

2. Globalization became the master frame for diaspora studies in the 1990s, and not surprisingly, migrations to the United States predominate (Cohen 1997; Green 1997; Harper 1997; Humphrey 2000; Jain 1998; Jusdanis 1996; Kearney 1995; Nurse 1999; Ong and Nonini 1997; M. Smith 1994; Werbner 1999; Wong 1997).

3. That this is a phenomenon of all diasporic roads leading to the new Rome is brought out in debates between scholars of American foreign policy, who argue about whether

Aden, and the pilgrimage to his tomb is one of the largest festivals in the annual life of the city, drawing tens of thousands. So closely is he identified with Aden that he is commonly referred to simply as al-ʿAdanī, "the Adeni." The Adeni died in 1508, and his tomb rests with those of companions under a cupola in Crater, the old center of the city nestled within the rim of an extinct volcano. Arriving at the Adeni's sanctuary, the armed men found themselves unopposed and set to work in groups. Graves were exhumed and their bones burnt. Into the flames went the wooden ark built over the saint's grave, together with the elaborate, five-hundred-year-old wooden doors to the sanctuary. When I saw the place a few weeks later, the old doors had been replaced by plywood and were secured with deadbolt and padlock. All that remained of the ark was a small lattice window with the words "In the Name of God the Merciful, the Compassionate" carved into its lintel. Now restored to the foot of the Adeni's grave, it stood there precariously balanced, a delicate testament to the affections the saint still commands.

The destruction was not a rampage; it showed every sign of systematic action. The sanctuary's keepers recounted how the attackers had examined the books in the sanctuary one by one, separating out for burning those inscribed as gifts in perpetuity *(waqf)* to the sanctuary. Even copies of the Qur'an were consigned to the fire in this way. Outside, the desecrators did not spare the graves of the common people. The headstones of tombs in the large graveyard out front were broken, giving the impression of a field of decapitated bodies strangely arrayed in rows. A smaller graveyard in one corner resembled a rubbish dump, littered with broken stones and planks. A bulldozer had apparently been brought in and put to work there, leveling the graves. The object of destruction was not only the saint but the community that had gathered around him.

The attack on the Adeni's grave had an electric effect elsewhere in the country. In Hadramawt, armed guards were immediately posted around the clock at the graveyards and tombs of other saints. Nevertheless, further incidents of tomb desecration occurred, leading to fatal clashes in the town of Tarim half a year later.[4] The visiting of graves was obviously a matter that engendered violent debate. Why? We will not try to say that

immigrant diasporic minorities distort (T. Smith 2000) or promote (Shain 1999) American national interests abroad.

4. "Wary Calm in Hadramawt after Clash and Two Fatalities," *Al-Ḥayāt,* 27 April 1995, pp. 1, 6.

FIGURE 2. Community of pilgrimage. Mosque-domed tomb complex of the Adeni, with graves in foreground denuded of headstones after 1994 desecration. Photo by B. Haykel and the author.

the destruction of graves was about something else, such as political disputes or economic interests. Rather, we will begin with what is seen and heard and assume that it was about the graves themselves.

These graves are, above all, sites of pilgrimage *(ziyāra, ḥawl)*. As such, they lie within circuits of movement. First is the movement of persons. People move for many reasons; their itineraries are numerous and so are the durations of travel. Subsequent chapters trace the curves of these movements of persons. Second, pilgrimage sites are located within the movements of texts. These texts may be pilgrimage manuals and prayer litanies compiled from other texts—such as the Qur'an, poetry, genealogies, and biographies—that connect the names of the saints to others. At the graves, these names of persons dead and gone become embodied in the voices of reciters and ring forth again in prayers and poems. Subsequent chapters follow the movements of these texts as they travel through countries, genres, and representational media. The graves of saints are places where these mobile persons and mobile texts meet. A pilgrimage is a return to a place. Each return is different because the events of each journey away and back are different. Each pilgrim brings new experiences to a place. These pilgrimage centers do not reveal their secrets when reduced to the usual rea-

FIGURE 3. Silk-draped ark over the Adeni's tomb in happier times. Photo purchased by the author at Hūd pilgrimage.

sons of politics or economics. They are better approached as places of increase. While tombstones are mostly signs of absence, and mostly silent, at times of pilgrimage they are noisy with the sounds of many presences. Movement makes all the difference. We cannot understand the grave, the destination, without paying attention to the journey beyond it.

The controversy over the graves may thus be viewed with profit, more generally, as having to do with issues of mobility. This book presents the results of research on one field of mobility, that of the Hadrami diaspora across the Indian Ocean. The material focuses on three moments—burial, travel, and return—that are conceptually separate yet are parts of a continuously connected process of movement.

FIGURE 4. The Adeni's tomb after the desecration in 1994. Photo by B. Haykel and the author.

Scholars often see mobility as an attribute of modernity and tend to associate it with the rise of the West (Asad 1993; Braudel 1992; Hegel and Hoffmeister 1975; Lerner 1964; McNeill 1963). Thought by westerners to be open, adaptable, and dynamic, Western societies and Western individuals were, in Lévi-Strauss's terminology, historically "hot." Non-Western societies, in contrast, were historically "cold." Anthropologists since Lévi-Strauss have sought to show that societies outside the West also had history (Sahlins 1985; Wolf 1982). More recently, they have also sought to show that non-Western societies are mobile as well (Appadurai 1988). But in doing so, they have largely documented the mobility of non-Western societies only in recent times, and in Western-pioneered vehicles that are overwhelmingly technological and modern (Appadurai 1996; Augé 1995; Bauman 2000; Clifford 1997; Hannerz 1996). For reasons yet to be explained, the new anthropology of mobility has reintroduced a teleology of progress that had previously been derided and, so it seemed, discarded. Like the early-twentieth-century Italian Futurists, this technological mobility of modernism is again obsessed with speed. Its compression of time creates a bias away from absence toward presence.[5] It ignores absence and has difficulty recognizing ways of effecting presence that take time. Yet societies, cultures, and religions have been mobile for a long time. Before modernism, experiences of mobility involved complex and subtle interplays between absence and presence in many dimensions: tactile, visual, auditory, affective, aesthetic, textual, and mystical. Beyond the urban sway of modernism, they still do (Helms 1988; Munn 1986; Myers 1986; Rosaldo 1980; Tsing 1993).

To understand why violent controversy erupted at the grave of the Adeni in Aden in 1994, we need to explore how mobility—how absence as well as presence—is experienced in these dimensions. The Adeni's troubles are especially instructive for us because they are rooted in presences that developed over long stretches of time. They are "hot" historically, politically, and discursively. They are rooted in the presences and absences of a diaspora that arose in the past half-millennium, in Arabia and the Indian Ocean. This diaspora was mobile before Columbus went to America. It was present in Calicut on the pepper coast of India, before Vasco da Gama rounded the Cape of Good Hope and arrived there to find a wealthy, vibrant community of transregional Muslim merchants. In the next section, let us consider a number of spaces and times through which explanations for the Adeni's troubles might move.

Explanations

The visiting of graves is a common legal and ritual site on which boundaries between Sufis and their fundamentalist detractors take shape in Is-

5. Theorists of media have long recognized that each medium of communication produces a bias toward one of the bodily senses (Innis 1950; McLuhan 1964; W. J. Ong 1982). The printed text effects a profoundly visual orientation, for example, while electronic media create a virtual aural sensorium. Anthropologists of postmodern mobility, who have an interest in all media, exhibit a bias toward the whole body itself, a sort of writ of ethnological habeas corpus, which, as happens, has been a hallmark of the Malinowskian tradition all along.

lamic societies. The divisions grow up around questions such as: Can a dead person hear a supplicant? Does she/he have power to benefit a supplicant? If we attribute this power to humans, and dead ones at that, are we usurping what belongs to God alone? What is the maximum height to which a tombstone can be raised—to prevent its becoming an idol?

Disagreement about such issues creates the divisions we see within one discursive tradition. The process gives rise to standard accusations and standard rebuttals. The question of mediation, *tawassul,* for example, asks, Is it legitimate for a person to mediate between God and someone else? Close on the heels of *tawassul* usually comes another question, that of *istighātha,* seeking assistance: Can one legitimately seek assistance from the dead? The answers that people develop for these questions stand within one discursive tradition in the sense that they draw on the same texts, authorities, and assumptions to a degree that is seldom acknowledged.

The vandals who smashed the gravestones in 1994 answered a resounding No! to these questions by their actions. In reply, partisans of the saint, although traumatized by the physical force accompanying that interdiction, motioned to other, less visible forces to prove their point. They said that the vandals had rigged the dome with explosives, but the explosives had mysteriously failed to detonate. They pointed out that the desecrators who had a hand in exhuming the graves died within those graves in subsequent battles with government troops. And a final triumph was that one of the fundamentalists was injured and paralyzed in the violent course of events, and his mother now came to the saint seeking forgiveness and assistance for her son.

The division can be expressed within a textual world, as one between those who read literally (thus the term *fundamentalists, uṣūlī,* to describe those who narrow and pare down to fundamental sources, *uṣūl*, the number of texts and their meanings) and those who provide wide latitude for interpretation, including "auditions," *samāʿ*, of the rhyme and musical performance of texts, such as Sufis. At one level, then, the violence at the Adeni's tomb complex is part of a common and widely staged debate with textual referents (Haykel 2003; al-Ḥibshī 1976; de Jong 1999; Knysh 1997; Memon 1976; Peskes 1999; Sirriyeh 1999).

The extraordinary feature of the attack on the graves was the scale of the destruction and its organization, inviting historical comparisons (El Amrousi 2001: 174–75; de Jong and Radtke 1999: 1). In the early nineteenth century, as northern Arabians imbued with the literalist, fundamentalist ideas of Wahhabism conquered Arabia and created a state, they smashed tombs and sacred places in Hadramawt (bin Hāshim 1948: 120;

al-Kindī 1991: 321), as well as in Iraq and the Hejaz (El Amrousi 2001: 10–54; Ibn Bishr 1982: 280, 288; Daḥlān 1887: 278–79), just as the early Muslims had smashed idols in the time of the Prophet. While the contentious discourse of grave visitation is generic and everyday, individual utterances may be loud enough to register as historical events. In the Saudi-Wahhabi case, the destruction of tombs of saints and prophets was a speech-act that inaugurated a state.

So why Aden 1994? Because the destruction of the Adeni's grave in that year essentially buried a state, the Democratic Republic of Yemen, which had seceded from a united Yemen during the Yemeni civil war of 1994. Apart since the British occupation of Aden in 1839, northern and southern Yemen had remained separate states after the independence of the South in 1967. A Cold War border divided the northern, U.S.-leaning Republic of Yemen from the southern, Soviet ally, the People's Democratic Republic of Yemen. The two fell into uneasy unity in 1990, after the fall of the Berlin wall. This unity was disrupted when civil war broke out in May 1994, and southern leaders formed a separate state, with the "People" expunged from the old name. They thereby repudiated socialism and sought entry into the fold of the bourgeois democracies. In the final stages of that war, Aden suffered a prolonged siege, which lifted in early July when northern tanks rolled into the city, ending the fighting. The Adeni's tomb was destroyed two months after southern capitulation and seemed like a final act in the hostilities. This impression was plausible given that northern tanks had made a special effort to blast the unusual, oversized graves of socialist martyrs, each topped by a prominent red star, on the way south to Aden. In the fighting, northern forces had the help of auxiliaries from fundamentalist groups, including the veteran "Afghan Arab" fighters home from their victory over the Soviets, so the Adeni's tomb was thought to be spoils for them. In this reading, the specifically historical scale and timing of the Aden tomb destruction resides within the politics of states and Cold War borders.

Yet the shapes of those states and their borders are hardly clear because they are porous to religious debates and sectarian rivalry. The Adeni's partisans noted that some sermons in Riyadh, such as those of one Sulaymān Fahd, supported the attack on the Adeni's tomb. In northern Yemen, Muqbil al-Wādiʿī, the influential leader of a fundamentalist movement in Yemen and beyond (Haykel 2002), had voiced his support for the action on cassette tapes, which were widely circulated. In response, the head *(manṣab)* of the Adeni's sanctuary, one of his descendants who stood as surrogate *(qāʾim bi-l-maqām)* for him, issued a written response; northern Zaydis, who themselves opposed Muqbil al-Wādiʿī, published this response. The *manṣab* received great expressions of support from individuals and organizations in Saudi Arabia, and from the governments of Abu Dhabi, Oman, and Kuwait. The foreign minister of Oman offered to finance the rebuilding of the complex.

In its moment of vulnerability and exposure, something of the transregional reach of the Adeni's grave was revealed. Persons absent and far away showed their interest in the events surrounding it. The grave became a site of contention among constituencies whose power and reach were transregional, even international. Among these social actors, states and religious movements were visible and easily recognized players. Less easy to see was the constituency of the saint, the Adeni, the absent actor at the center of events. His grave was able to play host to such wide-ranging rivalries only because it projected some sort of power, influence, or meaning over equally large geographies. What, then, was and is, the nature and extent of the Adeni's constituency?

The Adeni is, in the first instance, a migrant. He was born in Tarim, Hadramawt, in a family of sayyids, descendants of the prophet Muḥammad. Tarim houses the largest population and graveyard of sayyids in Hadramawt and southern Yemen and is a center of sayyid activity. Collectively, these sayyids descend from one person, Aḥmad bin ʿĪsā, who arrived in Hadramawt from Basra in Iraq in the tenth century. This founder of sayyid presence in Tarim, in Hadramawt, and in southern Yemen more generally, is known by the epithet al-Muhājir, the Migrant. The term resonates in Islamic discourse because the Prophet himself founded the original community of believers when he emigrated from his hometown, Mecca, to safety. The Muslim calendar begins with this migration as its Year One.

When the Adeni went to Aden in 1484, the city was a burgeoning port hosting transregional trade between Europe and Asia. The commercial activity was accompanied by heightened religious activity in the region (al-Ḥibshī 1976; al-Khazrajī 1914a; Knysh 1999b). The Adeni traveled around the region—to Ethiopia, Mecca, Medina, and northern Yemen—and became well known throughout. He is credited with converting communities of Ethiopians to Islam. When he died and was buried in Aden, his grave became a point of ritual focus for a growing city of Muslims who had come from elsewhere. Weber has defined a city as a place whose residents come from elsewhere. This description has fit Aden over long periods of its history. Even the rulers in the Adeni's time, the Rasulid sultans, were foreigners. That the annual pilgrimage to the Adeni's grave takes place on the thirteenth day of the Islamic month Rabīʿ al-Thānī seems fitting. This date is not the day he died, which is the normal day of celebration at saints' festivals, but the day he entered Aden.

The Adeni's migration to Aden, then, echoes the migration of Aḥmad bin ʿĪsā the Migrant to Tarim. The two men's lineage and graves provide a Prophetic focus for a new community. Following the Adeni, other members of his lineage migrated across the Indian Ocean, to East Africa, western India, and Southeast Asia. Throughout this region, the graves of members of this lineage have become pilgrimage destinations. They are explicitly connected to each other by elaborate genealogical books and charts prominently displayed at the tombs and in homes. The graves share common rituals and liturgical manuals, and some of their annual pilgrimages—such as those of Ḥabīb Ṣāliḥ in Lamu, Kenya; Ḥabīb ʿAlī al-Ḥabshī in Sayʾūn, Hadramawt; and Ḥabīb ʿAlwī bin ʿAlī al-Ḥabshī at Masjid Riyāḍ in Solo, Indonesia—are synchronized on 20 Rabīʿ al-Thānī annually. The Adeni's grave is the first of such pilgrimage destinations outside of Hadramawt and thus has become a point of return for subsequent pilgrimage centers across the ocean.

The Adeni was born in Tarim but died in Aden. It was at the place of death and burial that he became famous, the focus of pilgrimage and controversy. The same is true of those who followed him across the Indian Ocean. In all these cases, what is important is not where they were born but where they died and were buried. Seen in this way, the Adeni, his saintly colleagues, and their graves were not simply like a diaspora but indeed gave representational shape to one.

In 1994, this diaspora included a majority of the cabinet of the southern secessionist state. When leaders announced the new state of the Democratic Republic of Yemen during the war, with its capital in Aden, observers noted that nine of the sixteen cabinet members were from Hadrami sayyid lineages, including the president, his deputy, the prime minister, and holders of the all-important finance and oil portfolios. The northern media took this array of Hadramis as proof that the secession was run by a narrow cabal of *ancien régime* elements who harkened to the days of British colonialism. Darker, more muted mutterings saw a contemporary Saudi hand behind this fragmenting of Yemeni territorial integrity. The League of the Sons of Yemen, the secessionist vice president ʿAbd al-Raḥmān al-Jufrī's party, was a direct resuscitation of the preindependence League of the Sons of South Arabia, which had comprised pro-British elites such as sultans, sayyids, and urban notables. Indeed, the party was commonly referred to as "the League" (al-Rābiṭa), eliding the distinction between old and new. Despite having spent a quarter century in exile in Saudi Arabia in opposition to the socialist government of South Yemen, al-Jufrī mysteriously surfaced in Aden from Saudi Arabia during the war and took charge of its defense. The very idea of this staunchly antisocialist businessman barking out orders to armed socialist cadres was one of the eye-openers of the war and strengthened the perception of a Saudi hand at work. The secessionist president, ʿAlī Sālim al-Bīḍ, had abruptly abandoned the capital of Aden to sit out the war in Hadramawt, inexplicably leaving the defense of the capital city to al-Jufrī. It was widely believed that Saudi Arabia had always coveted an outlet to the Arabian Sea, from the time H. St.-John Philby embarked on a long trek to the southern coast of Hadramawt from Riyadh in colonial days. A deal must have been cut between the secessionists and the Saudis, with al-Jufrī as the point man. Furthermore, in this view, al-Jufrī did not act alone but had behind him the Hadramis of Saudi Arabia, the largest and wealthiest concentration of Hadramis in the diaspora today. The separation of South from North Yemen, then, was not so much a secession as an annexation of the Hadrami homeland by its diaspora. This reunion of Hadrami people and land amounted to a plan for the fragmentation of the South, with Hadramawt going its own way as a newly minted province of Saudi Arabia. The idea was not entirely far-fetched because some individuals abroad, such as the foreign ministers of Oman and Indonesia, were in a position to help secure international ratification. Like the secessionist leaders, both ministers were of Hadrami sayyid descent, the latter even being a cousin of the secessionist prime minister. On the ground, bedouin and other Hadramis on the border between Saudi Arabia and Hadramawt had already been receiving Saudi identification papers for years. In a remote place like Kharkhīr, a desolate sand dune near the Empty Quarter, the Saudis had set up a bedouin chief with a building, gas station, and tents. For ten thousand shillings one could get a ride there and apply for Saudi papers, upon answering questions such as where the local watering holes for goats and camels were and who owned them. The word was that if and when a border dispute were to arise, a plebiscite would reveal the residents to be Saudis, having possession of Saudi papers.

There were other, less alarmist theories about the composition of the secessionist cabinet. It was all easily explained: the core of the secessionist leaders was those who had run the country before unification with the North in 1990. They were simply picking up where they had left off when unity became untenable. They had emerged as the leaders of South Yemen only because the Yemeni Socialist Party, which ruled the South until unification, had been rent by regionalist factionalism. Throughout the southern state's postcolonial history, its leadership had mostly been in the hands of a dominant region. A series of internal purges and struggles in 1969, 1972–73, 1978–79, and 1986 (and 1993–94, forming a curious, seven-year cycle of bloodletting) had successively lopped off the heads of the party, replacing one regional elite with another. In socialist parlance, "the revolution eats its own." Never unified before independence (no road even connected the whole country; the British administration made do with comparatively cheap air-force transport), the country was most united immediately after independence. Subsequently, each region whose leaders were defeated in national contest fell away. The Hadramis ascended to rule in the last bloody putsch, of 1986, simply because they had not stuck their necks out throughout the history of southern power struggles. Hadrami sayyids in the cabinet were there not because they were sayyids but because they were well-qualified members of a generation who had received a modern education. They had been bright young students sent to Cairo to study in the 1960s and had returned to take part in building the new, independent state, serving party and country until they were thrust into leadership positions in 1986.

Other theories emerged as well, more conspiratorial, ambitious, nuanced, confused, and complicated—more cycles within cycles. What concerns us here is that regardless of the comings and goings of factions, interests, elites, and cliques—and of genealogical, sectarian, regional, ideological, or generational groupings—a common front appeared to line up at the critical moment: southern, separatist, sayyid. In this sense, the Adeni lying in his grave under a cupola could easily have been one of them as well. The attack on his tomb, the questions about who he was, what he stood for, which side he stood on, and the ambiguities surrounding these questions, were launched into discourse. These questions deepened, intensified, and added to the talk about sayyids, about strange absences and presences, about socialism, religion, morality, and about relations between North and South. Such talk was already making southern Yemen in general, and Hadramawt in particular, a very "hot" place. The attack on the Adeni was an "incitement to discourse" (Foucault 1990: 17), one in a string.

The pilgrimage to the Adeni's tomb that year was carried out on schedule on the thirteenth of the month of Rabīʿ al-Thānī. In 1994, this day was 16 September, two weeks after the attack on the tomb. The victorious president of Yemen, the northern ʿAlī ʿAbd Allāh Ṣāliḥ, personally

FIGURE 5. Community of cadres. Graves of socialist martyrs on a ridge along the revolutionary mountains overlooking Aden. Photo by B. Haykel and the author.

guaranteed security for the event and commanded that it proceed. About three thousand pilgrims showed up, far fewer than the usual number. But the city of Aden was grateful for the little mercies after the war, siege, and defeat. The saint's surrogate thanked the president for his magnanimity. Pilgrims thanked the saint for surviving the president's guns, or the quarter century of socialist rule, or the armed fundamentalists, depending on whom you talked to.

Though the Adeni had been dead for five hundred years, he could command a contemporary following and stand at the center of a swirl of violent conflicts. His was an absence of monumental proportions, one that resounded across countries and centuries.

Diaspora and Experiences of Absence

There are smaller absences as well. While the grand absence of someone like the Adeni commands pilgrims once a year in large numbers, the smaller absences of commoners and one's family members are chronic, everyday affairs. Yet they too can be highly significant. This simple matter is often overlooked. Contemporary studies of diasporas seldom appreciate the degree to which absence shapes diasporic experience. To be in one place is to be absent everywhere else. Moving between places, mobility leaves in its wake a trail of absences. Important persons in one's life may be far away and hard to reach. When a mobile person leaves behind dependents, his or her absence may loom large in their daily existence.

The following story illustrates the power of such absences. Every day, Muḥammad wishes his two brothers were in Hadramawt. Muḥammad came to his father's hometown in Hadramawt from Uganda when his father died, killed in Idi Amin's purges. His Swahili mother had remarried, and he took advantage of free air passage provided by the South Yemeni government for its nationals when Idi Amin began expelling Indians and Arabs from Uganda. He knew his father had sent money home to Hadramawt. The family had used this money to buy pumps and open up farmland, and Muḥammad hopes to claim his inheritance. His father's brother, who runs the affairs of the family back home, was welcoming when he came, even arranging for him a marriage to a particularly lovely cousin. But try as he might, Muḥammad has not been able to redeem his inheritance from his uncle. The old man's reasoning is impeccable. He cannot divide the land until Muḥammad's two brothers return and everyone can agree on the terms. Otherwise, if the brothers quarrel after the division of the land, they will all blame the uncle. What could he do then? In the meantime, Muḥammad has to wait. Getting the three brothers together is more difficult than one would suppose. One of the brothers, born in Kenya, has obtained Saudi papers and is working in the police force in Saudi Arabia. He either cannot get leave or is fearful of being unable to return if he leaves Saudi Arabia. The other brother is working in a part of Yemen where the phones seldom work.

The continued absence of his two brothers has left Muḥammad in limbo, unable to move away for fear his uncle will sell the land in his absence and unable to settle and build a house. The absence of others keeps Muḥammad from setting down roots in Hadramawt, his father's hometown, and from true repatriation, even though he has been living in the vicinity for a good number of years now. If Muḥammad's problem appears to be insurmountable so far, it is actually a relatively simple one, for it rests on the inability to get three brothers, or one generation, to be jointly present.

ʿAlī, who was born in Hadramawt, faced a more complicated problem but has found a more happy outcome than Muhammad has. In his case, property and the intertwining of rights and obligations have involved three generations spanning three countries, not to mention three changes of governmental regime in South Yemen. The absences of those dead or distant have created problems that ʿAlī could overcome only when a number of presences were effected simultaneously, by chance and cunning.

Unlike Muḥammad, ʿAlī is doing well and just had a little triumph. He escaped from Kuwait, where he was working, when Iraq invaded in 1990, and even was able to bring his car, which he now uses as a taxi. His mother owned some houses in Singapore, which her father left her when he died there. As she had no one there, she put the property in the hands of an agent in town, who arranged for the collection of rents in Singapore and paid her in Tarim. After independence in 1967, however, when the socialists came to power, the agent absconded to Saudi Arabia and died there after some years. Many people had placed their property in his hands, and they saw neither the income from their houses nor the titles with which they could have sold the houses. One day, after the reunification of the Yemens, when people began to return from exile, ʿAlī heard that the deceased agent's son was in town. He initiated a court case against the son for restitution. The son claimed that his father was only an employee of the investment company that managed the Singapore houses, not an agent. ʿAlī however had a record of the document that had granted the agent powers of attorney and found the document, complete with relevant numbers, registered at the local court, in a ledger from the time of the sultans and the British. Furthermore, he acquired a list of local property owned by the original agent, of which his son had inherited a quarter. The property included some of the largest mansions in town. The agent's son was shocked when he saw the list. The court could seize this property in lieu of restitution. While the case was being heard, the agent's son tried to abscond, like his father, but was stopped at the airport until one of his relatives stood surety for him.

As these examples intimate, invisible hands play a big role in the economy of the Hadrami diaspora, namely in inheritances from the dead and remittances from the distant. The absent continue to be present in their effects, for good or for ill. Inevitably, then, the absent stimulate talk, speculations, and theories. The diaspora is a society in which the absent are a constant incitement to discourse about things moving. We may call the diaspora "the society of the absent" as a convenience and a theoretical position because in it, discourses of mobility appear as both cause and effect and are inseparable from diasporic life, saturating its internal social space.

In the society of the absent that is the Hadrami diaspora, one sees a great hustle and bustle of movement. Persons flee war and famine, agents abscond with assets, parents die, orphans travel to distant relatives, migrants move to seek fortune elsewhere. People travel through countries with such varying national histories that one would be hard put to speak in any systematic way of an "international economy" in which they make a living. Life trajectories appear as so many outcomes of unpredictable external events. One often comes away from ethnographic fieldwork feeling that the great organizing nouns—culture, society, or life—are simply heaps of mishaps artificially sorted out by the priests of science, and not very convincingly at that. Should a researcher want to participate in such an enterprise? The question really is an artificial one, and the choice an illusion, for the ethnographic field yields no raw data. In doing field research, living among people, the researcher inevitably participates in discourses that objectify, systematize, and interpret the things seen by all.

The examples above describe attempts to gather the patrimony of patriarchs, which is scattered for various reasons. Such descriptions can be seamlessly augmented with narratives from the point of view of patriarchs, injecting reasons into incidents. The disrupted incomes, failed investments, and recovered inheritances of a fragmentary, unsystematic international economy can be embedded in a systematized discourse of mobility. Historians are producers of such discourses. Consider how situations such as those above might appear in the words of a contemporary Hadrami historian:

> Because of their love for the homeland, and desire to raise and educate their sons in it, and to provide them the leisure to pursue a life of study and Sufism and a comfortable existence, they preferred investing in real estate—as if they had pensioned themselves and their inheritors off, by this means. Thus there came to be, after a time, a generation idle on account of inheritance, and unprepared to follow what their forefathers had laid out for them in the way of a life of learning and knowledge, except for a very few. (al-Shāṭirī 1983: 417–18)

In this rendition, geographically mobile wealth was plowed into the ground, whether abroad in Singapore or at home in Hadramawt, and rendered immobile, in order to transform value into something that moves more securely through time instead: spiritual value embodied in offspring pursuing a life of study and Sufism. In the historian's discourse on mobility, land has unique properties precisely because it is immobile, and it thereby contains the potential for moral transformation. Yet in the historian's judgment, such transformations were not easy to effect and could just as well digress into channels that were purely monetary, listless, and corrupting—"as if they had pensioned themselves and their inheritors off."

The discourses of historians mix and mingle with yet others of independent provenance, such as the words and deeds of the prophet Muḥammad, known in Arabic as the *ḥadīth*. The *ḥadīth* may be translated as "Traditions" or "discourses and practices" of the Prophet. Not to be confused with the words of God, which are set forth in the Qur'an, the discourses of the Prophet have been systematically compiled by a number of encyclopedic titans into collections that bear their names, such as the famous *ḥadīth* compilations of Bukhārī, Muslim, and Tirmidhī. Passed on from person to person as unit texts since the time of the Prophet himself, these discourses are only as reliable as the chain of human transmitters. The encyclopedists stand by the robustness of each act of transmission in their compilations. Their specialized knowledge represents systematic, methodologically self-conscious arrangements of the Prophet's discourses systematized to a degree matched by few narrative historians.

The discourses of the Prophet suffuse and inform social practices common in Hadramawt. Available to the learned in multiple volumes with indices and concordances, they are also passed around in common talk, as pious homilies or ironic explanations. The historian al-Shāṭirī's unflattering view of the inheritors is a common one throughout the Hadrami diaspora. The view is generally an ironic one, for it acknowledges the gap between intentions and consequences. The intentions of those who pensioned off their sons cannot be faulted, for they are pious ones guided by Prophetic discourse. A *ḥadīth* of the Prophet states, with variations, that "when a person dies, nothing of him or her remains except for three things: beneficial knowledge, a pious son praying for one's soul, or continuing good works."[6] The Prophet's *ḥadīth* are words and works to be emulated, and this particular *ḥadīth* allows for variations in personal circumstance. Scholars who apply themselves writing books produce beneficial knowledge, even if they are without progeny or wealth. But few are or can be scholars. Those with money build mosques and leave gardens, lands, religious books, and income for coffee and dates in perpetuity to further the cause of pious practice. These objects permanently

6. Commonly quoted and referred to as the *ḥadīth* of *'amal jārī,* continuing good works, this *ḥadīth* is found in a number of authorities: Abū Dā'ūd *(Kitāb al-waṣāyā)*, Aḥmad *(Bāqī musnad al-mukaththirīn)*, al-Nisā'ī *(Kitāb al-waṣāyā)*, Muslim *(Kitāb al-waṣiyya)*, and al-Tirmidhī *(Kitāb al-aḥkām)*.

serve the cause of piety because as endowments *(waqf)*, they are immobilized, literally stopped from the onward movement of economic exchanges. These endowments are good works whose effects continue to be present. Tarim alone has three hundred and sixty endowed mosques (Bukayr Bā Ghaythān 1973). The mosques are commonly held up as a dramatic sign of the hold that Prophetic discourse enjoys over this community and of the ways in which such discourse guides social practice. Beyond the circles of the scholarly or the wealthy, each Muslim has the organic capacity to create progeny and the moral will to bring up a pious son praying for one's soul. The words of the Prophet speak not to the elect but to all, if only they would listen.

In this light, the investments in real estate that al-Shāṭirī mentions aimed to produce all three enduring presences—knowledge, pious sons, and endowed buildings to house and feed the scholarly offspring—even if they hardly succeeded. In this way, the absent planned to continue shaping the present, thereby securing their place in it. Prophetic discourse provides one theoretical or normative perspective from which we may clarify and evaluate the investments judged by al-Shāṭirī, or the movements described in the ethnographic examples above.

A Theoretical Opening

The discourses of mobility that are part of pilgrimages such as those to the Adeni's tomb—of the social experiences of absence in a diaspora and that combine so easily with the discourses of the Prophet—are not obstacles, prohibitions, interdictions, or similar edicts of negative compulsion. Neither are they backed by any kind of institutional state power. Rather, they are spurs to action, encouraging people to provide for, build, create, and travel on the right path. They are perhaps in the same spirit as the saying in English "God helps those who help themselves." One hears a similar message as a constant rhyming refrain: *ʿalayk al-ḥaraka, wa-ʿalā Allāh al-baraka* ("it is yours to move, and God's to bless"). Mobility is to be encouraged, not repressed. The point at issue is not movement as such but its moral direction.

There are many reasons why this might be so in the diasporic society of Hadramawt. Mobility widens the field in which people can engage and amass resources and powers. At the same time, forces from a distance may disrupt established accommodations in any locale. Power, domination, and rulers have long come from the outside. The discourses of mobility, by their pervasiveness, are ways in which movements are represented and objectified. This creates the conditions of possibility for movements to be channeled, controlled, diverted, and argued over. As the Hadrami diaspora developed across the Indian Ocean over the past five centuries, a powerful discursive tradition developed across this space as well and helped give it shape.

The *ḥadīth* of the prophet Muḥammad exemplify how both reverent emulation and contention attach to tradition in Islamic discourses. A number of traditions hold that just before the Prophet died, he asked his community to hold fast onto two things: the Book of God and the family of the Prophet. Other traditions maintain that the two things were the Book of God and the Prophetic examples *(sunna)*, as found in the *ḥadīth*. The different implications of these two sets of traditions constitute a long-running argument between Sunnis and Shia in Islam since the seventh century (Mottahedeh 1980). They also fed into the conflict over the Adeni's tomb that opened this chapter. The Adeni is one of the family of the Prophet. Pilgrimage to his tomb can thus signify that one is holding fast to the family of the Prophet and thereby keeping faith with one of the Prophet's traditions. But this interpretation is not the whole story, for in 1994, the Adeni also became associated with socialists, secessionists, Sufis, and Saudi ambitions. How these associations emerged is not obvious. Nonetheless, they could be made and were worth making precisely because the Adeni was already a powerful figure—one who, while stationary, stood at the junction of a number of paths and projects.

In the terms of Sufi discourse, the Adeni is described as a *quṭb*, an "axis" around which others revolve (al-ʿAydarūs 1985; Baḥraq al-Ḥaḍramī 1988; al-Shillī 1901). In systematized versions of this discourse, the axis is the highest station of spiritual attainment. Below him are four surrogates *(abdāl)*, then a larger number of pegs *(awtād)*, and so on. This hierarchy of states receives systematic elaboration in the writings of Sufi theorists such as Ibn al-ʿArabī but are looked on with suspicion by legists for pretensions to forming a rival cosmology to that of the Qur'an (al-Ḥibshī 1976; Chittick 1994; Chodkiewicz 1993; Knysh 1999b). I have neither the qualifications nor the intention to comment on such theological disputes. What I would like to do here, at the end of this chapter, is to outline the elements of a discursive tradition that imbues graves such as the Adeni's with great significance as part of a larger, transregional world. The terms of my analysis are anthropological. They derive from a Western tradition of social analysis that is by no means Islamic or Sufi, and they thereby inject into an already contentious discursive arena yet another set of terms, terms shaped in their own troubled history with Christianity (Asad 1993, 2003). While conducting field research, I have been both berated and shown much kindness in carrying out this enterprise. Both treatments are acknowledged here, and in apology—for one has to apologize for an intrusion—I can say only that these terms and their use have no doctrinal or normative ambitions. Their purpose is neither to fish in muddy waters nor to clean them up. Rather, they seek to present the results of observations of movements in the large space of the Hadrami diaspora. Those movements themselves are constituted in and through discourses of mobility that are rich in terminologies and teleologies. At places, these terms meet with those I introduce, and it is to be hoped that the resulting encounters be mutually intelligible and rewarding. One arranges such points of contact by embedding them in extended narratives, hoping that they become so many doors through which others may pass to different worlds, in both directions. It is for the sake of greeting, exchange, and self-transformation that an anthropologist prefers translation to voyeurism, shows up without an invitation, and seeks open doors rather than windows.

One such door is the grave. The grave is a productive starting point because it is a particularly dense semiotic object, a compound of place, text, person, and name. Subsequent chapters follow these categories as they move through diasporic Hadramawt and its discursive tradition. Put in motion, these categories trace extended historical itineraries and fill out social landscapes. To conclude this chapter, I offer a capsule outline of how these categories relate to each other in a dynamic of signification.[7]

Within the grave is a person. Very close by is a tombstone inscribed with text, representing the name of the grave's inhabitant. By means of writing, the name is attached to a rugged material object, stone, and thereby made durable in time. The person in the grave and the engraving on the tombstone point to each other in a silent spatial relationship of proximity that exists independently of visitors and reciters. The person who

7. Eickelman and Piscatori's *Muslim Travellers: Pilgrimage, Migration, and the Religious Imagination* is a pioneering volume that uses the concept of travel to explore interconnections among semantic fields in Muslim traditions (Eickelman and Piscatori 1990; also, Shari'ati 1980, on the significance of migration in Islam). In a similar spirit, studies of Christian pilgrimage have been pushing away from place-centered theories to explore broader fields of meaning and action through concepts of motion (Coleman and Eade 2004), travel narrative (Coleman and Elsner 2003), and combinations of place, text, and person (Coleman and Elsner 1995; Eade and Sallnow 1991). History plays an important role in creating these semiotic complexes and is particularly germane to the practice of Mormon traditions, where it is part of theology (Davies 1989, 2000; Mitchell 2003).

was nameless at birth becomes known as a name attached to a specific body for his or her lifetime, and is known forever as a name inscribed on the tombstone at death. The act of burial fixes this terminal relationship of metonymy in a place. The relationship of place and named person that a grave and inscribed tombstone represent is a base or foundation on which to create potentials. As a compound of place, person, name, tombstone, and text, the grave enacts a passage from silence to vocalization. The Prophet is said to have greeted the dead when passing by their graves, and the practice is encouraged even by critics of grave visitation (Ibn Taymiyya 1998: 177–78). Writing enables visitors to greet the dead by name. Here, inscription acts as an agent of transformation. Writing is a visual signifier; itself silent, it can provoke meaningful speech. Present on the surface of the tombstone at one end of a chain of signification, it enables the dead and silent person within the grave to be launched into discourse. Reading the name on a tombstone, a Muslim passing by can greet the dead within. Writing is an inert switch that converts the grave from a silent to a sonorous state when activated by the approach of a living Muslim person. In this sense, writing is a foundational step in the creation and realization of potentials for signification. It is precisely to cap the further development of such potentials that some Islamic jurists have specified limits on the structures built above graves, and the kinds of utterances allowed there, such as prayers and supplications. Otherwise, graves may be aggrandized and become mosques, congregations that are God's alone (Ibn Taymiyya 1998: 184–86). They may become famous and gain an expansive constituency on grounds other than the authorized one of revelation.

Ibn Taymiyya, the fourteenth-century jurist often cited to denounce the cult of graves, is clear on this point. He opposes the cultivation of graves not because such action is driven by superstition *(khurāfa)*, as modern opponents allege. Superstition is the misunderstanding of true causality; it does not work. Grave visits are to be opposed because they do work. They create powerful dynamics of signification with the potential to create communities based not on revelation but on something autochthonous and incipient in the grave complex. The idols that pre-Islamic Arabian communities worshipped were created by such processes: "It was veneration of a pious man's grave that eventually gave rise to the worship of al-Lāt," says Ibn Taymiyya, referring to one of the most famous pre-Islamic divinities, whose following preceded and rivaled that of Allāh's Muslims (Ibn Taymiyya 1998: 191; Memon's translation, 1976: 264). Even after the triumph of Islam, the possibility remains that new religions may originate from the cultivation of graves:

> If, however, one intends to pray at a prophet's grave or of a pious man, hoping that prayer offered in such an area would bring him beatitude, this is, then, exactly departing from, and opposing, the religion of God and His Messenger. It, moreover, amounts to originating a religion without divine sanction. (Ibn Taymiyya 1998: 193; Memon's translation, 1976: 265)

"Originating a religion": my purpose here is not to press on a delicate point of dispute as to whether rivals to God are being cultivated in the cult of graves. It is rather to point to the common ground of agreement: that graves and their visits are meaningful semiotic complexes that can set in motion powerful and expansive dynamics of signification. Not only are graves taken up in discourses of mobility, they frequently become the object of movement itself, the destination of pilgrimages. On this common ground, disputes over the moral consequences of such dynamics play out.

The next chapter moves back in time to Hadramawt, where the Adeni came from. We take in a view of the social geography of the country, where the moral qualities of persons have to do with the way they move through its landscape.

CHAPTER 2

Geography, a Pathway through History

Buried as he is in the port town of Aden, on the southwestern corner of the Arabian Peninsula, the Adeni lies between two geographical media: land and water. Buried in 1508, he also lies between two historical periods: the fifteenth and the sixteenth centuries. This double location is significant because it marks the point in space and time at which the Hadrami diaspora ventured out into the Indian Ocean, and thus into the new currents of what many historians now call world or global history (Eaton 1990; Frank 1998; Pomeranz 2000; Wallerstein 2004). The Indian Ocean, which hosted trade routes connecting the countries surrounding the South China Sea, Red Sea, Mediterranean Sea, and the North Atlantic, saw in the sixteenth century the arrival of silver and gold from the Americas, brought by the Portuguese and Spaniards via the Atlantic and Pacific oceans. What had been an international economy now became a global one, literally. From the sixteenth century on, too, Hadramis sojourning and settling in India became known as religious teachers, Sufis, and court and civic figures. Subsequently, from the eighteenth century on, they came into prominence farther east in the Malay Archipelago, in established religious roles as well as new ones such as adventurers, sultans, merchants, diplomats, and landlords. These new developments in the Hadrami diaspora moved roughly in parallel with and in counterpoint to the establishment of European colonies in the region, as the Portuguese, Dutch, and English expanded their activities eastward to India and the Malay Archipelago. But they moved in different ways.

Unlike the Europeans, whose activities combined conquest and trade and who maintained monopolies by navies, Hadramis entered into wide-ranging exchanges with peoples in the Indian Ocean, especially in modes that come under the broad banner of religion. Their travels traced out pathways across the ocean marked by mosques, graves, and schools. Some have called these pathways a Sufi order—the ʿAlawī *ṭarīqa,* or ʿAlawī Way (al-Attas 1963; Serjeant 1957; Trimingham 1973). The Arabic term *ṭarīqa* is a second-order derivative of the basic noun *ṭarīq,* which means "path." As a conceptual abstraction from the basic noun, the word may translate as "method," "way," or "pathway" in English. Applied to organized Sufism, it usually translates as "Sufi order," referring to the institutional complex that commonly comprises a combination of lodge, leader, mystical genealogy, particular texts, litanies, chants, and ritual practices. The eponymous ʿAlawī refers to an ancestor of the Hadrami sayyids, the grandson of the Migrant, Aḥmad b. ʿĪsā, and denotes genealogical descent from him; it connotes descent from the prophet Muḥammad as well.[1] I use the terms *ʿAlawī Way* or *pathway* interchangeably to name an institutional complex. That this complex is characterized by a term indicating movement is particularly apt, as we will see. Although the diaspora is a larger phenomenon than the Sufi ʿAlawī pathway, the latter has dominated its collective representations; it is difficult to separate the two before the late nineteenth century, since most of the written sources available for the diaspora were generated by the ʿAlawī Way.[2] Our interest here is the distinctive ways of moving through history and geography. These pathways are discourses that mobilize places, texts, and persons in meaningful narratives of travel.

A study of the Hadrami diaspora and of the ʿAlawī Way provides a thread through the history of the Indian Ocean. The telling of that history has been pioneered by historians of cross-cultural trade, notably K. N. Chaudhuri, Simon Digby, Ashin Das Gupta, J. C. van Leur, Michael Pear-

1. The Muslim world is rife with communities known by variants of the name ʿAlī, such as those rendered the Alawis, Alevis, and Alawites in the English-language literature. Among them, a connection to the prophet Muḥammad's family is important, be it in genealogy, theology, or history. The Prophet had no surviving sons; ʿAlī b. Abī Ṭālib, who was his cousin and his daughter Fāṭima's husband, is the progenitor of all the Prophet's descendants. Essentially, ʿAlī's name is often taken by those claiming descent from Muḥammad. This singular exception to the usual patrilineal reckoning of Arab descent gives rise to much discussion, especially in Shia circles. The Shia, short for *shīʿat ʿAlī*, are literally "partisans of ʿAlī," in reference to ʿAlī's position in historical disputes about the succession to Muḥammad. The interweaving of genealogy, theology, and history is precisely the focus of this study.

2. The preponderance of ʿAlawī writings and perspectives gives rise to controversies in the twentieth century, which I take up in chapter 6 and beyond.

son, B. Schrieke, Neel Steensgaard, and Sanjay Subrahmanyam. Their work has been built primarily on the documentary trail left by the European trading companies, which operated as virtual governments in the Indian Ocean. Ashin Das Gupta, who used Dutch archival records to elicit stories of non-European merchants, lamented the dearth of sources apart from those of the European trading companies (Das Gupta 1982: 408). An important exception to such sources has been known for a while, in the documents of medieval Jewish merchants in Cairo studied by S. D. Goitein (Goitein 1966). Recently, these have been fictionally exploited by the anthropologist-novelist Amitav Ghosh; his *In an Antique Land* (1992) is a combination ethnography-history that connects Egypt and Aden in Yemen with Malabar in India through the relations between a Jewish merchant and his Indian trading agent/slave—and at the same time the fantasy alter ego of an Indian anthropologist doing fieldwork in Egypt. Others, working on pilgrimage (Pearson 1996), prayer (Parkin 2000), textiles (Barnes 2005), gravestones (Lambourn 2003), and combinations of textual genres such as travelogues and poetry (Bose, forthcoming), have begun to retrace similar paths across the ocean but through different sets of materials.

The Hadrami diaspora, especially the ʿAlawī Way, provides a continuous set of records that enables us to imagine yet another pathway through the history and geography of the Indian Ocean. Discovering and interpreting the narratives embedded in them pose a challenge. Although the majority of these records exist in manuscript form and are difficult to access, some have been in print for decades. One of the main obstacles to discovering the narratives has been the fact that they were written in different parts of the ocean, such as Zanzibar, Mecca, Hadramawt, Surat and Malabar in India, and the Malay Archipelago. The texts were thus known as belonging to different national literatures, separated from each other, rather than as parts of a unified phenomenon in dialogue with each other. By reading these formerly separated texts together, as the literary output of one diaspora that traveled across the Indian Ocean during half a millennium, one begins to hear echoes across the countries and centuries and to recognize names, families, motifs, styles of expression, and ideas that connect the texts. At the same time, the task is eased because the scattered contents in this material are in discursive modes that express the experiences of mobility out of which they emerged. An appreciation of the fact of mobility itself attunes us to the narratives strung across these texts and to their slender threads across the ocean. The idea of mobility becomes an interpretive key. Furthermore, understood as discourses, the narratives

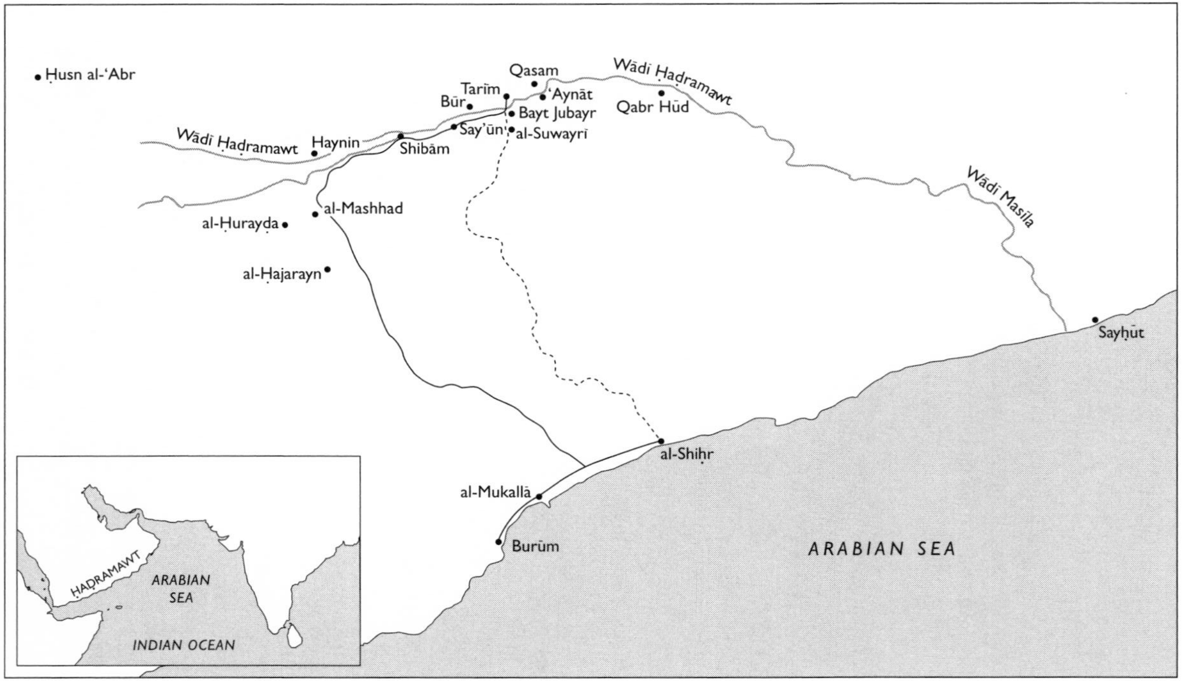

MAP 2. Hadramawt

are not restricted to texts but circulate orally in numerous arenas of social life as well.

While such discourses of mobility developed and were transformed in the Indian Ocean from the sixteenth century on, they had prior existence on land, in the homeland of Hadramawt. In both arenas, they charted the creation of new communities, which emerged from the interaction between transregional and local social groups. Such communities are composed of individuals who are creoles and local cosmopolitans. By local cosmopolitans, I mean persons who, while embedded in local relations, also maintain connections with distant places. They thus articulate a relation between different geographical scales (Ho 2002b).

This chapter moves backward from the Adeni to the homeland Hadramawt before the sixteenth century. We look at how a certain kind of place is created by the movement of a diaspora through it. In the longer view, Hadramawt is not only a homeland; it is a destination of earlier migrations. Marks on the landscape become significant as they are embraced by the stories of mobile persons, as points on an itinerary. The ʿAlawī Way of the Hadrami sayyids is such an itinerary. Landmarks became signs within the discourse of mobility, and particular places became signposts in the historical formation of the ʿAlawī Way. Conversely, as the ʿAlawī Way settled and developed in Hadramawt, the significance of the place changed, transforming from a destination to an origin. Through a narrative of geography, then, this chapter outlines the historical origins of the sayyids in Hadramawt, and the early roots and routes of the ʿAlawī Way there.

Hadramawt: Wadi and Society

Hadramawt has been a population center since ancient times. Incense burned in Roman temples before Christianity was shipped overland from its source in Ẓufār (in present-day Oman) via Hadramawt. Among the earliest reports of Hadrami migrations are those recording Hadrami participation in the Islamic conquests outside the peninsula, in the seventh century C.E. (al-Balādhurī 1936; Ibn Hishām 1955: 653). The Banī Hilāl, whose famous epic poetry traveled with them to Egypt and the Maghreb (Reynolds 1995), are said to be from this region. Ibn Khaldun, the Maghrebi historical sociologist, is, in Hadrami reckoning, one of their most famous sons (Bā Maṭraf 1984 vol. 4: 315).

Hadramawt consists of a system of wadis flowing into one main watercourse. The system is the largest of its kind in the Arabian Peninsula. North of the Arabian shore of the Indian Ocean, this main wadi runs west to east for about eighty miles. At its eastern end, it dips southward and drains into the ocean. If one moves north from the seashore, one crosses a stony plateau fifteen hundred to two thousand meters high for almost a hundred miles before coming to the system of gorges carved into the plateau. The plateau, the *jawl,* is literally a range, a "place of roaming." To the settled Hadramis, the *jawl* is a transitional barrier, an obstacle to cross, between the sea and the wadi. It is populated by bedouin, who once made a living transporting goods by camel between wadi and coast and still roam with their herds of goats today. Before motorized transport, one could cross this distance in seven days (al-Bakrī al-Yāfiʿī 1936: 161), and today the trip takes up to ten hours by car. As one descends into the wadi, the temperature rises by a few degrees. But within the wadi are towns with gardens of date palms, where the temperatures again cool down. Early European travelers in the twentieth century remarked that they could walk in Thibī, near Tarim, for hours in the shade of these trees without seeing the sun.[3] This fact is remarkable because perhaps fifty miles north of Hadramawt begins the Empty Quarter, the dry sandy desert that is iconic of the Arabian Peninsula.

The cardinal points within the wadi (except east) are not referred to by their usual Arabic names. While the north is called *najdī,* in reference to the populated plateau region of North Arabia, the south is called *baḥrī,* or seaward, and the west, *qiblī,* or the direction of prayer—that is, Mecca. The substitutions for the cardinal points indicate something of the major concerns of the Hadrami population in these directions. In the Najd are tribes like the bin Qumlā, who have ridden to Hadramawt in offense, such as during the raids of the iconoclastic Wahhabis at the beginning of the nineteenth century, destroying tombs of saints and tipping books of mysticism into wells (bin Hāshim 1948: 120; al-Kindī 1991: 321). To the west is Mecca, which Muslims in Hadramawt face when praying. To the south is the Indian Ocean, where Hadramis have gone in large numbers, to make a living and to seek fortunes and converts to Islam.

Within the wadi, the main towns are the triplets Shibām, Sayʾūn, and Tarim (moving west to east), which straddle roughly the center of the main wadi. Shibām and Tarim are pre-Islamic towns, mentioned by

3. The existence of endless shade near the desert is a motif associated with mythic places in Yemeni folklore, such as the great dam of Maʾrib before its ruin (al-Khazrajī 1914a: 52).

medieval geographers such as al-Qazwīnī, Yāqūt al-Hamawī, and al-Hamdānī. Say'ūn was founded late, in the sixteenth century. Seasonal monsoon rains in the summer, if they come, result in floods, which rush through the wadi system and rapidly discharge in the ocean. The orientation of Hadramawt reflects the overall downward tilt of the peninsula from west to east, from the mountains of Yemen by the Red Sea to the Persian Gulf. Thus, the waters in the main wadi run west to east, gaining volume as they flow downward. They are met along the way by flood waters running north and south from the branch wadis into the main channel. For agriculture, the best-watered places in Hadramawt are at the confluences of these perpendicular streams. Water diverts from the floods to fields in a system of spate irrigation.[4] As well, underground aquifers become charged and make water available for farming via wells. The main towns above are thus strategically located; this gives rise to the naming of directions within the wadi. While west in general is *qiblī,* to head west is to head "upward" *(yas'ad)*, while going east is moving "downward" *(yaḥdar)*. Settlements in the western end of wadi Hadramawt are smaller and sparser; their wells strike water at perhaps a hundred feet down. In the central towns such as Tarim, the waterline may be at fifteen feet. Farther east, near the tomb of the prophet Hūd, where the wadi turns south toward the sea, the water appears at ground level in the form of a stream, almost perpetual in some parts; it is a miraculous sight so close to the Empty Quarter. Nevertheless, the central towns are better suited for agriculture than are places at the eastern end. In the east, the wadi becomes wide, and few side wadis appear. Water concentrates in the main stream, which is an impossible situation for agriculture because of the torrent that rages through at the height of the rains.

The lay of the land gives shape to the social formations and political relations within it, patterning themes in its history and quickening the flow of events. In the thirteenth century, the Nahd tribes from the dry west of the wadi laid siege to the central towns, occupying Tarim for three years. Only when the rains came did the tribes cease their attacks, hurrying back to their fields (al-Bakrī 1936). A Marxist philosopher who teaches aesthetic theory at the college of education in al-Mukallā, Sālim al-Khuḍar, has crafted an argument that ties geographical base to social superstructure in Hadramawt (al-Khuḍar 1989). He argues that the drier western end of the wadi supports small farms, small families, and a more egali-

4. For a treatment of this unusual system in the comparable region of Laḥj, see Maktari 1971.

FIGURE 6. View of the wadi. Perpetual spring between massive plateau walls, beside the tomb complex of Prophet Hūd. Photo by the author.

tarian social system; in contrast, the central wadi supports large farms, large landholdings, bigger families, a landless peasantry, and more hierarchical and oppressive social relations. He himself is from the west.

In the central areas, a majority of the tribal groups are cultivators, having in that respect more in common with the nontribal townspeople than with other, less sedentary tribes. However, their hold on the country is more extensive and secure than that of the townsmen, as their country kin extend north and south on the plateau beyond the narrow wadi. In the central wadi, the main tribal confederation is that of the Shanāfir, whose domain stretches from west of Tarim to Shibām. The Kathīrīs are the foremost group within this confederation. Surrounding Tarim and to its east is the Banī Ẓanna confederation. The chief family of this confederation, the bin Yamānī, once controlled lands along the main wadi where the main water channel divides into two, loses velocity, and becomes gentler, making cultivation possible. Their wealth stemmed from the long rows of date palms they cultivated near the bifurcated streams. The Kathīrī land was drier. The Kathīrīs originally lived on the coast, at Ẓufār in the fifteenth century; given that they were relative latecomers to power in the wadi, their lands were poorer. Their presence in the interior dates from the sixteenth century, when their legendary chief Badr Bū Ṭuwayriq defeated the bin Yamānī chief (bin Hāshim 1948: 34–54). Badr Bū Ṭuwayriq is celebrated in Hadrami history as the leader who repelled the Portuguese from the Hadrami coast; modern scholars consider him to be the first nationalist, the first to unify all of Hadramawt within one state (Bā Wazīr 1957: 119–34). The chiefs of both tribal confederations maintained slave armies off their incomes. A historical irony flows from their differential endowments: the poorer Kathīrīs made more of migration, and from wealth they gained as officers *(jamadar,* "fief holders") in the Nizam's army in Hyderabad, India, in the nineteenth century, were able to recruit slaves from East Africa, creating the strongest armed force inland (ʿAkāsha 1985; Gavin 1975). The Quʿayṭī sultanate, which ruled the coast from the late nineteenth century until independence in 1967, also got its start from expatriate Hadrami officers in the Hyderabad Nizam's army; the Quʿayṭī's sultanate back in Hadramawt was supported by the British from the 1880s on.

Tarim: A Special Place

The town of Tarim lies roughly at the boundary of the Shanāfir and Banī Ẓanna confederations. The eastward creep of Shanāfir influence over the past four centuries has its counterpart in the westward motion of the Banī Ẓanna: Tarim feels pressure from both sides. The town was surrounded by a wall before the imposition of a universal peace by the independent socialist government in the early 1970s. Pulling down such walls was a favorite activity in the mobilization of populist militias of Maoist inspiration during the campaigns of the 1970s, known as *intifāḍa*s, against internal class enemies. According to sayyid history, the town of Qasam, now home to the bin Yamānī chiefly lineage of the Banī Ẓanna, was founded by sayyids, who invested money reportedly in the amount of 20,000 dinārs (al-Ḥāmid 1968: 460; Bilfaqīh 1994: 107) to create the settlement by planting date palms there. The sayyid ʿAlī b. ʿAlawī, the Endower of Qasam *(Khāliʿ Qasam),* named Qasam after his family's grand palm estate in Basra, Iraq. The estate was taken over by the head of the Banī Ẓanna confederation, ʿAbd Allāh b. Aḥmad b. ʿAbd al-Shaykh bin Yamānī, at the beginning of the nineteenth century (A. R. al-Saqqāf 2002: 566). In the past century, Tarim has been more or less under siege by the Banī Ẓanna, whose subtribe the Tamīm surrounds it. Despite the agonistic rhetoric between the Tarim-based sayyids and the Banī Ẓanna in their history and folklore, the groups have enjoyed more mutuality than is commonly acknowledged. The first domed grave in Tarim, with a cupola *(qubba)* usually associated with sayyid saints, was that of the founder of the bin Yamānī state, Masʿūd b. Yamānī b. Lubayd al-Ẓannī, who died in 1250 (bin Ḥāshim 1948: 14). Al-Ẓannī had come under the sway of Sufism taught by his Tarim teacher, ʿAlī al-Khaṭīb, and gave up power for spiritual pursuits, presenting some of his wealth to religious institutions as endowments.

Tarim, with its natural irrigation potential, has a recorded existence from pre-Islamic times. Its lore shares characteristics with those of other ancient places in the peninsula, such as the assimilation of etymology to genealogy. Tarim is by some accounts named for Tarim ibn (son of) Hadramawt. Its natural endowment has also earned it the sobriquet *al-Ghannāʾ*, "the abundant and self-sufficient." Yet its most notable and famous wealth is not that residing in its trees. Rather, it is the wealth of stories, which in their circulation continue to realize values that can take tangible forms. These accounts were a constant refrain while I lived there; they also appear in the old texts, as the citations below indicate.

It is said that during the wars of apostasy that plagued the nascent Islamic polity upon the death of the prophet Muḥammad, Tarim was one of the first places to return to the fold. Muḥammad's successor, the caliph Abū Bakr, sent seventy men to Tarim, and with the help of the locals, defeated the apostates on a battleground just outside the town, at the fort of al-Nujayr. This battleground is today identified with the open land around the settlement of Mishṭa. From that point on, Tarim was one of the most secure Islamic provinces. A slightly different account has it that the ruler of Tarim, Ziyād b. Labīd al-Bayāḍī the Companion, was the first to pledge allegiance to Abū Bakr upon the death of Muḥammad; Ziyād had been appointed by Muḥammad himself (Ibn Hishām 1955: 648). Only a minority of fighters, led by the indigenous al-Ashʿath b. Qays al-Kindī, rejected Abū Bakr.[5] They were besieged by Ziyād. Pleased with their loyalty, the caliph Abū Bakr prayed for three things for Tarim: that it would always be populous, that scholars would sprout in it like plants, and that God would bless those in it. Even more, it is also said that one of the gardens of heaven is located beneath Tarim[6] and that on Judgment Day, Abū Bakr will take all of Tarim in his hand and fling its citizens to heaven, the pious and the sinners alike. For this reason, Tarim is also known as the

5. Al-Kindī had previously led a deputation of Kinda to the Prophet at Mecca, where he pledged acceptance of Islam (Ibn Hishām 1955: 641). His biography is recorded by the Hadrami historian Saʿīd ʿAwaḍ Bā Wazīr (1954).

6. "On the authority of ʿAbd al-Raḥmān al-Saqqāf, . . . on some of his teachers in Mecca" (al-ʿAydarūs 1985: 76; al-Shillī 1982: 279).

city of Abū Bakr al-Ṣiddīq ("the Truthful/Honest").[7] In this sense, another appellation of Tarim, "the Protected," al-Maḥrūsa, transcends the old town walls and the territorial tribal confederations pressing in upon them, and portends a higher salvation.[8]

Like its copious aquifers, Tarim's further wealth lies underground. In the fifteenth century, ʿAbd al-Raḥmān al-Saqqāf, whom we will meet later, used to say that ten thousand saints lay in the graveyards of Tarim (al-Shillī 1982: 279). The seventy Muslim warriors sent to Tarim by the caliph Abū Bakr are Companions *(ṣaḥāba)*, or the first generation of Muslims who accompanied the Prophet and saw him daily; they are first in the ranks of the pious. They are reportedly buried in Zanbal, one of Tarim's three graveyards. Aḥmad al-Junayd, whom we will also meet later, was given to pointing out their resting places during his habitual walks in the cemetery. Tarim's significance and fame in the wider world rests not with the Companions, however, who are also identified with places in present-day Jordan and Syria. Tarim is known throughout the Muslim communities of the Indian Ocean littoral as the home of the Prophet's descendants, the sayyids, whose spread in those regions accompanied that of the religion itself. The Hadrami sayyids trace their history in Hadramawt to a single ancestor, who arrived three centuries after the advent of Islam. The telling of that history takes many forms. These forms are a major concern of this study, for the sayyid historiography of Hadramawt is an active agent in the history itself. Its evolution is a large part of the story of the Hadrami diaspora, at home and abroad. The next section tells that history in a form common to different genres of Hadrami historiography, as an itinerary of places.

The ʿAlawī Way: Routes to Roots

DESCENT

The sayyids of Hadramawt descend from a common ancestor, Aḥmad b. ʿĪsā the Migrant. The Migrant left his homeland in Basra, Iraq, and traveled in the Hejaz and the Yemen before finally entering Hadramawt in

7. The caliph Abū Bakr earned this title because he was the first to believe the Prophet's account of his night journey to Jerusalem and his ascent to the heavens.

8. ʿUmar al-Muḥḍār dubbed Tarim the Town of Medicine *(bilād al-ṭibb;* al-ʿAydarūs 1985: 74). Other Yemeni and Arabian cities, such as Ṣanʿāʾ and Dhammār, also have the appellation of "the Protected."

TABLE 1. The ʿAlawī Way: Foundational Figures

Year of Death	Name	Significance
622	**I. Prophet Muḥammad**	Prophet of Islam, ancestor of all sayyids
956	Aḥmad b. ʿĪsā the Migrant	Founding ancestor of sayyid line in Hadramawt
	ʿAlawī b. ʿUbayd Allāh	Eponymous ancestor of all Hadrami sayyids
1135	ʿĀlī Endower of Qasam	First sayyid buried in Tarim; founder of Qasam town near Tarim and investor in its productive date palms
1161	Muḥammad Principal of Mirbāṭ	The ancestor in whom all Hadrami sayyid genealogical ascent lines meet
1255	**II. The First Jurist**	Initiator of sayyid, Sufi ʿAlawī Way
1416	**III. ʿAbd al-Raḥmān al-Saqqāf**	Originator of ritual forms that mark the beginning of the institutionalized ʿAlawī Sufi complex
1430	**IV. ʿUmar al-Muḥḍār**	Originator of geographical form (sanctified landscape); first leader of a formal sayyid association
1451	ʿAbd al-Raḥmān al-Khaṭīb	Originator of textual form; non-sayyid author of Tarim Sufi biographical collection, *Garden of Heart Essences/ Transparent Essence*
1461	ʿAbd Allāh al-ʿAydarūs	"Sultan of Notables"; progenitor of al-ʿAydarūs lineage, the lineage most famous abroad and with the greatest number of sovereign settlements (*manṣab*ates) at home
1513	Abū Bakr al-ʿAydarūs the Adeni	Saint of Aden; founder of first translocation of the sayyid Sufi complex outside Tarim
1522	Aḥmad b. Ḥusayn al-ʿAydarūs	Founder of the first sovereign settlement under a sayyid (*manṣab*ates)

932 C.E. He first stayed at al-Jubayl, in Dawʿan, at the dry, western end of the wadi, encouraged by its inhabitants to settle there. He soon moved eastward, to al-Ḥajarayn, where he acquired land and date palms, and lived there for a number of years. He then moved again, gifting his land and trees to some followers, and moved farther east to the hill of Banī Jushayr near Būr, in the central part of Hadramawt. He finally settled nearby in al-Ḥusaysa, a place between Sayʾūn and Tarim. He died and was buried there in 965 C.E. His grave sits under a white cupola some distance up the side of a wadi, at the top of a dramatic flight of steps carved into the rock and painted white.

In the genealogies, the Migrant is a ninth-generation descendant of the prophet Muḥammad. For five generations more, his descendants kept moving east along the main wadi, as the Migrant had. This movement can be read off their graves, whose white cupolas appear as so many dots on the landscape, connected by the main flood line down the wadi. Thus, his son ʿUbayd Allāh was buried in Bur; his grandson ʿAlawī, in Sumal; and his great-grandson Muḥammad, in Bayt Jubayr (d. 1054), as was Muḥammad's son—until the burial of Muḥammad's grandson, ʿAlī, the Endower of Qasam, in Tarim (d. 1133 or 1135). This sequence is often told in accounts of sayyid origins in Hadramawt orally and in books (A. Q. al-ʿAydarūs 1985: 75; al-Mashhūr 1911: 17). With ʿAlī's burial in Tarim, a new phase in the history began, in which the sayyids were considered to have settled in Hadramawt, with Tarim as their base.

ʿAlī is known as the Endower of Qasam for having founded the settlement of Qasam by investing twenty thousand dinārs in planting date palms there. This investment and its telling are significant. They affirm that the sayyids brought value to Hadramawt; their immigration was not at the expense of locals. Cultivating date palms is a long-term project that requires start-up capital. From the time of planting, the trees may take up to fifteen years to bear fruit. In the meantime, farmers have to be paid to care for the trees and draw water for their irrigation. Once established, however, the trees are sturdy because their roots reach deeply into the ground. They withstand drought better than other species do, and they repay the initial investment for many years. Islamic law provides for ownership and usufruct rights to land that lies fallow; with conditions, rights may be given to those who cultivate the land. This procedure for establishing ownership of fallow land is provided for in legal manuals under the chapter head "Revivification of the Dead" *(Iḥyā' al-Mawāt;* al-Shāṭirī al-ʿAlawī al-Ḥusaynī al-Tarīmī 1949: 115). The legal possibility of acquiring "dead" land in this way answers a question posed by those who would oppose the sayyids: No land is ownerless; how did the sayyids come in and make a living? The question is not a trivial one, and it has resonance in Islamic history. When the nascent Muslim community moved to Medina to escape persecution in Mecca, the new arrivals were unable to make a living, as all gardens were occupied. The Prophet created a system that paired up each male immigrant Muslim with a local Medinese brother, who aided him;[9] in the cycle of Islamic sacred history, the Medinese are called "Helpers" *(Anṣār)*. Beyond that assistance, the Muslims began raiding the Meccans for booty.

The sayyids eventually entered into relations with Hadrami locals, whom

9. This pairing is known as the *mu'ākhāt,* or "brothering" (Donner 1981; Ibn Hishām 1955). I am grateful to Fred Donner for pointing out this parallel.

FIGURE 7. Grave of the Migrant. Restoration in concrete after vandalization. Photo by the author.

they called Helpers, but raiding was out of the question because the Hadramis were already Muslims. The investment of ʿAlī the Endower of Qasam left them an inheritance that provided a legitimate livelihood. His significance is evident in his appellation *the Endower.* ʿAlī is also the first sayyid to be buried in Tarim (al-Mashhūr 1911: 17; al-Shillī 1901: 230). Historically, he stands for the settlement of the sayyids in Tarim (Bilfaqīh 1994: 107) and their ability to put down roots in the locality, like his trees. ʿAlī is a sixth-generation descendant of the Migrant and died two centuries after him.

The significance of ʿAlī the Endower of Qasam's domestication in Tarim is established with hindsight, as his son Muḥammad, "the Principal of Mirbāṭ," *(Ṣāḥib Mirbāṭ)* moved away to Mirbāṭ, a cape and bay on the Indian Ocean coast in present-day Oman (Tibbetts 1981: 442), and is buried there. Some accounts indicate that Muhammad organized trading caravans into the interior, while others hint at political problems that necessitated his removal to the coast. The Principal of Mirbāṭ is of special significance because the lines of ascent of all Hadrami sayyids meet in him.[10] Past him, the single line of descent begins to bifurcate: to his grandson Muḥammad b. ʿAlī "the First Jurist" *(al-Faqīh al-Muqaddam),*

10. Knysh (1999a) has published a critical discussion of the position of this figure.

and to his son ʿAlawī, "Uncle of the Jurist" (*ʿAmm al-Faqīh*). All Hadrami sayyids trace their ancestry to one of these two men.

Saints and Sufis

With the First Jurist, a new element appears. To the line of Prophetic descent is now added a spiritual line, from the Sufi saint of Telemcen in Morocco, Abū Madyan Shuʿayb (Cornell 1996, 1998). Abū Madyan had sent his student ʿAbd al-Raḥmān al-Maqʿad to Hadramawt to spread his teachings there. Al-Maqʿad died in Mecca and did not fulfill his task. But before dying, he instructed ʿAbd Allāh al-Maghribī to go to Hadramawt to meet with the First Jurist, the sayyid Muḥammad b. ʿAlī, son of the Principal of Mirbāṭ. Al-Maghribī was to invest the First Jurist with the cloak of Sufism *(ilbās khirqat al-taṣawwuf)* and serve him his appointment *(taḥkīm)* as the representative of Abū Madyan's Sufi pathway.

The Hadrami historian al-Shāṭirī notes that before Abū Madyan's mission, the people of Hadramawt practiced a "general sufism" *(taṣawwuf ʿāmm;* al-Shāṭirī 1983: 253) of cleansing hearts and shunning worldly vanities. With the First Jurist's induction into Abū Madyan's pathway, Sufism in Hadramawt became organized, adopting the technical vocabulary of pathway *(ṭarīqa)*, appointment *(taḥkīm)*, license *(ijāza)*, mantle *(khirqa)*, litany *(dhikr)*,and so on. Far from being an isolated backwater, Hadramawt participated in important contemporary developments in the wider Islamic world. In the thirteenth century, an elaborate theoretical discourse joined with institutional organization to shape the practice that became known to subsequent centuries as Sufism (Chodkiewicz 1993: 10). Ibn al-ʿArabī, who died in 1240, just fifteen years before the First Jurist's death (1255), set out a vision that was synthetic and systematic yet subtle. His technical vocabulary was adopted throughout the Islamic world, including in Hadramawt. For Ibn al-ʿArabī, Abū Madyan represented the complete fulfillment of spiritual potentiality—of what he understood sainthood to be. While some spiritual seekers flee from the mundane world and others reach God, the full saint is one who, having attained such spiritual heights, then returns to the mundane world to act within it. This path is modeled on the making of the prophet Muḥammad, who went into retreat, received the revelations from God, and then returned to spread the message among his people. For Ibn al-ʿArabī, the fully realized saint was a guide for humanity, a teacher *(ʿālim)* who is the inheritor *(wārith)* of the prophetic role (Chodkiewicz 1993: 171).

The terms set by Abū Madyan and Ibn al-ʿArabī on the meaning of sainthood inform Hadramis' understanding. Ibn al-ʿArabī's notion of the saint as inheritor of the prophet Muḥammad is broadly understood in genealogical terms, as descent. Abū Madyan's notion of the saint who combines knowledge and action *(ʿilm wa-ʿamal)*, who engages both religious and mundane worlds *(dīn wa-dunyā)*, provides the theoretical underpinning for a tradition of social engagement that marks Hadrami Sufism. Within this tradition, the ʿAlawī sayyids, descendants of the Prophet, form a core and provide leadership that is not aloof but participates in society at large.

For these reasons, the First Jurist represents a new level of participation in the local community of Tarim by the recently settled sayyids. The First Jurist was already a jurist when Abū Madyan's deputy arrived. Upon his investiture with Abū Madyan's cloak, he broke his sword over his knee, angering his teachers in the law, especially Shaykh ʿAlī Bā Marwān. This action inaugurated the sayyid tradition of pacifist Sufism and is a major plank in sayyids' self-identification as independent arbiters of the peace between armed tribes. With this act, the sayyids were no longer partisans in local disputes. Unable to defend themselves by force of arms, they tied themselves irrevocably to the general good and began to work for its achievement. The totalizing (or "global" in Chodkiewicz's terms) discourse of sainthood is the theoretical expression of this new role in society. Together with the Hadrami sayyids' repudiation of arms, a global discourse enhanced their capacity for mobility across a landscape troubled by tribal rivalries, since they threatened no one. As such, their settling in Tarim was not a confinement but the beginnings of a new mode of mobility. This form of mobility carried with it specific notions of primacy in legal, spiritual, and genealogical matters, which the First Jurist brought together.

The Hadrami version of a "cult of saints" resonates with recent arguments by Peter Brown (1981), Michel Chodkiewicz (1993), and Vincent Cornell (1998). While Brown focuses on Christian rather than Muslim saints, studies of both have been hobbled by a pervasive Humean distinction between the popular polytheism of the unlettered masses and the textual monotheism of the learned elite (Hume 1976). This distinction became received wisdom in the social sciences under Robert Redfield's banners of Little and Great traditions (Singer 1976), even though Redfield himself was concerned with their interconnections (Redfield 1967). Following Brown's lead, scholars of religion have begun to see a much stronger literate hand in saints' cults than was previously supposed. The Sufi movements influenced by Ibn al-ʿArabī are virtually integrated with saints' cults, because the role of such guides is central to the language and practices of such movements. Organized Sufism brings together literate and illiterate believers, elite and follower, and connects such movements to the world beyond local communities. In Islamic countries, saints' cults were patronized by major states such as the Fatimids, Ayyubids, Mamluks, Ottomans, and Mughals and became mass organizations, relative to the size of earlier groups. Sufism, in van Ess's view, was incorporated into the establishment very early (van Ess 1999). While in Hadramawt the ʿAlawī Way was free of state patronage because states were weak there, the situation was different in the diaspora, as we saw in chapter 1.

For the Hadrami sayyids, the First Jurist represents a unique station in the temporal motion of their ancestral genealogy. He marks the point at which the transmission of religious piety in its organized Sufi form converged with patrilineal descent from the Prophet. The confluence makes him the identifiable starting point of the sayyids' mission in Tarim and Hadramawt, and outward. From his time, the Hadrami sayyids were both a lineage and a distinct school of Sufism, a way distinct from other ways.[11] He was a foundational figure for whom his ancestors in Hadramawt were material precursors, as it were. Subsequent to him, the intertwining of religious and genealogical statuses continued to play out in many ways. The First Jurist is buried in Tarim, and when émigré Hadramis, especially sayyids, return to Tarim, he is the first ancestor they call upon. In ritualized visits to the graveyards of Tarim, pilgrims visit his grave first—hence the "First" in his appellation. He did not leave any writings behind.

Four generations past the First Jurist came his lineal descendant, ʿAbd al-Raḥmān al-Saqqāf (d. 1416). Al-Saqqāf stands at the beginning of a new phase in the history of the ʿAlawī Way: the development of an institutional complex of Sufi practices. This complex comprises the suite of cultural forms that still characterize the Hadrami sayyids and their way. The suite includes identifiable clusters of ritual, geographical, and textual forms, each of which has ties to an individual originator.

RITUAL

ʿAbd al-Raḥmān al-Saqqāf is most famous today for the ritual of "presencing," which is associated with his name. The Saqqāf Presencing

11. Syed Naguib al-Attas, in his study of Sufism among the Malays, makes the point thus: "In certain respects the *ʿAlawiyyah* is different from the rest. Its primary distinction is its *silsilah* or spiritual genealogy, which is also of a biological nature. For the *silsilah* of the *ʿAlawiyyah* Order is the family tree, and the *Ṭarīqah* is more or less a family concern." (al-Attas 1963: 32)

(ḥaḍrat al-Saqqāf) takes place every Monday and Thursday in Tarim at the mosque that also bears his name. Al-Saqqāf composed litanies *(Rātib al-Saqqāf)* which are used at the Saqqāf Presencing and introduced the use of flutes and tambourines to accompany its performance (al-Shāṭirī 1983: 264). His descendants have directed it until today.

Al-Saqqāf's great-great-grandson, Aḥmad b. Ḥusayn al-ʿAydarūs, brought singers and musicians specially from Egypt to form an ensemble of seven to accompany the Saqqāf Presencing. They settled in Tarim, and their descendants continue to fill these roles today. The musicians are known as the "servants of al-Saqqāf" *(akhdām al-Saqqāf)*, and the positions are hereditary in a few families; one of these families has the surname "the Egyptians" *(Āl Bā Miṣrī)*. The musicians receive no payment for accompanying the Saqqāf Presencing: they play "for the facing of God" *(li-wajh Allāh)*. Beyond their playing at presencings, they have performed invocations to God at the funerals of sayyids since the sixteenth century, and since the nineteenth century, they have played their instruments at the weddings of sayyids; for these services, they receive honoraria. They are in demand beyond Tarim and perform their services in towns at some distance.

PLACE

ʿAbd al-Raḥmān's son ʿUmar al-Muḥḍār (d. 1430) is famous for his ascetic rigors in isolated places. Stories of his actions abound in oral and written accounts, such as that of his spending a month at the tomb of the prophet Hūd consuming the while only one pound of dried fish (al-Ḥāmid 1968: 749). During such retreats, he reportedly saw his ancestor the prophet Muḥammad regularly. Following in his footsteps, pilgrims today trek annually to the tomb of Hūd, beginning at a large rock above the river, known as ʿUmar's Rock, with two of the prostrations *(rakʿatayn)* prescribed in normal and supererogatory Muslim prayers.[12] The Hūd pilgrimage is the largest annual pilgrimage in Hadramawt. ʿUmar's stature associates him with another of the largest annual gatherings in the region as well. The al-Muḥḍār mosque in Tarim, which bears his name and which possesses a high minaret visible from over a mile, is the venue for the final prayers *(khatm)* of the fasting month of Ramaḍān. On this occasion, devotees come from towns sur-

12. Two prostrations are customary out of respect for a mosque; the place is thus treated as one.

FIGURE 8. Umar's rock, the first station of pilgrimage to Hūd, under a new prayer platform, by the perpetual stream. Ablutions in foreground. Photo by the author.

rounding Tarim and overflow onto the streets performing their prostrations. The prayers at this mosque close the holy month of Ramaḍān in Tarim and its vicinity.

ʿAbd al-Raḥmān al-Saqqāf and ʿUmar al-Muḥḍār initiated ritual and spiritual practices that continue to be observed today. The association with them across the centuries and down the generations bestows an aura upon these practices: they are relics. The enactments of these virtual relics are indissolubly tied to places—ʿUmar's Rock, al-Saqqāf's Mosque—in complexes that cannot be fully reproduced elsewhere. Spiritual meaning is grounded in ritual locale.

A notion exists of an ultimate source of value, to which subsequent avatars stand in a relation of derivation by emanation: from God to the prophets to the prophet Muḥammad and to his descendants. The latter are certainly mobile, and one can trace them with well-honed genealogical methods. The litanies and musical instruments too are portable, as texts and instruments. What is absolute and irreproducible here is the historical convergence of these streams in this one place, in one distinct complex. The graves, the mosques, the hills, and the rocks—these are the relics of an original convergence. Reproduction is possible, but only as a reduction: its value is less than that of the original. Replicas always relate to relics as satellites relate to their sources, and they always point back to their sources. The emergence of replicas of the relics itself signals the advent of a structure of memory, in which reduction is a prime feature. The relation of difference between replica and relic frames the progress of time as a process of decline. With the passing of the generations, the exaltation of the ancestors intensifies (al-Shāṭirī 1983: 255).

TEXT

The coalescing of the institutional complex that is the sayyid Sufi way was accompanied by a major literary production: *Garden of the Heart Essences, Apothecary for Incurable Maladies,* a collection of biographies of Sufis of Tarim by ʿAbd al-Raḥmān al-Khaṭīb, who died in 1451.[13] The author was a self-confessed enthusiast of the saints, who wrote because he feared that the saints, Sufis, and scholars of Tarim were in danger of being forgotten, "unbeknownst even as their graves were trodden underfoot." The book comprises five hundred stories of preternatural acts and events in the lives of saints. The accounts are not didactic in the sense of fostering pious imitation. Rather, they are replete with awe-inspiring acts that are in fact inimitable. The sources of charisma are not apparent. He cites a report of the jurist Aḥmad Ibn Ḥanbal, to whom a man commented disparagingly, "These sufis sit in the mosques without knowledge." Ibn Ḥanbal replied, "My son, their sitting is their knowledge."

Although al-Khaṭīb was not a sayyid, his position in the development of the institutional complex was crucial. He was a student of ʿAbd al-Raḥmān al-Saqqāf and died three and a half decades after him. Unlike the many other books about the sayyids, al-Khaṭīb's book is not organized genealogically. It contains a chapter on the blessings in the water, cemeteries, and hills of Tarim and one on the virtues of the house of the Prophet. The book groups its biographies of saints into four generations, the last being the nearest to the author's own time. Abd al-Raḥmān al-Saqqāf and his son ʿUmar al-Muḥḍār, whom al-Khaṭīb knew, were dominant figures in the last generation. In the earlier ones, the accounts and figures were more varied, including a number of non-sayyids. The rich accounts in al-Khaṭīb's book became a seminal source for subsequent biographies and histories. To the ritual and geographical innovations of al-

13. The Arabic title is *Bustān al-qulūb al-jawāhir wa-taryāq al-ʿilal al-muʿḍalāt* (al-Khaṭīb n.d.).

Saqqāf and al-Muḥḍār, al-Khaṭīb's stories added an abundant narrative vehicle that portrayed vividly the doings of the saints in the locale of Tarim, amongst its mosques, graves, hills, and gardens. The limpid quality of its imagery gave its subjects a familiar immediacy, and it became known by another title, *The Transparent Essence, Recounting the Marvels of the Sayyids of Tarim, and Their Contemporaries in It of the Greatest, Gnostic Saints.*[14]

The Transparent Essence stands in a transitional position, looking backward and forward at the same time. In its explicitly testamentary motivation, it makes a very local, oral world available, accessible, and reproducible to others removed in space and time. It launches that world into discourse. Through the book, the stories of the saints became detachable documents, and these documents became authorities upon which later authors drew for their own compositions. I explore the textual reincarnations of the hagiographies in the second part of this book, "Genealogical Travel." Here, we need to mark the inauguration of the textual form of the institutionalized Sufi complex, placing it beside its ritual and geographical counterparts.

By the middle of the fifteenth century, the constitutive elements of the ʿAlawī Way had been brought together in a complex that is recognizable today. This complex institutionalized a canon of saints, texts, rituals, special places, and genealogies. As a Sufi way, it has not been well understood, and Trimingham has characterized it as a limited "family way" (Trimingham 1973: 3; also al-Attas 1963: 32). Viewed as a complex, however, the ʿAlawī Way is a malleable discourse that evolved over time, as it confronted new historical and cultural situations. As a complex, too, its beginnings can be approximated.

Shifting Trade Routes: The Transregional Context

The development of the ʿAlawī Way in Hadramawt, and its engagement with the Hadrami landscape, was part of a dramatic and dynamic shift in the wider world of the Red Sea, Indian Ocean, and beyond. During the period between the First Jurist (d. 1255) and al-Khaṭīb (d. 1451), southern Arabia, from Zabīd near the Red Sea to Hadramawt off the Arabian Sea, was under the rule of the Rasulid state (1235–1457). The Rasulid era

14. The Arabic title is *al-Jawhar al-shaffāf fī dhikr karamāt man fī Tarīm min al-sādāt al-ashrāf wa-man ʿāṣirhum fīhā min al-awliyāʾ al-akābir al-ʿarrāf.*

was the golden age of premodern southern Arabia, a time of wealth, luxury, sumptuous buildings, and courtly cultivation of the arts (Croken 1990; Ibn al-Daybaʿ 1979; Jāzim 2003; al-Khazrajī 1914a, 1914b; Varisco 1994). Like its counterpart in Egypt, the Mamluk state (1250–1517), the Rasulid state benefited from a recent shift in long-distance trading routes.

The shift is marked by the Mongol conquest of Baghdad in 1258 (Abu-Lughod 1989: 120; Schrieke 1960: 9). Up to that point, the maritime half of long-distance trade between the East (China, the spice islands of the Malay Archipelago, India) and Europe went through the Persian Gulf, up to Baghdad, and from there to the Levant (the Silk Road across Central Asia was the overland counterpart). Chinese junks and Arab dhows traversed the entire distance of this long route, from China to Iraq, stopping at the port of Quilon in Malabar on the southwestern Indian coast. With the fall of Baghdad and the Mongols' relocation of their rival capital to Tabriz, the caliphal peace across the Fertile Crescent shattered, with disastrous consequences for the transport of goods. The maritime route from the East across the Indian Ocean shifted from the Persian Gulf to the Red Sea, arriving at the Mediterranean farther south, in Alexandria in Egypt rather than on the Levantine coast. This rerouting of long-distance trade brought into prominence a series of cities now vitally connected to each other: Venice, Alexandria, Cairo, Jedda, Aden, Cambay (subsequently Diu, Surat, Bombay), Calicut, and Pasai (subsequently Melaka, Aceh, Banten) in north Sumatra. In the Indian Ocean, this new route quickly became identified with Muslim merchants and states. By the first decade of the fifteenth century, the rulers of Cambay in Gujarat were Muslim, as were those of Aceh and Melaka in the Strait of Melaka and Gresik on the north Java coast. Muslim tombstones in Pasai date from 1290. The Venetian Marino Sanudo noted these developments as early as 1306:

> Earlier the largest share of the Indian merchandise transported to the West used to make its way over Baghdad to the ports of Syria and Asia Minor; in those days both spices and other Indian products were cheaper and more abundant than nowadays. Now they are for the most part unloaded at Aden and from there transported to Alexandria; in that way a third of their value flows into the treasury of the sultan of Egypt. The profits along that route come only to the advantage of the Arab traders, for the sultan does not allow a Christian to travel through his territory to India. (Quoted in Schrieke 1960: 11–12)

The intrepid Janet Abu-Lughod has argued that in this period, from around 1250 on, a "world system" of trade came into being "before European hegemony" (also the title of her book; Abu-Lughod 1989), connecting China with Europe on both ends. While she sees the intensity of exchanges start to fall off in 1350, this situation was less marked in the Red Sea–Indian Ocean sector.[15] In this sector, the chain of port cities forged connections in ever-denser networks of trade, interstate relations, and religious movements (A. Lewis 1973; Mortel 1995; Tibbetts 1981). The consolidation and expansion of this transcultural realm of social exchanges were crucial to the formation of the ʿAlawī Way both at home and abroad. Hadrami sayyids' rise to prominence in Gujarat in the sixteenth century and in the Malay world in the eighteenth was part and parcel of the expanding transregional, cosmopolitan Muslim ecumene which got its start in the thirteenth-century shift in Indian Ocean trade routes. By locating the formation of the institutional complex of the ʿAlawī Way in the first century of this Indian Ocean "new world" of Islam, we are better able to relate its early formation in the homeland to its later developments in the diaspora. In the thirteenth century, energized trading links enhanced the mobility of religious scholars and their ideas.

In al-Khaṭīb's *The Transparent Essence,* the fourth generation, which begins with ʿAbd al-Raḥmān al-Saqqāf, sees the introduction of a new motif of light. Light plays an important role in the synthetic thought of Ibn al-ʿArabī, as the generative primordial Light of Muḥammad. Al-Saqqāf lived in a period when the influence of Ibn al-ʿArabī reached its apogee in Yemen, when his partisan Ibn al-Raddād was appointed to the supreme judgeship of the Rasulid state (1235–1467) (al-Ḥibshī 1976: 138; Knysh 1999b: 248). Al-Saqqāf and Ibn al-Raddād died within a year of each other (1416 and 1417, respectively). During the period of the Rasulids, new states in the Red Sea–Indian Ocean region—in Egypt, Yemen, India—were formed by nonnative slaves, *déraciné* mercenaries, and Turkoman conquerors who patronized scholars and Sufis in building their regimes (al-Muḥibbī 1966; Ulughkhānī 1910–28; Wink 1997). The Rasulids had inherited such traditions quite directly from their Ayyubid predecessors and Mamluk contemporaries in Egypt. Scholars were indispensable as administrative institution builders and shapers of popular opinion, while Sufis often served as personal counselors. In many cases, the prevailing intellectual culture meant that scholars often were Sufis too. The celebrated Saladin the Ayyubi, while preparing to fight

15. The notion of a broad decline in this period is a consensus view among economic historians; Lopez, Miskimin, and Udovitch (1970) locate Middle Eastern trends with broader ones in Eurasia.

the Christians, had been advised to channel funds for scholars and Sufis to soldiers instead. He refused, saying, "How possibly can I withhold the pensions of a people who, while I am peacefully asleep in my bed, fight on my behalf with arrows that never miss a target. You want me to spend their money on people whose arrows might miss? Never! They even have a share in the public treasury" (Memon 1976: 49).

Knysh has definitively established the trajectory of Ibn al-ʿArabī's influence in Rasulid Yemen and concludes that the rulers there were able to divide their potential critics, the learned, by selective patronage of factions (Knysh 1999b: 268). Whatever the reasons, Muslim states had already begun to patronize Sufis and saints, with the Fatimid celebrations of the birth of the Prophet *(mawlid)* in their courts. In the century and a half from the time of Hadramawt's First Jurist (d. 1255) to that of ʿAbd al-Raḥmān al-Saqqāf (d. 1416), the southern part of Yemen saw an unusual development of interest in Ibn al-ʿArabī. This period is captured in the lives and careers of Ibn Jamīl (d. 1253), al-Jabartī (d. 1403), and Ibn al-Raddād (d. 1417). Ibn Jamīl was one of the first to introduce the "auditory gatherings" *(samāʿ)*, which became popular among followers of Ibn al-ʿArabī.[16] During these sessions, followers sang and chanted hymns and litanies in unison (al-Ḥibshī 1976: 31). Subsequently, al-Jabartī introduced musical instruments into the sessions, such as flutes and tambourines. His gatherings became popular, and he commanded a huge following as a result. Even Rasulid kings such as al-Mujāhid, al-Afḍal, and al-Ashraf attended. The sounds were so potent that listeners would become agitated, and some threw themselves from high places (al-Ḥibshī 1976: 32–33). In 1386, the sultan went to the seashore with a retinue of Sufi shaykhs and their families to hold such sessions in the evening; the sultan remained there almost a week (al-Khazrajī 1914b: 197).[17] In this period, Hadramawt had close ties to Aden, and the Rasulids maintained a governor in the coastal Hadrami town of al-Shiḥr (al-Ḥāmid 1968: 547 ff.). Hadramis were among the scholars the Rasulids supported generously (Knysh 1999b: 227). Given the royal patronage and prestige of Ibn al-ʿArabī's followers and their activities, it is not surpris-

16. *Samāʿ* gatherings are associated with Ibn al-ʿArabī's followers, even though he considered them a sign of immaturity (Knysh 1999b: 233). ʿAbd al-Raḥmān al-Saqqāf reportedly detested them initially, before he came round to embracing them (al-Shillī 1982; Bā Wazīr 1961: 135).

17. I am indebted to Lucine Taminian for sharing this reference and for her infectious enthusiasm for the Rasulids, whom she first brought to my attention.

ing that their ideas and practices were taken up in other parts of the Rasulid realm.[18]

Thus, in Hadramawt, ʿAbd al-Raḥmān al-Saqqāf introduced the auditory gathering, with its developed complement of flutes and tambourines, and incorporated it as one of the distinguishing features of the ʿAlawī Way, the Saqqāf Presencing. Even his employment of the troupe at life-cycle events of sayyid families had precedent; al-Jabartī had been the first to introduce it on family occasions (al-Ḥibshī 1976: 32). The combination of hymns and musical instruments was subsequently carried to other places, to Sayʾūn in Hadramawt, by the saint ʿAlī al-Ḥabshī, and to Lamu in Kenya, by Ḥabīb Ṣāliḥ (El Zein 1974). Together with the flutes and tambourines of the auditory gatherings that El Zein reported in Lamu, he recorded the genealogical liturgies. A chart of one of these liturgies opens his book, tracing through early generations the same Hadrami lineage of the Prophet that we have seen here, the canonical founders of the ʿAlawī Way.[19]

Within a century of the death of al-Saqqāf, the auditory gathering was reintroduced to Aden by a great-grandson of al-Saqqāf, Abū Bakr al-ʿAydarūs the Adeni, the saint of Aden (d. 1508), whom we met in chapter 1. By this time, the influence of Ibn al-ʿArabī's followers had waned in the region, as their opponents gained the upper hand in the mid-fifteenth century.[20] The Adeni wrote poetry and litanies that were sung and accom-

18. References to Ibn al-ʿArabī among Hadrami historians are usually guarded rather than explicit. Bā Wazīr states that some of the Hadramis placed importance on reading his books, although the books were kept out of the hands of beginners and young students (Bā Wazīr 1961: 90–91). The saint of Aden, Abū Bakr al-ʿAydarūs the Adeni, remembered being scolded and beaten by his father only once, when his father caught him with a copy of Ibn al-ʿArabī's *Meccan Conquests* (Baḥraq al-Ḥaḍramī 1988: 9). His father forbade him to read Ibn ʿArabī's works but ordered him to maintain a good opinion of the man: Ibn al-ʿArabī was among the greatest of gnostics and scholars, whose books contained truths known by the loftiest but harmful to beginners. The son replied that he was of the same opinion. Like the attitudes among Talmudic scholars, circumspection is justified by the saying attributed to Malik and al-Junayd (and al-Ghazzālī by some): "Whoever becomes a sufi before knowing the law has become an atheist *(Man taṣawwaf qabla an yatafaqqah tazanddaq)*." (al-Shāṭirī 1983: 253)

19. That this consensus exists is evident in works by non-sayyid authors. One of these, Saʿīd ʿAwaḍ Bā Wazīr, whose *Thought and Culture in Hadrami History* attempts to redress an imbalance in favor of sayyid personalities in Hadrami historiography by including a minimum of sayyid biographies, pares down the number of sayyids he mentions from the twelfth century onward, essentially leaving us with a list of the founders of the ʿAlawī Way (compare with table 1): Muḥammad Principal of Mirbāṭ; the First Jurist (II in table 1); ʿAbd Allāh Bā ʿAlawī, ʿAbd al-Raḥmān al-Saqqāf (III), ʿUmar al-Muḥḍār (IV); ʿAlī b. Abī Bakr b. ʿAbd al-Raḥmān al-Saqqāf; ʿAbd Allāh al-ʿAydarūs (V) (Bā Wazīr 1961: 126–40).

20. The trajectory of the rivalry is traced in al-Ḥibshī 1976 and Knysh 1999b.

FIGURE 9. Tambourines and flutes of the "servants of al-Saqqāf." The wedding of a Java-born sayyid in a tribal town some distance from Tarim. Photo by the author.

panied by musical instruments. He was religiously musical in the new ʿAlawī Way. He was skilled in combining textual, vocal, and instrumental media. In Aden, Abū Bakr was able to reconstitute the practice that had become (or was becoming) identified as a Hadrami-ʿAlawī mode of religiosity in Aden. His own tomb became the destination of an annual pilgrimage in which pilgrims used ritual paraphernalia similar to those of his ancestors in Tarim. In this area, he was a pioneer for Hadramis. Aden was a transshipment node in the burgeoning trade between Gujarat and the Hejaz in the Red Sea (Barbosa 1918 [1518]). Within a couple of generations, his agnates of the ʿAydarūs family achieved position and renown as influential religious figures in major transregional trading centers such as Ahmadabad, Broach, and Surat in Gujarat, as well as in developing Muslim principalities such as Bijapur off the Konkan coast of India. In the books of biographies, success abroad is summarily judged by whether pilgrims visit one's grave, and those whose graves are visited earn titles such as the Principal of Aḥmad Ābād. Part 2, "Genealogical Travel," explores these travels and their narratives.

From the sixteenth century on, as members of the ʿAydarūs family made their mark abroad and remitted wealth home, their brothers and cousins in Hadramawt branched out from Tarim to create new settlements with date-palm gardens over which they exercised a form of sovereignty. These gardens were the *ḥawṭas,* whose sayyid heads were known as *manṣab* (bin ʿAqīl 1949: 47), a term possibly borrowed from Indian Mughal imperial ranks (Ali 1966, 1985; Moreland 1998 [1936]). One of the first *mansab*s was Aḥmad b. Ḥusayn al-ʿAydarūs (see table 1) and others followed, a majority of them ʿAydarūses. As a result of these expansions abroad and at home, the ʿAydarūs family became the grandest of the sayyid lineages. Its eponymous ancestor, ʿAbd Allāh al-ʿAydarūs, father of the Adeni, is thus invoked in the graveyard of Tarim with the honorific "Sultan of Notables."

The creation of such new settlements, *ḥawṭa*s, was an important way for sayyid families to establish themselves across the country (bin Hāshim 1948: 112). *Ḥawṭa*s were created for several reasons. Among them was the basic idea of a sanctuary. Similar concepts are embodied in the terms *hijra* in North Yemen—linked with the extension of Zaydi sayyid settlements in tribal lands (Gochenour 1984)—and *ḥaram,* to describe the holiest sites of Islam (Serjeant 1962). In Hadramawt, *ḥawṭa*s were established and maintained by the agreement of two parties—typically a sayyid and lineages of the tribe whose commons the *ḥawṭa* was carved out of or adjoined.[21] Together, the parties provided guarantees of protection, both spiritual and mundane. Under the protection of these parties, the places became sanctuaries within which arms and violence were proscribed (bin ʿAqīl 1949: 47–48). Other activities, such as trade, pilgrimage, and agricultural investment, then became possible. In *ḥawṭa*s, sayyids might feature in multiple roles, as *manṣab,* investor, dispenser of justice, spiritual protector, and recipient of tithes *(khums,*

21. Documents of such agreements, such as those between sections of the Bā Jaray tribe and the ʿAydarūs sayyids about the settlement of Būr, are in the Sayʾūn Museum Archives, dating to 1665 and 1865 (SMA 1, SMA 17). Copies of the latter and other agreements were submitted to the British by the ʿAydarūs *manṣab* laying claim to sovereignty over Būr in

FIGURE 10. Flag and following. Progress of the manṣab of ʿAynāt into Hūd during the annual pilgrimage, after bin Shihāb entry. Photo by the author.

the one-fifth set aside for the Prophet's family, sometimes assimilated by the state) and sumptuary benefits. Oral accounts of such agreements often depict the sayyid returning to Hadramawt with wealth from abroad, making an investment in partnership with local tribes on their land. Hagiographies offer varying accounts. In one instance, the charismatic sayyid ʿAbd Allāh Bā ʿAlwī (d. 1331), grandson of the First Jurist, was granted a quarter of a garden belonging to a lineage of nontribal farmers, the Āl Bā Najjār, as a votive offering (*nadhr*). Tribesmen of the Āl Kathīr had been looting the dates in the garden, but with part of the land belonging to the sayyid, most of the Kathīr now kept their distance. When one of them cut off some dates and ate them, the Bā Najjār called out to the sayyid in supplication; the man who ate the dates subsequently developed an injury in his hand, which proved fatal. The sayyid, for his part, made his share of the garden into an endowment for some mosques (al-Shillī 1901 vol. 2: 189). Closer to our time, within living memory in the settlement of ʿAynāt, it was mandated that each household rear a

1945, as colonial authorities imposed a garrison and began to tax the town (IORL, R/20/C/1475, "Affairs of Bor and Other Mansabates (Kathiri State).")

goat belonging to the *manṣab (dhabīḥat al-manṣab)*, a sacrificial animal for festive occasions.[22]

Sacred History: Discourse of Frontiers, Transformation of Landscapes

The ʿAlawī Way was the convergence of a number of streams in Tarim. These streams coalesced in the context of a transregional shift in Indian Ocean trade routes from the Persian Gulf to the Red Sea. A line of descent from the prophet Muḥammad, brought from Iraq, and a spiritual genealogy from Abū Madyan, brought from the Maghreb, coalesced into a Sufi way organized around ritual, geographical, and textual institutions. Tarim was the point at which the streams met. The skeletal outline I have presented so far, which draws on time lines and itineraries to show how things came together in one place and time, does not adequately represent the accomplishments of the historical accounts from which it draws. For the itineraries that featured so prominently as a basic genre element within these accounts created effects that go beyond the ambitions of positivist historical reconstruction. In telling of the travels of various figures, they created a discourse of frontiers that ultimately transformed landscapes. The discursive effect on Hadramawt in general, and on Tarim in particular, was to transform a place from a destination to an origin. Such effects were created through intertextual narratives that continuously wove the movements of sayyids in Hadramawt with the journeys of the early Muslims in Islam's formative period of sacred history, in Medina and Mecca. Such narratives act most strongly on persons with developed historical sensibilities, who can readily see parallels and recognize continuities and connections being invoked. Where such sensibilities are lacking, the repeated telling of the narratives themselves becomes a form of education. It is thus not surprising that education is often cited as the reason for their travels. In this way, travelers open up frontier lands.

Unlike the nineteenth-century American idea of Manifest Destiny,

22. British colonial officials, intent on extending the tax collector's brief into such settlements in the 1940s and usurping the sovereignties of sayyids and tribes alike, portrayed such practices as oppression of the people (IORL, R/20/C/1475). But the goats were part of a broader set of local exchanges, within which the *manṣab* maintained a communal kitchen (referred to by the Indian term *langgar*) that was financed by endowments in Hyderabad, India.

frontiers in Hadrami sayyid discourses of mobility are not devoid of people but full of them. Newcomers such as the sayyids found places for themselves—as educators—in lands that were already full. This theme has been a constant one throughout the Hadrami diaspora around the Indian Ocean, beginning with Hadramawt itself in the early days. This chapter concludes by looking at how the landscape of the Hadrami homeland itself was shaped by continuous engagement with sacred history over centuries, as the diaspora of sayyids moved through and settled the area.

Islam became established as a world religion when it erupted out of one corner of Arabia (Donner 1981). Originating in a dry trading outpost peripheral to the densely populated centers of civilization at the extremities of the peninsula, Islam reversed the geographical valences, turning well-watered lands into frontiers. This powerful, founding expansion is usually known as "the openings/conquests" *(al-futūḥāt)* in which the geographical and religious frontiers were one and the same. One of the classical accounts of this expansion and establishment of Islam is al-Balādhurī's *The Conquest of the Countries* (*Futūḥ al-Buldān;* al-Balādhurī 1932). The concept of a geographical and religious frontier is also easily sublimated and internalized into that of a spiritual one, as in *The Meccan Openings (al-Futūḥāt al-Makkiyya;* Ibn al-ʿArabī 1972) by the controversial Sufi theoretician Ibn al-ʿArabī. Migration carries a powerful religious charge, being a movement forward in both space and time. In the Islamic calendar, the year of the Prophet's migration from Mecca to Medina is Year One, as we have noted.

When Aḥmad b. ʿĪsā the Migrant arrived in Hadramawt, the Hadramis were already a Muslim people. However, sayyid historiography still made of the country a religious frontier. One of the most common ways of doing so was to characterize the inhabitants as bedouin. While this characterization may not have been entirely accurate, it activated a field of semantic associations among landscape, people, and moral quality etymologically grounded in a shared triliteral root. Throughout the Arabian Peninsula, the countryside or desert, *al-bādiya,* has had the reputation of being incompletely covered by religious discipline. Correspondingly, its inhabitants, the bedouin, *al-badū,* have been stereotyped as religiously lacking. In Hadramawt today, for example, townsmen tell of other locals visiting prostitutes in bedouin encampments on the edge of town. Bedouin life, *al-badāwa,* has had and continues to have the romantic image of being carefree. The characterization of the countryside as religiously lacking has been mapped onto time as well. The speech of bedouin is often supposed, again romantically, to be closer to the original, prerevelation Arabic of the Age of Ignorance. Arabic lexicographers in the towns of Islamic Iraq—an Arabized *(musta'rab)* but not originally Arab country—used to interview bedouin in the markets as part of their scholarly effort to gain insights into the past of the language. Most concretely, the religious shortcomings of the bedouin are proved by their lack of a Friday congregational mosque, which is enjoined by Islamic law wherever Muslims settle (al-Shāṭirī al-'Alawī al-Ḥusaynī al-Tarīmī 1949: 51). By definition, bedouin do not settle; as a consequence, they do not have Friday mosques and are thereby less Muslim, in the spatial logic of townsmen.[23] In contradistinction to bedouin, sayyid historiography stresses sayyids' mosque-building activities wherever they settle, their nature as learned people, and their forswearing of arms. The sayyids have come to spread the religion among the ignorant bedouin of Hadramawt.

No country is ever too full for another mosque. The Hadrami town of Tarim, the sayyid center *par excellence,* boasts three hundred and sixty mosques. A stranger newly arrived in town with nowhere to go can always "go sleep in the mosque." Key sayyid texts, such as the seventeenth-century *The Irrigating Fount* (al-Shillī 1901) and the eighteenth-century *The Sublime Benefits* (*al-Fawā'id al-saniyya;* A. H. al-Ḥaddād n.d.), dedicate entire chapters to mosques consecrated by their ancestors. The building of mosques is often undertaken by Hadrami sayyids where they settle. Mosques are ready-made models for public spaces and are of abiding interest to community leaders and rulers of states. As a result, those who organize their construction often enter into relations with masters of the locale. Even in the socialist People's Democratic Republic of Yemen of the 1980s, those who donated imported materials to build mosques enjoyed the benefit of importing other items tax free as well. The sayyid 'Umar al-Junayd, who was invited by the English founder of Singapore to relocate his business from Sumatra in the early nineteenth century, established the first mosque on the island, and his descendants were prominent Muslim leaders of the city for generations. Today, schools, streets,

23. Urban, Arabian sentiments are prominent more generally in Islamic literature (Donner 1981). Strictly speaking, a Friday mosque need not be a physical building. However, I have listened to Hadrami bedouin consulting the jurist Sayyid 'Abd Allāh al-Ḥaddād of al-Mukallā about whether they were obliged to construct a Friday mosque. The discussion was lengthy, with the bedouin explaining the complex temporal rhythms of their movements to the jurist and the jurist interpreting these movements in the categories of Islamic law.

an industrial estate, a parliamentary constituency, and a subway station in Singapore bear their name.

Not only did the sayyids push back the frontiers of religious ignorance in the countryside, they pushed back the countryside (uncultivated, unsettled land) itself. The manuscript "The Journey Intent on Beholding the Shrine" (A. H. al-ʿAṭṭās n.d.), a contemporaneous account of the founding of the pilgrimage town al-Mashhad by its founder, the sayyid ʿAlī b. Ḥasan al-ʿAṭṭās, described the area as empty except for bedouin and thieves when he arrived. One of his founding acts was the discovery of an ancient well, which magically sprang to life when he came upon it, like the old well of Zamzam in Mecca that was rediscovered by the Prophet's paternal grandfather, ʿAbd al-Muṭṭalib. The discovery of a well is a precondition for the creation of a pilgrimage destination, as pilgrims need to be watered in great numbers.[24] A well also provides the irrigation necessary to open up new land for farming, enabling people to settle. As we have seen, revivifying "dead" land was how the Endower of Qasam created a legally sound, economic basis for descendants of the Migrant to settle in Hadramawt, when they were still newcomers to the country.

The account of how sayyids first settled in Sayʾūn , the modern capital of interior Hadramawt, uses similar motifs from sacred history. The first residence of a sayyid in the new Kathīrī capital of Sayʾūn, in the sixteenth century, was at the invitation of its sultan, the famous Badr Bū Ṭuwayriq (who reportedly created the most powerful Kathīrī state ever and repelled the Portuguese): "that we may have a light and a lamp to guide us, for my town does not have a single one of the family of the Prophet" (al-Kindī 1991: 202–04). The sultan invited the Ḥabīb ("beloved sayyid") ʿUmar al-Ṣāfī of Tarim to marry and settle in Sayʾūn, to which some of the latter's followers had migrated from Tarim. Sayyid ʿUmar married a Sayʾūn woman of the Āl Bā Najjār and returned to Tarim, leaving in Sayʾūn the issue of that union, his son Ṭaha b. ʿUmar al-Ṣāfī. When Ṭaha grew up, he repatriated to Tarim, whereupon the sultan rushed after him to plead with the sayyids there for his return to Sayʾūn. Sayyid Ṭaha would not budge until the sayyids of Tarim presented him with a

24. The association with Zamzam draws upon even deeper springs, because the well came to life when Ismāʿīl, ancestor of all Arabs, struck the ground with his foot. Ismāʿīl had migrated to Mecca with his Nubian mother, Hagar, and was close to dying of thirst when his mother ascended Ṣafā and Marwa to plead with Allāh. Allāh sent Gabriel to Ismāʿīl, as he was later to be sent to the prophet Muḥammad.

writ confirming that the area of his residence in Say'ūn was a sacred, protected enclave *(ḥawṭā)*, a sanctuary similar to that of Mecca *(al-Ḥaram)* and an integral part of Tarim. Subsequently, Ṭaha established near Say'ūn a mosque and a well, where the water of the holy Meccan well Zamzam was found, possessing thaumaturgic properties.

The story of Ṭaha's residence models a relationship between Say'ūn and Tarim similar to that between the holy cities Medina and Mecca. The prophet Muḥammad's grandfather ʿAbd al-Muṭṭalib had been born in Medina (then Yathrib) of a woman of the Banū Najjār (a section of the Yemeni, Qaḥṭānī tribe of Khazraj, one of the two dominant tribes of Medina), and his place of residence was subsequently an issue between his maternal and paternal (Meccan) kin. When the orphan ʿAbd al-Muṭṭalib was oppressed by his paternal uncle Nawfal after his repatriation to Mecca, the maternal uncles rode down from Medina to Mecca on eighty camels to his defense. Moreover, ʿAbd al-Muṭṭalib was the one who rediscovered the holy well of Zamzam in Mecca and controlled pilgrimage to the Kaʿba, feeding and watering pilgrims. Two generations later, the Banū Najjār affines were to play a prominent role as early supporters of the Prophetic cause, some of whose most vehement opponents were agnates.

The narrative parallel between the holy towns of Mecca and Medina and the Hadrami towns of Tarim and Say'ūn makes of the Hadrami landscape a valenced structure in which a specific relation exists between political and religious power: the sultan is the follower and helper of the sayyid; the Say'ūnīs are affines of the Tarim sayyids. In Hadramawt and abroad where sayyid communities settled, the term *khawwālnā,* "our mothers' brothers" is used in the sense of "the locals"; the other common term is *muḥibbīn,* "devotees." In Islamic history, the first Muslims migrated from the Prophet's home town of Mecca to Medina, whose residents supported the Prophet. In the vocabulary of sacred history, the former, called the Migrants *(al-muhājirūn)*, are religiously prior to the latter, the Helpers (*al-anṣār*); together, they formed the community of Muslims. Some of the non-Prophetic lineages of religious notables (the shaykhs, such as the al-Khaṭīb) in Hadramawt trace their origins to the Helpers today.

Sayyid accounts of settling Hadramawt tell of their transformation of the built landscape. The transformations conferred new spiritual potencies upon places that had been religiously empty in their previous incarnations. These activities figured whole regions as frontiers even as the sayyids brought them within the precincts of the City of God.

In discursive terms, sayyid migrations to and through Hadramawt

FIGURE 11. Pilgrims at the tomb of Ḥabīb ʿAlī al-Ḥabshi, Sayʾūn. Photo by the author.

brought the country within the ambit of sacred history. In settling the country, the sayyids transformed its landscape from a destination to a series of moving origins. These origins are marked by the eastward movement of graves, as we have seen: that of the Migrant in Ḥusaysa, of his son ʿUbayd Allāh in Būr, of his grandson ʿAlawī in Bayt Jubayr, and so on, until that of ʿAlī the Endower of Qasam in Tarim. The white cupolas above the graves dot the Hadrami landscape. They provide geographical orientation for the traveler and mark a pathway through history for the initiated.

Tarim: From Destination to Origin

In this chapter, we have traced the migrations of the Migrant Aḥmad b. ʿĪsā and his descendants along wadi Hadramawt, and their settling in Tarim. In this early period, between the tenth and the twelfth centuries, Tarim was a destination for the diaspora of the ʿAlawī sayyids from Iraq. The appellations of the early ancestors—Aḥmad b. ʿĪsā the Migrant, ʿAlī the Endower of Qasam—acknowledge their position as incomers and bespeak the self-consciousness of the newly arrived. Yet these newcomers were unusual in their self-portrayals. They brought things of value that had not been available before, such as Prophetic descent and an organized Sufi way, and vested them in the locale of Tarim—in its rituals, mosques, hills, graves, and other places. These mobile persons brought with them portable valuables, which they then interred in Tarim and its environs. The Endower of Qasam built the premier sayyid mosque, the Bā ʿAlawī mosque of Tarim, with mud bricks specially brought from the earth of Bayt Jubayr, where he was born and where his father and grandfather were buried. The Endower of Qasam also invested his twenty thousand dinārs by planting date palms; pious, successful migrants put their money in real estate to foster learning among their offspring; many built mosques; others sank wells, thereby creating new agricultural lands, population settlements, and pilgrimage destinations. Such actions "revivified dead land" (al-Shāṭirī al-ʿAlawī al-Ḥusaynī al-Tarīmī 1949: 115). Understood within the broader context of such actions of improvement by interment, burial can come to signify an investment of mobile values to create potentials in a locale. With burial, the dead bring a place to life, as it were. The narrative of the first six generations of sayyids in Hadramawt, whose burial plots trace a line moving toward Tarim (from the Migrant buried in Ḥusaysa to the Endower of Qasam buried in Tarim), forms a synecdoche that models movement as investment and becomes a trope for sayyid historiography: "Each land they descend upon is brought to life, as if making thrive the most ruined of countries" (A. Q. al-ʿAydarūs 1985: 75). Hadrami history books usually state where persons are buried as a basic fact, and the place of burial carries with it wider significances in social life.

The discourses of mobility that describe the founding activities of migrants such as the sayyids shape the historiography of Hadramawt. Within this corpus, the abundant narrative references to the sacred history of Islam in Mecca and Medina do not only parallel Prophetic precedence; they connect to and continue Prophetic activity as well, now in Hadramawt, by the Prophet's descendants. As Hadramawt came within the fold of sacred history, its landscape was transformed. With the arrival of the Migrant and his descendants, the land that had been a frontier country populated by impious bedouin became a repository of religious value. Over the course of centuries, burials of sayyid saints in the earth of Tarim accumulated to transform Tarim from a destination into a source, or origin.

This transformation of place entailed a coordinate transformation of the persons who migrated to it. As Tarim shifted from a destination to an origin, the sayyids who settled it gradually ceased being foreigners and became locals. In this chapter, we have seen something of what this change involved, in the distant past. Yet such work is never complete. Every generation faces the task anew, even in very personal and intimate ways. The next chapter looks more closely at why such tasks arise and how people confront them. How do individuals become conscripted into a long-term project of place making? In addressing this question, we shift from a historiographic to an ethnographic mode, and adopt the perspectives of persons resident in the town of Tarim itself, in the nineteenth and twentieth centuries. What is it like to live in a special place such as Tarim, origin and home of the ʿAlawī Way known throughout the Muslim Indian Ocean as a fount of Islamic virtue?

CHAPTER 3

A Resolute Localism

Resident Aliens

In the early 1990s, when one entered Tarim, one of the largest towns in the southern Yemeni region of Hadramawt, one had a choice of perhaps two restaurants for lunch, if that. At the edge of town, right by the cemetery and bounded by remnants of the ancient town wall encircling the settlement—the wall had been torn down by socialists dismantling feudal ramparts—stood the Kenya Restaurant. While the restaurant was unlikely to have a full hot meal ready to serve, it was likely to be open and to serve tea and snacks such as French fries and sugar-glazed doughnut holes called *kalimati.* If one bothered to ask, the African youth serving the food would draw on linguistic resources that were equal parts English and Arabic to explain, with an apologetic grin, that *kalimati* is a Swahili word, and the treats are an African specialty: Aren't they sweet and tasty? The other dining option was the Tanzania Restaurant, on the main road toward the center of town, run by dark men of African descent. There, the hungry traveler could sit down and be served without a word: invariably, the restaurant offered a choice of fried fish with red-tinted rice vaguely reminiscent of Indian *biryani,* cooked in *ghee* (Indian clarified butter) and spiced tomato sauce, or more of the same. At either place, nevertheless, one could count on a ready pick-me-up: a stiff cup of Hadrami tea, an unmistakable, astringent brew of Ceylon leaves distilled by prolonged double boiling in a small teapot perched over a large kettle of hot water, samovar style. "Hadrami whiskey," the mischievous would say in jest, and the color was about right.

When I first visited Tarim in 1991, and on many subsequent occasions

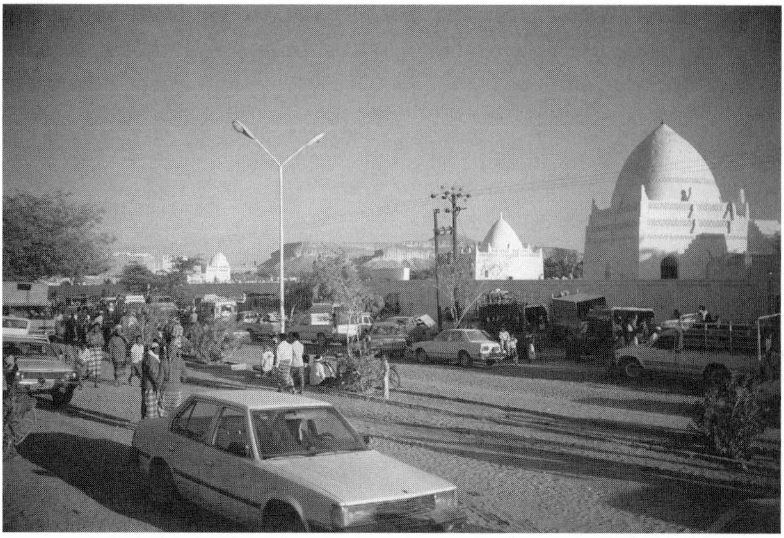

FIGURE 12. Graves of Tarim and their cupolas, ensconced behind the wall. The road is a major flood path. Kenya Restaurant at end of line of cars, to the left. Photo by the author.

between 1993 and 1995 while resident there, I spent time at the Kenya and Tanzania restaurants, too lazy to cook but busy with fieldwork. The restaurants were natural places for "hanging out," as the town had few other eating spots or open public spaces. Only later did I realize, after minor admonishment, that these places were expressly not frequented by persons from good families, or by self-respecting locals, for that matter. People who wanted their fish and rice but couldn't cook, such as work crews, ordered takeout from the Tanzania. That explained the big pots and few customers. From hearing accounts of restaurants in Hong Kong and Beijing, I had assumed that the poor state of the local ones here—so symptomatic of the "postsocialist transition" to a market economy—was the legacy of a quarter century of Marxist government, geared to production rather than services: feeding the people rather than serving foreign tourists. The only Marxist state in the Arab world, South Yemen had a ruling politburo that was communist enough to pursue bloody struggles between "Chinese" and "Soviet" factions through the 1970s and 1980s. As it turned out, however, the restaurant service problem predated the Marxist one.

The very notion of a place where one could eat and drink in public was not just foreign but base in Hadramawt. The first modern, printed history of Hadramawt, al-Bakrī's *Political History of Hadramawt* (al-Bakrī al-Yāfiʿī 1936), mentions coffeehouses and bars in the same breath—as institutions of ill repute on the coastal regions of the Red Sea, in areas populated by lowly Africans and their descendants. Foreign mercenaries could be hired at such establishments for attacks on legitimate local authority. In 1806, Isḥāq b. ʿUmar b. Yaḥyā gathered such a crew from Red Sea bars and coffeehouses and with them, attacked the Kasādī emir of al-Mukallā, a principal Hadrami port on the Indian Ocean coast (al-Bakrī al-Yāfiʿī 1936: 118).

In Tarim, Kenya and Tanzania referred not just to the restaurants that posted these names on signboards above their doorways. They stood for the countries they named, the Africans found in them, the inferior quality and cleanliness of their food, and the troubling moral quality and activity of their denizens—the sum total of the normative distance between the desirable home and the undesirable foreign. The hierarchical nature of this distance took on further dimensions when some of the old men I met at the Tanzania Restaurant admitted that they had in the past, before the independence revolution, been slave soldiers of the local Kathīrī sultans and were descendants of East African slaves. The Africans in the Kenya and Tanzania restaurants of Tarim were as unwitting participants as I was in social associations that enjoyed sufficient consensus and durability for people to enact and realize them in urban space and reiterate them across centuries and regimes. After the Yemeni civil war of 1994, in which northern forces subdued southern secessionists, we were to be joined by other outsiders, poor northern Yemenis who sold *qāt* and snacks by the old wall and cemetery next to Kenya Restaurant. They lived and slept where they traded and were apparently devoid of places in which to take baths. In the cool of the evenings, this area became a rather lively place for Africans, northerners, and even wayward sons of good families to gather, drink tea, watch TV, and endlessly chew *qāt*. Having grown up on the array of delicious foods littering the streets in Malaysia, and imbued with the anthropologist's penchant for public culture, I naturally gravitated to these points of low social standing. Moreover, I had not received many invitations to dine in.

I had my first taste of a "real" Hadrami meal when an acquaintance had some visitors from out of town to his home for a spread, laying out dishes of meats and vegetables on plates, the staple of steamed white rice, and saucers of condiments on mats on the carpets. Each guest had his own plate of rice and added bits of meat, vegetables, and condiments from the shared dishes throughout the meal to flavor the rice. The spread was essentially the type of meal that the Dutch in Indonesia came to call *rijsttafel,* or "rice table." The condiments were *sambal, achar,* and a sweet, thick soy sauce poured over the chicken, called *kichap.*[1]

"So," my host asked, "is it like what you have in your country?" I replied in the affirmative, quite amazed at the similarities, even though some dishes were not exactly the same and not exactly my favorites.

He explained to me, with a triumphant flourish, that in the good houses, I would find pure steamed white rice, unlike the greasy stuff that Africans eat, like the rice I had in the Kenya and Tanzania restaurants, and not like the animal-fat rice preferred by the bedouin in the countryside. Further, most of the large houses in town were built by grandfathers who had migrated to Jāwā (Java, a synecdoche standing for "island Southeast Asia" in Hadrami parlance), and the cuisine I was having was passed down from Jāwā grandmothers within those houses. In fact, a number of those repatriated women were Chinese women who had been adopted by or married to the Hadrami grandfathers in Jāwā. This intermarriage was one reason why the scions of the good houses were often of a fairer aspect. I digested this between fistfuls of my white rice and red-chili *sambal.* On another such occasion, an Indian visitor commented to the Hadrami host on the light complexion of his little son, who burst in during the meal; he noted that the fair boy was quite handsome ("he doesn't look Arab"). This statement was taken as a great compliment.

While color informs hierarchical valuations of persons and places, the semantic domain of *Jāwā* encompasses other potent associations. *Jāwā* comes from the time of ancestors and is about descent, wealth, and inheritance, as well as about cuisine and phenotype, the constituents of tangible human substances. "The food was better when granny was around." For the good families in the great houses, the era preceding that

1. *Sambal* is pounded chili flavored with shrimp paste. It is common in Southeast Asia; the word derives from the Hindi word *sambar. Achar* is an acid and salt fruit relish, usually pickled lime in Hadramawt. It is widely known by the same term in most of the Indian vernaculars, Siam, Burma, and the Malay world. Limes in this form were used by Muslim Malabaris (descendants of Arabs, called Choolias by the English) to protect against scurvy when they sailed from Malabar to Southeast Asia in the eighteenth century. The term was common in Anglo-Indian usage, applied to pickled products of the English firm Crosse & Blackwell; it may have originated from the Latin *acetaria* and come to India via the Portuguese (Yule and Burnell 1994 [1903]: 3). *Kichap,* from Malay, stems from the Hokkien Chinese *koe chiap,* a compound of paste and sauce (with a consistency between the two). The word was also adopted into English usage, as *catsup* and finally *ketchup,* the American tabletop icon.

of the Marxists, who took power soon after independence from Britain in 1967, was one of nostalgia for a century in which good things came from the Jāwā regions, in goodly numbers. The Javanese Days, the *ayyām Jāwā,* were a lost golden age to the generation that grew up under Marxist rule. The connections were broken when the Marxists came to power, and the golden age slipped into the past. Families that identified with tribal groups *(qabā'il,* adjective *qabīlī)*, or with descent from the prophet Muḥammad, were categorized as bourgeois[2] and subdivided into big, medium, and small bourgeoisie. Families with wealth and remittances from Jāwā were called "big bourgeoisie" and were dispossessed of houses and lands.

One has to understand the celebration of Jāwā in Hadramawt in the context of the dissolution of the Marxist state in South Yemen, after the fall of the Berlin wall and the unification of North and South Yemen in 1990. The return of valuable land and houses confiscated by the Marxists, the lifting of surveillance on communications and restrictions on international travel, and the return of religious scholars and rich uncles from exile abroad all created excitement at the prospect of recuperating the past glory signified by "Jāwā" today. Indeed, students from Jāwā are beginning to come again to Tarim, the spiritual home of Islamic scholars and the Prophet's descendants in the Indian Ocean, signaling its reinstatement as the fount of religious education and value for Jāwā and the Sawāḥil (Swahili East Africa). A new university, founded in 1995, has been built with funds from migrants in the Persian Gulf. The architect for the buildings is a Malaysian of Hadrami descent.

Jāwā was not always so celebrated. In the late nineteenth century, when wealth began to pour into Hadramawt from the tens of thousands of Hadrami migrants there, Jāwā was bemoaned as a foreign source of corruption. "Forget *Jāwā,* stay home and water the fields"[3] was the best-known line from a celebrated poem condemning Jāwā and its sowing of discord and corruption of morals in the homeland. The poem's author, the judge Muḥsin b. ʿAlawī al-Saqqāf, fielded numerous commercial disputes between migrant Hadramis coming out of Jāwā.[4] But the biggest disputes of the era were not commercial. They accompanied the rise in

2. At times, other stigmatized terms were used in place of *bourgeois,* including *iqṭāʿī* ("feudalist") and *kahnūtī* ("priestly").

3. *al-sināwa wa-lā Jāwā*

4. One of these cases is described by his descendant, the notary public Jaʿfar al-Saqqāf (1993).

Southeast Asia of a new movement against the erstwhile social precedence of the descendants of the Prophet, the preeminent citizens of Tarim.[5]

The morals of Hadrami offspring born of foreign mothers, the creoles called *muwallad,* were a great concern.[6] Books were written for their edification, schools were started in the homeland for their education, and wills were written granting them inheritance on condition they spent their formative years in the homeland.[7] Stereotypes of the Jāwā *muwallad*s from the late nineteenth/early twentieth centuries are similar to those of the African youths who loiter about the Kenya Restaurant today. Those Africans are also *muwallad*s, Hadrami creoles from Kenya and Tanzania. But in their social and spatial marginalization, they fill positions vacated by the Jāwā *muwallad*s, who have since gained ancestor status.

In Hadramawt, the identification of people, places, and things as foreign or local is relativized by history and framed in hierarchy. Designations of "foreign" and "local" are parts of an apparently stable, public, consensual structure of valuation. Despite the processual parade of persons, places, and things through time, such as the foreign Jāwā *muwallad*s who have become localized, a relatively stable structure of perception seems to persist, which valorizes the local and diminishes or even demonizes the foreign. In the face of a scientific—that is, a historical—analysis that can map the trajectory of a cultural item from despised-foreign to valued-local status, we can call the insistence on valorizing the local a resolute localism. It is resolute because it is not always unaware of the trajectories of localization; it is resolute despite that knowledge. The apotheosis of the Jāwā *muwallad*s is one example. Naturalization is never complete because local folklore within circles of family and community, and sometimes even individual memory within one lifetime, tells of such incorporations.

Material culture, such as items of food, provides other examples. The books of Hadrami history and biography are replete with firsts: the first person to introduce tea to Hadramawt was the sayyid Ḥāmid b. ʿAbd Allāh al-Junayd, for example, according to Muḥammad b. Aḥmad al-Shāṭirī in his *Epochs of Hadrami History* (al-Shāṭirī 1973: 71). Religious law

5. This topic is discussed in chapter 6 and subsequent chapters.

6. Chapter 8 elaborates on this theme.

7. The largest of these wills was that of Shaykh b. ʿAbd al-Raḥmān b. Aḥmad al-Kāf, which was drawn up in Singapore in the first decade of the twentieth century; payouts lasted until the last decade of the century. See IORL, R/20/A/3874, "Probate No. 176 of 1910 (Will of Shaykh al-Kaff)."

and practical morality of past centuries register debates about the admissibility of coffee, tea, and tobacco for human ingestion by Muslims.[8] When tobacco first appeared in Hadramawt in the sixteenth century, it was initially taken up by soldiers, bedouin, and cameleers. Muslim jurists campaigned against its use, and in the seventeenth century, al-Ḥusayn, the son of the great Hadrami saint Shaykh Bū Bakr bin Sālim of ʿAynāt, issued a *fatwā* (jurisprudential opinion) pronouncing it illegal. He commanded the governors of the country to stop its entry at the ports and personally bought up all supplies in the country to prevent its spread (al-Shāṭirī 1973: 72). His home base of ʿAynāt was a major caravan center in the Hadrami interior for goods from the coast, and from there, the message that tobacco was contraband went out to other markets in the country. Nonetheless, these items of material culture are now thoroughly integrated into local Hadrami religious practices and everyday pursuits of sociability.

As novelties or stimulants, foreign items find ready assimilation into legalistic categories and subsequent evaluation. They easily fall under the religiously prohibited classes of "reprehensible innovations" *(bidʿa makrūha)* and "intoxicants" *(khamr)*. They are thus foreign not only to the particular geographical locale of Hadramawt but also to the global community of Muslims. To bear the label *foreign* is to carry the burden of a legal charge of illegitimacy.

Such charges can focus on personal spirituality as well. The famously pious Aḥmad b. ʿAlī al-Junayd of Tarim (1783–1858) had two brothers: ʿUmar, a migrant in Singapore, and ʿAbd Allāh, a migrant in Ṣanʿāʾ, in North Yemen. Annually, ʿUmar sent Aḥmad a gift of five hundred "French riyals," while ʿAbd Allāh remitted a hundred.[9] Of these gifts, Aḥmad would say, "I find more blessing *(baraka)* in the hundred of ʿAbd Allāh than the five hundred of ʿUmar." ʿUmar also regularly sent him fine garments from Singapore, heavy ones for winter and light ones for summer. Yet Aḥmad simply stored them away in a box or cupboard and never wore them. His

8. By 1532, coffee had gained acceptance in legal circles. In that year, the chronicler of the Hadrami diaspora ʿAbd al-Qādir al-ʿAydarūs, resident in Gujarat, recorded a discussion of the beneficial and deleterious effects of coffee and whether its nature was hot, cold, dry, or moist (al-ʿAydarūs 1985: 124). Yet even at the end of the nineteenth century, the Hadrami sayyid ʿAlawī b. Aḥmad al-Saqqāf, son of the mufti of the Shāfiʿī school in Mecca, saw a need to author a volume on restraining desires associated with the consumption of coffee, tobacco, and *qāt* (al-Mashhūr 1984: 243).

9. French riyals were the silver, Austrian Maria Theresa thalers used in Yemen until recent times.

sartorial choices were considered: he reasoned that using the foreign garments would throw the local weavers of Tarim out of work and cause their finished stocks to go to ruin. Moreover, the Tarim weavers were Muslims who invoked God while they went about their spinning and weaving, and their products were charged with blessings, unlike foreign cloth made by unbelievers (A. Q. al-Junayd 1994: 122).

The lore of Aḥmad al-Junayd is legion among his numerous descendants in Tarim and those of his brother ʿUmar in Singapore today. To them, his ratiocinations on the relative merits of foreign and local must be tempered by a certain historical irony, for ʿUmar in Singapore was the one who established the family fortunes and built the mosque that today stands as the oldest such structure in downtown Singapore. The ʿUmar Mosque on ʿUmar Road was built in 1820, a year after the founding of British Singapore. While al-Junayds in Singapore enjoy the prestige of residing in a modern city-state where streets, a subway station, and an industrial park bear the family name, their cousins in Tarim live in great houses (some with indoor swimming pools, now dry) built by grandfathers who were repatriated from Singapore: the *Jāwā muwallad*s.

These stories of Aḥmad, ʿUmar, and their descendants appear in a thick family history published in Singapore (A. Q. al-Junayd 1994) and distributed *gratis* in Hadramawt and elsewhere. The book's author, Sayyid ʿAbd al-Qādir b. ʿAbd al-Raḥmān al-Junayd, is the Tarim-born leader *(imām)* of the Friday mosque of Dar es Salaam in Tanzania. The personage of Aḥmad al-Junayd, the most religiously celebrated member of this family since its ascent two centuries ago, carries gravitas that grounds the self-regard of the family. As Sayyid ʿAbd al-Qādir recounted to me while the work was in progress, the idea for the family history evolved from work that began as a biography of Aḥmad al-Junayd, which remains the kernel of the volume. To guide his additional research and composition, he drew up a family genealogy with the help of his brothers in Tarim and Singapore and of relatives elsewhere; this tree also has since been published and distributed. In the making of the book and genealogy, family members reexperienced and tightened the bonds of family that had been created during the Javanese Days, as they rediscovered distant kin and resumed contacts. The book assembles and caps the glory of one family gained over an expanse of space and time. Within its covers, the juxtaposition of photographs of urban landmarks in Singapore that carry the al-Junayd name with the biography of Aḥmad al-Junayd, the resolute localist, domesticates all that was foreign to Aḥmad and brings the foreign home to the realm of religious virtue, ancestors, and homeland. The possibility that he himself might have simply stored away such a gift does not matter: storage is the point, for it is an act of intimacy. Thus, the enchantment of cupboards and boxes.

Foreign Intimates: Naturalization

For a place that has long been connected with the outside world, Hadramawt presents a surprising binary valuation of local and foreign. As we know, migration is a chronic feature of Hadrami life. At times in the past, when external connections were disrupted, such as during the Second World War, the country experienced famine (Hartley 1961; Van der Meulen 1961). Famine and isolation are vividly inseparable in memories of the recent past. In the longer view, the denigration of the foreign makes little sense and appears hypocritical or paradoxical. This is not how I choose to approach the question. What is more interesting is to consider how cultural items are marked in the first place, for what is foreign can be domesticated and made intimate.

A preliminary notion of the domestic can be expressed by the Arabic term *bayt,* which approximates the English "house" in both its literal and metaphorical senses: as a structure of bricks piled one atop another or as a descent group similarly stacked (Geertz 1979; Mundy 1995; Munson 1984). Within the *bayt,* exotic foods, novel appliances, foreign wives are removed from observation, evaluation, and talk; these matters are *ḥarīm,* which denotes both respected women and respected places—off limits, at least to outside men. Within the genealogical *bayt,* creole ancestors are similarly regarded. Thus, both meanings may equally be invoked in the transgressive act of cursing.[10] Outside the house, creole children on the dusty streets are noticed, questioned, remarked upon. Yet such probing inevitably places them within the cover of a known descent group, or house. Outside the physical *bayt* but inside the genealogical one, the ambivalence of reception that creoles often sense in such encounters is not uncommon and itself induces a sense of marginality.

10. An early altercation over the issue is recorded in the prophet Muḥammad's biography: "'Umar b. al-Khaṭṭāb wrote to Salmān b. Rabī'a al-Bāhilī . . . when he was in Armenia ordering him to show preference to those who possessed pure Arab horses, as against those who owned mixed breeds, when distributing spoils. Accordingly he mustered the cavalry and as he passed by 'Amr b. Ma'dī Karib's horse he said: 'This horse of yours is of mixed breed.' 'Amr was furious and said: 'A mongrel knows a mongrel like himself!' Qays sprang at him and threatened him." (Ibn Hishām 1955: 695)

While one hears disapproving or disparaging remarks about creoles, one never hears anyone fault their fathers for bringing home foreign wives or slave concubines.

The binary of local/foreign can and often does serve as a discursive platform for elaborate, derivative suites of associations between white and black, pure and tainted, original and fake, sacred and profane, desirable and loathsome, modest and wanton, and even Japanese and Taiwanese, in reference to original and imitation parts for Japanese cars. Indeed, it easily and naturally draws charge from such conjunctions. In use, the binary often occurs in a field of agonistic exchange between subjects. This image is a familiar one in the ethnographic literature from the Mediterranean. The social value of binarism lies, in Herzfeld's words, "entirely in the processes of accommodation between intimacy and its defense—the protection of the secrets of the house from the glare of the public space by householders who are busily probing the defenses of their neighbors at the same time" (1997: 172). At street level rather than from on high, the local/foreign binary appears not as a map of paradox, hypocrisy, or culture but as a practical problem of negotiating one's way through an itinerary fraught with the potential of intimacy unveiled: caught between houses, for example, or seen entering one. Under conditions of intimacy, within the boundaries of what by definition is acceptable, such as the *bayt,* charges of the foreign are not possible. The problem arises typically when things are in transit, before they enter the *bayt* or final destination. The itinerary itself is a large part of the problem: *muwallad*s on the streets, or *muwallad*s who have yet to attain ancestor status. While white rice is unavailable in restaurants open to the streets, the lack of restaurants itself is not a problem if one is local and has a house to return to.

The problem of itinerary is one a woman faces every time she contemplates leaving the house. She avoids main roads and has to consider the hour so as to bypass secondary streets when they are busy. Sometimes she must make circuitous treks between destinations, being sure to cross a road farther along where it narrows into an alley, and sometimes the trip is better postponed. Young girls who are used to playing outside have to relearn their bodily relation to the streets when they get older. They do so during a period of relative confinement, which promotes the required spatial amnesia, from the age of ten or eleven until marriage, which may be as early as fourteen. While women cook, vegetable markets are only frequented by men. The latter do the daily marketing, and as such, everyday maintenance of the household entails constant coordination of itineraries between genders. *Muwallad* girls repatriated from abroad commit many mistakes of deportment in this regard, such as buying their own groceries. Running out of onions has its hazards. The eventual discipline is not one they entirely conform to or are pleased with. Yet it is one they will learn regardless, because not doing so carries its price. The foreign that is on display is by nature problematic; the exhibition itself is a transgression of local norms of rectitude and standards of conformity. Small children feel free to throw pebbles at foreign women in the streets, for example. Older ones cast stones with words. In doing so, they act squarely within the social and moral matrices in which the binary of local/foreign resides—that is to say, within their rights. These are actions for which they do not expect to be beaten by their superiors, the elders—or by their inferiors, the foreigners. Unless they want to remain inferior, *muwallads* learn to be local.

Alienations and the Usurpation of Local Ends

Within Marx's oeuvre is a kernel that is the logical premise and temporal beginning of his theory of capitalism as world history. This core idea is the notion of a primordial state in which the working subject is owner, producer, and consumer. It is a condition prior to exchange and before their historic separation, in which raw materials, tools, and products jointly exist in the material form of land:

> In the best case he relates not only as worker to the land and soil, but also as proprietor of the land and soil to himself as working subject. Ownership of land and soil potentially also includes ownership of the raw material, as well as of the primordial instrument, the earth itself, and of its spontaneous fruits. Posited in the most original form, it means relating to the earth as proprietor, and finding raw material and instrument on hand, as well as the necessaries of life created not by labour but by the earth itself. . . . This is historic state No. 1 . . . (Marx 1978: 264)

In *German Ideology* and *Grundrisse* (the source of the above quotation) Marx traces history as the separation of these elements out of their original commingling. As private property, the means of production become divorced from labor, the division of labor progresses with specialization and a wider exchange of goods in trade, and money arises as a means and measure of value, facilitating expanded commerce. This history is represented in the opening chapters of his *Capital,* as the logical transformation of the commodity form into money and capital. Beginning his exposition with a Janus-like commodity that is exchanged for a sensuously different commodity, use value for use value, Marx correlates the expanding circulation of commodities with the increasing development and domination of the second aspect of the commodity, its exchange value. From the last third of the seventeenth century on, precious metals like gold and silver became specialized commodities, prized for their exchange value. Their natural properties of rarity, portability, divisibility, and durability rendered them suitable to stand as universal equivalents of value quantities, and their use and exchange values merged into one attractive body that was both physical and symbolic: "although gold and silver are not by Nature money, money is by Nature gold and silver" (Marx 1967 [1867]: 89).

Commodities were originally the ends, to be used in the satisfaction of human needs. Money was originally a means for exchanging commodities. As means, money was subsidiary to the ends, commodities. Somewhere along the line, these two elements traded places, with money emerging as the ends, usurping the place of commodities. Means and ends became reversed.

These developments result in the production of goods by human beings, not to satisfy human needs but to increase capital, so that money can beget money. In the form of capital, commodities produced by the worker exert an objective power over him; this dynamic is the alienation of labor, which separates labor's living form from its dead, congealed form, which then becomes dominant. The dominance also extends into space, with markets becoming worldwide, and labor's advent in this form gives rise to foreign competition for workers, capitalists, and whole countries alike.

A near-contemporary of Marx, Aḥmad al-Junayd, whom we met above, also noted the phenomenon of foreign competition. Because of his concern for the weavers of his native Tarim, Aḥmad al-Junayd mothballed the luxurious garments his brother sent him from Singapore and continued to use the simpler local product. With access to neither Hegel nor the British Library, his actions were not grounded in a complex theory of alienation. Nevertheless, the power of capital-based production to swamp the local artisanry was patent to him; he saw it as a problem of alien nations instead. Against the blandishments of foreign finery, he posited a moral end in local cloth: the product was virtuous because God-mindedness was woven into the very warp and woof of its fabric. More correctly, as it appears in his biography, the action of this spiritual incorporation is denoted by the Arabic verbal noun *gh-z-l,* which vowelized as *ghazl* means the spinning of yarn; as *ghazal,* the word evokes the love poetry of Sufi mystics sung in praise of the divine (A. Q. al-Junayd 1994: 122).[11]

Al-Junayd's preference for the local is shared by Aristotle. For Aristotle, the ground of the local was not divinity but the household *(oikos)*, the basic unit of his theory of Greek sociability.

> It was out of the association formed by men with these two, women and slaves, that the first household was formed; and the poet Hesiod was right when he wrote, "Get first a house and a wife and an ox to draw the plough." (The ox is the poor man's slave.) This association of persons, established according to the law of nature and continuing day after day, is the household, the members of which Charondas calls "bread-fellows." (Aristotle 1962: 27)

In Aristotle's ontology, each thing has a nature and a teleology, the final cause or end toward which it is directed and provided for "according to the law of nature." The end of the household is its independent maintenance, or reproduction, under the administration of the master. This end may be called "household management."

As a thing of nature, the household is already provided for. No need exists "for this kind of money-making (for which) the end provides no limit, because wealth and getting money are themselves the end" (Aristotle 1962: 44). Enough resources lie close at hand to provide for the *oikos*—in nomadism, farming, piracy, fishing, and hunting:

> Getting a living in this self-supporting way is clearly given by nature herself to all her creatures . . . plants exist for the sake of animals . . . all other animals exist for the sake of man . . . If then we are right in believing that nature makes nothing without some end in view, nothing to no purpose, it must be that nature has made all things specifically for the sake of man. This means that it is part of nature's plan that the art of war, of which hunting is a part, should be a way of acquiring property. (Aristotle 1962: 39–40)

Moneymaking to provide for the household is a part of its administration, as is warfare. But both are only means for household ends. Moneymaking for itself or warfare for itself deviates from the task of household management, which is providing for the *oikos.*

Exchange begins originally because of relative shortages and surpluses

11. Messick (1987) offers a suggestive perspective on how weaving may constitute a whole discursive arena that is silent or subordinate and that interlaces meaning and thread simultaneously in a semiotics of resemblance rather than representation.

in different areas. Thus, it occurs socially and spatially beyond the household. In Aristotle's rustic naturalism, restricted exchange merely restores natural equilibria. The imbalances that motivate exchange are a result of naturally occurring differences in resource endowment within the realm, not of socially generated causes. The problem of generalized exchange arises when exchanges cross national boundaries, whereupon media of exchange appear. First, traders use precious metals; then, fiat money. The notion emerges that wealth is a pile of coins, and the pursuit of money for its own sake begins. This idea is easily debunked by Aristotle's naturalism, for fiat money is arbitrary and easily debased when political authority falters, and "it will often happen that a man with plenty of money will not have enough to eat" (Aristotle 1962: 43).

Here, we are far from the original purpose of providing for household consumption. The prudent go home to the restricted economy of autarky, pursuing domestic production for domestic consumption. Self-sufficiency (which includes slavery and piracy) is a virtue in this economy and is an end grounded in the static "law of household nature," or *oikonomos,* "economics." For Marx, in contrast, no possibility exists of going home to the primordial, as the circuits of exchange and mediation carry an inner necessity. Laws of motion drive the system forward and ever outward: congealed alienated labor and the cumulative social power of generations.

This excursus helps us understand why Marx's near-contemporary Aḥmad al-Junayd might have more affinity with Aristotle than with Marx. While all three partake in a nostalgia for true ends in a world increasingly dominated by means, their responses diverge. For Marx, extensive, large-scale sociability, including foreign trade, is coterminous with large, multiple circuits of exchange that create their own necessary dynamic and ends. Rejecting them *in toto* is out of the question; they are the limits of the known social world. They represent the living cumulative social power of dead generations. The issue is how to restore human needs as the ends of the system, directing rather than rejecting its power.

For Aristotle and Aḥmad, respectively, such social power is unnatural and ungodly; power from large, multiple circuits of exchange is inherently destructive. Engagement with these means of exchange is a choice, not a necessity. Such choices deviate from the true ends, of maintaining the *oikos* or of maintaining God-minded livelihoods such as weaving. They transgress the law of nature or of God. Aristotle and Aḥmad both valorize self-sufficiency as moral virtue. In economic terms, they promote the return to autarky: consuming at the site of production, "historic state No. 1"—in anthropological terms, the apotheosis of the domestic group, defined by kinship or religion. In this perspective, the ends reside at home, where they are attainable. Aristotle's solution is a relatively trouble-free return to the equilibrium state of the household. Aḥmad's is a resolute valorization of an end conjoined with communal intimacy—donning the blessed cloth of the Tarim weavers—on the one hand, and a containment of the intrusive, destructive foreign, on the other—putting a lid on the luxurious foreign cloth.

The three thinkers' differences directly confront each other in their views on weaving. Aḥmad's view we already know. As for Aristotle:

> So any piece of property can be regarded as a tool enabling a man to live. . . . suppose that every tool we had could perform its function, either at our bidding or itself perceiving the need, like the statues made by Daedalus or the wheeled tripods of Hephaestus, of which the poet says that "self-moved they enter the assembly of the gods"—and suppose that shuttles in a loom could fly to and fro and a plucker play on a lyre all self-moved, then manufacturers would have no need of workers nor masters of slaves. (Aristotle 1962: 31)

Dispensing with workers, precisely Aḥmad's point; dispensing with slaves, against the natural constitution of the Greek *oikos,* in Aristotle's view.

In contrast, Marx observed that:

> That labour which from the first presupposed a machine even of the crudest sort, soon showed itself the most capable of development. Weaving, earlier carried on in the country by the peasants as a secondary occupation to procure their clothing, was the first labour to receive an impetus and a further development through the extension of commerce. Weaving was the first and remained the principal manufacture. The rising demand for clothing materials, consequent on the growth of population, the growing accumulation and mobilisation of natural capital through accelerated circulation, the demand for luxuries called forth by the latter and favoured generally by the gradual extension of commerce, gave weaving a quantitative and qualitative stimulus, which wrenched it out of the form of production hitherto existing. Alongside the peasants weaving for their own use, who continued, and still continue, with this sort of work, there emerged a new class of weavers in the towns, whose fabrics were destined for the home market and usually for foreign markets too. (Marx 1978: 180–81)

Aḥmad al-Junayd's reasons for putting in a box the luxurious cloth he received from Singapore have ample support from Aristotle and Marx. Yet his principled stance is not without its historical ironies. The ascent of the great sayyid families within Hadramawt—the founding of sanctuary settlements *(ḥawṭa)* there under their authority (in "*mansab*ates") and their rise to regional fame, as represented by the saint Abū Bakr al-ʿAydarūs of

Aden in the sixteenth century—correlates with their contemporary prominence in Gujarat, the textile-producing center of the Indian Ocean (Chaudhuri 1990), whose natural market stretched from the Middle East to Southeast Asia. When the industrial production of batiks and sarongs took off in Java in the late nineteenth century, not long after al-Junayd's principled rebuff of the luxurious Singapore textiles, Hadramis were among the leaders of the powerful marriage of capital and industrial technique. In the middle of the twentieth century, an al-Junayd was one of the largest manufacturers, as well as president of the Federation of Indonesian Batik Manufacturers (Vuldy 1987: 175–77, 226).[12] Desirable Indonesian sarongs today bear trademarks named for well-known Hadrami lineages, such as al-Jufrī, al-Junayd, al-ʿAṭṭās, Bā Ḥashwān, bin Sumayṭ, and bin Sunkar.

Aḥmad al-Junayd's distrust and rejection of the foreign was not only because of principles. His experiences confirmed his convictions. These experiences are recounted in his biography by his descendant. The author's sources are stories passed down orally within the family, private documents such as personal correspondence, and published histories. In the oral telling and retelling of these stories, and their inevitable accommodation to the authority of written histories, the accounts take on a recognizably paradigmatic character. Hagiography is one of the dominant forms of history writing in Hadramawt, and it exerts a standardizing influence on lesser biographies.[13] Biographies, in turn, which are regularly and widely compiled from oral accounts after a person dies, are the primary source material for Hadrami historians. In consequence, we should not be surprised to find in Aḥmad al-Junayd's biography elements and themes that resonate with those in the history books. The connection is not coincidental. As he explained to me, Aḥmad al-Junayd's biographer ʿAbd al-Qādir al-Junayd was motivated to write because Aḥmad had participated in political reform in the general interest. While the activities of his associates had been recorded in the histories, Aḥmad's role had not.[14] The biographer wanted to show that Aḥmad was a figure in line with the classic Hadrami sayyid saint personalities, who combined scholarship and ac-

12. I am grateful to Michael Gilsenan for the reference.

13. The well-known Lebanese historian Shakīb Arslān was quite taken with a rhyming line that often opens Hadrami biographical accounts: "He was born in Tarim, and memorized the Qurʾan, the *Karīm*" (al-Mashhūr 1984: 54; al-Shillī 1982: 7).

14. The events in question concern sayyid figures such as Imam Ṭāhir b. Ḥusayn bin Ṭāhir, Ḥasan Ṣāliḥ al-Baḥr, and the "Seven ʿAbd Allāhs," who campaigned with the local tribal Kathīrī sultans to repel the foreign Yāfiʿī interlopers (al-Ḥāmid 1968; bin Hāshim

tion.[15] Writing Aḥmad's biography made the example of this predecessor didactically available for mimesis by his successors; Aḥmad himself composed such history lessons, as we will see in chapter 7.[16] Aḥmad's son and one of his students had begun writing notes on his biography, but they died before bringing it to completion.[17] 'Abd al-Qādir inherited these notes from his teacher when the latter died and took them with him when he migrated to Africa, finally to complete the task.

The books of biography and history echo ways in which similar elements and themes occur today in the telling of events and the interpretation of their meanings. While in Hadramawt, I spent a significant amount of time reading history and biography with friends. We read biographies of their friends' ancestors, family histories, and more general histories of Hadramawt. My friends were always quick to locate members of their families and ready to point out analogies between the content of the texts and the current situation. These lessons were constant demonstrations to me of the high degree of interpenetration of oral and written media in Hadrami social life, to the extent that these media merge into a single discourse to one who works with these sources over time.

1948; al-Kindī 1991). They are represented in the genealogical table and discussion in chapter 7. The term *Seven 'Abd Allāhs (al-'Abādillāh al-Sab'a)* derives from the writings of Ibn al-'Arabī. Its use in Hadramawt demonstrates familiarity with his doctrines, in this case the specific idea of saints as the inheritors of prophets (Chodkiewicz 1993).

15. This combination is represented by the pairs *'ilm wa-'amal, dīn wa-dunyā* (knowledge and works, religion and mundane world). A tradition of social engagement is part of the sayyids' self-image of their brand of Sufism. The interrelation of knowledge and action means that hagiography and historiography are intimately related in Hadrami literature. One can trace this combination of "theory and practice" in an Islamic idiom to the early lights of Hadrami Sufism. Abū Madyan Shu'ayb emphasized the complementarity of knowledge and action, *'ilm* and *'amal* (Cornell 1998: 135), while Ibn al-'Arabī's concept of the "perfect human being" *(al-insān al-kāmil)* was elaborated upon by 'Abd al-Karīm al-Jīlī, a disciple in Yemen, to show how the prophet Muḥammad could be a living reality "made manifest in a Sufi saint" (Cornell 1998: 208; for more on al-Jīlī in Yemen, see Knysh 1999b). Cornell's work reexamines the troubled relation between model and history in writings on Islamic saints. Differences between mystics and orthodox legal scholars have been exaggerated by generations of Orientalists. Often, legists were Sufis. The Prophet's *ḥadīth* are both sources of law and models for spiritual imitation. Hadrami luminaries lay claim to both labels of legist and saint.

16. Dresch (1990) has noted the active role that learned historiography with a unified narrative plays in constituting states, even from fragments, in his study of the Zaydi imamate in North Yemen.

17. Ahmad's student was 'Abd al-Raḥmān al-Mashhūr, the nineteenth-century author of the sayyid "total genealogy" and abridger of Aḥmad's graveyard manual (discussed in chapter 7).

Such at least was my experience. On that basis, I will explore further the ways in which foreign and local forces interact within Aḥmad al-Junayd's biography. In its telling are themes that recur in subsequent chapters of this study.

A House Divided

Aḥmad al-Junayd lived at a time when major towns in Hadramawt were ruled by foreign sultans who had originally been brought in as mercenaries to repel other outside conquerors. These mercenaries were Yāfiʿīs, from the Yāfiʿ mountains two hundred miles to the west, near Aden. They had been brought in by Shaykh Bū Bakr bin Sālim, the Saint of ʿAynāt, to repel the forces of the northern Yemeni imams of Ṣanʿāʾ, the Qāsimī dynasts, in the seventeenth century (al-Ghālibī 1991; Haykel 2003; al-Ḥiyed 1973). The historiography of the period symbolically marks the beginning of Hadrami rebellion against the Qāsimī occupiers by the limit of Hadrami patience. The Hadramis reached this limit when the Qāsimī governor changed the call to prayer from that common to the Shāfiʿī (Sunni) school, which is dominant in Hadramawt, to that of the Zaydis (Shia), which was the doctrine of the Qāsimī.[18] The Yāfiʿī mercenaries, in their turn, gradually took over the Hadrami towns they were meant to liberate. During most of Aḥmad's life, his hometown of Tarim was ruled by Yāfiʿīs. Hadrami histories that reflect a sayyid point of view consider the period one of occupation by the foreign Yāfiʿī tribes. Against them, two local forces—the sayyids and the Kathīrī leaders of the Shanfar tribal confederation (centered in the region around Sayʾūn town)—created a partnership. Aḥmad al-Junayd associated closely with sayyid leaders of this alliance, and was himself put forward as a candidate to lead their efforts, at one point. The histories portray Yāfiʿī rule as driven by lust and therefore opposed to the rule of religious law and justice. They characterize the period as one of tribal disorder riven by rivalries amongst Yāfiʿī tribal groups themselves. Disorder was exemplified by the division of rule in Tarim among three rival groups of Yāfiʿīs from the Yāfiʿī region of Labʿūs: the Gharamah, the Ibn ʿAbd al-Qādir, and the Humām. Each group controlled one part of Tarim, and as a consequence of their internecine jealousies, the townsfolk could not pass from one section of town to another.

18. A number of Hadrami histories cover this period (al-Bakrī al-Yāfiʿī 1936; al-Ḥāmid 1968; bin Hāshim 1948; al-Kindī 1991; al-Shāṭirī 1983).

Sayyid historians hold up the spatial division of Tarim as a prototypical case of unjust rule that contravened Islamic law. This was exemplified by the inability of the townsfolk to constitute a unified religious community that prayed together at the congregational mosque every Friday. The injunction for a local settlement to form a single Friday mosque community has the status of an obligatory rule in Islamic law, as we noted (al-Shāṭirī al-ʿAlawī al-Ḥusaynī al-Tarīmī 1949: 51).

In Tarim, the market center where the Friday mosque stood was ruled by the Gharamah chief. Aḥmad al-Junayd lived in another part of town, Nuwaydira, ruled by another Yāfiʿī chief, Ibn ʿAbd al-Qādir. Aḥmad insisted on fulfilling his religious obligation to pray at the congregational mosque in the market center on Fridays and obtained special permission from the Gharamah to do so. He went to the mosque with an escort of Gharamah tribal guards under their formal guarantee, known as *siyāra* under tribal custom. But when he arrived, he was arrested and thrown in prison. His biography explains this turn of events—unusual because the Gharamah violated their own guarantee—in the following way: Aḥmad's cousin Ḥusayn bin Sahl, his father's sister's son, lived in the market center under the Gharamah's rule and sought to ingratiate himself with the ruler. He did so by informing the Gharamah that his rival, Ibn ʿAbd al-Qādir, was being instigated by Aḥmad: Aḥmad received large sums of money from his wealthy brother in Singapore and was bankrolling the Ibn ʿAbd al-Qādir's efforts against the Gharamahs. The Gharamah was incensed and imprisoned Aḥmad when he went to the mosque within the Gharamah's jurisdiction. Ahmad's biographer quotes him as follows: "It was not the Gharamah who imprisoned me, but Ḥusayn bin Sahl" (al-Junayd 1994: 142). The biographer notes that Ḥusayn acted in this way despite the fact that Aḥmad was his mother's brother's son.

The narrative of this incident moves between two poles: Aḥmad sought to fulfill religious ends, and he was thwarted by irreligious foreign powers. These powers are represented not just by the Yāfiʿī chiefs but also by the money from Singapore, which turns out to be a curse. Yet these foreign powers do not operate of their own accord. They realize their ends through the agency of a local subject, an intimate: Aḥmad's cousin Ḥusayn. The biographer strikes a poignant note in this regard: after quoting Aḥmad on the true identity of his jailer, he volunteers almost as an afterthought that Ḥusayn's mother, Aḥmad's aunt, would send her nephew food while he was in jail, "for it was close to her house" (al-Junayd 1994: 142). Whatever the stakes are in this story (a historical struggle for political dominance over Hadramawt itself? local rivalries? family jealousies? the transgression of God's laws?), it is taking place at very close quarters. The spatial compression itself seems to increase the complexities; the aunt sent the food not out of remorse, nor concern, but simply because "it was close to her house," by way of explanation. And perhaps that explanation is the best one can do under the circumstances. Were internal family problems the original cause of the whole affair? Or the money from Singapore? Or the intrinsic unjustness of foreign rulers? We will never know. And indeed, no one ever knows the complete story in the majority of such cases. Such incidents are only single episodes in a stream of events whose origins recede into the horizon. Accounts of them seldom leave the audience with the feeling of having gotten to the bottom of the matter. Rather, they reinforce the overall sense of being overwhelmed by powers from afar whose workings are not known, and they underscore the violation and corrosion of intimate relations within a domestic community, be it a town or a family. Actions that were originally means to achieve local ends—importing mercenaries to liberate the Hadrami towns, sending money to help a brother at home—turn out to usurp the ends instead.

The telling of such incidents tars the notion of external instrumentalities itself with the broad brush of illegitimacy. Only in this way can we interpret the poem below, by the judge Muḥsin b. ʿAlawī al-Saqqāf (M. A. al-Saqqāf n.d.), which counsels against the most common and powerful means known to Hadramis to improve one's situation: migration abroad.

Oh people of Say'ūn, what's this silliness and stupidity?
How odd! How strange! This harshness and severity.
To one in the flower of youth they say, "To Java with thee!
Hand over the dough, we'll marry you and throw a party!"
Forget Java. By the wells you stay, for here is ease;
Contentment is wealth, in it well-being and peace.
The satisfied stay with their folk, to Java they don't.
Ah the clean life, with neither meddling nor discord.
Oh people of now, what's this dimness of sight?
Your cares over money, the cause of enmity.
Oh shabby smelly spit, throw a cover over it!

Perhaps the nadir of Aḥmad al-Junayd's residence in his hometown of Tarim under foreign Yāfiʿī occupation occurred after his son and brother in Tarim died. Aḥmad felt alone and without helpers, and he asked his other brother, ʿUmar, to return from Singapore to aid him and keep him company. ʿUmar came back with all his sons and a cousin. But soon after their arrival, the family members were imprisoned by the Gharamah ruler. The latter had become used to jailing Aḥmad regularly for ransom, and ʿUmar from Singapore represented a bigger catch. When ʿUmar was finally released, after surrendering a substantial cash ransom, he immediately prepared to leave Tarim. He appealed to Aḥmad to go with him; he would take the family to live in Mecca. Aḥmad declined. ʿUmar left immediately for Singapore, never to return. Aḥmad al-Junayd was devoted to his hometown, tied to it by powerful attachments he could not break. In this devotion he was not alone, for Tarim is a special place in the Hadrami imagination, at home and in the diaspora.

Traces of the Ancestors

Aḥmad al-Junayd was reluctant to leave Tarim for Mecca, despite his constant imprisonment by the Gharamah, because he was attached to the graveyards of Tarim. The story is recounted today as one of his distinguishing preternatural acts (*karāmāt*) that even during his incarceration, he was spotted at night visiting the tombs.[19] His enthusiasm for them was part of a larger project that was his life's work: to seek out and revivify the "traces of the ancestors/predecessors" (*āthār al-aslāf*). This commitment involved architectural projects of restoration—seeking out ruined mosques of the ancestors and rebuilding them in accordance with available knowledge of the original architectural styles. Beyond repairing cracks in walls and replacing whole roofs, he underwrote the expenses of keeping a mosque in use and inducing men to prayer: the salaries of custodians, oil for the lamps, coffee, and incense. Among the major Tarim mosques he restored are the al-Saqqāf, al-Muḥḍār, and Bā ʿAlawī. He made trips to surrounding settlements especially to locate and restore mosques that had fallen into disuse. His devotion to his famous pious ancestors drove him to acquire the houses they had lived in. He had the house of the First Jurist rebuilt and constructed around it a dwelling for himself. He ended up owning fifteen such houses. In the cemeteries, he identified graves that had fallen into oblivion and rebuilt their tombstones. Gravestones of outstanding individuals he had raised and coated with polished white quicklime, "that their light may radiate outwards." Polished quicklime is an expensive material used in the houses of the wealthy. Its production is labor intensive, in-

19. Attributed to saints, *karāmāt* are ontologically inferior to the miracles of prophets, *muʿjizāt*.

volving quarrying, breaking, and firing limestone; long hours of pounding with clubs; and hand polishing the resulting dry paste on a surface with stone to achieve the desired smooth, reflective surface. The local term for quicklime in this form is *nūra,* the feminine form of the Arabic word for light, the material being named for its function. With the quicklime's exposure to the elements, the treatment has to be renewed every few years.

Thus revivifying the traces of the ancestors is constant, unending work. A continual expenditure of energy is required just to keep at bay the corrosive action of the elements and of forgetfulness. Ahmad's biography reports that he volunteered the reason for his efforts in this way: "to procure for the imagination[20] its share of the historical traces" (al-Junayd 1994: 119). The traces were sensuous media that connected men directly to their pious ancestors, and this conjunction itself he supposed had creative consequences in consciousness. How direct is the connection? It is strongest at the grave. The *Sublime Benefits* explains the significance of the graves of the pious thus:

The grand shaykh ʿAbd Allāh b. Abī Bakr al-ʿAydarūs was asked:

> what is the meaning of "to be blessed by the remains of the pious ones (*al-tabarruk bi-āthār al-ṣāliḥīn*)?" He said: "Blessing is by their remains and devotions and their clothes, because their places (graves) are in contact with their clothes; their clothes cover their bodies; their bodies dress their souls; their souls adorn the presence of their God." Then he sang, "the fragrance of souls we find in their clothes, when coming close to knowledge of the abode." (A. H. al-Ḥaddād n.d.: 71)

This statement gives formulation to the practice, which is general in the Islamic world at the graves of saints, of passing both hands over the tombstone or its cloth cover, then drawing one's hands to one's face and inhaling. In Hadramawt, bits of clothing of saints are collected in small, triangular bundles *(qubuʿ)* and paraded on certain ritual occasions. At the conclusion of the parade, they are made available to devotees *(muḥibbīn,* literally "lovers"), who perform the same action as at the graves. The olfactory interpretation of the connection also plays a role in the practice of what has been erroneously called "kissing hands," which in Hadramawt is performed on a great scholar, pious person, sayyid, or family elder. One takes the right hand, stoops while raising it to one's face, and makes a sniffing

20. See the discussion below on the relation between imagination and sense perception in Ibn al-ʿArabī's thought.

gesture, which consists of short, sharp, shallow inhalations, rather than kisses.[21] The gesture is a hovering of the nose above the back of the hand, rather than physical contact. In *The Transparent Essence,* the earliest and least inhibited collection of Hadrami Sufi hagiographies, the flamboyant saint ʿAbd Allāh Bā ʿAlawī is reputed to have been liberal in his use of perfumes, and his presence could be discerned from a distance.[22] The sacred has a scent. In Hadramawt, it is usually encountered as the aroma of smoldering sandalwood, the incense that Aḥmad al-Junayd paid for to attract men to prayer. The incense is a dark-colored variety with a sweet, buoyant musk; it is extracted from the jungles of Southeast Asian islands such as Timor and sourced from creole Hadrami middlemen in Penang, Singapore, Surabaya, and other regional centers. It cost three hundred dollars per kilogram in the mid-1990s, more than the monthly salary of a schoolteacher. At mosque gatherings, during pilgrimages, and at weddings, it is carried aloft through the crowd and taken round in a censer to each person in the gathering. In a gesture similar to the action at the grave, one cups one's hands above the smoke and draws it to the face, breathing in. In addition, one may wave the incense toward one's clothes, tucking it, as it were, into the recesses of the folds.

The remains of the ancestors exist only as traces, in small quantities and almost beyond recognition; often they are physically buried and no longer protrude into the visible realm. Their recuperation by those who know of them involves making their signs sensible and accessible. Making them available for direct perception by the less privileged requires mobilizing all the human senses and their material stimuli. This was how Aḥmad al-Junayd proposed, in his various projects, "to procure for the imagination its share of the historical traces." Elevating sepulchral monuments and illuminating them with gleaming white quicklime made them available to sight. Incense, working through the same olfactory pathways as those that induce appetite for food, even in the absence of sight, arouses a sensation of presence in anticipation of the contact of taste. As for taste itself, the stimulant coffee viscerally promotes wakefulness and exerts an energizing effect on the imagination. Its use has been traced to Sufis of the Shādhilī order in the Red Sea areas around Aden and Zabīd in the fifteenth century, including the Adeni of chapter 1, who ingested it during their nighttime vigils of invocation, or *dhikr* (Hattox 1985). Coffee

21. Serjeant understands the action as that of kissing, denoted by the Arabic word *taqbīl,* but correctly notes that colloquially it is *shamma,* which is to smell or sniff (Serjeant 1957: 14).

22. ʿAbd al-Raḥmān al-Saqqāf had similar tastes; he is discussed below (al-Shillī 1982: 328).

FIGURE 13. Coffee implements at the grave of the Migrant. Photo by the author.

finds use in Hadramawt today on religious occasions, such as during ritual mosque activities, in the breaking of the fast, at pilgrimages to graves, and for special social occasions such as weddings and the annual ibex hunt. While it is normally prepared with sugar, it is preferred unsweetened by "old men" and for religious occasions. The term for such coffee, intriguingly, is *Shādhiliyya* ("of Shādhilī"), which appears to be a direct reference to its historical provenance.[23]

23. While the social origins of coffee have not been conclusively established, much evidence points to its usage by Sufis on the Red Sea coast in the fifteenth century, before

The mobilization of the senses is directed toward a prototypical goal: the "presencing" *(ḥaḍra)* of the prophet Muḥammad. The ability to perceive the Prophet's presence while awake is a high station of Sufistic achievement. Its method and ontological basis have been the subjects of extensive refined elaboration by the thirteenth-century mystic and theoretician Ibn al-ʿArabī, whose ideas, often glossed as "monist," continue to inform much Sufi thought and practice in the Islamic world (Chittick 1994; Chodkiewicz 1993; Corbin 1997 [1969]; Hoffman 1999; Knysh 1999b; O'Fahey and Radtke 1993). Chapter 5 discusses some of Ibn al-ʿArabī's influence on Hadrami religious writings, tracing the development of a canon of texts. For now, I would like to note that one can speak of a vernacularization of his doctrines in the daily practice of religion in Hadramawt.

A number of religious rituals, held on a regular basis, formally focus

---

the European rush for it at the Red Sea port of Mocha in the seventeenth century. Botanists believe that Ethiopia was the source of coffee beans. In the fourteenth century, Muslim Somali pastoralists waged a war of conquest against Christian Ethiopia under Aḥmad Granye. The Muslims were supported with gunpowder and finance from the Hejaz and the Turks and used the Yemeni towns of Zabīd and Aden as logistical bases. They were finally defeated by the Ethiopian emperor Galawdewos with artillery assistance from the Portuguese, who had long been in search of the legendary Prester John, a Christian king lost in infidel lands. A relatively large number of émigré Hadrami sayyids participated in these events, and many are recorded in Hadrami genealogies as martyrs in that context. The Muslim base in the Ethiopian highlands was Harar, which even today is known as a coffee-producing region. Antonine Besse, who founded St. Antony's College at Oxford and built his fortunes in Aden on his uncanny ability to grade coffee, discovered that he could mix the cheaper Harar beans with Yemeni ones without customers being any the wiser. This practice is one indication of the possible closeness of the Yemeni and Ethiopian varieties. The introduction of coffee to the Red Sea coast of Yemen itself may have been a consequence of this war. The chronology would support this interpretation, and the itinerary retraces the path of war booty such as slaves and ivory back to the Arabian Peninsula. The Hadrami sayyids who participated in the Ethiopian war were also Sufis with Shādhilī affiliations, and they had a presence in the town of Zabīd, which was a regional center of Sufism in the Indian Ocean under the patronage of the Rasulid court. The al-Ahdals, the preeminent scholarly family of Zabīd, reputedly entered Yemen as companions of the ancestor of the Hadrami sayyids, from ʿIraq. The Yāfiʿīs from near Aden, who have a relationship with the Shaykh Bū Bakr sayyids of ʿAynāt in Hadramawt as spiritual clients and political allies, have sent annual votive offerings to Hadramawt in the form of coffee since the seventeenth century. Mood drugs seldom are able to cast off associations with the risqué. In this regard, the choice of coffee over other alternatives has received an interesting interpretation by the very eminent and very Protestant historian of Islam, Marshall Hodgson. While wine was associated with singing slave girls and drunken madness, hashish effected a "dreamy play of the imagination," causing a loss of responsibility but "called for no women." Coffee was the most innocuous of these substances, "more adaptable to peaceable all-male gatherings than wine, bringing a certain mental excitement or relief without loss of responsibility" (Hodgson 1974: 568).

on the Prophet. One of them is the presencing, or *ḥaḍra;* the other is the celebration of his birth, or *mawlid*. Coffee and incense are used on these occasions. But they are the enabling paraphernalia of other special social occasions as well, such as weddings, receptions for important personages and long-absent migrants, and the annual ibex hunts. Such gatherings usually have masters of ceremonies who choreograph the performance of etiquette. Throughout the event, they call out regularly at certain moments, such as the entrance of important participants: "Prayer for the Prophet!" *("Ṣalā ʿalā al-Nabī!")* and those present respond as a chorus: "God's prayers and peace be upon Muḥammad!" *("Allāhuma ṣallī ʿalā Muḥammad wa-sallim!").* The call to pray for the Prophet figures in Ibn al-ʿArabī's writings as the act of *taṣliyya* (an onomatopoeic neologism), whose repetition effects presencing of the Prophet (Hoffman 1999; O'Fahey and Radtke 1993). What I am suggesting is that such special social occasions are conducted as if they were Sufi presencings geared to the beatific *visio Muḥammadi*. Their specialness is marked by their reiteration of cues such as the *taṣliyya*. Within the religious tradition that has developed in Hadramawt, the traces of the ancestors, and especially of the prototypical ancestor—the prophet Muḥammad—loom large as signs in and for the imagination, whose care and feeding became Aḥmad al-Junayd's life's work. Their sensuous apprehension indeed received much theoretical elaboration in Ibn al-ʿArabī's thought as the concepts of sight *(ru'ya),* taste *(dhawq)*, and hearing *(samāʿ).*[24] As signs, the consumption of coffee and the inhalation of sandalwood align two distinct hierarchies of value (Sahlins 1976: 179 ff.). While coffee finds use in special religious and social occasions, its cheaper substitute, tea, facilitates social pleasantries on more mundane occasions, such as the daily family gathering after lunch. Similarly, frankincense, a cheaper incense, serves as a deodorant in the home. The choice of substances in these cases aligns hierarchies of social occasion and location with hierarchies of monetary rarity *qua* price, serving as a common structure of signs for separate domains of value. The choice between costly polished quicklime and basic matte whitewash,

24. For Ibn al-ʿArabī, the imagination lies between spirit and body and is a composite of meaning *(maʿnā)* and sense perception *(ḥiss)*: "Revelation is a meaning. When God wants meaning to descend to sense perception, it has to pass through the Presence of Imagination before it reaches sense perception. The reality of imagination demands that it give sensory form to everything that becomes actualized within it. There is no escape from this. If the divine revelation arrives in the state of sleep, it is called a 'dream-vision,' but if it arrives at the time of wakefulness, it is called an 'imaginalization,' *takhayyul*, . . . That is why revelation begins with imagination" (Chittick 1994: 74–75; Ibn al-ʿArabī 1972: II 375.32).

which Aḥmad al-Junayd constantly confronted in his restoration projects, reflects coordinate considerations.

As signs, the sensuous media we have discussed thus far are arbitrary in the long view. As we saw in chapter 2, some of these media are of foreign origin and have been localized and assimilated into the indigenous scheme of things. Tea became a substitute for coffee at home, and foreign sandalwood at some point probably displaced frankincense in ritual function. Foreign cement and industrial paint are now beginning to make inroads as alternatives to local quicklime, whitewash, mortar, and adobe. The blessed cloth of Tarim, ranked by Aḥmad al-Junayd above the foreign textiles, has now been completely supplanted by the foreign goods and no longer exists. Those fabrics, sourced today from Indonesia and bearing Hadrami names as trademarks, themselves constitute hierarchies of religious and social use values, whose sartorial deployment functions in precise ways to mark status, position, and occasion. At religious or social gatherings, for example, the religious notables, sayyids and shaykhs, are easily recognized at the head of the group, striking in their long white cotton gowns and their white turbans tightly wrapped in a spiral with ends tucked in. On these occasions, notables also don white sarongs of fine cotton with light, thin lines outlining large, subtle grids. Others sport white skullcaps or colored turbans loosely tied with ends sticking out, and some wear darker sarongs of industrial Tetron in browns or blues with shaded checkered prints, a coarser design for everyday use that is less susceptible to soiling. At dance processions during pilgrimages, townsmen who are neither sayyids nor tribesmen cover their heads with red-and-black headdresses of *ikat* textile, a distinctive eastern Indonesian design that is woven with the dye wet on the weft, resulting in diffuse, bleeding patterns as in a Rorschach test. Local weaves from al-Shiḥr, made on narrow looms and barely covering the kneecaps when worn[25]—with their bright polychrome patterns, open ends, and loose fringes—mark the wearers as bedouin from out of town. Interestingly, while the Indonesian textiles are adapted to local categories in their usage, they impose a major distinction of their own: that of gender. Checkered sarongs in bitonal shades are for men, while polychrome batiks with botanical motifs are for women, in accordance with Indonesian usage. That principle is scrupulously respected and retained in Hadrami consumption of the imported cloth.

25. Because covering the kneecaps is enjoined in Islamic law, this attire carries a hint of the risqué in the eyes of the religiously aware.

FIGURE 14. Texts in a niche by a grave within a dome. Photo by the author.

Coffee, sandalwood, the *taṣliyya,* musical instruments, sarongs, and liturgical texts are detachable media. They are the mobile paraphernalia of ritual events such as *ḥaḍra* and *mawlid* that can be reconstituted in modular fashion and performed elsewhere (J. Z. Smith 1992). In the diaspora, in East Africa, India, and Southeast Asia, communities of Hadramis, or of Muslims under Hadrami tutelage, regularly held such sessions, which had a distinctive Hadrami cast. They continue to do so today. Yet such sessions relate to the ones in Tarim as satellite to source, and in that sense, something gets lost in the transmission. There are things emplaced in Tarim that cannot be replaced or modularly reproduced elsewhere.

These are the traces of the ancestors, which kept Aḥmad al-Junayd at home and kept him busy in lifelong projects of restoration. In the most immediate sense, the traces of the ancestors are their bodies interred in the graves of Tarim. Their location enables unique and inimitable presencings. In these performances, participants are moved not only by the action of their sensory organs from a distance. Rather, it is their whole bodies that gravitate to the graves and tilt toward the ancestors lying within.

CONCLUSION TO PART I

Making Tarim a Place of Return

In the historiographic descriptions of chapter 2, it was possible to maintain a narrative of a one-way flow of value arriving with the sayyid descendants of the Prophet in Tarim in the twelfth century, and then outward from Tarim. From Tarim, mobile sayyid migrants bore the gift of revelation, which no return could equal. Their very persons were in a sense gifts to local populations. In the ethnographic descriptions of the current chapter, however, the unidirectional flow cannot be upheld. People and things keep coming into Hadramawt and Tarim from the outside: mercenaries, *muwallad* creoles born abroad, brothers, nephews, money, textiles. Their absorption or rejection continuously creates work. Creoles with foreign manners repatriated from abroad learn to be local. Their families work to maintain the good name of their *bayt,* the physical house within which everything is by definition domestic and the genealogical house within which descendants are by definition native.

In representational terms, whether something comes wholly from the outside or is merely returning from the outside, having originally come from Tarim or Hadramawt itself, makes all the difference. The conversion of foreign to local involves the work of transforming a place from destination to origin, as chapter 2 points out. Aḥmad al-Junayd was certainly kept busy by both these tasks, in which he persisted through all the problems he confronted: the family quarrels at close quarters that led to his incarceration; the foreign rulers of Tarim; the upkeep of ancestral houses, mosques, and graves falling into ruin; the corrosive effects of goods and monies coming from abroad; the confusion of relatives coming and going but not staying. Throughout these trials, he remained home

FIGURE 15. ʿUmar al-Junayd's mosque, the first mosque in Singapore. Photo by the author.

in Tarim and kept faith with the place, maintaining a resolute localism that kept him working in a deliberate manner, selecting, restoring, constructing, composing, and making a place to which others would want to return. In all this, the graves of Tarim provided an absolute vertical axis to ground and fix all that was of value, whether mobile or sedentary, foreign or local. Burial initiated a process of return.

Al-Junayd's constant polishing of the traces of the ancestors sought to create a model of movement as return to source, to ancestors. The polished quicklime, the aroma of incense wafting over, coffee, and the light from oil lamps all beckoned whole bodies to the mosques and graves of the ancestors. Al-Junayd aimed to cultivate a bodily attitude, or tilt, toward the ancestors in Tarim. In this work, he helped make the town a place of origins, to which others, like his successful brother in Singapore, would return, or so he hoped.

The idea of return is a denial of the possibility of true exchange. Things that return to Tarim were originally from there, and therefore do not add something new or alien. Things that return are also not equivalents, given in exchange for something of equal value from Tarim. Rather, they are inferior, copies derived from a source. In this place that is the homeland of an old diaspora, where people and things keep coming in from the outside, the puzzling denigration of people and things foreign amounts to a resolute localism, resolute in the face of the constant entry of the external. The acceptable foreign is only that which enters on a return journey, as a pilgrimage back to an ancestral source. Such returns are movements of descendants toward ancestors, and of inferiors toward superiors. All others are aliens or guests, who cannot fully enter and be incorporated. In this sense, reciprocity is not possible. Tarim's gifts can only flow one way: outward. Returns are tributes, acts of obeisance.

This figuration of movement is centered on a Tarim that was no longer a destination for migrations but had become an origin. It creates a moral geography in which qualities are attached to places, and places in turn become signs for values. The diaspora of Hadramis across the Indian Ocean was already a geographical system of such signs when Aḥmad al-Junayd worked on the Tarim end of it in the nineteenth century. Before him, in the sixteenth and seventeenth centuries, others had worked at elaborating such a moral geography, but from abroad. In the diaspora, in places such as Gujarat and Mecca, other Hadrami sayyids worked with materials lighter than Aḥmad al-Junayd's gravestones and mud bricks, composing books of history, biography, and genealogy. Although their creations are works of travel, while al-Junayd's are works of burial, both participate in a larger, cumulative project that harnesses mobility to the purposes of morality.

In part II, we examine canonical texts of the ʿAlawī Way that were written abroad in the diaspora. We look at diasporic experiences that provide the contexts for these compositions. And, in turn, we discuss the consequences these texts had for the social mobility of Hadramis abroad and at home.

PART TWO

Genealogical Travel

CHAPTER 4

Ecumenical Islam in an Oceanic World

Cambay chiefly stretches out two arms, with her right arm she reaches out towards Aden, and with the other towards Malacca.

Tome Pires (1944:43)

The three continents of the Old World are therefore essentially related, and they combine to form a totality. Their distinguishing feature is that they all lie around a sea which provides them with a focus and a means of communication. This is an extremely important factor. For the connecting link between these three continents, the Mediterranean, is the focus of the whole of world history. With its many inlets, it is not an ocean which stretches out indefinitely and to which man has a purely negative relationship; on the contrary, it positively invites him to venture out upon it. . . . It is the centre of world history, in so far as the latter possesses any internal coherence.

Georg W. Hegel (Hegel and Hoffmeister 1975: 171)

Travel Writing

In part I, "Burial," we saw how Tarim was transformed from a destination to an origin, as the ʿAlawī sayyids from Iraq moved in and became domiciled, and their ʿAlawī pathway developed and became discursively interlaced with landmarks on the ground. By the mid-nineteenth century, Tarim had become a place of return as well, for persons from across the Indian Ocean. Between origin and return, a story remains untold, a whole history of travels. This middle part of the book, "Genealogical Travel," tells that story. The story is not complete, for not all travels became tales. And not all tales were written down. The material for this part of the book, then, comes from a subset of a subset of journeys, those which were written about. Who were the travelers, and who wrote about them? Why did they write? And what were the consequences of doing so?

The history of Hadrami migrations across the Indian Ocean is something of a fabulous tale, in which secrecy and exaggeration follow one another in quick succession. It is also a grand one: in Africa, India, and the Malay Archipelago, many reports tell of noble descendants of the Prophet being received with reverence, receiving the hands of princesses in marriage, and becoming leaders and rulers of Muslim states. Exaltation naturally has its detractors. Western writers, such as Richard Burton (1966 [1856]) in East Africa and Snouck Hurgronje (1906) in Aceh, noted—with a mixture of awe and resentment—the apparent ease with which foreign Hadrami sayyids, descendants of the Prophet, entered the ruling echelons of native society in these very different places. They saw them as worthy competitors for native affections. Whether a figure of pure virtue or the center of a vortex of intrigue, the stranger-sayyid was a known type across the Indian Ocean. How could this be?

One simple reason is that the lands around the Indian Ocean were in communication with each other from very early on. When the earliest Dutch fleets went into the Indian Ocean, they were able to go from one end of it to another by carrying letters of introduction from Muslim sultans on various shores. At the turn of the seventeenth century, the Dutch fleet from Zeeland landed at the island of Anjouan in the Comoros off the East African coast. There, the Dutch mariners obtained a letter of recommendation to the sultan of Aceh all the way across the ocean in Sumatra. On 23 August 1601, they sailed into Aceh. In Aceh, they received introductions from its sultan to the great Mughal emperor Akbar when they set out for Cambay in Gujarat the next year (Schrieke 1960: 44). The letters the Dutch obtained from the Muslim sultans facilitated their travel across the ocean. The journeys of men across the ocean went hand in hand with those of writings. Persons and texts traveled together. During this period, Europeans other than the Portuguese were newcomers in the ocean they called an "Arab lake," by analogy with the "Roman lake," the Mediterranean. Initially, Europeans like the Dutch traveled under the writ of Muslim sultans.

The places that the Dutch visited—the Comoros, Aceh, and Gujarat—were frequented by Hadramis also. The difference was that the Hadramis, especially the sayyids, brought their own texts as letters of introduction;

in that sense, they were more mobile than the Dutch were. From the sixteenth century on, the Hadramis began to carry texts written by Hadramis on their journeys. Like the letters obtained by the Dutch, these Hadrami texts facilitated Hadrami movement across the ocean and were to have great historical consequences as well. Written in Arabic, these texts borrowed from the genres available in that language, with authors creating their own hybrid versions. Chapter 5, "Hybrid Texts," examines two of these works, written in Gujarat and Mecca. Viewed together with other Hadrami texts, they form a canon, which evolved with the movement of the Hadrami diaspora across the Indian Ocean. The social composition of these writings changed as the canon developed. Early instances portray a broad range of Hadramis and other Muslims, while later texts narrow the concern to the ʿAlawī sayyids. A continuing thread through this evolution was the genealogy form, which connects the texts but appears in changing shades as it shares the page with other literary concerns, such as those of chronological history and legal disputation.

In the development of this canon, genealogy took on specific meanings for the Hadrami diaspora and its sayyid component. Chapter 6, "Creole Kinship," explores the meaning these genealogical understandings had for the conduct of kinship and marriage relations in the Malay Archipelago, both among Hadramis and between Hadramis and non-Hadramis. This cultural analysis of genealogy elucidates links between writing and social practice. Genealogy provides a conceptual bridge between the two because it is not a static category of culture but a historical product that evolved as the diaspora moved between societies and contexts. First, however, we need to describe these movements and to establish with some care their local contexts. This chapter takes up that task.

New Polities along New Trade Routes

The shifting long-distance trade routes of the Indian Ocean, and their creation of new Muslim polities across this space, provide the maximal framework for considering the Hadrami migration and the canonical formation of the ʿAlawī Way. Chapter 2 showed how the foundational elements of the ʿAlawī Way came together in the crucible of extensive transregional communications, beginning in the thirteenth century. The shift in East-West trade routes, from the Persian Gulf to the Red Sea, brought Hadramawt and Aden into greater contact with Egypt, the Hejaz, and India. This shift, and the new polities it brought forth, had a singular historical result: the creation of a transoceanic "new world" for Islam, symbolized by a common allegiance to the Shāfiʿī school of Islamic law. I use the term *new world* because this expansion was over water, whereas elsewhere, Islam had expanded territorially, like the preceding empires of the Romans and others. Ultimately stretching from Cape Town on the southern tip of Africa to Timor at the limit of the Malay Archipelago, this new world of an enlarged Islamic ecumene became a transcultural space that numerous Muslims, among them Hadramis from Arabia, traversed and settled in with relative ease and great profit, participating in the creation of new ports, polities, and even peoples.

While historians who work strictly with trade data speak of rises and declines along these routes between periods, a progressive intensification of contacts is detectable from the thirteenth century on if one looks at the phenomenon in broader cultural, political, and religious terms. Specifically, the route through the Red Sea brought into new prominence established cities along it, such as Cairo and Aden, and threw up new ones like Cambay and Calicut, in the thirteenth and fourteenth centuries. Farther east along the route, in the fourteenth and fifteenth centuries, other cities such as Pasai and Melaka in the Strait of Melaka rose to prominence as transregional emporia. In all these places, foreigners arrived in increasing numbers, and new societies formed as a result of their intercourse. In Calicut, for example, the Hindu ruler known as the Zamorin (or *samudri raja,* "ruler of the sea") hosted four thousand foreign Muslim traders in the fourteenth century, while Muslim Melaka in the fifteenth century hosted many Indian merchants from Cambay, Calicut, and the Coromandel coast, who became officers of the Malay court and some of the wealthiest merchants. Elsewhere, in Egypt, Yemen, and Gujarat, foreign soldiers and slaves settled and became rulers, military officers, and state officials. The Mamluks in Cairo, Rasulids in Aden, and Muzaffaris in Cambay were among these dynastic states run by foreigners and slave officials. This newly energized trade route and the new Muslim polities along it made possible the celebrated travels of Ibn Battuta, the Maghrebian Muslim scholar, in the mid-fourteenth century. Like many other itinerant Muslim scholars and soldiers in this period, he earned his keep serving these new states, in his case as a judge. In each place, he took local women as wives and slave-concubines. The descendants of such unions between traveling men and local women became the mobile, creole natives of this new, Indian Ocean world of Islam.

In the sixteenth century, this process intensified, as the Ottomans overran first Egypt, then points down the Red Sea until they reached and occupied Aden. The governors, officials, and soldiers in these places were foreigners who came from different parts of the Ottoman imperial realm. In India in the same period, the Mughals established their dominance, and their ruling institutions were manned by similar itinerants. In the same century, the Safavid dynasty established its rule in Persia and secured the coastal regions. The simultaneous rise of these three extensive territorial empires in the age of gunpowder, and the shrinking of space between them, energized commercial and political relations in the western Indian Ocean. Furthermore, aggressive Portuguese depredations, in the first and last thirds of the sixteenth century, drew together Muslim states across the ocean. In the former period, Muslim naval forces from Diu and Calicut combined with those of the Ottomans against the Portuguese on the west coast of India. In the latter, Turkish artillery was sent to Aceh to counter the Portuguese there,[1] while Muslim Bijapur and Golconda combined against Portuguese Goa. Together, Golconda and Aceh sent arms and men to push the Portuguese out of Melaka (Reid 1969, 1993). In the 1570s, the Arab jurist and historian of Malabar, Zayn al-Dīn al-Mulaybārī (also al-Malībārī or al-Maʿbārī), detailed the events and geography of this international conflict and formulated an explicit theory of *jihād* against Christians who invaded Muslim lands (al-Maʿbārī 1987). In contrast to graphic acccounts of Portuguese violence, al-Mulaybārī portrayed the expansion of Islam in Malabar as the result of a peaceful history of trade and intermarriage, beginning with the apocryphal Cherumal Peraman. Peraman, the ancestor of Calicut's Zamorin rulers, had established the divisions and ceremonial insignia of state, been converted to Islam by traveling Sufis, and followed them to Hadramawt, dying in its port city of al-Shiḥr.

The rise of port cities from the thirteenth century on, and of large territorial states in the sixteenth, meant that new Muslim states and polities were being created out of old ones with the arrival and incorporation of foreigners in positions of rule and influence. Such a process is difficult to imagine in today's postcolonial, nationalized world. The racialized privileges and jealousies of late nineteenth-century colonialism have given foreigners, European and otherwise, a bad name. They became thought of as aliens who could not be absorbed and as interlopers who threatened and exploited indigenous sovereignty and wealth—rather than as partners

1. In the late 1990s, the Turkish scholar Cemil Aydin met persons in Aceh who claimed to be descendants of these Ottoman artillerymen; I appreciate his relating this remarkable encounter to me. Ottoman and Portuguese artillery also faced off in Ethiopia in the same period, as auxiliaries in the Christian-Muslim wars there.

with whom new persons, polities, societies, and economies could be created. Yet precisely the constitution of new polities and persons by mobile Muslims was the important dynamic in the expansion of Islam across the Indian Ocean. Hadramis, especially the sayyids, were a strong current in this restless ocean.

The Two Arms of Cambay

By the beginning of the sixteenth century, the long Persian Gulf–China oceanic route had been broken up and consolidated into three sectors. From the Red Sea to Gujarat, and between Gujarat and Melaka, trade was carried by Gujarati and Arab merchants. Onward from Melaka to China, it was carried by their Chinese counterparts. Competition between Chinese and Arab merchants on the long route had been resolved into component sectors under separate dominance. This had been preceded by violence against Muslim merchants in Canton and against Chinese merchants in Malabar. The Muslim sector now had an eastern terminus in Melaka, where it articulated with the western one of the Chinese. On each side, the new division meant a shorter sailing season for ships and faster turnover of capital. This reorganization of the routes provided the conditions under which, in the fourteenth century, port cities around the Strait of Melaka simultaneously rose in significance as transregional emporia and became Muslim. Melaka's predecessor, Pasai, was Muslim, and Portuguese accounts of Melaka's founding tell of Arab merchants in Pasai advising the Melaka chief to convert if he wanted to attract trade (Pires 1944).[2] In Hadramawt, scholars told me that Malabar derives from the Arabic word *maʿbar,* meaning "crossing," which Arabs used to refer to their destination when crossing over the ocean from Aden. Similarly, some people in Hadramawt claim that Melaka derives from the locational participle of the Arabic verb "to meet," *l-q-ā/y.*

The two Muslim sectors spanned the breadth of the Indian Ocean. Between them, Gujarat served as a natural fulcrum, a linking node for exchange between them, grounded by its own dominance in textile pro-

2. In the fifteenth century, a theological debate that had begun in Yemen over ʿAbd al-Karīm al-Jīlī's interpretation (composed in Yemen) of Ibn al-ʿArabī's doctrine of "the perfect man" *(al-insān al-kāmil)* was pursued in Pasai and Melaka, providing evidence of vital intellectual relations between the two regions (al-Attas 1966; Knysh 1999b). Al-Jīlī himself was an Indian scholar who studied, taught, and wrote in Yemen.

duction.[3] Its natural market included both Egypt and Southeast Asia (Chaudhuri 1990). Its major port was Cambay. The Portuguese accountant Tome Pires, writing in Melaka at the end of a surveying journey around the ocean, could see this role very clearly: thus, the two arms of Cambay.

On the "right" arm of Cambay, stretching to Aden, Hadrami maritime activity is evident. The Portuguese observer Barbosa noted that al-Shiḥr ("Xaer") on the Hadrami coast was a very large emporium. Frankincense was exported from there to Cambay, where al-Shiḥr horses were also in great demand, outclassing the Arabian Hormuz and local Gujarati Kathiawar breeds (Barbosa 1918 [1518]: 65–66). Central Asian horsemen played an important role in the Muslim conquests of India, and Barbosa estimated an annual supply of three thousand first-quality animals from al-Shiḥr. Hadrami and other Arabian maritime records exist as well. When the intrepid Vasco da Gama crossed over from East Africa to India after rounding the Cape at the end of the fifteenth century, his guide was an Arab pilot, Ibn Mājid al-Najdī, whose detailed knowledge of the ocean was set down in writing (Tibbetts 1981). Sulaymān, the other famous Indian Ocean navigator from the period whose knowledge was recorded, was from Mahra, the region adjoining Hadramawt (Hourani 1951). The contemporary Hadrami chronicler of al-Shiḥr, Bā Faqīh, noted events in Ethiopia on one side of the ocean and Gujarat on the other (Bā Faqīh 1999). Despite their intrinsic interest, these writings, which cover a wide geographical field, played no role in the development of the sayyid canon. For that role, we have to examine the particularities of Muslim rule in Gujarat.

The Independent Muslim Sultanate of Gujarat

The Muslim sultanate of Gujarat, based initially in Cambay, was declared independent by its governor in 1407, when his Tughluq overlord in Delhi succumbed to the Timurid invasions. Five hundred Bukhari Sufi sayyids had accompanied Timur (Tamerlane), and some of their descendants remained court favorites and leading divines throughout the tenure of the Gujarat sultanate, which ended with incorporation into Akbar's Mughal

3. The combination of location and production (shared by pepper-producing entrepôt regions such as Malabar and Aceh) enhances survival over long periods, Gujarat and Malabar being significant from Greco-Roman times (Hourani 1951: 37). Aden and Singapore provide contrasting examples from recent times. After gaining independence in the 1960s, Singapore augmented entrepôt trade with production, whereas Aden lost trade and emphasized production under socialist models: the results are apparent to the casual visitor.

empire in 1573. As in Anatolia, Sufis were important figures in the early armies of the Central Asian conquerors of India, serving as warriors in combat and seers of omens in strategy (R. M. Eaton 1978; Ulughkhānī 1910–28). Their roles subsequently evolved and multiplied: they served as spiritual patrons of dynasties, leaders with local followings, and foci of tomb cults, or *durgah* (R. M. Eaton 1978), scholarly promoters of Islamic law, state officials with ranked bureaucratic sinecures (Pearson 1976), sources of imperial information attuned to the pulse of public opinion (Bayly 1996), and arbiters in the formulation of public consensus in urban centers with mixed, mobile populations, such as the port of Surat (Das Gupta 1979). To retain a sense of the historical plasticity, I will refer to such persons by the general term *religious adept* and reserve the terms *Sufi, saint,* and *scholar* for specific contexts. These players were often foreigners, such as Bukharis and Hadramis, and their changing roles have to be seen in conjunction with those of their peers and fellow itinerants. The latter were the slave-soldiers common in the Middle East and South Asia in this period.

Imposed upon large, sedentary populations, the numerically inferior Muslim conquerors of India regularized rule by parceling out fiefs to subordinates. On that basis, an intermediate stratum of military nobles emerged, responsible for raising and commanding cavalry from local revenues.[4] The dislocations of conquest had created mobile persons, goods, and precious metals, monetizing the conquest frontier and creating new opportunities for accumulating power and wealth (Wink 1997).

In the processions of the Cambay sultans, Yāfiʿīs and Mahrīs from southern Yemen took the lead, as the fiercest of their mercenaries, followed by Javanese, Turks, and Portuguese (Ulughkhānī 1910–28: 290–91).

4. In the developed Mughal administration, these benefits were, strictly speaking, not fiefs but rotating "revenue assignments" (Habib 1963: 257) of three to four years that aimed to prevent the buildup of local power by the assignees. Known as *jāgīrs,* the assignments effectively created garrisons throughout the Mughal realm that could respond immediately to local contingencies. The assignees were usually holders of formal Mughal ranks known as *manṣab* (Moreland 1998 [1936]). A parallel system of "revenue grants," known as *madad-i maʿāsh* (literally, "subsistence aid"), was created in a religious-charity mode for indigents, impecunious nobles, scholars, and Sufis. Reminiscent of Saladin's designation of salaries for those "whose arrows do not miss," the emperor Jahangir called the religious functionaries who received these grants his "army of prayer," which was as important as the military (Habib 1963: 310). In 1690, Aurangzeb made the grants hereditary. Aurangzeb's tilt toward religious orthodoxy was accompanied by the expansion of state surveillance, and we can view the strengthening of the grants system in that context. C. A. Bayly has drawn out the significance of religious functionaries and other "information elites" for the "information order" of the Mughal empire (Bayly 1996).

Besides foreign soldiers, Circassian, Turkish, and Ethiopian slave elites populated the ranks of the new nobility, forging a mobile class out of mobile wealth. These people were non-Muslims who had undergone a "social death" (Patterson 1982) by being wrenched out of their home societies in youth and were now incorporated into Muslim polities as loyal fighters. Their re-creation as new social persons involved a process of education in two important fields: horsemanship, to serve in the all-important cavalry; and the rudiments of Islam, to inculcate identification with the Muslim polities to which they now belonged.[5] For those who rose to become commanders and administrators, the fruits of lifelong pursuit of religious cultivation became an adjunct of personal social success. Out of such ambitions, they associated with Muslim scholars and Sufis—religious adepts—and shared with them their worldly gains.[6]

Religious Adepts and Nobles

Examples from al-Ḥājj al-Dabīr Ulughkhānī's *Victory of those Fervent for Muẓaffar and his Folk* (Ulughkhānī 1910–28), a history of the independent Muslim sultanate of Cambay in the fifteenth and sixteenth centuries, give us an idea of how widespread such associations were and the regard in which religious adepts were held. Ulughkhānī was born in 1539 in Mecca, to which his father had been sent by the Cambay sultan to administer his property, and he repatriated to Cambay in 1554. He was very familiar with the mobile, foreign Muslims who came to Gujarat.

Rayḥān Badr al-Dīn Jahangir Khān was a slave in the sixteenth century who had been educated while in the service of his master. He was cultured, literate, and wise. He displayed proficiency in writing and handling his master's financial affairs and was appointed a minister. Evidently a wealthy man, he associated closely with Hadrami sayyids. One of these associates was Shaykh b. ʿAbd Allāh al-ʿAydarūs, a fifth-gener-

5. Gunpowder and mounted archers are the two major factors that historians credit for the military successes of Central Asians in the Middle East and South Asia. The slave-soldier model was developed earlier in the Levant and Egypt, under the Ayyubids and Mamluks (themselves of military-slave origin) and has been credited by historians for Muslim successes against the depredations of the Crusaders.

6. In the early sixteenth century, a number of these Ethiopian slave-soldiers and Hadrami Sufi scholars would already have been acquainted with each other before arriving in Gujarat. The slaves were captured in war between Muslims and Christians in Ethiopia and sold to Turks in Yemen on the Red Sea coast, such as on the island of Kamaran. The Turks brought them to Gujarat.

ation descendant of ʿAbd al-Raḥmān al-Saqqāf, who established the basic rituals of the ʿAlawī Way, and great-grand nephew of Abū Bakr al-ʿAydarūs, the Adeni, whom we met in the first chapter. His grandfather had the name Shaykh b. ʿAbd Allāh al-ʿAydarūs as well, so I will refer to him as Shaykh (II) al-ʿAydarūs.[7] Shaykh (II) al-ʿAydarūs was born in Tarim in 1513 and entered India in 1551, being the first al-ʿAydarūs to do so. He remained there for over three decades, until his death in Aḥmad Ābād (also Ahmedabad), the capital of Gujarat, in 1582. Of Rayḥān's disposition toward Shaykh (II) al-ʿAydarūs, the Arabic historian of Gujarat wrote:

> He loved the pious, and devoted himself to serving the wali of the holies, sun of suns, Shaykh b. ʿAbd Allāh al-ʿAydarūs (God sanctify his secret and benefit us through him). He was encompassed by the ʿAydarūsid attention,[8] and through al-ʿAydarūs the creed was perfected within him until he became famous for it. Thus he gave al-ʿAydarūs his due in many poems that he composed, and expended whatever he possessed in his service. He became a shining exemplar, and both this slave and all that he owned was for his master al-ʿAydarūs. Rayḥān loved the Hadramis, especially the sayyids, but also other Hadramis. He was fond of those closest to the sayyids, and in this way his charity extended to those of the Arab race.[9] (Ulughkhānī 1910–28: 612)

Rayḥān enjoyed being in the reflected glow of the ʿAydarūs light, which afforded him the chance to display his literary culture in composing eulogies, and to achieve renown for his piety. Hadrami sayyids who were held in such regard, such as Shaykh (II) al-ʿAydarūs, were correspondingly well rewarded for their ability to bestow such favors.

Another of the ʿAydarūses who received the attentions of Rayḥān was Shaykh (II) al-ʿAydarūs's son, the sayyid Aḥmad b. Shaykh (II) al-ʿAydarūs. The historian al-Ḥājj al-Dabīr Ulughkhānī was a constant companion of Rayḥān, in whose service he worked as a scribe, and affords us a firsthand account. In his writings, the successes of slave-administrators such as Rayḥān and Hadrami sayyids are closely linked. When Rayḥān

7. Shaykh here is a personal name, not the honorific, which is more common. In turn, Shaykh (II) al-ʿAydarūs's grandson in Bijapur was also named Shaykh b. ʿAbd Allāh al-ʿAydarūs (R. M. Eaton 1978: 127). A fuller discussion of this lineage appears in the next chapter.

8. The term is *ʿināya,* which means care, attention, favor, protection. It is often used in relation to God, who extends it as a cover to one who has been singled out to receive it as a divine gift.

9. The term translated here as "loved" is *walah,* a common term in Sufi discourse that denotes a state of infatuation and rapture.

assumed a new ministerial position in Aḥmad Ābād, Aḥmad al-ʿAydarūs was resident there. Ulughkhānī described him in this way:

Axis of the witnesses/seers, master of revelations of the majestic and the beautiful, rapture of the holies, the greatest manifestation, our master star of the religion Aḥmad b. Shaykh al-ʿAydarūs (God sanctify his secret and benefit us through him). Rayḥān exerted himself in his service, took him as his sole guide, achieved perfection in Sufism through him, and became his follower and partisan. In his attraction to al-ʿAydarūs, he found it proper to remove himself from the affairs of the world, remaining under the shade of his supreme virtues; he was content to be worthy of al-ʿAydarūs's blessings. As he said of al-ʿAydarūs during a number of his states of rapture, "My shaykh, he and I are in heaven." . . . Rayḥān was in communication with the nobles of his race and with residents of the port-towns, with whom he corresponded, and because of this he did not send me away in the daytime and for part of the night. Thus I saw the good fortune he had in rule, enjoying God's support in the way of rewards and results. (Ulughkhānī 1910–28: 612)

One of the slave-nobles, Sharwan Khān, was given to the good life, almost never seeing the crescent moon once in a month in a sober state (Ulughkhānī 1910–28: 609). He was an Ethiopian leader in the army in Baroda, in the time of Chingiz Khān. His annual income was two hundred thousand Maḥmūdīs, with which he was liberal in charity, helping the needy and founding a "society of friends," which made him "eternally glorious and famous." He particularly favored ʿAbd Allāh Saʿīd al-Hadrami al-Yamanī, a Hadrami Sufi, for his musical abilities (Ulughkhānī 1910–28: 610).

Ghālib Khān, yet another of the slave nobility, had been purchased in Yemen and grew up to be both a horseman and an administrator. He was treated kindly and became something of a scholar. He "completed the Qurʾan, studied books of jurisprudence, *ḥadīth* and commentary, distinguished between the permitted and the prohibited, was read in literature and known for it" (Ulughkhānī 1910–28: 610). Unlike Sharwan Khān, Ghālib Khān consulted with Hadramis on matters of jurisprudence, and "even when he was travelling, a party of Arab sayyids and theologians of Yemen remained in his house" (Ulughkhānī 1910–28: 611).

The Ethiopian slave-commander Bijlī Khān was known for a number of things, including his services to the Hadrami sayyids of Tarim, to the extent of providing slave-concubines to those who were impatient for marriage, thereby preserving them from sin.[10] He would pay the way of sayyids who were guests in his house but had become indigent and wished

10. Apart from relations with wives, sexual relations are legally permitted with slave women in Shāfiʿī law.

to return to their homeland. When these guests first arrived in Gujarat, his custom was to distribute them among the most eminent of his friends, provide for their expenses during their stay, and furnish them with supplies and mounts when they journeyed (Ulughkhānī 1910–28: 544).

These brief examples demonstrate that Hadrami sayyids found broad opportunities for patronage among the foreign slave nobility of Gujarat, persons who spent a lifetime cultivating themselves after their "social deaths" in slavery. Hadrami religious adepts of different talents could find reward with such patrons for musical ability, legal erudition, luminous fame, and the chance of transport to paradise. Bijlī Khān's particular devotion to the sayyids of Tarim indicates that Tarim's reputation as the origin of the ʿAlawī sayyids had spread to Gujarat by this time. The usual categorization of Hadrami divines as Sufis is somewhat misleading and certainly not exhaustive, for in addition to possessing musical and poetic skills, the Hadramis pursued jurisprudential cultivation. The dominant modes that biographers assigned to individuals are just partial views, as all these skills were included in the curriculum of any Hadrami educational experience. Historical scholarship that studies soldiers, Sufis, and scholars as separate types fails to perceive the links among individuals, peer groups, generations, and diasporic families. Such links are usually invisible in the specialized secondary literature, except in chance remarks in footnotes, but are abundant in the original sources.

Religious Adepts and Sultans

In their patronage of religious adepts, the nobles emulated their betters, the sultans. As I have noted, Sufis had been integral members of the conquering armies of Muslim India, and they remained in the entourages of sultans throughout the period of Muslim rule there.

The "balance of power diplomacy" (Misra 1982: 164–65) that Gujarat pursued with its neighboring states, such as Malwa and Khandesh, was rife with intimacy and intrigue. Internal actors such as religious adepts and kinsmen of sultans were likely to conspire with neighboring rulers, and death by poison was common. One episode, between Sultan Quṭb al-Dīn of Gujarat and Sultan Maḥmūd of Malwa in 1451, involved a corresponding contest between Sayyid Jalāl al-Dīn al-Bukhārī, the "spiritual patron" of the Gujarat dynasty, and a rival Sufi, Shaykh Kamāl (Pearson 1976: 147–48; Ulughkhānī 1910–28: 6, 204, 304). The Malwa sultan offered Shaykh Kamāl a refectory for the poor, which would increase his following, and a stipend of three million rupees (equal to that of Shaykh Aḥmad Khattu, spiritual patron of the first Gujarat sultan) if he aided his conquest of Gujarat. The shaykh accepted and issued a public call for the Malwa sultan to invade Gujarat. Sultan Quṭb al-Dīn had just ascended the throne, and his hold on it was not yet secure; he requested that the shaykh help prevent the invasion but was rebuffed. In the event, the attack failed, and Shaykh Kamāl died. Spiritual precedence remained in the hands of the Bukhari sayyids until the demise of the Gujarat dynasty.

In another encounter a century later, in 1566, the Gujarat sultan Chingiz Khān assured himself of victory by rewarding the Sufis before he marched. The Bukhari sayyid Ḥāmid received a thousand *ashrafīs*, as well as robes embroidered with gold, an Arab horse, and other precious items (Ulughkhānī 1910–28: 499). The thousand *ashrafīs* was equivalent to the sum paid another Sufi, the Hadrami sayyid Shaykh (II) al-ʿAydarūs whom we encountered above. He had sent an envoy to the sultan saying that the city under contest was "a bride at a wedding. She will not be married without bridewealth, proposal and consent" (Ulughkhānī 1910–28: 499). The sultan asked how much the bride price was, and the envoy replied, "One thousand *ashrafīs* up front, and an equivalent amount in estates" (Ulughkhānī 1910–28: 499). The sultan accepted and at the same time sent for the Bukhari sayyid and others, to whom he gave the same amount.

While influence at the courts of sultans must have been a heady and rewarding experience, proximity to power and its intrigue carried risks in a place like Gujarat. The prolific Hadrami author (his books are still studied in Hadramawt today), jurist, and administrator Baḥraq discovered this reality at great personal cost.

In his biographical collection of eminent Hadramis, the modern Hadrami historian Saʿīd ʿAwaḍ Bā Wazīr praises the shaykh Muḥammad b. ʿUmar Baḥraq as a "distinguished, self-made man" who "became great and famous not by descent or inheritance, but by ability and merit" (Bā Wazīr 1957: 142). Baḥraq was born in the new Hadrami town of Sayʾūn in 1465. His family was not sayyid but traced its descent to the ancient Himyarites of Yemen. He traveled and studied with the great Sufis, jurists, and historians of his time: ʿAbd Allāh b. Aḥmad Bā Makhrama in Aden; Abū Bakr b. ʿAbd Allāh al-ʿAydarūs the Adeni; Ḥusayn al-Ahdal in Zabīd; and Shams al-Dīn al-Sakhāwī, the Meccan jurist and historian of wide repute. His ability won him positions, but Baḥraq's career was to be checkered, and he gained and lost favor a number of times. He had been a judge in al-Shiḥr but quit when the governor interfered with his court. His uprightness impressed the great Kathīrī sultan Badr Bū Ṭuwayriq (1496–1569), who sent him on a military expedition to conquer Mahra. He became governor of the Mahrī capital Qishn, which was a prosperous port (Barbosa 1918 [1518]). In this time, he put down revolts in the western interior of Hadramawt in the service of Bū Ṭuwayriq, at Haynin and al-Ḥajarayn. Originally from the coast, the legendary Bū Ṭuwayriq put the Kathīrī state on a firm footing, allying himself with the Ottomans and extending his hand over the Hadrami interior, aided at times by both Turks and Portuguese (bin Hāshim 1948: 34–54). But Baḥraq subsequently fell out of favor, and he left for Aden, protected by its ruler in exchange for scholarly duties teaching and issuing *fatwā*s. When this patron died, Baḥraq went farther away and arrived in Gujarat.

Baḥraq was highly regarded by Ulughkhānī, who detailed his teachers, listed his books, and praised his forty days of ascetic retirement in Zabīd: "On completion of it, he said that parts of his body too were in remembrance of God" (Ulughkhānī 1910–28: 118–20). Baḥraq was well received by the Gujarati sultan Muẓaffar b. Sulṭān Mahmūd Begarha, who "elevated him, kept him near himself, promoted him and showed him extensive favour" (Ulughkhānī 1910–28: 119). He became famous in Gujarat and dedicated books to his patron. Baḥraq enjoyed the sultan's favor until he provoked the jealousy of an Indian named Khudawand, who spread slanderous tales about him. He was forced to remove to Cambay, where he died of poison in 1524. His Hadrami biographer reports poignantly that "This is how the learned Baḥraq came to an end, a stranger far from family and home, may God have mercy on him and be satisfied with him" (Bā Wazīr 1957: 148). But succumbing to poison was a fate that Baḥraq shared with successful Gujarati sultans and nobles. Favor at court was a fickle affair, and when fortunes changed, religious adepts moved away to more receptive places. This pattern is evident in the career of the grandson of Shaykh (II) b. ʿAbd Allāh al-ʿAydarūs, who was also named Shaykh b. ʿAbd Allāh al-ʿAydarūs; I will call him Shaykh (III) al-ʿAydarūs.

Shaykh (III) al-ʿAydarūs was born in Tarim in 1585 and arrived in Surat, then becoming the dominant port of Gujarat, in 1616.[11] He had previously visited Mecca and Medina, where he acquired affiliations with numerous Sufi orders, including the Qādirī, Shādhilī, Jabartī, Madīnī, Suhrawardī, Rifāʿī, Kāzirūnī, and Ahdalī. His father had bestowed on him the "noble mantle" of Sufism numerous times. His brother Muḥammad and pater-

11. This account is from al-Shillī's *The Irrigating Fount,* which we discuss in the next chapter (al-Shillī 1901: 117–19).

nal uncle ʿAbd al-Qādir b. Shaykh (II) al-ʿAydarūs (author of *The Travelling Light Unveiled*, which I discuss in the next chapter) were in Surat when he arrived and bestowed upon him further scholarly and Sufistic credentials. From Surat, he traveled to Aḥmad Nagar on the Deccan plateau, where he was well received by Sultan Burhān Nizām Shāh and his nobleman Malik ʿAnbar. There he benefited many with his learning, and was honored by the sultan. But in a turn of events we have seen before, in the case of Baḥraq, he was slandered and therefore moved away, to Bijapur, another city on the Deccan off the Konkan coast, between Gujarat and Malabar.

Bijapur was a sultanate that retained its independence from the Mughals, and its sultans welcomed itinerant Sufis and scholars.[12] There Shaykh (III) al-ʿAydarūs taught law, Arabic, and Sufism. He had numerous students, to whom he passed on Sufi credentials, and had a wide circle of acquaintances. His success bred resentment, and he was again the target of slanderous speech. But he had learnt an effective counter: he habitually sent gifts and apologies to his detractors.

Shaykh (III) al-ʿAydarūs was credited with extraordinary powers by his Hadrami biographer al-Shillī, and these reports were transmitted onward by Urdu biographical sources, which Eaton has analyzed (Eaton 1978). Echoing earlier associations between Hadrami religious adepts and Ethiopian slave elites, al-Shillī attributed the success of one of the latter, Ḥabash Khān, to the intervention of Shaykh (III) al-ʿAydarūs. Habash Khān had been thin and dull when he arrived in India. He sought out Shaykh (III) al-ʿAydarūs, who prayed to God to make him abundant in learning and physique, and the prayers were answered. More dramatically, when Shaykh (III) al-ʿAydarūs met the sultan of Bijapur, Ibrāhīm ʿĀdil Shāh, he found the sultan stricken with pain in the buttocks, which prevented him from sitting and resting. The sultan had been cursed by another Hadrami sayyid, ʿAlī b. ʿAlawī al-Ḥaddād Bā ʿAlawī. Shaykh (III) al-ʿAydarūs commanded the sultan to sit down evenly, and when the sultan did so, he found himself cured. Not surprisingly Shaykh (III) al-ʿAydarūs subsequently wielded great influence over the sultan; he enjoined him to wear Arab clothing, which the sultan reportedly did most of the time. When Sultan Ibrāhīm died, Shaykh (III) al-ʿAydarūs again moved, this time to Dawlat Ābād, under the rule of Fatḥ Khān, son of his for-

12. Eaton's *Sufis of Bijapur* (1978) covers five hundred years of Bijapur history and is one of the most comprehensive accounts of a regional tradition in India. Shaykh (III) b. ʿAbd Allāh al-ʿAydarūs appears in his volume as "the shaykh ʿAbd Allāh al-ʿAydarūs."

mer patron Malik ʿAnbar. There he was well provided for until he passed away in 1631. Al-Shillī records that his tomb is well known and visited by pilgrims.

Voice of the Port City: Hadrami Sayyids and the General Interest

By the beginning of the eighteenth century, families of Hadrami sayyids like the ʿAydarūses had established wide reputations in the region. They were no longer solely tied to individual patrons such as nobles, or subject to the vagaries of sultanic favor—struggling as individual immigrants abroad without supporters, dying from poison alone like Baḥraq. In eighteenth-century Surat, the primary port of Mughal India, the ʿAydarūs sayyids were quite at home. Predecessors had established prestigious lineages locally, which were constantly reinvigorated by relatives from Hadramawt and the Hejaz. During this century, Surat went into decline, to be supplanted by English Bombay nearby.

Surat's fall to provincial status was part of the general decline in Mughal fortunes and was punctuated by a series of crises in which ʿAydarūs sayyids featured as authenticators of public opinion. The retreat of imperial power cut cities off from the surrounding countryside and from each other. The governors of Surat lost their rural incomes to resurgent local Maratha chiefs and increasingly lived out of the pockets of the urban merchants, by turns through compulsion and debt. Merchants themselves were unable to obtain supplies of cloth from looms in the surrounding countryside for their main business, export to the Red Sea Yemeni port of Mocha;[13] carts transporting goods between towns were heavily taxed by local warlords; and the flow of pilgrims from the north Indian interior, headed for Mecca on Surat ships, dried up. Gubernatorial excesses provoked revolt by merchants, while financial crises moved those with control over the

13. By the seventeenth century, Gujarati merchants had abandoned the great exchange between Indian cloth and the Indonesian "fine" spices, having been edged out by armed Dutch monopoly. Instead, they concentrated on Red Sea trade, the erstwhile "right arm" of Cambay (Das Gupta 1967). Yemeni exports of coffee were a key source of specie into Mocha, which buoyed the markets for Gujarati products. These coffee exports dried up through the eighteenth century, as Dutch coffee plantations in Java, started with trees smuggled out of Yemen around 1699, began undermining the Yemeni product. The compromises of those early days can be tasted today in the continued existence of the first blended coffee, Mocha-Java.

means of violence, such as the Ethiopian-commanded Mughal navy and English and Dutch Company traders, to blockade the port as a means of exacting dues.

In these maneuvers, rival blocs of merchants and military units—normally at odds with each other—temporarily formed coalitions to counter a common imperative or threat. They needed help in holding together. Wavering parties had to be convinced that public opinion stood behind them, to prevent their breaking ranks. At such moments, personalities from the ʿAydarūs family were conspicuous in giving their blessings to plans and in giving voice to public opinion. The fractious city had common, generalizable interests at certain rare moments but had few nonpartisan figures in a position to express them.

In 1732, the merchants of Surat, even those who were bitter rivals, came together to overthrow the governor, Sohrab Khān, who had squeezed them once too often. They carried with them the Ethiopian slave-commanders of the Mughal navy, the English traders, and eventually the Dutch as well. To dissuade participants from changing their minds, the organizers obtained a public pronouncement from the Hadrami sayyid Zayn al-ʿAydarūs that their cause was just. Sayyid Zayn gave his blessings to the venture, pronouncing the governor worthy of punishment, and brought the qadi and mufti over to their side as well (Das Gupta 1979: 224). The armed standoff between governor and merchants lasted almost a month; it ended with the governor's defeat when Maratha commanders from outside the city gave their support to the urban merchants. Muḥammad ʿAlī, an eminent Bohra merchant and prime instigator of the revolt, raised and maintained two thousand fighting men for the duration of the hostilities.

Three years later, in 1735, the Mughal navy itself threatened to blockade the port just as the ships of the Surat merchants were fully loaded with goods for the annual convoy to the Red Sea, and a thousand pilgrims were gathered for passage to Mecca. Maritime affairs had never been a priority of the rulers of the subcontinent, and the Mughal navy was manned by Ethiopian slaves who had been brought over by Turkish warships sent to repel the Portuguese in Gujarat in the early sixteenth century.[14] They remained the core personnel even as the navy evolved into a standing force, paid out of Surat customs revenue by the governor. The

14. Pearson argues that the Portuguese were able to control the Indian coasts because maritime affairs were insignificant to the overlords of the subcontinent; customs contributed only 6 percent of the state revenues of Gujarat (Pearson 1976: 24). Such trifling matters

blockade in 1735 was born out of the desperation of the Ethiopian seamen, whose wages were long in arrears. The Ethiopians were further impelled by English plans to take over their role as the Mughal navy.

The blockade threatened the economic life of the city as a whole, and normal activity within it came to a standstill. Messengers hurried between the merchants, the navy, the governor, the English factory, the Dutch lodge, and the principal ʿAydarūs sayyid. The merchants pressed the governor to accept English arbitration in his dispute with the navy, and when public anger against the governor became critical after six days, the latter relented and agreed to arbitration by Sayyid Zayn al-ʿAydarūs, the principal Surat merchants, and the English factor. "Once this agreement had been reached, Sayyid Zayn led the whole city to prayer and it seemed the crisis had blown over" (Das Gupta 1979: 267).

Why were the ʿAydarūs sayyids able to play such mediating roles? One reason is that they were the only party in all these negotiations that never overtly posed a threat to any other. The governors milked the merchants; the merchants had deposed a governor (and maintained correspondence with officials in Delhi, through whom they could pressure and undermine governors); the navy had threatened both governor and merchants; and English and Dutch traders had on occasion called in their Company warships against all the above, in pursuit of sometimes private interests. The traders were Company representatives who traded on their own account, and they could get away with using coercive force at Company expense to juggle personal debts, dues, and profits if they did so in moderation. The sayyids, in contrast, had a history of cooperative relations with most of these groups. With rulers they had served as counselors and administrators; with slave elites such as the Ethiopians, they had been Muslim cultural mentors; with the merchants, they were familiar as judges and arbitrators in commercial disputes. Europeans often found that the sayyids could help or hinder their dealings, whether they involved obtaining houses or blockading the city (Das Gupta 1979: 35–36, 257).

Furthermore, reputation was a significant factor. We have seen something of the sayyids' peregrinations in courts and major textile-producing towns on the west coast of India: in Surat, Aḥmad Ābād, Bijapur, and

---

were left to the maritime merchants to sort out under their own lights. The Mughal navy's slaves were booty captured in the war in Ethiopia between Imam Aḥmad Granye's Muslim forces and Christian Ethiopia led by the emperor Galawdewos, with assistance from Portuguese artillery. Abir (1980) clearly lays out the geostrategic dimensions of this war.

Dawlat Ābād; Hadrami sayyids were also present in Broach, Randir, Aḥmad Nagar, Malabar, and elsewhere. At the Red Sea destinations of the Gujarati ships—in Aden, Mocha, and Jedda—they were well known as judges, scholars, Sufis, and saints. A single lineage, that of the ʿAydarūses, for example, could be prominent in most of these places. Through correspondence and travel, persons were familiar with distant conditions and personalities throughout the diaspora. Indeed, internal sources indicate that most of these cities housed tombs of family members that were the objects of regular cult pilgrimages. A common family name, across this space and through generations of immigrants and local-born creoles, effectively made the Hadrami sayyids a known quantity.

Perhaps most important was their development of sophisticated techniques in handling their names. These names in combination comprise their genealogies. We can think of the genealogies as accumulative projects that folded within themselves multiple generations, familiar geographies, and known histories. While as onomastica they harbored a restrictive set of names, their serialization contained rich possibilities for narrative elaboration and engagement. The genealogies provided multiple points of contact that articulated with the experiences of other peoples, and in that sense, were public documents whose inscription and spheres of circulation embodied a whole multicultural diaspora. Their contents were copied and reemerged in historical and biographical compilations by non-Hadramis in Arabic and in other languages such as Swahili, Urdu, and Malay, in India (R. M. Eaton 1978; Mulkapuri 1912–13), East Africa, the Hejaz, Syria (al-Muḥibbī 1966), and Southeast Asia (Raja Haji Ahmad and Raja Ali Haji 1997). The next chapter retraces the distance we have covered in this one, but through the window of evolving genealogical texts.

CHAPTER 5

Hybrid Texts: Genealogy as Light and as Law

Traveling Texts, a Diasporic Canon

The advent of a new world of ecumenical Islam in the Indian Ocean gave rise to new opportunities abroad for Hadramis, who traveled, settled, or were born abroad, and chronicled parts of the diasporic experience in texts. In the main, the authors of such accounts were sayyids, and the resulting volumes, which chain-link back to predecessors, themselves form a coherent genealogy. The two main works I examine in this chapter were composed in Gujarat and Mecca. In later centuries, subsequent titles were written in Hadramawt, Southeast Asia, and elsewhere. They were abridgments and augmentations that conformed to a pattern set in the seventeenth century. In other words, we are dealing with the formation of a textual canon.

The major texts of this canon developed abroad. Yet they were intimately concerned with the homeland, in particular Tarim: its hills, rocks, mosques, graves, and ancestors. In these texts, an image emerges of the history we reviewed in chapter 2, the formation of the ʿAlawī Way. The inscription of that history is simultaneously a process of canonizing the ʿAlawī institutional complex. The foundational figures of the canon (see table 1 in chapter 2)—the First Jurist (d. 1255), ʿAbd al-Raḥmān al-Saqqāf (d. 1416), ʿUmar al-Muḥḍār (d. 1430)—are buried in Tarim. Within a century of al-Muḥḍār, the descendants of these ancestors traveled abroad to India and elsewhere, carrying with them the paraphernalia of the complex and replicating it abroad following the example of Abū Bakr al-ʿAydarūs the Adeni (d. 1508). Recording their practical successes as history stabilized the canon and gave it a distinct if hybrid generic form.

The traveling texts we examine in this chapter are a key part of the dynamic of signification we explored in chapter 1 at the grave, and expanded the circulation of names and their significances throughout the Hadrami diaspora in the Islamic Indian Ocean. Such textual transmigration gave the ancestors buried in Tarim visibility far beyond the narrow confines of their graves. Conversely, these texts helped repatriate the now-augmented fame of the ancestors as well. The reciprocal motion that was set up within a textual medium was a process of schismogenesis, in which home and the world, in their interaction, came to be dichotomized as source and satellite, relic and replica. Late in the day, one of the most celebrated Hadrami poets of the nineteenth and twentieth centuries, the sayyid Abū Bakr bin Shihāb (1846–1923, d. Hyderabad), who spent long years abroad in East Africa, Southeast Asia, and India, rhapsodized about Tarim, his hometown:

> Were we to visit her, we would find her earth
>   fragrant, perfumed as ambergris breathing;
> Well mannered, we would tread barefoot in her villages,
>   beholding that in a sacred wadi were we walking.
>
> (Editor's introduction, al-Shillī 1982: 8)

The first text of interest is *The Travelling Light: Accounts of the Tenth Century*[1] (al-ʿAydarūs 1985). The title also translates as *The Light Unveiled;* I will refer to it as *The Travelling Light Unveiled*. The book was completed in Aḥmad Ābād, the capital of Gujarat in India, in 1603 by a creole sayyid, ʿAbd al-Qādir b. Shaykh (II) al-ʿAydarūs (d. 1628), son of an immigrant Hadrami father (Shaykh (II) al-ʿAydarūs of the previous chapter) and an Indian mother, a manumitted Indian slave *(umm walad)*. I will refer to him as ʿAbd al-Qādir al-ʿAydarūs. *The Travelling Light* commemorated the end of the first millennium of Islam, and chronicled events and personalities of the tenth Muslim century, which corresponds almost exactly with the sixteenth century C.E. It covers a region stretching from Gujarat through the Horn of Africa and the Hejaz to Egypt, providing a window on the cosmopolitan Muslim world of the western Indian Ocean that greeted the Portuguese when they arrived.

The second preeminent text of the sayyids of Hadramawt, *The Irrigating Fount: Biographical Virtues of the ʿAlawī Sayyids* (al-Shillī 1901, 1982), was written in late seventeenth-century Mecca by Muḥammad b. Abī Bakr

1. The Arabic title is *Taʾrīkh al-nūr al-sāfir ʿan akhbār al-qarn al-ʿāshir.*

al-Shillī (d. 1682; henceforth, al-Shillī), a Hadrami sayyid who was born in Tarim, sojourned in India, and settled in Mecca. The book appropriates the diasporic accounts of *The Travelling Light Unveiled* and the local Tarim stories of *The Transparent Essence,* synthetically recasting the whole.[2] In it, the breadth of the Indian Ocean, from Ethiopia to Sumatra, became a frontier for missionary settlement by the Hadrami sayyids. Geography receives a religious significance, driven by Prophetic genealogy. The genealogy was sophisticated, augmented by law in the form of *ḥadīth.* Whereas persons of all origins appear in *The Travelling Light Unveiled* and *The Transparent Essence,* only sayyids have roles in *The Irrigating Fount.* The expansive space of diaspora was now fitted into a cosmogony that was at once universal and historical yet particularistic.

The sixteenth/seventeenth century is a particularly effervescent period in Yemeni historiography, giving rise to a crop of chronicles where few existed before.[3] Yet none was as ambitious as the hybrid texts we are concerned with here; they remain individual period pieces to be trawled and plundered for data by positivist researchers. The chronicles did not determine the future shapes of their readings, unlike the hybrid texts, which did so by forming a canon shaped as a self-referential genealogy of predecessors and successors.

The Traveling Light: Textual Constitution of Diasporic Space

I detect from you an aroma I have not known.
ʿAbd al-Qādir b. Shaykh al-ʿAydarūs (1985: 75)

ʿAbd al-Qādir al-ʿAydarūs completed *The Travelling Light Unveiled* in Gujarat in 1603, at the end of the tenth Islamic century. The book was a cen-

2. *The Transparent Essence* is the foundational compendium of Sufi biographies of Tarim by ʿAbd al-Raḥmān al-Khaṭib (d. 1451), which we have encountered in the formation of the ʿAlawī institutional complex. I draw on but do not incorporate a few other Tarim-authored predecessors in this study, including al-Shaykh ʿAlī b. Abī Bakr al-Sakrān Bā ʿAlawī (1928) and Muḥammad b. ʿAlī Kharid (1985).

3. Manuscripts by non-sayyid Hadramis include *Qilādat al-nahr* and *Tārīkh thaghr ʿAdan* by al-Ṭayyib ʿAbd Allāh b. ʿAbd Allāh Bā Makhrama (1980, 1987), *Tārīkh al-qarn al-ʿāshir* by ʿAbd Allāh b. Aḥmad Bā Sanjala, and *Bahjat al-samar fī akhbār bandar saʿād al-mushtahar* by Sālim b. ʿAwaḍ Bā Sabāʿ. *Tārīkh al-Shiḥr* by the sayyid author Muḥammad b. ʿUmar Bā Faqīh (1999) incorporated historical material from Bā Sanjala's *Tārīkh* and from draft

tenary biographical chronicle, recording the important personages and events of the previous hundred years. This genre had been pioneered by the Egyptian *ḥadīth* compiler Ibn Ḥajar al-ʿAsqalānī (d. 852/1449) in his *Concealed Pearls* (Ibn Ḥajar al-ʿAsqalānī 1972–76) for the eighth Islamic century. Ibn Ḥajar was followed by Shams al-Dīn al-Sakhāwī (d. 902/1497), who wrote for the ninth century (al-Sakhāwī 1992), al-Ghazzī (d. 1061/1651; al-Ghazzī al-Dimashqī 1981–82) and al-ʿAydarūs (d. 1037/1628) for the tenth (al-ʿAydarūs 1985), al-Muḥibbī (d. 1111/1699) for the eleventh (al-Muḥibbī 1966), and al-Murādī (d. 1206/1791) for the twelfth Islamic century (al-Murādī 1997).

Ibn Ḥajar is known for his large *ḥadīth* compilations. His encyclopedic impulse, which was shared by his contemporaries, may be viewed in the context of the Kārimī merchants of Egypt, whose trade with India gave them a broad geographical outlook. They were the most prominent beneficiaries of the reorientation of trade routes to the Red Sea in the thirteenth century, dominating the pepper trade between Calicut and Cairo. Ibn Ḥajar was from a Kārimī family whose members had intermarried with others in the trade. Indeed, the genre he pioneered progressed in tandem with a continuous history of trade and imperial expansion on the Egypt-Hejaz-Yemen-India route. His book charted the rise of that new route, in the century after the fall of Baghdad in 1258, with entries stretching down to Aden and across to India.

The new route was an expansion in which flag followed trade in a Muslim mode. In the fifteenth century, the Kārimī business in pepper and spices was taken over by an Egyptian state monopoly under the Mamluk sultan Barsbāy, who reorganized and secured the route down to the Hejaz.[4] This route was subsequently extended and administered by the Ottoman Turks, who colonized the Hejaz and Yemen after their conquest of Egypt in the sixteenth century and who projected naval power into the Indian Ocean, as we have seen. The ascendance of three major Muslim empires around the western Indian Ocean in this century—the Ot-

notes by ʿAbd Allāh b. ʿUmar Bā Makhrama, both now lost (Bā Faqīh 1999: 6–9, editor's introduction). Serjeant's pioneering work (1950a, 1950b, 1974 [1963]) discusses some of these titles and their locations.

4. Historians suggest that the new state monopoly, which reduced transport costs by securing the route between Alexandria and the Hejaz, prompted a 50 percent decline in pepper prices at Venice in the fifteenth century (Ashtor 1976; Lane 1968). This finding removes one reason often given for the Portuguese push into the Indian Ocean: a rise in European pepper/spice prices.

toman Turks, Persian Safavids, and Indian Mughals—energized trade and communications between port cities along the length of the route.

Writing *The Travelling Light Unveiled* in Gujarat at the opposite end of the same route, essentially facing Ibn Ḥajar in Egypt, as it were, ʿAbd al-Qādir al-ʿAydarūs chronicled newsworthy events and personalities throughout the space between them. Among the reports in his chronicle are death notices (obituary being the occasion for biography) of jurists, historians, saints, pious persons, and kings; stories of floods, fire, rain, lightning, earthquakes, eclipses, comets; reports of shipwrecks; and comments on novelties such as coffee, *qāt,* and Portuguese attacks. The juxtaposition of these accounts on the flat pages gives the book the feel of a newspaper, where events separated geographically jostle each other in parallel columns, sharing the space of a common time. A dominant image of the diasporic space emerges: one in which localities are held together by a skein of common reference books in religion, language, and law; by scholars whose itineraries and generations span the space, in their writing of abridgments, commentaries, and copies; and by intellectual genealogies of teachers licensing students to teach those texts. The dominant legal-educational curriculum that emerges is that of the standardized Shāfiʿī, Sunni school of Islamic law.

Unlike the Portuguese accountants whose concern was with the movement of trade goods (Barbosa 1918 [1518]; Pires 1944), ʿAbd al-Qādir al-ʿAydarūs was concerned in his text with the movement of scholars. Kings, princes, and ministers, in contrast, appear as local, parochial, territory-bound potentates who either help or hinder the activities of the religious scholars. An example of the relative weights al-ʿAydarūs gives to rulers and scholars is his entry for the Islamic year 904. In it, he spares one brief sentence for the killing of the sultan of Egypt al-Nāṣir Ibn Qāʾitbāy. Next to it, the obituary of a pious woman of Zabīd, Asmāʾ bint Mūsā al-Ḍajāʿī, takes up eight lines: she read Qurʾan, hermeneutics, and *ḥadīth;* taught women; was buried next to her father on Thursday morning the day after she died; prayers were said for her at the Ashāʿir mosque (al-ʿAydarūs 1985: 38).

In *The Travelling Light Unveiled,* the attitudes of rulers in particular places and times appear as capricious accidents, mundane states liable to change. The book depicts good rulers who support schools, mosques, and scholars as establishing periods of flourishing justice, scholarship, and piety, while bad rulers suppress them. In several episodes, scholars stand up to the depredations of sultans; these scholars figure as landmarks in the diasporic space. In the Islamic year 907 (1501), for example, the "saint, pious ascetic, judge and jurist" ʿAbd Allāh b. Muḥammad bin ʿAsīn the Shāfiʿī died in the Hadrami port of al-Shiḥr and was buried in the Bā Faḍl cemetery. The people were saddened at his loss. Bin ʿAsīn had been famous for standing up to the Kathīrī sultan of al-Shiḥr. On one occasion, the sultan had bought a horse but refused to pay the seller, claiming that the horse was defective; he wanted to return it. The sultan complained to bin ʿAsīn, the judge, who responded by summoning him to court. When the sultan came, the judge paid him no attention and did nothing to ease his way, favoring him with not even a word. This sultan had commandeered the endowment of the Friday mosque meant for teachers and schools. Bin ʿAsīn took it out of the sultan's hands, and his reorganization of educational finances led directly to the arrival of ʿAbd Allāh b. al-Ḥājj Faḍl, who organized classes in the mosque and benefited many with his scholarship.

The achievements of such upstanding scholars attract others. In their mobility and their common curriculum, the scholars as a whole encompass the sultans, verging on Louis Dumont's sense of hierarchical superiority. Tyrannies are islands surrounded by a wider sea of Sunni Shāfiʿī scholars; this sea ebbs and swells locally but ever dominates the horizon globally, possessed of multiple sources and resources.

In this transregional space, the journeys of goods, emissaries, pilgrims, and religious adepts, while usually sharing the same ships and caravans, describe social geographies of different shapes. The routes are material chains along which travel different sets of social relations, making for a nonhomogeneous surface. A city could serve as a node in different circuits, being central in one but peripheral in another. Cambay, for example, the fulcrum of Indian Ocean trade in a linear dimension, was merely a recipient of Islamic *ḥadīth* scholarship in Arabic, where that road ended, so to speak;[5] the obverse was true of Medina, a world center of *ḥadīth* studies and the resting place of the prophet Muḥammad. While these cities were cosmopolitan in different ways, true metropoles such as Cairo were centers on many counts: religion, politics, trade. Leaving Cairo, one moved down in almost all dimensions. Yet such global peaks were few, and the distinct hierarchies of separate social geographies kept in play a multitude of places as way stations and regional destinations for persons moving from different starting points. In the expansion of trade, religion, and geostrategic diplomatic alliances across an ever-larger, connected sur-

5. However, Gujarat is credited with introducing *ḥadīth* studies to the rest of India.

face, the separate regimes of value embedded in these distinct hierarchies came into close proximity, creating potentials that allowed mobile actors to profit from a kind of geographical arbitrage between them. Over a number of centuries, the cumulative results of such actions and movements in the Red Sea and Indian Ocean reshaped this space, the relative positions of places within it, and the distribution of diasporas around it.

In Egypt, the long-distance, private pepper trade of the Kārimī merchants became so important to the fiscal position of the Mamluk state that it was made a state monopoly. In officially aligning commercial and state interests, Sultan Barsbāy also began a geographical movement that eventually incorporated the religious center of Mecca.[6] The Ottomans subsequently extended this thrust when they succeeded the Mamluks in Egypt. From the other direction, the enhanced security of the Hejaz provided not only profits for Gujarati merchants but succor for Gujarat's Muslim sultans. In times of insecurity, Gujarati sultans would send their families and treasures to the Hejaz for safekeeping. The historian al-Ḥājj al-Dabīr Ulughkhānī's father escorted one such sultanic delegation to the Hejaz. The sultanate indeed fell, in 1573, and the triumphant Mughal emperor Akbar retained his services, giving him charge of pious endowments in Gujarat dedicated to Mecca and Medina.

As traders and mercenaries, Hadramis participated in this multifaceted social space and its expansion. They were best known throughout the region as religious adepts, however, and as a distinct grouping put their inland wadi Hadramawt and the town of Tarim on the map. When the ill-fated Hadrami jurist Baḥraq moved from Aden to Surat in Gujarat, he probably was already known there, from his time as judge in al-Shiḥr and governor in Qishn, Hadrami ports frequented by Surat merchants (Das Gupta 1979: 71). The itinerary Tarim-Shiḥr-Aden-Mecca-Zabīd-Aden-Gujarat is common in Hadrami biographies of this period, and we have seen that impecunious Tarim sayyids stranded without means at the end of this road had their expenses in Gujarat and their passage home underwritten by the pious Ethiopian slave-official Bijlī Khān. Along the way, successful Hadrami religious adepts in Gujarat—such as Baḥraq, Shaykh (II) al-ʿAydarūs, and Shaykh (III) al-ʿAydarūs—sojourned in Mecca and

6. John Meloy recently provided a more nuanced view of the Mamluks' incorporation of the Hejaz, emphasizing that the exercise of control was periodic—timed with the arrival of Indian Ocean trade ships on the monsoons—and that the local Meccan sharifs remained indispensable political brokers in the maintenance of Mamluk overlordship (Meloy 2003).

Medina, studying with influential scholars of transregional fame such as Shams al-Dīn al-Sakhāwī and Ibn Ḥajar al-Haytamī (or al-Haythamī), before returning home or traveling abroad to take up careers as teachers, jurists, administrators, and Sufis.

They went north (Cairo, Mecca, Medina) to learn, and south (the Indian Ocean) to teach. While this directionality remains one of the verities of the Hadrami *longue durée,* the rising stature of Hadrami religious adepts abroad in the sixteenth century caused the topography of scholarly exchanges to morph in their favor, according to individual itineraries. By the late seventeenth century, al-Shillī was able to state in his autobiography that he went from Hadramawt to Gujarat to learn from Hadrami luminaries there, and despite moving on to Mecca to learn from its luminaries, was pressed into teaching—with great reluctance—at the preeminent al-Ḥarām mosque when his teacher there, ʿAlī b. al-Jamāl, died:[7]

> When our shaykh ʿAlī b. al-Jamāl died, a group of my teachers (including ʿAbd Allāh Bā Qushayr) ordered me to sit in his place in Masjid al-Ḥarām. But I excused myself, saying I was busy studying with teachers before they passed away. This to me was more important than teaching. They did not accept this [excuse] and reviled me for it. So I sat teaching in al-Ḥarām mosque for a number of years. Then I stopped because of a serious illness. A group asked to study with me at home, where I was recuperating, and we did this. Subsequently I was asked to return to al-Ḥarām mosque. I was not happy with this. So they asked me to write on the science of timing. So I wrote a treatise on the science of *Mujīb* and the students benefited from it. Then I wrote a commentary on it and they benefited from it. Many from Egypt, Yemen and India copied it down. (al-Shillī 1982: 38–41)

In this account, the usual flow of knowledge from Mecca to Tarim, as from center to periphery, is reversed. This reversal was a studied and unabashed conceit that al-Shillī allowed himself, but such dispositions were common among the great transregional encyclopedists of the era—such as Ibn Ḥajar al-ʿAsqalānī and al-Suyūṭī, authorities popular among the Hadramis—and merely confirmed him as one of them. As is still true among academics today, ego expands with spatial spread. For provincials newly arrived in the centers after detours in manufacturing towns such as Surat and the like, that space of achievement and pride could be a particularly large one.

7. Al-Shillī's journey reversed the center-to-periphery flow of knowledge from Hadramawt to Gujarat. The account is also given in the autobiography in his history *Nafāʾis al-Durar* and is reproduced in al-Muḥibbī (1966).

The Travelling Light Unveiled reflects this shifting geography in its biographical accounts, in which Hadramis are one stream in a universal concourse of Muslim scholars, Sufis, and rulers. In presenting this broad view, the book is like the other centenary biographies. However, if one reads it with an eye for detail and pays attention to regional origin, family name, and transgenerational genealogical links, a complete and almost self-sufficient network of Hadramis fills the space. Over time, Hadramis established themselves and became known in all the key centers. One could embark from the Hadrami homeland, travel, and receive an education solely from Hadramis throughout the diaspora. If one were a sayyid, perhaps of the al-ʿAydarūs family, many of the teachers in foreign lands might in fact be close agnates: fathers, brothers, uncles, cousins. The Hadramis were well placed along the Gujarat-Aden-Hejaz axis, in relation to which interior Hadramawt was eccentric. But in ʿAbd al-Qādir al-ʿAydarūs's rendering, the locational disadvantage of the homeland was overcome by a decided spiritual advantage. In speaking of Tarim, he says, "Many of those mentioned in this history died in that blessed town; and some of them died elsewhere, such as Shibām and Dawʿan of Hadramawt" (al-ʿAydarūs 1985: 61). The value of Tarim's cemetery lies with the historical personalities buried in it. Going by this interpretation, al-ʿAydarūs's statement means that the cemetery and all that is associated with it is constantly on the increase. That increase enables it to become a generative fount for the wider world.

In the out-migration of religious adepts from Tarim, and the return to its graves, *The Travelling Light Unveiled* models a process of exchange over generations in which home and the world are mutually engaged, ideally in a virtuous cycle. Shipwrecks, such as the one at Cambay in 1567 in which ten Hadrami sayyids drowned, disrupt that cycle, but the deceased nevertheless earned places in heaven as martyrs who perished migrating in the path of God (al-ʿAydarūs 1985: 286). For the Holy Qur'an says, "Those who migrate on the path of God, and are slain or die: God will provide well for them. Truly, God is the best of providers" (22: 58, Pilgrimage). In another sunk boat, reported by al-Shillī, the very successful Shaykh (III) al-ʿAydarūs lost the many rare books and wealth he was repatriating from India to Hadramawt. He had intended to build tall buildings, plant gardens, and establish pious foundations *(awqāf)* for sayyids in Hadramawt (al-Shillī 1901:118). These reported exceptions highlight the normal, ongoing process of augmentation in Tarim's cemeteries, libraries, gardens, pious foundations, and fortunes, as other ships steered safely home to port.

The Traveling Light of Muhammad Unveiled: Genealogical Figures

> If a person knows news of those who have passed,
> it would be as though he had lived a long time;
> for he would have lived the times of he who was knowledgeable.
> Generous, patient, he would have gained a long life.
>
> ʿAbd al-Qādir al-ʿAydarūs (1985: 5)

Embedded within the annalistic, year-by-year frame of ʿAbd al-Qādir al-ʿAydarūs's *The Travelling Light Unveiled* is an alternative chronology that is seen to exist in real history and geography: that of Muḥammadan Prophetic genealogy. In a sporadic way, the book makes large claims for this genealogy, even though the genealogy does not dominate the narrative as a structuring principle. While its appearance in the volume is desultory, the genealogical assertions are in no way reticent. Rather, the apparent subordination of genealogy to the steady march of the years—punctuated by floods, droughts, and deaths of sultans—underscores its historicity. In the same way, interdigitation of the educational careers of Hadrami sayyids within suites and series of non-sayyid teachers and students places them firmly within the social context of a diaspora of Hadrami religious adepts, and links them to a cosmopolitan network of like persons, superiors, and inferiors. The genealogical exclusivism and contest of later centuries does not appear here. Indeed, non-sayyids, such as Baḥraq, wrote hagiographies of sayyids such as Abū Bakr al-ʿAydarūs the Adeni (Baḥraq al-Ḥaḍramī 1988). In the expansive spirit of *The Travelling Light Unveiled* and its times, Prophetic genealogy does not appear as a scarce commodity subject to contestation. Rather, it is merely the front of a rising tide that lifts all boats.

ʿAbd al-Qādir al-ʿAydarūs's alternative chronology begins with a cosmogony in which the prophet Muḥammad figures as the primeval, first substance before the rest of Creation. In the introduction to his detailed chronicle of the tenth Islamic century, al-ʿAydarūs starts over fifty thousand years earlier. The introduction takes the reader from Creation to the birth of the Prophet and the historical accounts of his early mission on earth, before entering the world of the tenth Islamic century:

> Know that God, when He wanted to bring His creation into existence, brought out the Muḥammadan Reality. From His eternal Lights. In His blessed presence. Then He peeled from it all the worlds, the highest and the lowest of them, in accordance with what He demanded of him, the Prophet: completeness of wisdom,

precedence in knowledge and will. Then His Exaltedness told him of his perfection and his prophethood. And charged him with spreading his call and his message. And told him that he was the Prophet of Prophets. And intermediary for all the pure ones. Whilst his father Adam was still between spirit and body. Then there gushed forth from him gems of spirits, emerging possessed of extension in their realm, which is prior to the world of appearances. He was the loftiest of all the species, and the greatest father of all persons and existence. Even though his corporeal existence was subsequent, he was distinguished from the rest of the worlds by his elevation and his precedence, for he is the repository of the eternal secrets, and highborn, singled out for the merciful succour. As the true *ḥadīth* report by Muslim has it, the Prophet said: "God Almighty wrote the dimensions of human beings fifty thousand years before making the skies and the earth, while His throne was still on the water." (al-ʿAydarūs 1985: 7)

This opening illustrates in small compass a central feature of the prevailing intellectual culture of the Islamic Indian Ocean, in which ʿAbd al-Qādir al-ʿAydarūs participates. Here, legal and mystical discourses found a common locus in Prophetic *ḥadīth.* The question of what the first created things were—the Pen, the Inkpot, Water, the Throne, the Light of Muḥammad—had been the subject of debate by *ḥadīth* scholars, who marshaled their arguments from allegorical interpretations of the Qurʾan augmented by variant *ḥadīth* reports attributed to the prophet Muḥammad (al-ʿAydarūs 1985: 8; Chodkiewicz 1993: 60). ʿAbd al-Qādir al-ʿAydarūs's chosen answer is the Light of the prophet Muḥammad, but this answer gives rise to another question. If Muḥammad was the last of the prophets, how could he be the first to have been created?

Al-Ghazālī explains the Prophet's description of himself in possession of prophethood before the existence of his substance in the *ḥadīth,* "I was the first of the prophets to be created, and the last to be sent," by saying that creation was recognition *(al-taqdīr),* not existence *(al-ījād/al-wujūd).* Before he was carried by his mother, he had not been created and did not exist. However, the intention and the perfection were prior in recognition, even though subsequent in existence. For the Prophet said: "I was a prophet, that is in recognition, before the creation of Adam, who was not brought forth except to have Muḥammad and his actualization flow from his seed." The house which exists in the mind of the architect is the real, mental cause of external existence—and precedes it. God Almighty recognizes, then in accordance with that recognition, builds and brings into existence. (al-ʿAydarūs 1985: 6)

In this explanation, which sounds to our ears neo-Platonic on first hearing, al-ʿAydarūs invokes an ontological realm between the sensible physical world and the realm of the divine—an isthmus *(barzakh)*. It is an intermediate realm in which angels and spirits exist. In the ontology of Ibn al-ʿArabī, this realm is an "imaginal world" *(ʿālam al-takhayyul)* of images or forms (Chittick 1994). The entities that subsist in this realm share the forms of objects in the physical world but not their corporeality. They are nonphysical images. These entities have the qualities of two realms: on the one hand are the light and incorporeality of the spirits, and on the other are the forms of the sensible world. The images that populate the dreams of human beings in sleep are a central instance of such nonphysical images. They are perceived by the faculty of imagination, which is distinct from that of reason. Reason perceives ideas that are abstract and devoid of sensory correlates; in contrast, the imagination perceives ideas in the images given by sense impression, which subsist in a material substrate, even though the same images are nonphysical within the imagination itself. The organ of this faculty of imagination in human beings is the heart *(qalb)*. The heart is apt because it is an organ of flux: it perceives and is inconstant, subject to change *(yataqallab)*: *heart* and *change* derive etymologically from the same triliteral root, *q-l-b*. What is in flux is not the form of the images of the intermediate realm but their transient partaking of the divine Light. The forms themselves are "immutable prototypes" *(al-aʿyān al-thābita)*—determined, specific, and unchanging in themselves. In evoking these ideas through terminology, al-ʿAydarūs participates in a discourse dominated by Ibn al-ʿArabī, although he does not name him.[8] Thus, at the beginning of his historical annal, al-ʿAydarūs opens up an imaginal topos that communicates with the world of names, dates, and countries—that is, of history.

Revelation is one such communication. In revelation, God sends

8. For an erudite history of the polemic surrounding Ibn al-ʿArabī and his ideas, see Knysh (1999b). Despite widespread condemnation in the later centuries, Ibn al-ʿArabī continues to exert a profound influence. Among Hadramis, he continues to enjoy a subterranean following, which emerges cautiously such as when ʿAbd al-Qādir al-ʿAydarūs volunteered in an obituary that the deceased was an enthusiast of Ibn al-ʿArabī's and possessed the only copy of Ibn al-ʿArabī's *Meccan Conquests* remaining in Hadramawt (al-ʿAydarūs 1985: 309; the same account is found in Bā Faqīh 1999: 401). The saint of Aden, Abū Bakr al-ʿAydarūs, reminiscing on his father's good nature, recalls being beaten by his father only once—when he caught him reading Ibn al-ʿArabī (Baḥraq al-Ḥaḍramī 1988: 9; also quoted in Bā Faqīh 1999: 402). In my discussions with Hadrami savants, many terms and concepts were unintelligible to me until I came across them in the context of Ibn al-ʿArabī's ideas. I am indebted to Knysh, who first confirmed the hand of the "Greatest Shaykh" and himself searched in vain for Ibn al-ʿArabī's books in one of the vigorous new schools in Tarim (Knysh 2001: 410).

Meanings down to the sensible world. For these Meanings to be understood by humans, they have to be "imaginalized," or procured for the imagination, by taking on the forms and images of objects in the sensible world. Prophets apprehend these meanings either in the imagination or in sense perception. The knowledge of God's qualities or attributes proceeds by understanding the meanings' similarities with forms perceived through sense perception. A large part of revelation is therefore conveyed as images, or in auditory linguistic forms. This form contrasts with reason, which proceeds abstractly by establishing separation and difference. Thus revelation, as a communication of divine meaning to history—to historical peoples via their historical prophets—is the introduction of similarities into a world of differences.

The successive dispatching of prophets into the mundane world constitutes a series of such similarities. Each prophet is similar to the others: he appears among a specific people, conveys revelation in their distinct language, is repudiated, and sees his people destroyed or punished by God; he is followed by another prophet (al-Qadi 1988). The succession of prophets is not a series of events that one can explain in relations of cause and effect along one temporal dimension (Hempel and Oppenheim 1965 [1948]). Mundane time does not provide adequate coordinates for charting this process, which begins before recorded history, understood as a flow of contiguous units (years). The intermittent appearance of prophets is conceived of as a descent from another realm, an intervention from on high, as and when God deems the time right. Nevertheless, these prophets are real historical figures sent to real historical peoples. They appear in a sequence that is conceived of not annalistically but figurally. Auerbach calls such a conception "figural interpretation," which he describes in the following way:

> Figural interpretation establishes a connection between two events or persons, the first of which signifies not only itself but also the second, while the second encompasses or fulfils the first. The two poles of the figure are separate in time, but both, being real events or figures, are within time, within the stream of historical life. Only the understanding of the two persons or events is a spiritual act, but this spiritual act deals with concrete events whether past, present, or future, and not with concepts or abstractions; these are quite secondary, since promise and fulfilment are real historical events, which have either happened in the incarnation of the Word, or will happen in the second coming. (Auerbach 1959: 53)

Auerbach locates the major origin of Christian figural interpretation in Paul's transformation of the Old Testament, from a canon of law and history identified with a specific people into one of universal prophesy, foreshadowing things to come. The Pauline emphasis was one of "grace versus law, faith versus works: the old law is annulled" (Auerbach 1959: 50). Formulated against attacks in a hostile environment, this transformation had consequence for the spread of the new religion in the western and northern Mediterranean:

In this form and in this context, from which Jewish history and national character had vanished, the Celtic and Germanic peoples, for example, could accept the Old Testament; it was a part of the universal religion of salvation and a necessary component of the equally magnificent and universal vision of history that was conveyed to them along with this religion. In its original form, as a law book and history of so foreign and remote a nation, it would have been beyond their reach. (Auerbach 1959: 52)

ʿAbd al-Qādir al-ʿAydarūs's *The Travelling Light Unveiled* conceives the reversal of ontological actuality (as that between the Old and New Testament prophets, the precedent reduced to the role of prefiguring the subsequent—what Auerbach calls figural interpretation) more boldly: as imaginal cosmogony. This cosmogony begins with the primordial creation of the Muḥammadan Light.

So he became a prophet, and his name was written upon the throne, that the angels and others would know his noble standing with God. For his reality was present from that time onwards, even if his noble body which was described by it arrived later. When He brought him prophethood and wisdom and all the attributes of his reality and perfection, it was early. That which came later was created and transported in backbones and pure wombs until the Prophet appeared. (al-ʿAydarūs 1985: 8)

This Light is occluded from sight as it is transported through history in suitable vessels. The pre-Muḥammadan prophets are such vessels, which contain and move the Light; occasionally, it is glimpsed.

It appeared that when God created Adam, he put the Light in his backbone. And it shone from his forehead. When he died, his son Seth was the executor of his wishes, as was his son after him, in regard of what his father had ordered of him: that this Light would not be placed in any but the purest of women. This order was carried out until the Light arrived to ʿAbd Allāh (father of the prophet Muḥammad) in a pure state, from the fornication of the Jāhiliyya, as the Prophet has said in numerous *ḥadīth*. (al-ʿAydarūs 1985: 9)

As vessels, the pre-Muḥammadan prophets are no longer only prefigures, signs that point to something similar which comes after and completes them. They stand in relation to one another and to Muḥammad, both metaphorically and syntagmatically. From Adam, his son Seth, and down to ʿAbd Allāh and his son Muḥammad, the prophets have become genealogical figures. The external genealogy, which these figures, taken together, constitute, describes a traveling light that is in occultation. With the appearance of the prophet Muḥammad at the end of the line, that traveling light is unveiled. It is not figural prophecy (Auerbach 1959: 58) but genealogical prophecy.

In ʿAbd al-Qādir al-ʿAydarūs's history, as in the early universal histories of Islam, that genealogy began moving before Muḥammad appeared to the Arabs as a prophet. But what transpired after Muḥammad? Like figural prophecy, genealogical prophecy has a tentative quality. It moves toward a future existence, but its signs are ambiguous and hard to read. Muḥammad had no surviving son. His descendants are the progeny of his daughter Fāṭima, in union with his cousin ʿAlī. What became of the Light of Muḥammad?

Jameson has built upon Auerbach's ideas to present the concept of the life of Christ as a master narrative (Jameson 1981: 29). He conceives of the movement from what he calls a "literal" reading of the Old Testament to the "allegorical" interpretation of the New Testament life of Christ as a double one. It restricts the narrative to a single biography yet opens the text up to multiple readings. This opening up enables the religion to spread in the western Mediterranean and beyond (Jameson 1981: 30), as Auerbach has noted. The master narrative becomes an "interpretive code" that prepares the text for further "ideological investment." Ideology here simply means a structure of representation that allows the individual to imagine his or her relation to the larger whole, be it society or history (Jameson 1981: 30).

Muḥammad was the last prophet to be sent; there was to be no other. Thus, beyond him, genealogical prophecy became Prophetic genealogy. In this reversal, Muḥammadan genealogical Light underwent a double movement similar to that of the life-of-Christ master narrative. Its pre-Muḥammadan spiritual travel became geographical travel, as his descendants spread out with the early Islamic conquests and beyond. Through conquest, marriage, concubinage, clientage, alliance, diarchy, and other modalities of exchange, this genealogy assimilated and engaged with the self-conceptions of other peoples—sayyids and non-sayyids, Arabs and non-Arabs—and became numerous and widespread. At the same time, it became restricted to only one of God's peoples, the Arabs, and a small subset of them, the sayyids. Furthermore, the idea became widespread that Prophetic genealogy was very similar to genealogical prophecy, retaining some of its spiritual properties and potencies. But the appearance of those qualities could never be regular, or regularly apprehended. Thus, the most restrictive version of that line became an occult genealogy, surfacing now and then with its special signs. These signs were hard to read or establish, and methods arose for interpreting them by comparing them with other segments of the genealogy that prefigured them. The recording and handling of those genealogies took on many forms, such as visual representations as trees or parallel lines, prose elaborations, mnemonic poems, long individual names, liturgies, and sepulchral monuments. Like the individuals who constitute them, these forms themselves are so many genealogical figures, composite ones, in whose shapes, evolution, and assessment mingle imaginal and historical worlds.

In the course of ʿAbd al-Qādir al-ʿAydarūs's chronicle, the imaginal and the historical come together in individual figures who are genealogically linked. At times, these genealogies are occult, and at others, they are conspicuous. At each point, the space between the visible and the invisible is bridged by preternatural acts, dreams, and names. A series of such bridges arches across the years in ʿAbd al-Qādir al-ʿAydarūs's tenth century, creating an alternative chronology in the form of a luminous genealogy, which emerges out of occultation as it travels through years and countries. To summarize, the main stations of the series are as follows:

Creation of the Muḥammadan Light—

—Transmission of the Light through the prophets—

—The birth of Muḥammad (buried in Medina)—

—The main events of Islamic sacred history—

—The geographical location of Hadramawt/Qurʾanic figures in it, such as the prophet Hūd (buried in Hadramawt)—

—The virtues of Tarim (and those buried in its graveyards)—

—The arrival of Muḥammad's descendant the Migrant in Hadramawt and the sayyid settlement of Tarim—

—The death of Abū Bakr al-Aydarūs the Adeni—

—The biography of Shaykh (II) al-ʿAydarūs (buried in Gujarat, India)—

—The birth of ʿAbd al-Qādir b. Shaykh (II) al-ʿAydarūs (author of *The Travelling Light Unveiled* and son of Shaykh (II) al-ʿAydarūs).

In this genealogy, ʿAbd al-Qādir al-ʿAydarūs creates a master narrative in Jameson's sense, one that effects both a narrowing and a broadening. The creation of this effect is evident in the range of authoritative sources he draws upon to authenticate the narrative. The introduction, which we have discussed as cosmogony in content, also serves as a liturgical text in its form. In tracing the creation and birth of the prophet Muḥammad, it employs prose with internal rhymes (*sajʿ*) as well as regular metrical verse (*qaṣīda*). This rhyming mimics the texts used in ritual gatherings celebrating the birth of Muḥammad, the *mawlid*s, in which the oral musicality of the narrative enables a reciter and his audience jointly to create an auditory performance, as leader and chorus. Such gatherings take place regularly in Hadrami communities and enact modalities of "presencing," as we have seen in chapter 3. The introduction thus provides a ritual stamp, a benediction if the term be allowed, that prefigures the Prophetic genealogy to follow. Subsequently, his conspectus of the celebrated events in the establishment of Islam during the Prophet's lifetime—such as his emigration to Medina, formalization of brother pairs of émigrés and Medinese, change in the direction of prayer, institution of the fast of Ramaḍān, and battles against the infidels—draws from standard accounts such as those in Ibn Isḥāq's authoritative life of the Prophet, complete with dates.

The next significant station in our series is an excursus on the geographical location, description, and mythology of Hadramawt. This lengthy section bulges conspicuously beyond the parsimonious, linear confines of the annalistic chronicle. It draws from the metropolitan Arab geographers of Cairo, Baghdad, and Mecca, who in previous centuries had incorporated mathematical cartography and filled out the dimensions of the known world with travelers' reports, establishing a global conception of geography within Islamicate literature. To the best of my knowledge, *The Travelling Light Unveiled* is the earliest instance in which the global metropolitan frames of scientific geography appear in the literature of Hadramawt itself, as a way for Hadramis to define their homeland. Subsequent works, even those authored in the homeland (such as A. H. al-Ḥaddād n.d.), followed ʿAbd al-Qādir al-ʿAydarūs's lead. That this new self-consciousness of location first appears in the work of a creole Hadrami living in the diaspora is perhaps not surprising. The appearance is even less surprising if we bear in mind the ambitious nature of his work: to "put on the map" a homeland that was geographically, commercially, and religiously eccentric to the Cairo-Hejaz-Gujarat axis.

If Hadramawt was in one sense peripheral, it was by no means parochial. Al-ʿAydarūs cites copiously metropolitan geographers such as al-Qazwīnī, whose compilations engage the geographical lore of Hadramawt. Al-Qazwīnī was the preeminent authority among the geographers of the Ottoman imperial court. In particular, ʿAbd al-Qādir al-ʿAydarūs reproduces *in extenso* accounts of the prophet Hūd, the people of ʿĀd, the country of al-Aḥqāf, and the Broken Well *(Biʾr muʿaṭṭala*; Qurʾan 22: 45). For not only are these people and places identified with Hadramawt, but they are also mentioned by God in the Holy Qurʾan. Hūd is the earliest of the Qurʾanic Arabian prophets, and the reputed site of his tomb in Hadramawt is the focus of the largest annual pilgrimage in the region. His presence there bestows a primacy of Qurʾanic dimensions. In such names, the Qurʾanic verses are interwoven with the extensive local folklore and ritual geography of Hadramawt. In addition to citing geographers such as al-Qazwīnī, ʿAbd al-Qādir al-ʿAydarūs draws on the work of the Hadrami al-Khaṭīb, whose foundational *Transparent Essence* is a voluminous repository of stories of Sufi luminaries of Tarim, as we saw in chapter 2. Themes like the ones we encountered there, such as the burial of seventy of the Prophet's Companions in its graves, the special relation between Tarim and the caliph Abū Bakr, the location of one of the gardens of paradise under its Red Hill, the stories of ʿAbd al-Raḥmān al-Saqqāf, all draw from al-Khaṭīb's work and are reproduced in al-ʿAydarūs.

Al-ʿAydarūs's section on Hadramawt sits astride the chronicle at the Islamic year 914 (1508 C.E.). This year is significant because in it the Saint of Aden, Abū Bakr al-ʿAydarūs the Adeni, passed away. Indeed, the obituary of the Adeni follows immediately upon the account of Tarim. The link is a direct one: the Adeni was born there in 1447, the great-grandson of ʿAbd al-Raḥmān al-Saqqāf, initiator of the ritual forms of the ʿAlawī Way. In the narrative, the move from Tarim to the Adeni is a motion in which Tarim becomes an originating point; the Adeni's powerful biography effects a reorientation in spatial cognition. For the Adeni is a key figure in the geographical expansion of the Tarim sayyids: he was the first among them to achieve renown as a saint outside of Hadramawt. He is the patron saint of Aden, and the annual pilgrimage to his tomb remains a central festival in the urban life of the city. Aden and the Adeni became the geographical and genealogical point of departure from which other Hadrami sayyids were to achieve renown throughout the Indian Ocean. We saw something of his contemporary significance in chapter 1.

Whereas ʿAbd al-Qādir al-ʿAydarūs's eclectic use of authoritative texts created a broad base by hybridizing genres, thereafter his focus narrowed to a genealogical one—in fact, to the genealogy of his own family.[9] However, this lineal narrowing was at the same time a broadening, as the genealogy threaded its way through countries and centuries.

In ʿAbd al-Qādir al-ʿAydarūs's *The Travelling Light Unveiled,* the authentication of the Adeni's spiritual prowess is socially diverse and spatially wide (al-ʿAydarūs 1985: 77–85). Born in Tarim, the Adeni spent a quarter century in the port town of Aden, where he died. As a measure of his social standing there, he had thirty sheep sacrificed daily during Ramaḍān to feed his visitors. For this generosity, he accumulated a debt of two hundred thousand dinārs, which was paid off by the emir Nāṣir al-Dīn ʿAbd Allāh Bā Ḥalwān just before the Adeni's death. His teachers included his father's brother al-Shaykh ʿAlī, non-sayyid Hadramis such as the jurist Muḥammad b. Aḥmad Bā Faḍl, and the famous historian of Mecca Shams al-Dīn al-Sakhāwī, author of a much-cited centenary biography of the ninth Islamic century. The Adeni's position as the "axis of the age" is authenticated in the biographies of others, such as that of the jurist Muḥammad b. Aḥmad Bā Jarfīl and of the sharif Ḥusayn b. al-Ṣiddīq al-Ahdal, spiritual leader of Zabīd, the foremost center of religious scholarship in Sunni Yemen. The following three examples of the Adeni's preternatural acts, which ʿAbd al-Qādir al-ʿAydarūs cited in his obituary, reflect the nodal position of Aden as a port city strategically located on the main route of transregional shipping:[10]

The slave-emir Marjān was in battle surrounded by enemies on the road north to Ṣanʿāʾ when his horse was injured. In desperation, he called out the Adeni's name. The Adeni appeared, grabbed the emir and his horse by their forelocks, and snatched them out of the enemy's reach. The horse expired upon arrival on safe ground.

9. A similar phenomenon is found in Christianity. According to Peter Brown, "The progress of the Christian community, which can seem so homogeneous at first sight, rapidly dissolves into a loose bundle of family histories. For the historian Sozomen, the story of Christianity in Ascalon and Gaza was the story of his own and of a neighboring family: 'The first churches and monasteries created in that country were founded by members of this family and supported by their power and beneficence toward strangers and the needy'" (P. Brown 1981: 30).

10. In the parlance of the shipping industry today, this location enjoys "zero deviation"—that is, deviation from the main Europe-Asia route. Aden sits halfway between Rotterdam and Singapore, the two terminals, and bulk breakage there entails no loss of time for the supercontainers of today, unlike the situation for Aden's Arabian competitors Salāla and Jabal ʿAlī. Today's postsocialist reinsertion of Aden into the arteries of world capitalism is in the hands of a consortium comprising a Hadrami family based in Saudi Arabia, the bin Maḥfūẓ, and the Port Authority of Singapore. The diaspora perennially harbors resources available for investment in the homeland when political winds turn favorable.

On his way back from the pilgrimage to Mecca, the Adeni stopped at Zaylaʿ, the Muslim port town on the Ethiopian coast. There he found the Muslim ruler Muḥammad b. ʿAtīq on the verge of madness as his wife lay prone in death. The ruler swore to him that if God did not revive his wife, he too would die, with faith in no one. The Adeni shouted at the wife by name, and she responded and was resuscitated. In saving her, he also saved her husband's faith in God.

The Sufi devotee Nuʿmān b. Muḥammad al-Mahdī was traveling on a ship to India when the vessel sprang a leak. Everyone on board prayed to God, and each called out to his shaykh. Nuʿmān called out to the Adeni and saw him in the ship, proceeding toward the leak with a white handkerchief in hand. He shouted the good news to his travel companions, and sure enough, the travelers found the hole plugged up with the cloth.

The pithy account of the second incident indexes more than is apparent. The Adeni has been credited with introducing the oldest Sufi order into Harar in Ethiopia (I. M. Lewis 1955). He entered Zaylaʿ in 1483 (al-Mashhūr 1984: 95), when the Muslim rulers of Zaylaʿ were, from their up-country base of Harar, conducting large-scale warfare against the Christians for domination of Ethiopia. Many Hadrami sayyids participated in the events, and their genealogies record that many of them died there as martyrs, including the descendants of ʿAbd al-Raḥmān al-Saqqāf from his great-grandsons down (al-Mashhūr 1984; al-Shillī 1901).[11] Significant finance came from the Hejaz, to which returned ivory and captives as slaves. This exchange was the source for the Ethiopian slave-officials in Gujarat.

The three accounts of the Adeni, located in the entry for the Islamic year 914, are linked figurally and genealogically with one much later in the chronicle. In the Islamic year 990 (1582), the death of Shaykh (II) al-

11. These events had geostrategic significance, as the Christian Ethiopians sought the aid of Portuguese artillery to achieve parity with the Muslims, who had Turkish gunpowder and gunners sent from the Yemeni town of Zabīd. The final defeat of the Muslims with Portuguese help in 1543 meant that no Muslim state would be established in Ethiopia. Thus, the Hadrami sayyid lineages lost opportunities for state service of the sort they encountered in Gujarat and moved south along the East African coast. As well, descendants of those who perished in Ethiopia later showed up in India. In the main, the Muslim warriors in the war were Somali pastoralists, whose genealogies meet maximally in descent from the prophet Muḥammad (I. M. Lewis 1958) and connect with Hadrami ones. In the course of my research in Hadramawt, I met many Somalis who had fled the civil war in their country and who found acceptance among local Hadrami lineages when they recited shared genealogical links going back generations. Hadrami sayyids have a long history of involvement in the region (for example, al-ʿAydarūs 1954; Burton 1966 [1856]; I. M. Lewis 1955; Martin 1971), and a number of fine, in-depth studies have been written (Bang 2003; Romero 1997; el Zein 1974). *The Travelling Light Unveiled* records close relations between the Muslim rulers of Zaylaʿ and the family of the author.

ʿAydarūs is recorded (al-ʿAydarūs 1985: 333–39) (see chapter 4 on Gujarat). Like the Adeni, he had spent long years away from his hometown, Tarim, and died abroad celebrated as the leading light of his age by consensus of the gnostics of his time. In his final resting place at Aḥmad Ābād in Gujarat, Shaykh (II) al-ʿAydarūs too had a dome lofted above his tomb and was sought by pilgrims.[12] His teacher, the renowned Egyptian *ḥadīth* scholar Ibn Ḥajar al-Haytamī, had been a student of the Adeni's teacher, Shams al-Dīn al-Sakhāwī. Shaykh (II) al-ʿAydarūs's paternal grandfather, Shaykh (I) b. ʿAbd Allāh al-ʿAydarūs, was the Adeni's brother. As the Adeni was dying, he had asked his nephew ʿAbd Allāh b. Shaykh (I), who was in his service, to make a wish. ʿAbd Allāh asked for nothing more than blessings and prayers that he beget devout descendants. The Adeni then told him that to him would come such-and-such sons, mentioning them by name. Among them was Shaykh (II) b. ʿAbd Allāh al-ʿAydarūs, whom the Adeni singled out, saying, "Truly, he is my son and master of my mystery, and the mother of his mother is the daughter of al-Shaykh ʿAlī" (al-ʿAydarūs 1985: 334).[13]

The author discusses the significance of the name Shaykh, drawing comparisons with the prophet Muḥammad. Inspired by God, the Prophet's folk had given him his name, Muḥammad, which means "the praised one," before his praiseworthy qualities appeared. This naming of Muḥammad by his folk, of course, was prefigured by God's giving him his name before his body appeared. In like wise, Shaykh (II) al-ʿAydarūs became a shaykh, like his name, in a number of ways: he lived to an elderly age *(shaykhūkha)*, he was shaykh (leader) of the Sufis of his time, and he was the shaykh (teacher) of students in the exoteric sciences. "Thus he was a shaykh in name and in qualities by every estimation" (al-

12. Shaykh (II) al-ʿAydarūs's tomb exists today in Ahmadabad, off Relief Road in the Pranjapole neighborhood behind the Edrus building. He is buried next to a brother and sons under a dome, bathed in a soft light coming through *jali* latticework in the walls. Visitors, many Hindus, light incense and strew flower petals over the ʿAydarūs graves daily and associate Shaykh (II)'s tomb with al-ʿAydarūs tombs in Broach and Surat, as linked pilgrimage shrines. The domed tomb of his son ʿAbd al-Qādir al-ʿAydarūs—author of *The Travelling Light Unveiled*—a short distance away along Relief Road behind the Arab Masjid is an even grander affair; guarded by tall pillars beyond the latticework walls in the middle of a garden, its structure resembles the *dargah* mausoleums of the great sultans and Sufi saints of Ahmadabad, such as that of Shaykh Aḥmad Khattu at Sarkhej. The graves of father and son are sometimes referred to in Gujarati as "big" and "little" ʿAydarūs, *Bade Aydarus* and *Chhote Aydarus* (Khalidi 2004: 333).

13. Al-Shaykh ʿAlī is al-Shaykh ʿAli b. Abī Bakr al-Sakrān (d. 1490). He is the first sayyid author of biographies.

ʿAydarūs 1985: 333). God had inspired his folk in naming him Shaykh, "in order that he realize his inheritance from his predecessors—just as God had inspired the folk of the chosen Prophet in naming him The Praised One before his praiseworthy qualities appeared" (al-ʿAydarūs 1985: 333).

In his numerous discussions of names, the author brings into play genealogical and figural links between beings separated in space and time. The requisite shuttling between seen and unseen, unknown and to be known, potential and actual, and present and future draws a tissue of nominal connections between the imaginal world of immutable entities and the historical world of changing places and times. These connections cluster around genealogical figures whose names at least are available to sense impression, even if their full import is not always apparent. ʿAbd al-Qādir al-ʿAydarūs's chosen method for demonstrating that import was to engage these figures with the dimensions of the known world, space, and time. Yet his method had a fundamental drawback. For those who did not bring to their reading of his text a basic, preexisting familiarity with the names and lineages—those who were not in some way native to the world within and containing his text—the names, rather than emerging into the light, remain buried in a morass of differences. To these readers, many figures in the book are irretrievably lost in the strange seascape of an unfamiliar diaspora. Ironically, too, the small number of names in the text does not simplify matters but adds to the confusion.[14] Their repetition and alternation within one genealogy quickly creates confusion between nominal and figural similarities. Undoubtedly, the reader of this study has also been much inconvenienced by such features of a restrictive onomasticon made to bear a great interpretive load. This problem was to be addressed in al-Shillī's *The Irrigating Fount,* to which we now turn.

Gathering the Roots and the Branches

> Once God showed me, in the way in which a dreamer sees, that I was circumambulating the Kaʿbah with a group of

14. The small number of names itself is not unusual. In England around 1700, for example, eight Christian first names reportedly accounted for 90 percent of the male population (J. C. Scott et al. 2002: 8). The unusual aspect of the Hadrami sayyid names is the amount of symbolic work they had to do.

> people whose faces I did not recognize. They were reciting two lines of poetry, one line of which I remember and the other of which I have forgotten. The one which I remember is this: For years we have turned, as you have turned, / around this House, all together, each of us. . . .
>
> One of them spoke to me, calling himself by a name that I did not recognize. He said, "I am one of your ancestors."
>
> I said to him, "How long ago did you die?"
>
> He replied, "Forty thousand and some years."
>
> I said to him, "But Adam himself did not live that long ago."
>
> He said, "Which Adam do you speak about? Are you speaking about the closest one to you, or about another?"
>
> Then I recalled a *ḥadīth* in which the Prophet says, "God created one hundred thousand Adams." That ancestor to which I go back could have been one of those.
>
> Muḥyī al-Dīn Ibn al-ʿArabī (Quoted in Chittick 1994: 90)

One hundred thousand Adams, forty thousand some years, one ancestor. Names establish figural connections in dreams, across years, between imaginal and historical realms. Yet the power of figural interpretation in creating similarities comes at the cost of imprecision in defining differences. This problem was not an issue in *The Travelling Light Unveiled* because its dominant narrative structure was annalistic and geographical rather than figural. The author undertook the task of identifying the genealogical figures in situ, within already differentiated space and time. He assumed that readers had preexisting knowledge of the persons, places, and times he invoked. In an oxymoronic sense, his book was a local chronicle of a diasporic society written for readers native to that society. Precisely because of its fidelity to the spatiotemporal lineaments of that society, it reproduced a locality—albeit a large one—to which it became confined. For readers in other places and times, its figural genealogies remained obscure because the primary genealogies themselves were confusing. To the imaginations of readers beyond its own society, *The Travelling Light Unveiled* of ʿAbd al-Qādir al-ʿAydarūs in fact could not travel. Some of the untouched readers who were born later and elsewhere, in a transformed diaspora in which most of the landmarks had changed, included persons whose own ancestors figure in the chronicle, like poor Ibn al-ʿArabī in his dream, a waif lost in the mirrors of figural genealogy—son of the unknown Adam.

Nominal multiplication breeds anonymity. The irony is not lost on Ibn al-ʿArabī, who, in his monism, speculated on the potential of God's ninety-nine names for actualization in each human being. While floating signifiers that are detached from referents may be celebrated by undisciplined anthropologists these days, this approach makes for intractable history and genealogy. Al-Shillī was to compose a text that organized the names in a systematic fashion, *The Irrigating Fount: On the Virtuous Biographies of the Noble Sayyids, Descendants of the Patriarch ʿAlawī* (1901, 1982). He was familiar with ʿAbd al-Qādir al-ʿAydarūs's text and had written an appendix to it (al-Shillī n.d.), while also trying his hand at a similar chronicle for the following century (al-Shillī 2003). He knew the names in ʿAbd al-Qādir al-ʿAydarūs's history; their families had been connected in Hadramawt and India by kinship and pedagogical links for generations.[15] In a customarily standard, self-effacing gesture, al-Shillī avers in his book that he is merely borrowing from his predecessors in content and form; he then allows that he added knowledge gained from his travels, as well as *ḥadīth.* He had sojourned four years in India away from Tarim, then settled in Mecca for a quarter century. While he was familiar with the people and places of al-ʿAydarūs's chronicle, al-Shillī did not assume similar familiarity on the part of his readers. His intellectual world was a larger and more cosmopolitan one than ʿAbd al-Qādir al-ʿAydarūs's, sitting as he did in Mecca composing his text. Although he had been inspired by al-ʿAydarūs's chronicle, he sought to improve upon it by employing a different structure of presentation. This form made it accessible to a wider audience that included both non-Hadrami contemporaries and Hadramis born in later times. *The Irrigating Fount* became one of the best-known Hadrami compositions throughout the diaspora and was published in book form in 1901 (al-Shillī 1901). In manuscript or in print, the book was eminently portable. Among the sayyids, it became something of a foundational, canonical text. Indeed, it locates itself at the end of a line of eminent predecessors (al-ʿAydarūs 1985; al-Khaṭīb n.d.; al-Sakrān 1928; Kharid 1985; al-Shillī 1982: 13–14).

The book has two main parts and an introduction. In the interests of continuity, we will begin with the second half. It addresses the problem of anonymity, paradoxically created by an abundance of names in figural genealogy.

15. ʿAbd al-Qādir b. Shaykh (II) al-ʿAydarūs's father, Shaykh (II) b. ʿAbd Allāh al-ʿAydarūs, had been a student of al-Shillī's brother, Aḥmad b. Abī Bakr al-Shillī. ʿAbd al-Qādir's grandfather, ʿAbd Allāh b. Shaykh (I) al-ʿAydarūs, had been a student of al-Shillī's father, Abū Bakr b. Aḥmad al-Shillī.

Like Climbers on a Rock Face: Names and Places

Al-Shillī addressed the problem of anonymity with apparent simplicity: he organized the biographies alphabetically by first name. Although such a scheme was not new in the Islamicate biographical literature and had been used by Ibn Ḥajar in his biographies of the eighth Islamic century, it had specific consequences for the kinds of biographies we are dealing with, given their figural and syntagmatic connections. A scheme that severed these relations was of no use, because it would destroy the meanings that emerge from their interplay within genealogy. As a first step to understanding what al-Shillī achieved by alphabetization, we need to look at how places were incorporated into personal names as geographical and genealogical expansion progressed hand in hand. Then we will discuss the consequence of alphabetization.

Places, like persons, have individual identities: they possess proper nouns that others have bestowed upon them. The point was made patent to me one day when, standing in a wadi bed in southern Yemen, I was almost swept away by a torrent of water that appeared from nowhere. As I stood clear of the flood a few minutes later, dripping wet, feeling scared and stupid, I was subjected to haranguing about wadi hydrology: "Don't you know, idiot, that this wadi A is joined by B, C, D, which are fed farther up by F, G, H, I, and so on? When the water starts running here, it is joined by a gush from B and B's branches after seven minutes, then by more water from C after ten minutes, and so on." Each time the joining occurs, the level of the main stream rises almost instantaneously.

The wadis in southern Yemen are individuated, counted, and serialized; they are known and named. They both nourish and extinguish, and they are objects of both attachment and dread. Like slaves, they are used and trodden upon. Sometimes they strike back, with fatal results. They possess strong features and individual character. Unlike slaves, such places seldom die; it is only their masters who do. Their masters attempt to follow them into perpetuity by imitating their permanence. This they do by naming sons after grandfathers. Thus, a name reappears in alternate generations.[16] This naming process is akin to leapfrogging backward to eponymous ancestors tied to places. Like climbers roped together on a rock face,

16. Goitein reports a similar practice of naming newborn children after their grandfathers among diasporic Jewish families in the Mediterranean, giving rise to recurring couplets of biblical names, such as "Sahlān IV b. Abraham III b. Sahlān III b. Abraham II b. Sahlān II b.

the generations together maintain a tenacious grip despite their precarious individual hold on the surface. In this way do the transient contrive to subjugate the perduring, converting eternal land into perpetual bequest. Something of this sort anthropologists call positional succession. It confers the blessings inherent in an ancestral name *(tayammun)* on a descendant, but a great name is also "a heavy burden to carry," as many will say.

Take the name Muḥammad b. ʿAlī b. ʿAlawī b. Muḥammad b. ʿAlī b. Muḥammad b. ʿAlī. In expanded form (with asterisks noting names that appear in table 1 in chapter 2), it is **Muḥammad** Lord of the Statelet; son of **ʿAlī** Lord of Darak; son of **ʿAlawī;** son of the First Jurist;* First of the Graveyard **Muḥammad;** son of **ʿAlī;** son of **Muḥammad** Principal of Mirbāṭ;* son of **ʿAlī** the Endower of Qasam;* . . . grandson of **Muḥammad** Prophet of God.*[17]

Although this expanded name is our first encounter with Muḥammad Lord of the Statelet, we can already locate him in the history of sayyid settlement in Hadramawt. Within this person's name are other persons and the places they are famously tied to. The name is both pedigree and provenance. Recalling table 1, we can map his movements in relation to early sayyid peregrinations in Mirbāṭ, Qasam, and Tarim, where the sayyids finally settled, and know that he was in some way native to these lands. The name suggests that he founded a settlement and had authority over it. Because of his fame, Muḥammad's cognomen Lord of the Statelet has become a family name, the patronym Mawlā al-Duwayla, and as such, serves as a place marker in the genealogy that enables people to take shortcuts within it in identifying one another. Though Muḥammad died more than six centuries ago, in 1364, one can readily link any of his descendants abroad today in Kenya or Indonesia or Dubai with people and places in the homeland through such shortcuts, even if these descendants are ignorant of their full names.

Of course, such names are never full; they gradually migrate, both in-

---

Abraham I b. Sahlān I b. Solomon I (probably regarded as the Hebrew equivalent of Sahlān) . . . ('*You* have given life to me, *I* ensure the perpetuation of your name.')" (Goitein 1978: 6). The practice also became common in post-Homeric Greece. Pindar called it "isonomy," and Svenbro reasons that "To give the child the name of a grandfather is to make it sound forth once again" (Svenbro 1993: 75–76). For contemporary ethnographic studies, see Herzfeld (1982, 1985), Kenna (1976), and Sutton (1997).

17. **Muḥammad** Mawlā al-Duwayla ibn **ʿAlī** Mawlā Darak ibn **ʿAlawī** ibn al-Faqīh al-Muqaddam **Muḥammad** ibn **ʿAlī** ibn **Muḥammad** Ṣāḥib Mirbāṭ ibn **ʿAlī** Khāliʿ Qasam . . . sibṭ al-Nabī **Muḥammad** Rasūl Allāh.

dividually and collectively, across a surface like our climbers on the rock face, pulling up pitons from behind and planting them ahead. The cognomens are like rare distant spikes left in place many scratches away in the rock, sticking out. The republican Yemeni government today considers a four-generation name definitive for its documentary purposes.[18] Any ancestors earlier than Muḥammad Lord of the Statelet are at too great a remove to be of practical use as patronyms in individual names—with two exceptions. As I have noted, the sayyids of Hadramawt are known by the ultimate patronym ʿAlawī, deriving from the grandson of the Migrant (see table 1 in chapter 2). ʿAlawī is nominally prefigured by ʿAlī b. Abī Ṭālib, cousin and son-in-law of the prophet Muḥammad, and he is the male progenitor from whom the Prophet's descendants issue. ʿAlī's descendants are known throughout the Muslim world as ʿAlawīs. Thus, as ʿAlawīs, the sayyids of Hadramawt are nominally linked to known ʿAlawī groups elsewhere, such as those in Morocco, Turkey, Egypt, and Syria.[19] Furthermore, the repetition of the Muḥammad-ʿAlī couplet in the genealogical chain of names replicates the initial male-male transmission of the Prophet's patriline. It occurs early in the sayyid settlement of Hadramawt.

In the discussions above on Gujarat and *The Travelling Light,* we encountered individual names that in fact form a chain of similar couplets:

18. Four generations is a surprisingly good bureaucratic innovation, reconciling Islamic law, local knowledge, and the reasons of state. Birth certificates are recent, and a person needing official identification can establish his or her identity on the testimony of two witnesses from the home locale. If these witnesses are of one's grandfather's generation, they would be familiar with four generations of names, if not the persons themselves. The official stance is indifferent to how far back the last name is taken. This policy was not always so. The socialist government in the south considered the patronym to be a tribal sign, a holdover from reactionary feudalism that the government sought to repudiate and expunge. Prudence too played its part in acquiescence by citizens, at least on paper. But in genealogical perspective, the quarter century of socialist rule is equivalent to only one generation, in lists that may run on for forty or more generations. James Scott and associates have written on the relationship between the rise of the permanent family surname and the needs of states (J. C. Scott et al. 2002).

19. Such links are ancient and weak but are of sporadic significance. The ʿAlawī sultans of Morocco have in the past sent money for distribution to the Prophet's descendants—the one-fifth of booty that is theirs by right—in Hadramawt. One of these remittances led to the composition of the earliest "genealogy of mothers," because the person charged with its disbursement took seriously the rules for calculating inheritance. Sayyids with non-sayyid mothers were to receive a share only through one parent, while daughters were to receive one-half the share of men. The identities of mothers needed to be known in order to avoid transgressing the religious laws of inheritance. The minute payouts that resulted from this exercise were perhaps compensated for by the wealth of knowledge it produced.

Shaykh (III) Principal of Dawlat Ābād; son of **ʿAbd Allāh;** son of **Shaykh (II)** Principal of Aḥmad Ābād; son of **ʿAbd Allāh;** son of **Shaykh (I);** son of **ʿAbd Allāh** the Grand ʿAydarūs, Sultan of the Notables.*[20]

We met ʿAbd Allāh the Grand ʿAydarūs, Sultan of the Notables, in chapter 5; he is the eponymous ancestor of the ʿAydarūses and lies under a grand white cupola that is one of the major stations of the graveyard visit in Tarim. Dawlat Ābād and Aḥmad Ābād, which appear in the name, are towns founded by Muslim rulers in India. Aḥmad Ābād was built by Sultan Aḥmad, grandson of the first sultan of the independent Muslim kingdom of Gujarat (1407–1573). Sultan Aḥmad put the kingdom on a firm footing in the early fifteenth century and crowned his glory by bestowing his name upon his new capital. For allied reasons but in the context of a different tradition, the sultan's territory-based immortality was subsequently incorporated into the names of generations of ʿAydarūs Hadramis in the diaspora, serving as a prop to their glory, in the name of Shaykh (II) Principal of Aḥmad Ābād. The term I translate as "principal" (*ṣāḥib*) also carries the meaning of "owner," "friend," or "companion" (as in travel).[21] Hadrami genealogists usually apply the term to a celebrated, pious person whose tomb is the object of the pilgrimage cults so evocative of the polysemy of the term.

Separated as they are by the years in ʿAbd al-Qādir al-ʿAydarūs's chronicle, the chain of names is not immediately apparent. In al-Shillī's alphabetical arrangement, however, the biographical entries of the three Shaykh b. ʿAbd Allāhs appear next to each other. Any possible confusion is easily resolved by comparing the juxtaposed entries, and the relations between them immediately become apparent. Alphabetization also makes al-Shillī's book a reference work accessible to any nonnative seeking information about an individual. To do so in ʿAbd al-Qādir al-ʿAydarūs's chronicle would involve reading the whole book, unless one had preexisting knowledge of the year of death, for example, or names of associates.[22] In his book, al-Shillī used alphabetization to systematize the biographies on the basis of the names themselves, rather than by place, time, or generation, and he did

20. **Shaykh** Ṣāḥib Dawlat Ābād ibn **ʿAbd Allāh** ibn **Shaykh** Ṣāḥib Aḥmad Ābād ibn **ʿAbd Allāh** ibn **Shaykh** ibn **ʿAbd Allāh** al-ʿAydarūs al-Akbar, Sulṭān al-Malaʾ. See table 1 in chapter 2 for Sultan of the Notables.

21. In British India, a similar cluster of meanings combining power and sympathy later became associated with the white woman, the wife of the imperial masters, the "memsaheb" (compound of "madam" and "ṣāḥib").

22. The objection could be raised that an index would achieve the same function as alphabetization of the body of the text. But for most of these books' existence, they were

so while retaining the semiotic figural and syntagmatic relations obtaining between the persons, rather than severing them.[23] This approach is an achievement if one keeps in mind the restrictive universe of the onomasticon: only some two dozen first names populate the hundreds of biographies.

In this second half of his book, al-Shillī compiled biographies from predecessors such as *The Travelling Light* and *The Transparent Essence.* Arrayed in his systematic presentation, the biographies became accessible to non-Hadrami scholars and reached a wider audience. Other scholars, non-Hadramis, borrowed from al-Shillī's book to create their own compilations. The best known of these scholars is al-Muḥibbī, resident of Damascus, whose biographical compendium of the eleventh Islamic century, *Khulāṣat al-Athar* (al-Muḥibbī 1966), is voluminous and finds great use (Sabbāgh 1986).[24] Through such textual pathways, the Hadrami names circulated beyond the Hadrami diaspora. Al-Shillī's biographies show that the diaspora was already wide in the late seventeenth century. In addition to numerous entries involving India, Yemen, and the Hejaz were many reports from Ethiopia. Fewer but already present were Hadramis who went east of India, like his paternal uncle who moved to Aceh in Sumatra, finally settling down there, betrothed to the daughter of a senior minister in the court of the female ruler of the time.

Place as Fount: Homeland as Patriline

The first half of *The Irrigating Fount* sets out in a definitive manner the pedigree of the Hadrami sayyids and their spiritual investment in Hadramawt, especially Tarim. The history of their settlement in the region,

---

manuscripts, so pagination differs between copies. One would have to index each copy individually, which would be no mean task. Alphabetical ordering of the entries probably begins with an index but supersedes it, creating a separate work unto itself. The problem also arises in arrangement by generation, as Rosenthal has noted: "The greatest and obvious drawback of *ṭabaqāt* (generational biographical) works was that it was extremely difficult for the historically minded to find in them that which they were looking for. In the famous *Ṭabaqāt al-fuqahā' of Abū Isḥāq ash-Shirāzī,* one needs about as much information in order to be able to locate a particular biography as one might expect to find in that biography once one has succeeded in locating it" (Rosenthal 1952: 84).

23. Al-Shillī allows for one exception to alphabetical order: he places the biographical entries beginning with the name Muḥammad first. In this case, figural considerations take precedence over purely alphabetical ones.

24. Though al-Muḥibbī lived in Damascus, his book's center of gravity is Mecca-Medina.

which was summarized in *The Travelling Light* before the biography of the Adeni, appears in full detail, drawing from very early sources such as al-Kharid's *Blaze* (1985) and al-Shaykh ʿAlī al-Sakrān's *Lightning Bolt* (al-Sakrān 1928).[25] The account is couched in a rhetorical, argumentative style that anticipates objections. Thus, al-Shillī tells us that when the Migrant first arrived in Hadramawt from Iraq, the natives challenged the veracity of his Prophetic descent. The response to this challenge is given in detail. The process of authentication takes the form of itineraries, in which Hadrami pilgrims to Mecca meet pilgrims coming from Basra, who confirm the Migrant's provenance.

Al-Shillī then traces the ascendants of the eponymous ancestor of the Hadrami sayyids, the grandson of the Migrant, step by step to the Prophet, and beyond. Having established the ascent/descent line, he presents sections on the mosques, graves, and hills of Tarim. These accounts draw heavily from stories such as those in the *Transparent Essence*, which we have encountered in chapter 2. But they are now fitted completely within the master narrative of the Prophetic genealogy of the Tarim sayyids; this is new. Whereas al-Khaṭīb's *Transparent Essence* and al-ʿAydarūs's *The Travelling Light* featured both sayyids and non-sayyids, al-Shillī's *The Irrigating Fount* retained only the former, featuring canonical ancestors such as ʿAbd al-Raḥmān al-Saqqāf and ʿUmar al-Muḥḍār.

The narrowing focus of the developing canon is evident in subtexts embedded within these texts. One genre of these subtexts is manuals for visiting graves. These manuals are short, early predecessors of more complex manuals, such as Aḥmad al-Junayd's *Salve for the Sickly in Organizing Visits to Tarim's Cemetery,* which I analyze in chapter 7. Such manuals appear in the earlier texts of ʿAbd al-Qādir al-ʿAydarūs and al-Shillī. ʿAbd al-Qādir al-ʿAydarūs includes as efficacious not only visits to the graves of Tarim but to those of Zabīd as well (al-ʿAydarūs 1985: 76), and he names the graves to visit there. He does not restrict his list to the graves of Hadrami sayyids. Al-Shillī, however, focuses only on those of Tarim and presents a how-to guide to visiting them, in a liturgical account that contains the basic structure of al-Junayd's later manual (al-Junayd n.d.; al-Shillī 1982: 283).[26] This account starts with the First Jurist and works its way through a number of names, stations, and prayers. It also begins

25. Muḥammad b. ʿAlī al-Kharid's (d. 1451; see table 1) book is the first major Hadrami sayyid genealogy. Al-Shaykh ʿAlī b. Abī Bakr al-Sakrān (d. 1490; see table 2) is the first author of Hadrami sayyid biographies.

26. Al-Shillī's section on "how to visit" the graves of Tarim is called *kayfiyyat ziyāratihim*.

with Zanbal, the graveyard of the sayyids, and moves on to al-Furayṭ, that of the shaykhs. Unlike ʿAbd al-Qādir al-ʿAydarūs's rendition, the liturgical movement in al-Shillī's version becomes driven by the larger, systematized narrative of Prophetic descent in which it has been placed. One can trace this systematization in the evolution of genealogical texts abroad, as we see here, and note that it provided paradigms for subsequent texts composed in the homeland, such as al-Junayd's. That al-Shillī wrote his text in and for the diaspora is not in question, as he ends abruptly his liturgical guide to the graves of Tarim, saying that "there is no use in lengthening the account here because he who is far from the place will not benefit from its description, and he who is there can easily find and ask reliable persons in the town" (al-Shillī 1982: 284). Aḥmad al-Junayd's manual for visiting the graveyards of Tarim, a repatriate descendant of al-Shillī's subtext written in and for the homeland, is best learned in the company of just such "reliable persons in the town," as we shall see.

In *The Irrigating Fount* of al-Shillī, non-sayyids and non-Hadramis disappear from the scene, and the scene is no longer a diasporic space emergent in the desultory accounts of events there. Rather, the text presents a didactic and developmentally systematic account of one patriline and one tradition, anchoring it in the homeland. The far-flung places that are intimates in ʿAbd al-Qādir al-ʿAydarūs's *The Travelling Light* appear marginally, as points in the biographies of mobile persons featured in the *Irrigating Fount*. In *The Travelling Light*, space and time are discrete, named entities that are of interest in themselves. The century gives its name to the book. Each year is individuated and numbered; some years stand out because of memorable events. Places too, such as Zabīd, have their own lives, narrated through alternation of floods, fires, droughts, and inflation.

In al-Shillī's *Irrigating Fount*, in contrast, space and time are not independent realities; they are harnessed to a narrative project—the unfolding of the genealogy of the prophet Muḥammad. This unfolding is almost Cartesian in its elaboration from first principles. The book opens with a discussion of this genealogy and marks the progress of time by the chainlike parade of predecessors and successors. Dates are often dispensed with; it is sequence that matters, the *silsila*, the onomatopoeia of "chain" that repeats itself. Places come into view not in their own right but because of the spirituality invested in them by specific persons of this genealogy. Whereas *The Travelling Light* incorporated a whole world of persons beyond the Hadrami sayyids—the ecumenical society of transregional Sunni scholars and Sufis in the Red Sea/Indian Ocean—*The Irrigating Fount* dispensed with all others in its focus on the sayyids. Others are retained only as teachers or students of individual Hadrami sayyids. The sense of the Indian Ocean as a universal concourse trafficking in scholars of all origins disappears.

The Irrigating Fount thus transforms *The Travelling Light* by reworking its materials into a new, tightly integrated form focused on the Prophet's patriline from Hadramawt. Al-Shillī's book converts the whole diasporic space of *The Travelling Light,* with its rhizomic quality and its diverse cast of actors, into a stage that displays the missionary telos of the Hadrami sayyids.

Patriline as Fount: From Figural to Literal Genealogy

> The science of genealogy is a grand art. It is part of the sciences of Prophetic *ḥadīth.* The Prophet has said: "Learn from your genealogies of your kinsfolk *(arḥām)* attached to them, for the bond of kinship *(ṣilat al-raḥim)* is love in family, riches in property and merit in the afterlife."[27] . . . Among its legal boons are descendants, suitability in marriage *(kafā'a),* avoidance of marriage with those prohibited, providing for those to whom one is obliged, knowledge of genealogical contacts with affines who inherit, knowledge of the female/matrilateral kin whom one is commanded to visit regularly and aid.
>
> Muḥammad b. Abī Bakr al-Shillī (1982: 65)

The introduction to al-Shillī's text constitutes a treatise on genealogy. But it is not the sort of genealogy we saw in ʿAbd al-Qādir al-ʿAydarūs's *The Travelling Light Unveiled.* While al-ʿAydarūs's introduction creates the philosophical and mystical space for a figural interpretation of genealogy, meditating on the mediations between its esoteric and visible forms, al-Shillī's introduction sets the terms on a completely exoteric basis: the clear light of Islamic law, a light that is in principle intolerant of ambiguity. Here, genealogy became an important adjunct to correct practice of the law. It was indispensable to knowing whom one could and could not marry, for example. It was necessary for calculating eligibility and shares in inheritance. Thus, al-Shillī classifies genealogy as one of the sciences

27. The attribution is found in the authorities al-Tirmidhī (*al-Birr wa-l-ṣila*) and Aḥmad (*Bāqī musnad al-mukaththirīn*).

of Prophetic *ḥadīth,* the latter a source of positive law second only to the Qur'an. While the two major halves of the book draw upon preexisting genres of Hadrami literature, the introduction is a distinct innovation within this corpus, in its tight integration of genealogy with the discourse of *ḥadīth* scholarship. This innovation represents a contribution from the Meccan wing of the Hadrami diaspora, as Mecca and Medina had maintained a self-regard as repositories of Prophetic *ḥadīth,* given that they were the original venues for Muḥammad's pronouncements and deeds (Dūrī 1983). Al-Shillī's work, written in this milieu, reflects the intellectual habitus of its scholars.

The *ḥadīth* orientation appears in the attention to each link in the chain of ascendants going from the Hadrami sayyids up to the Prophet, for example. Testing for weak links is a basic method in *ḥadīth* studies, which aim to ensure that the chain of transmitters of the Prophet's words and deeds is reliable and robust at every juncture. Genealogy in the hands of *ḥadīth* scholars takes on a tangible, substantive quality. As a *ḥadīth* scholar, al-Shillī's handling of genealogy in his introduction was completely different from ʿAbd al-Qādir al-ʿAydarūs's. Instead of wide-ranging figural similarities, the focus was now on clarifying fine distinctions, even within the genealogy itself. Those distinctions were made on the basis of *ḥadīth:* what the Prophet is reported to have said or done. The reports came in small, self-contained units of a few sentences, sometimes with variations. The contents of such reports were subjected to literalist readings by jurists. As such, arguments revolved around the authenticity of individual reports rather than their possible meanings. Interpretation lay in the choice of reports. The *ḥadīth* orientation predisposes al-Shillī's introduction to agonistic argumentation; ʿAbd al-Qādir al-ʿAydarūs's introduction, in contrast, doubles as a ritual "benediction." The divergence is evident in al-Shillī's approach to Prophetic genealogy, a topic of fundamental concern to both of them.

In his introduction, al-Shillī presents Prophetic genealogy in terms of a number of "issues" *(masā'il)* under contention. Why were descendants of the prophet Muḥammad special? If Muḥammadan Prophetic genealogy was special because it in some way continued pre-Muḥammadan genealogical prophecy—a transmission of light, for example—why should Muḥammad's patrilineal uncles and grand-uncles and their descendants not partake in some way and be classed with the sayyids? The Umayyad and ʿAbbasid caliphates, for example, derived their right to succeed the Prophet in temporal rule from precisely such agnatic ascendants of Muḥammad. Confronting such issues entails grouping and regrouping the Prophet's kin in various ways.[28] The ancestral branching of patrilineal genealogy provided a ready, major basis for making such distinctions. But it was not sufficient, because the relevant groupings formed on many other bases: matrilaterality, filiation, shared milk, historical rivalry, Prophetic fiat. In the generation of the Prophet's great-grandfather, for example, al-Shillī distinguishes between two sets of brothers (and their descendants in perpetuity): Hāshim (the Prophet's great-grandfather) and his brother al-Muṭṭalib, versus their brothers Nawfal and ʿAbd Shams (al-Shillī 1982: 43). The first two are classified as the *Āl* (which may be glossed as "folk," a maximal patriline) of Muḥammad and therefore are forbidden to receive Islamic charity taxes and alms, according to *ḥadīth,* which al-Shillī adduces. Their brothers who are not covered by this rubric, who are not *Āl* of Muḥammad, are permitted the monies. The definition of this grouping is based not on genealogical grounds but on Prophetic *ḥadīth,* such as "The sons of Hāshim and the sons of al-Muṭṭalib are one thing." This divide corresponds with long-term historical lineage rivalries that preceded and succeeded Muḥammad over generations.[29]

A more difficult issue is how to define the Prophet's descendants, the sayyids (or sharifs). Descent is reckoned patrilineally: "he who claims descent from other than his father is cursed" (al-Shillī 1982: 63). But the Prophet's descendants such as the Hadrami sayyids derive from his daughter Fāṭima; the Prophet had no surviving male issue. The exceptionalism of this link had to be accounted for and restricted to a single instance. This issue is a problem in the Shia creed in Islam, in which legitimate temporal rule is the prerogative of the Prophet's descendants. The Shia found many solutions, the more ambitious of which involve the esoteric transmission of Prophetic essence, via either Fāṭima or her hus-

28. Among the terms that al-Shillī defines or mentions for some of these groups are: *Dhawū al-qurbā, al-āl, al-ʿitra, ahl al-bayt, al-dhuriyya,* and *dhāt al-arḥām.*

29. Hāshim, ʿAbd Shams, and al-Muṭṭalib were full brothers, while Nawfal was of a different mother. The Umayyad caliphal dynasty traced descent from ʿAbd Shams through his son Umayy, while the rival ʿAbbasids traced descent from al-ʿAbbās, grandson of Hāshim and father's brother to Muḥammad the Prophet. Preceding the Prophet, Nawfal had seized a courtyard from Hāshim's son, the orphan ʿAbd al-Muṭṭalib (grandfather of the Prophet). The orphan's mother's brothers, the Banū Najjār of Medina, came to his defense. Roughly from the rivalries of these two generations arose the alliance of the Medinese, the Hāshimīs, and the al-Muṭṭalibs, on the one hand, and the Nawfals and ʿAbd Shamses, on the other. This division was to play out subsequently in Prophetic history. The four brothers Hāshim, ʿAbd Shams, al-Muṭṭalib, and Nawfal had established Qurayshi fortunes by securing trade guarantees with the distant rulers of Syria, Persia, Abyssinia, and Yemen.

band, ʿAlī (Conte 2001). But al-Shillī, like the Hadrami sayyids traditionally, was not Shiʿi. He restricted his solution to *ḥadīth,* claiming, for example, that "Every son of a mother has an agnatic group except for the two sons of Fāṭima, for I am their master and their agnatic group is mine" (al-Shillī 1982: 48).

If the sons of Fāṭima were patrilineal descendants of the Prophet, why weren't the daughters of Zaynab, another of the Prophet's daughters, and their sons? The same issue applied to the sons of the two daughters of Fāṭima. Al-Shillī's answer was to reassert patrilineality at the second generation: "the son of a sharīfa is not a sharīf (or sayyid) if his father is not a sharīf" (al-Shillī 1982: 48).

In al-Shillī, the definition of such groupings of the Prophet's kin, whether from genealogical division or Prophetic pronouncement, had legal consequences. It determined eligibility in inheritance, trusts, and marriage. How this determination was made in marriage was to be of particular significance in the Hadrami diaspora. For example, al-Shillī states that a Hāshimī—that is, a descendant of the Prophet's great-grandfather who is not also a descendant of the Prophet himself *(sayyid, sharīf, ahl al-bayt)*—is not eligible to marry a *sharīfa* (female descendant of the Prophet). The term he uses is *kafāʾa* ("sufficiency"): a Hāshimī does not possess sufficiency in hierarchical rank to match her. Marriage eligibility indexes an underlying rank that subsists in closeness to patrilineal Prophetic descent (of which unity is the maximum). Stated as a legal injunction, the maintenance of *kafāʾa* sufficiency amounted to a rule of hypergamy, which mandated asymmetrical marriage exchanges: sayyids could be wife takers but not wife givers.

The issue of *kafāʾa* in marriage gave theoretical jurisprudential formulation to an issue crucial to Hadrami sayyids throughout the diaspora. Abroad, the sayyids were a patrilineal Islamic people who settled among peoples who themselves could be patrilineal, such as the Somalis; matrilineal, such as the Malabar Nayars and Sumatran Minangkabaus; or bilateral/bilineal, such as the Malays. Generally, only male sayyids traveled or migrated. What kinds of marriage relations could they enter into with indigenes, and what sorts of marriage exchanges would the subsequent creole generations engage in? In this context, the maintenance of *kafāʾa* constituted an internal structuring principle of hierarchy that sayyids could actualize in asymmetrical marriage exchanges with locals in the diaspora, regardless of the nature of prevailing marriage practices. The upholding of *kafāʾa* had a number of historical consequences. When enforced over generations, the principle constituted a means of figuring agnatic self as superior to cognatic affines.[30] At the same time, it undergirded the creation and growth of localized patrilineages of sayyids. As wife takers who did not reciprocate, such lineages were net recipients of persons in ongoing exchange relations: they grew fast.

In the maintenance of *kafā'a* abroad, genealogy was formulated as an end in itself, an end conjoined with the maintenance and reproduction of the living community of the Prophet's descendants. In this way, it became the germ of a readily identified community that was portable. A similar process had transpired in the Hadrami homeland itself, in the centuries since the arrival of the Migrant.[31] As members of such sayyid communities were in many cases identified with the advent of Islam itself, the religion was perceived as coming initially in the form of a patriline of the Prophet. Host societies, or their elites who entered into exchange relations with sayyid strangers, did not necessarily distinguish between the two, or want to. Many uses may be found for luminous genealogies by others. These we will explore in the next chapter.

The Irrigating Fount sought to formulate collective social goals for descendants of the sayyids who populate its pages. Its numerous biographies of ancestors already discussed persons who were migrants and creoles in the Indian Ocean and what correct moral action in this space consisted of. It combined Prophetic *ḥadīth* with elements of the diasporic history and experience that we saw earlier in *The Travelling Light.* In this sense, the nature of *The Irrigating Fount* as a hybrid text was critical to its power and relevance—to its influence. It anticipated debates and had ready answers. What it could not do, however, was bring around those whom it had already excised from its foundational narrative: the nonsayyid scholars, Hadrami or otherwise. In this sense, its power cut two ways. In this sense, too, the text contained potentials for its own refutation.

The next chapter examines how the genealogical discourse that evolved in the Hadrami diaspora—in texts such as *The Travelling Light Unveiled* and *The Irrigating Fount*—became a focus of contention in another part of the diaspora, the Malay Archipelago. Indeed, al-Shillī's text itself featured in the controversy, over two centuries after its composition.

30. This view was not necessarily shared by affines, who could hold the inverse interpretation (that wife takers were inferior) perfectly well without jeopardizing relations. The cohabitation of opposed opinions, even over long periods, is of course not unusual in marriages.

31. The initial sayyid settlers in Hadramawt—in Bayt Jubayr, Tarim, and Say'ūn—married local women. Valued endogamous unions were possible only later, whereas marriage alliances with local affinal lineages have continued to the present.

CHAPTER 6

Creole Kinship: Genealogy as Gift

Genealogy as Theory and as Practice

We have seen that genealogy emerged as a genre of writing in the Hadrami diaspora and as a collective representation that could take on different guises. In ʿAbd al-Qādir al-ʿAydarūs's *The Travelling Light Unveiled,* genealogy is embedded in a plural world of places, dates, and persons, on the one hand, yet is somehow autonomous, on the other, beginning with God's earliest creations and moving through history in esoteric, mystical ways. In *The Irrigating Fount,* in contrast, genealogy becomes part of the exoteric science of law, a guide to moral action. As law, genealogy determines whom one can and cannot marry, how inheritance is distributed, and whom one should visit and aid. Nowhere is genealogy simply a straightforward reckoning of lineal descent.

ʿAbd al-Qādir al-ʿAydarūs's text began to separate the Hadrami descendants of the Prophet from the general run of Muslims, in spiritual ways. Al-Shillī's treatise took this process further, separating the Prophet's descendants out in precise legal terms, even making finer distinctions within the Prophet's line of ascent. If al-Shillī seemed to be drawing an absolute boundary around Prophetic descent, the division was not a total one. His *ḥadīth*-based argument did not rule against all exchange of human substance between sayyids and others. Rather, it mandated that exchanges be asymmetrical: men of the sayyid community could marry out, but women could not. Conversely, non-sayyid women could marry into the sayyid community, but non-sayyid men could not. This asymmetry meant that as a whole, the sayyid community would gain descendants and not lose them, since children are identified with the father's line.

In this way, not only did the diaspora move, it was able to populate itself, reproduce, and grow. This achievement is remarkable, if we remember that initially, only men migrated from the homeland. A diaspora consisting only of males was able to become self-reproducing. That achievement turned on the control of the community's women, especially daughters, and their marriage choices.

In reading these texts, we see the development of genealogical thinking in the far-flung society of Hadrami sayyids. The elaboration of genealogical concepts amounted to the creation of theories of and for a diaspora: how it moved through time and space, what kinds of exchanges it could and should have with other peoples, how it could maintain a corporate identity through generations of intermarriage with foreigners abroad, and whether imperatives existed for doing so. All diasporas, as peoples who are mobile, potentially face such questions, whether as individuals or as groups. Not all theorize them. Their different responses have consequences for whether their descendants assimilate into particular local societies or not.

By the seventeenth century, the diaspora of Hadrami sayyids had books that discussed these issues and elaborated concepts, terminologies, images, and visions for theorizing diaspora. The possession of such discourses in textual form is significant. Having texts that discoursed on diasporic issues helped the Hadrami diaspora persist despite its great mobility, and reproduce itself abroad. Indeed, the possession of texts is a feature often found among social groups that are very mobile yet persistent, such as old diasporas and the monotheistic religions of the book.

What roles, then, did genealogical texts play in the Hadrami diaspora? This chapter explores the question by looking at the projection of the diaspora into the Malay world, from the eighteenth century on. By this time, ʿAbd al-Qādir al-ʿAydarūs and al-Shillī had written their books. The aspects of genealogy they had written about—mystical luminescence, law, biography—all came into play in this new destination of the Hadrami diaspora. Movement of genealogical texts accompanied the movements of diasporic Hadramis. As Hadramis intermarried with non-Hadramis, their genealogical texts articulated with those of others. The possession of these texts allowed Hadramis to move not only geographically but transculturally as well. We will examine how this transcultural mobility transpired, first by understanding how others moved into Malay society, and second by looking at the specific ways in which Hadramis did so, in the late eighteenth and early nineteenth centuries. Although our narrative here is broadly chronological, coming after the discussion of Gujarat in the preceding centuries, it is not meant to be a continuous and complete history of Hadrami diasporic movement. Rather, it seeks to confront conceptual problems, in this case the question of how possessing genealogical texts inflected the mobility and integrity of Hadrami diasporic existence in the midst of intimate exchanges with foreign others in new places. Up to the present moment, professional historians have not established a historical baseline for the Hadrami diaspora. I suggest that this lack is due to the diaspora's complex geography and hope that a conceptual account of the modes of mobility through that geography will establish a maritime space, a seascape on which to view how the many threads of the diaspora come together, mingle, and separate.

The genealogies of the Hadrami sayyids are traveling texts that formulate discourses of mobility. Before the twentieth century, sayyids were the few Hadramis who created, used, and read such transcultural texts. In the late nineteenth and early twentieth centuries, however, the rise of a modern Arabic press, circulated by steamship, created a new sphere of public transcultural textuality that non-sayyid Hadramis in the diaspora could and did participate in. Journals published in Paris and Cairo by Muslim intellectuals, a vanguard commonly labeled as reformists, had wide influence throughout the Muslim world, and Hadramis were now a part of that world. With the emergence of this new public sphere, a critical reflection on the earlier, sayyid, genealogical texts became possible. The existence of two distinct realms of textual circulation gave rise to an active confrontation between the two. Conflict that started as disputes in the sphere of texts soon spilled over into disputes in the sphere of institutions, such as schools and mosques, and finally drew boundaries between groups of persons as well, including families.

To understand how these disputes started and widened, the first half of this chapter examines Hadrami diasporic experience in the Malay world before the twentieth century. It will explore the Malay world in order to understand how mobile foreigners were able to enter Malay societies and make themselves at home.

The second half of the chapter then looks at a debate in the early twentieth century, in which the genealogical texts and discourses of the Hadrami sayyids faced a new challenge. At stake in this debate were questions about the significance of the diaspora, the nature of moral action in it, and the simultaneous role of its denizens as members of a religion shared by different peoples, societies, and cultures. The sayyid discourses of mobility faced anew questions previously thought to have been done with. These questions ramified in many directions but kept returning to one key issue: the control of marriage choices by daughters of the sayyid community, on which al-Shillī seemed to have had the last word in seventeenth-century Mecca. We begin the first half of this chapter by now turning to the Malay world.

Domesticating Stranger-Sultans

The sometimes fabulous receptions accorded early Arab arrivals in the seventeenth and eighteenth centuries—as holy sayyids and sultans—can be viewed in terms of established ways in which Malay polities domesticated foreign forces. Precedents existed in Arab experience, in paradigmatic foundational narratives and in the incorporation of Buginese challengers in the eighteenth century. The Malay context needs to be kept uppermost in mind, as I try to show below, if we are to understand the profound ways in which Hadramis became integrated into various societies of the archipelago.

The Malay areas were the coastal perimeter of the Malay Peninsula, east Sumatra, Singapore, the Riau Archipelago, and southwestern Borneo. These locations were coastal trading settlements a few days' sailing distance from each other. They were the terminals of riverine systems connected to each other by the sea. Ports hosting transregional entrepôt trade provided the revenues on which major Malay states were built (Wolters 1970). These ports became prominent with the shift in Indian Ocean trade routes from the Persian Gulf to the Red Sea in the thirteenth century. The trade that made Cambay great in the fifteenth century did the same for Melaka, and they prospered together. Along this route, the narrow Strait of Melaka created a natural nautical funnel, which a succession of states sought to dominate: Srivijaya, Melaka, Aceh, Johor-Riau, the Portuguese, the Dutch, and the English. Politically, the non-European rulers in this Malay region acknowledged authority derived in one way or another from the fifteenth-century Muslim Melaka sultanate.

According to the sultanate's preeminent court chronicle, the *Sejarah Melayu,*[1] this ruling line derived from Sri Tri Buana, a descendant of Alexander the Great who had appeared at Si Guntang hill in Palembang after an underwater journey from India. Sri Tri Buana married the

1. *Sejarah Melayu*, "the Malay Annals," is the generic title by which the chronicle became known. The original title is *Sulālat al-salāṭīn, The Family Line of Kings,* the book being a genealogical king list (Roolvink 1970).

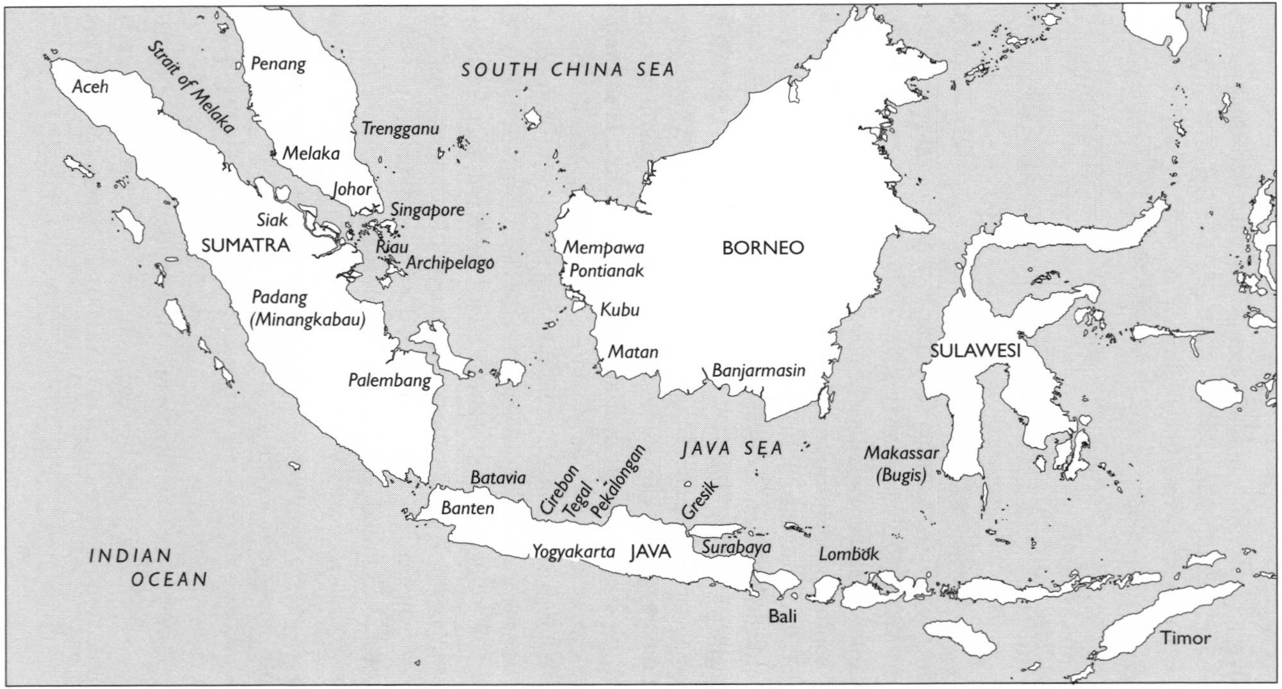

MAP 3. The Malay Archipelago

daughter of the local chief, Demang Lebar Daun, and was made king. The chief became the bendahara, or chief minister to the king. Subsequently, the bendahara line provided wives for the rulers. Representing the people before the stranger-king, the bendahara had sealed a pact with the ruler in which the people would never be disloyal however the ruler chose to behave. The new ruler pledged, in turn, never to treat the people badly. This mutual pledge of loyalty has been an important component of Malay political discourse and is repeatedly invoked in the histories of Malay states (Ho 1990). It reiterates the initial act of state creation described in the *Sejarah Melayu,* in which Alexander the Great vanquished the king of half of India, Raja Kida Hindi, converted him to Islam, invested him with robes of honor, wed his daughter, and continued east. In this story, the conqueror does not replace the vanquished but adds himself to the line of the latter. Conversely, the weaker dynasty grafts its kings onto the illustrious world-historical genealogy of Alexander the Great. The legitimacy of the local ruling house is not displaced but rather is augmented; it proceeds by accumulation rather than substitution.[2] Henceforth, the descendants of this house had two genealogies, one local and the other global.

In the founding myths of the *Sejarah Melayu,* confrontation between local sovereign and superior outsider does not result in the obliteration of one by the other. Rather, the weaker, local incumbent makes his opponent a son-in-law even as he surrenders the reins of state. Affinity provides an idiom for a sharing of interests and rights in sovereignty. Within that formulation is an inherent ambiguity: the father-in-law is putatively superior in rank but presumably inferior in bodily strength to his categorically younger son-in-law. In the Malay kingdom of Johor-Riau, the preeminent port of the Strait of Melaka in the eighteenth century, an affinal alliance of this sort was created between a local Malay ruling family and a family of alien Buginese warriors. The ambiguities inherent in the diarchic arrangement provided ample room for the tortuous conduct of politics between Malays and Buginese, creating a vortex that drew in others, including diasporic Hadrami Arabs, over the course of a century.

Malay polities were absorptive, accumulative entities that actively incorporated foreign elements into their symbolic constitutions. Centuries

2. The titles of postindependence kings of Malaysia are agglutinative philological marvels (incorporating various languages), which primary-school children learn by heart in civics classes: Duli Yang Maha Mulia Sri Paduka Baginda Yang diPertuan Agung Sultan . . . Ibni Almarhum . . .

of contact between local Malay polities, on the one hand, and diasporic Hadramis and Buginese, on the other, bred mutual familiarity, which was expressed in shared cultural idioms that captured the delicate states of being "separate, but not far away; close, but not touching" (Drakard 1990). Kinship idioms played an important role in the constitution of these polities, and therefore interethnic unions, creoles, cross-cultural alliances, multilingual families, and transregional networks of kinsfolk became integral to the social substance of such polities. Within this field, creole Hadrami Arabs were marked in a unique way. The ebb and flow of the Hadrami diaspora was in many ways inseparable from the gradual enlargement of ecumenical Islam in the Indian Ocean that began in the fifteenth century. In consequence, a particularly complex intertwining of religious and genealogical status has helped define what it means to be Arab in this wide field.

Mobility was an essential feature of the diasporic life of Hadrami Arabs here and elsewhere. At the same time, it was key to the dynamic constitution of polities in the Malay Archipelago. Mobility was important because spatial distance allowed people to make contradictory assertions without triggering confrontation. Distance provided a stage on which meanings could be doubled, hierarchies could be both confirmed and confounded, and ambiguities could play out *in extenso* with resolution chronically deferred.[3] Rulers in the region were skilled at trading on such ambiguities in constituting themselves as sovereigns, representatives of distant overlords, and vicegerents of God on earth.

The calm waters of the archipelago both foster mobility and allow easy entry to foreigners. The corollary of mobility is the challenge by ambitious usurpers from the outside. Where arms were inadequate or inappropri-

3. An ambitious Malay chief might parade in his demesne with the yellow umbrellas that are the sumptuary prerogative of the sovereign. Doing so in the court of the sultan, however, is a different matter. The custom of ritual prostration at court, the *sembah,* which is central to the inauguration of a Malay ruler, works precisely to revoke, for an instant, the spatial distance that so often harbors ambiguous intentions and contesting claims. Under the old system of tributary trade with China, the Malay sultan of Melaka himself ritually acknowledged the overlordship of the distant Chinese emperor. Yet in the *Sejarah Melayu,* the subordination could be reversed. In one episode of this court history, the Chinese emperor suffers a disease for which all cures fail until he bathes in water sent from Melaka that has been used to wash the sultan's feet. The sending of tribute by Malay to Chinese ruler, normally a sign of obeisance, is transformed into a virtual Malay-court prostration, a *sembah,* in which the Chinese sovereign pledges obeisance at the feet of his Malay counterpart. The great distance between the two courts provides a space of play whose virtual expansion and collapse in the episode confounds apparently fixed, unambiguous hierarchies of the international regime (Ho 1990).

ate, Malay states thwarted such threats by civilizing the barbarians, which often meant marrying them. The simple politics of warfare expanded into the complex politics of families; in such ways were conquerors conquered and their menacing energies dissipated. Correspondingly, as superior Buginese warriors from the East and spiritually potent Arab descendants of the Prophet from the West entered Malay areas, their incorporation into the Malay family generated an expanding skein of kinship relations that stretched from Sulawesi to the Hejaz, and was densest in the Strait of Melaka.

This cultural process resulted in the historical creation of a large sociogeographical seascape that peoples of different origins could navigate and inhabit. Within it, the difference between being Arab and being Malay, Buginese, Gujarati, Malabari, Acehnese, came down to subtle variations in the relative ease with which one could traverse and profit from different parts of this space. These experiential gradations animated the rhythms of regional political and economic history and determined where one could be arrogant or humble, rebuild a state or a career, trade, be ruined by deception, or find refuge with kinsfolk. The outcome in each case hinged on destinations rather than origin.

The next two sections of this book follow the experiences of diasporic Buginese and Hadramis as they negotiated entry into the Malay region in the eighteenth century. First, we will consider the Malay-Buginese diarchy of Riau, then the establishment of Hadrami sayyid sultanates in the region.

1700–1824: The Bugis Century

After the sacking of Melaka by the Portuguese in 1511, the royal line removed to Johor-Riau with its progeny intact. In 1699, Sultan Maḥmūd, the last of the Melaka line, was killed by one of his officials. His murder had been agreed upon by all the court nobles because of his cruel ways. Upon his demise, the bendahara assumed the sultanic throne, with the title Sultan ʿAbd al-Jalīl. This move was not accepted by a number of groups. Dogged by the shadow of ill-gotten gains, the bendahara-turned-sultan was plagued by constant revolts. These upheavals became more persistent with the appearance of a pretender prince in Siak (across the Strait of Melaka in east Sumatra), who claimed to be Sultan Maḥmūd's son, Raja Kecik, and was supported by the Minangkabau power of West Sumatra. Raja Kecik had been brought up at the court of the Minangkabau queen and thus became a vector for the projection of Minangkabau influence in the southern Strait of Melaka. Raja Kecik's forces overran Johor-Riau in 1718. He humiliated Sultan ʿAbd al-Jalīl by demoting him back to the rank of bendahara and forcing himself in marriage upon ʿAbd al-Jalīl's daughter Tengku Qamariyya.

Ex-sultan ʿAbd al-Jalīl's children plotted to restore their honor and state. At this time, the Malay lands were seeing the arrival of Buginese fighters from Sulawesi in the east, who had been displaced by wars in their homeland. In particular, five princely Bugis brothers—the Five Opu's—played a major role in subsequent events. ʿAbd al-Jalīl's children decided to ally themselves with the Buginese Opu's. Our main source for these events, the Buginese text *The Precious Gift*, or *Tuḥfat al-Nafīs* (Raja Ali Haji ibn Ahmad 1982; Raja Haji Ahmad and Raja Ali Haji 1997), says that ʿAbd al-Jalīl's son Raja Sulaymān suggested that his sister Tengku Tengah offer to be the wife of one of the Five Opu's, Opu Daeng Parani, to secure their help. But the text also provides a different interpretation, from the Minangkabau-oriented *Siak Chronicle,* suggesting that "it was Tengku Tengah who was intent on avenging their humiliation, and it was she who conferred with Raja Sulaymān" (Raja Ali Haji ibn Ahmad 1982: 50).

The difference between the texts—one saying that the brother gave his sister away, the other saying that the sister offered herself—is built on the apparent assumption that wife givers are the inferiors, as formulated in the customary relation between bendahara and sultan, and in its crude reenactment by the victor, Raja Kecik. Since the family had already been humiliated by Tengku Qamariyya's forced marriage to Raja Kecik, the suggestion that her sister Tengku Tengah marry the Bugis was no longer as big an issue. The delicate manner in which *The Precious Gift* handles the matter suggests that large room for ambiguity exists: in an act of apparent capitulation may lurk an iron will that could emerge superior. Further, great kings were known to give daughters to their vassals as acts of investiture. The key point was who initiated the action.[4] This ambiguity opens the next step up to interpretation. Once the Bugis princes had dined, "Tengku Tengah stood at the entrance to the guests' gallery, opened the screen and threw down her ear stud, saying, 'Oh, Bugis princes, if you

4. Lévi-Strauss's ambitious comparative exercise (1969), an "as if" thought experiment that gave bridal exchange, alliance, and hierarchy a seemingly autonomous existence, distracts us from seeing the possibilities of a single marriage. For example, when the sultan of Aceh defeated the Johor sultan in 1613, he summoned the Johor royal family to his court, married his own daughter to the Johor sultan's brother, and sent his new son-in-law home to rule Johor, under an armed guard of two thousand Acehnese (Andaya 1975: 24). Despite

are truly brave, avenge the shame of our family! When that is done, I shall willingly be your slave, and even if you ordered me to cook your rice, I would do it'" (Raja Ali Haji ibn Ahmad 1982: 50).

Opu Daeng Parani agreed to avenge their shame, and the two parties agreed to constitute a diarchic state in which one of the Bugis princes—and their descendants—would become the *Yang diPertuan Muda,* the junior ruler to the *Yang diPertuan Besar,* the Malay sultan, if the princes succeeded in restoring to power the ex-sultan ʿAbd al-Jalīl's family. This marriage established the difficult dual system of rule in Johor-Riau for the next century, whereby the Malay senior partner was often at the mercy of his Bugis junior, even if Tengku Tengah, as sister to the sultan, was saved from cooking Buginese rice. Though ex-sultan ʿAbd al-Jalīl's family negotiated from a position of weakness, the episode demonstrates that although conducting relations through women was a means of marking subservience, women were able to use their alliance-making ability to advance the interests of their families and male relations.

While Malay disunity following the regicide of Sultan Maḥmūd enabled the foreign Bugis to enter into Malay politics, the elaborate genealogical basis of Malay sovereignty prevented the stronger Bugis from ruling in their own names. Force of arms was a common factor in deciding gross outcomes, but the complex politics of apportioning indebtedness, revenge, booty, sexual favor, and trust were best pursued in the subtle medium of kinship and affinity. The Bugis joined the Malay family even as they entered Malay politics, and thus began the process of their disarmament. Four generations later, the Buginese-Malay chronicler Raja Ali Haji was to sum up that process as a splicing of Malay and Buginese genealogies, the story of his family:

> The story goes on to say that Raja Sulaymān had sixteen brothers and sisters, but only the following will be mentioned in this genealogy. First, Raja Sulaymān; second, Tengku Tengah; third, Tengku Qamariyya, generally known as Tengku Puan; fourth, Tengku Mandak. It was Raja Sulaymān who became king, raised up by the Bugis princes, that is, the Five Opu's who were Brothers. Their story will come later in this chronicle.

---

the appearance of affinal alliance, and the gracious conversion of the Aceh sultan's military superiority to generational precedence, the Johor princes knew full well that not only were they under guard, they were being watched from close quarters, by someone well placed to gather intimate local information and relay it abroad. Marital unions were also nodal points in overlapping circuits of information, here linked by subjugation.

Tengku Tengah became the wife of Opu Daeng Parani, and gave birth to Raja Maimunah, who married the Temenggung of Johor, giving birth to Daeng Cellak, Daeng Kecik and the Engku Muda. Daeng Cellak died in a gunpowder explosion on a keci which he had attacked. . . .

. . . Tengku Qamariyya married Raja Kecik of Siak and gave birth to Raja Maḥmūd, generally known as Raja Buang.[5]

Tengku Mandak married Opu Daeng Cellak and had two daughters, one named Tengku Putih and the other Tengku Hitam.

These are some of the daughters of Sultan Abd al-Jalīl whose lines were mingled with the Bugis and Siak princes. (Raja Ali Haji ibn Ahmad 1982: 20)

The Four Youths: Hadramis in a Bugis Century

During the three-way contest among Buginese power, Malay legitimacy, and Minangkabau counterlegitimacy in the early decades of the eighteenth century, other players with other genealogies arrived on the scene. These new arrivals were the Arab sayyids of Hadramawt, whose ancestor the First Jurist had broken his sword over his knee, renouncing violence. What they lacked by way of arms, they made up for with a genealogy that at a minimum matched that of the Malay sultans; both genealogies stretched back to an ancestor mentioned by God in the Holy Qur'an: the prophet Muḥammad and Alexander the Great.[6]

In the pantheon of foreign pioneers in the Malay lands, the Five Opu's of the Bugis are matched by their eighteenth-century contemporaries, the Four Youths of the Hadramis. Though these young men were by no means the earliest arrivals, they have, like their Buginese counterparts, been memorialized in Hadrami diasporic writings as inaugurators of a period the historians might be persuaded to call a Hadrami century as well.[7] They left Tarim, the religious center of Hadramawt, after receiving the permission of their teachers, and headed for the regions of the East to spread the call to God. They stayed four years studying in Malabar, learning from Hadramis such as the sayyid Muḥammad b. Ḥāmid and the sayyid Shaykh b. Muḥammad al-Jufrī, author of the *Treasury of Proofs* (al-Jufrī n.d.), before entering the Malay Archipelago. There, they were to achieve

5. "Tengku Qamariyya" is "Kamariah" in the Latin-based text.

6. In Alexander the Great's Islamic guise as Dhū al-Qarnayn.

7. The eighteenth century has been dubbed the "Bugis century" by historians of Southeast Asia (Andaya and Andaya 1982: 80).

fame and position as teachers, judges, and saints. The immediate progeny of three of the Four Youths, creole Arab sons of native mothers, went on to become rulers of states in their own names.

Each one of the Four Youths settled in a different locus of power in the Malay world: Malay, Acehnese, Minangkabau, and Buginese. Sayyid Muḥammad b. Aḥmad Karaysha settled in the Malay sultanate of Trengganu, where he spread the call.

Sayyid ʿAydarūs b. ʿAbd al-Raḥmān al-ʿAydarūs founded the town of Kubu in southwest Borneo. Kubu declined as Pontianak rose, and Sayyid ʿAydarūs moved to Aceh on the northern tip of Sumatra, where he died and was known as Tuan Besar Aceh (Grand Master of Aceh).[8] His son ʿAbd al-Raḥmān subsequently became ruler of Kubu, under Buginese tutelage.

Sayyid ʿUthmān b. ʿAbd al-Raḥmān bin Shihāb settled in Siak, where the Minangkabau held sway, and married the daughter of the ruler Raja ʿĀlam, a son of Raja Kecik. She was a granddaughter of the rivals Raja Kecik and Daeng Parani. The couple's creole son Sayyid ʿAlī eventually displaced the last of the ancient Melaka line of Malay sultans and replaced them with a line of sayyid sultans in Siak, the Āl bin Shihāb.

Sayyid Ḥusayn b. Aḥmad al-Qadrī lived in Matan in southwest Borneo for seventeen years, as teacher and judge; he married the sultan's daughter there. He finally moved to Buginese Mempawa and became known as the Lord of Mempawa, where he was buried. His son ʿAbd al-Raḥmān married a daughter of the sultan of Banjarmasin, and also married a sister of the Buginese sultan of Mempawa, cousin to the premier Buginese warrior Raja Haji. ʿAbd al-Raḥmān was to found the al-Qadrī line of sayyid Arab sultans in the new settlement of Pontianak in southwest Borneo.

The arrival of the Four Youths in these areas and their rapid rise appear to vindicate three centuries of Dutch awe and envy of the apparently magical powers of such personalities. Van den Berg, a sympathetic Dutch official who sought to counter stereotypes of Arabs within Dutch officialdom by conducting a comprehensive field survey and publishing his results, explained his motivations thus: "As compatriots of the Prophet's nation, the spiritual prestige of Arabs is minimal; yet it has become an *idée fixe* in European circles, and I should debunk it" (van den Berg 1989:

8. Aceh had been the dominant power in the Strait of Melaka in the sixteenth century, after the fall of Melaka in 1511 and before the rise of Johor-Riau. A number of the primary pilgrimage sites in Aceh are the tombs of Hadrami sayyids.

139). The ability of the itinerant mystic and holy man to enter and conquer sultans' courts and minds is standard fare in the anthropological literature. However, our Four Youths' geohistorical itinerary did not follow an ineffable mystical path that terminated in an inexplicable irruption of charisma. Rather, they percolated down a transregional spatial network of hierarchical centers and peripheries that was simultaneously commercial, religious, legal, political, and mystical.

This network spanned the transoceanic trade route that framed our discussions in chapters 2 and 4. We encountered it in the fourteenth and fifteenth centuries, at the height of Ibn al-ʿArabī's influence in Aden and Rasulid Yemen, when the institutional complex of the ʿAlawī Way was taking shape. We explored its participation in the making of Muslim Gujarat in the sixteenth and seventeenth centuries, at the courts of sultans and slave-administrators and in the ports of merchants. In the larger network of religious adepts beyond the diaspora of Hadramis, these places were oriented toward Mecca and Medina as religious, scholarly, spiritual, and institutional centers. From the sixteenth century on, with the Turkish assumption of suzerainty over Mecca and Medina, these holy cities gained fresh footing as centers of Islamic networks in a new, material sense. Sultan Salīm I grandly declared the whole of Egypt to be an endowment for the benefit of the holy cities, and lesser sultans from Yemen, Gujarat, and the Malay Archipelago followed suit, underwriting mosques and schools (Azra 1992: 153). These holy cities were a unique concourse where Muslims from all lands met and were more cosmopolitan than the port cities along the Indian Ocean route. Over the centuries, intellectual fashions and movements brewing in Mecca-Medina were to ripple out along the route, sometimes tending toward mysticism and at other times favoring law.

One of these movements has been called neo-Sufism by historians of Islam (Azra 1992; Rahman 1979; Voll 1982). These scholars believe that neo-Sufism originated in Mecca and Medina in the eighteenth century and then spread to the rest of the Islamic world, and they see its significance in its reconciliation of Sufism and Islamic law. In this view, medieval, ecstatic forms of Sufi practice became tempered by orthodox textual learning, producing a reformist ethic that reconciled the two, and even constituted an Islamic enlightenment (Schulze 1990). While the Hadrami material suggests that the Hadrami diaspora participated in a so-called neo-Sufi movement, it also suggests that the sharp distinctions suggested by the term *neo-Sufism* are artificial. In Aden in the fifteenth century, and in Gujarat in the seventeenth century, mobile religious adepts such as the Hadramis were Sufis as well as legal scholars. Neo-Sufism was neither a new phenomenon in the eighteenth century nor a reconciliation of a preexisting divide between mysticism and law.[9] A critique of the category of neo-Sufism has been offered by O'Fahey and Radtke (1993) on similar grounds, and the Hadrami material offers further complications.[10] Instead of seeing disjunctions based on historical periodization, a geographical orientation provides a view of the *longue durée* in which a multiplicity of travels, contacts, and exchanges takes place within one geographical space over time. Within this space, new impulses, say toward orthodoxy, are not completely novel phenomena that signal absolute change. Rather, they are ripples across a body of water that is already interconnected. The continuous record of Hadrami participation in this space shows that mobile religious adepts were always engaged in a range of activities and that a narrowing of focus was a matter of emphasis rather than wholesale change. Each new movement that coursed through this space was a wave that individual Islamic adepts could ride at the expense of others, rather than a "sea change." What was effected each time was a redistribution, in particular places along the route, of the favors of sultans and the allegiances of the local Muslim populace among rival itinerant Muslim scholars. Such shifts were reversible and were often marked by unannounced arrivals and unceremonious departures of influential divines. Accounts of such movements made copious use of the language of emotion. The narratives moved events along as much by attraction, love, manners, and jealousy as by the niceties of theological disputation, and at least one chapter in the history of Islam in the Indian Ocean ought to be written in this language.

Throughout, Muslims were interested in the person of the prophet Muḥammad. His *ḥadīth* provided precedence for law and models for spiritual emulation. Regardless of emphasis, what elements counted as religious knowledge was clear: the Arabic language, the Qur'an, *ḥadīth,* the

9. Indeed, van Ess (1999) argues that Sufism had become an integral part of orthodox, establishment scholarly circles very early, and even scholars considered to be authoritative sources of anti-Sufi arguments, such as Ibn Ḥanbal and Ibn Taymiyya, were themselves associated with Sufi lineages. Distinctions were being made at closer and more intimate quarters than one might gather from the heresiographical spirit of Orientalist scholarship.

10. The neo-Sufi idea, which expands to include a more general, unified Islamic revivalism, grew out of biographical studies of networks of scholars that focused on "who met whom"; the center of gravity was Mecca-Medina among *ḥadīth* scholars. Analyses of intellectual content, however, show that categorical divisions yield to complication (Dallal 1993; Haykel 2003).

Shāfiʿī legal textbooks, and scholarly pedigree. On these grounds, the linear trade route linking Makassar, Banten, Palembang, Melaka, Aceh, Malabar, Gujarat, Aden, Mocha-Zabīd, Jedda-Mecca-Medina, and Cairo was conceptualized as a hierarchy of centers and peripheries emanating out of the Hejaz. Scholarly itineraries, the difficulty of texts, the size of mosques and libraries, teacher-student relations, and the seeking and answering of jurisprudential opinions can all fit within this spatial hierarchy. Only recently have the outlines of such a network in the Indian Ocean begun to emerge. The pathbreaking work of Azra (1992, 2004) has spun the prosopographical web most clearly.

In their geographic focus, the Hadrami works we examined in the previous chapter looked toward the western Indian Ocean and the Red Sea. The regions east of India such as the Malay Archipelago receive the briefest of mentions, such as in the biography of al-Shillī's uncle, who settled in Aceh. In the seventeenth century, those regions were new frontiers for the Hadrami diaspora. In the terminology of Arab sailors, they were the lands "under the wind" *(taḥt al-rīḥ)*.[11] To get there from Aden normally entailed waiting for a second sailing season in India. Yet while these lands barely appeared in the Hadrami canon in the seventeenth century, when al-Aydarūs and al-Shillī completed their books, the opposite situation obtained on the frontier itself. There, Hadramis were instrumental in establishing new, canonical genres of Islamic writing in the Malay language. In particular, the role of Muḥammad b. ʿAlī al-ʿAydarūsī al-Rānīrī (d. Randir 1666) was singular and remarkable.

Al-Rānīrī, who arrived in Aceh in 1637, is a controversial figure in Malay letters and religious history. His family origin has not been conclusively established, and I have been unable to identify him with a Hadrami line of descent. Historians know that he was from Randir, a town in Gujarat across the Tapti river from Surat. He was educated in the Hadrami-Indian creole milieu of ʿAbd al-Qādir al-ʿAydarūs, author of *The Travelling Light Unveiled*. His teacher was a Hadrami sayyid born in India, ʿUmar b. ʿAbd Allāh Bā Shaybān (also known as Abū Ḥafs), who had studied in Tarim with the brothers of both ʿAbd al-Qādir al-ʿAydarūs and Muḥammad al-Shillī. Abū Ḥafs's teacher in Surat was a migrant from Tarim, Muḥammad b. ʿAbd Allāh al-ʿAydarūs, brother to Shaykh (III) al-ʿAydarūs Principal of Dawlat Ābād, and nephew of ʿAbd al-Qādir al-ʿAydarūs. Through Abū Ḥafs, al-Rānīrī was initiated into the Rifāʿī Sufi order, in a chain of initi-

11. The Malay term for the archipelago, *bawah angin,* derives from this origin.

ation stretching back to Abū Bakr al-ʿAydarūs the Adeni, Saint of Aden.[12] The "al-ʿAydarūsī" in al-Rānīrī's name indexes his membership in this chain of initiates, if he was not of the patriline. In the other direction, on the "left arm of Cambay," his family maintained close contacts with Aceh. His uncle had taught there in the 1580s, and his mother was reputedly Malay (al-Attas 1966: 12–13). Al-Rānīrī wrote in the Malay language.

From 1637 to 1644, al-Rānīrī was the most influential religious leader in Aceh, holding one of the highest religious positions *(Shaykh al-Islām)* at the Aceh court. He launched a campaign against mystics who, he claimed, believed God to be immanent in creation. At the height of his influence, he had some of them executed as heretics. In Azra's judgment, al-Rānīrī was the first neo-Sufi of significance in the archipelago. He campaigned to bring mysticism in Aceh in line with religious law. The full panoply of knowledge in the religious sciences that he brought to bear upon this task also made him the originator of important genres of Islamic writing in the Malay language:[13] basic prayer manuals, *ḥadīth,* and universal history (Azra 1992: 377–81). In addition to his personal ability, al-Rānīrī brought with him an intellectual genealogy that connected him with the well-known al-ʿAydarūs family of Hadrami sayyids.

In the figure of al-Rānīrī, who was a contemporary of al-Shillī, the influence of Hadrami sayyids in the Malay Archipelago comes into sharp focus, initially from the creole Hadrami-Indian community of Gujarat in the seventeenth century. From the perspective of the archipelago, such figures from the West, whether from Gujarat, Hadramawt, or Mecca, carried great authority. Their precise places of origin were always unclear. Where did Islam come from? is a vexed and ongoing question in the field of Islamic studies of Southeast Asia, originally conceived in the diffusionist paradigms of colonial-era scholars. From my perspective in this study, the source of the imprecision is clear: as diasporic creoles native to a transregional network of religious adepts and kinsfolk, these figures were from "all of the above."

In the seventeenth century, this authority from the lands "above the

12. The Adeni authored a biography of the founder of this order (A. B. al-ʿAydarūs 1970). Azra (1992) provides a detailed account of the teacher-student linkages in India and Arabia, including generations of al-ʿAydarūses and neo-Sufi luminaries in Mecca such as Ibrāhīm al-Kurānī and Aḥmad al-Qushshāshī. Azra's main sources are non-Hadrami compilers such as al-Muḥibbī (1966), who incorporated material from Hadramis such as al-Shillī; thus, his sources overlap with Hadrami sources used here.

13. In addition to knowing Malay, al-Rānīrī knew Arabic, Persian, Urdu, and Acehnese (Azra 1992: 375).

wind" began to take on a distinctly—though not exclusively—legal cast. Al-Rānīrī's persecution of the Acehnese mystics is a dramatic example.[14] The influence was most keenly felt in Muslim port cities along the trade route with those lands, such as Aceh and Banten bordering the Malay nexus of the Strait of Melaka. In 1638, the ruler of Banten received a writ from the Sharif of Mecca conferring upon him the title of sultan. He also received apparent impressions of the footprint of the Prophet, which were taken around in procession during celebrations of the Prophet's birthday, or *mawlid* (Azra 1992: 116). In 1699, the last of a series of four queens who ruled Aceh abdicated her throne, in obedience to a *fatwā* (in response to queries from Acehnese) from the chief mufti of Mecca declaring it illegitimate for a woman to rule (Azra 1992: 399). She stepped down in favor of her son, the creole Hadrami sayyid Ibrāhīm Zayn al-ʿĀbidīn b. Hāshim Jamal al-Layl, who ruled until 1702 (al-Mashhūr 1984).[15]

Given these experiences of the preeminent Muslim port sultanates of the region in the seventeenth century, it is likely that when the Four Youths arrived at relatively new or minor polities such as Siak, Mempawa, Matan, Kubu, and Pontianak in the next century, they were welcomed as prestigious figures descending from superior cosmopolitan centers to parochial backwaters. For religious personalities coming from Tarim via Malabar, it was the expansive, transoceanic network that authorized their entry into Malay Muslim courts and underpinned their successes there.

The Precious Gift of Genealogy

The eighteenth century saw constant demand for religious functionaries in the sultanates of the region. This demand echoed that in Gujarat in the fifteenth and sixteenth centuries but arose for different reasons.

14. The polemics and politics surrounding al-Rānīrī are still not well understood. In particular, his attacks on the mystical teachings of Hamza Fanṣūrī are puzzling, since the latter's doctrines are readily identified with Ibn al-ʿArabī, and his illuminationist terminology (al-Attas 1966) is very similar to that of ʿAbd al-Qādir al-ʿAydarūs's, in *The Travelling Light*. Al-Rānīrī apparently was respectful of Ibn al-ʿArabī and was formed in al-ʿAydarūs's milieu. Possible answers range from the influence of antieclecticism under the Mughal emperor Aurangzeb in India, political opportunism, and an inadequate command of Malay. Another possibility is that a difference of opinion lay in Fanṣūrī's monism, in which light was diffuse and prismatic rather than genealogically channeled, though this idea bears further research.

15. The Jamal al-Layl have also been rulers in the Comoro Islands and Perlis in Malaysia, the latter to the present day.

The need was more pressing in new port sultanates attempting to place themselves on the trading map. These little Melakas in the making competed with each other and needed a few key ingredients to thrive: foreign merchants, a measure of political security and freedom, low taxes, and institutions for the equitable resolution of commercial disputes. In the early stages of these ports' development, piracy was also part of the process of state making, providing a way to dip into someone else's tax base and channel traders away from rivals; it was a primitive form of accumulation in an otherwise-competitive field. Once a port-making project reached a certain size, however, such methods became counterproductive. Sultanates needed to show that they were now civilized and comfortable places for the peaceful pursuit of profit, and they needed to advertise their maturity. Few better ways existed to achieve such objectives than installing a resident Muslim jurist to refashion a grimy pirates' haven as a new sphere of civilian concourse, boasting a Friday congregational mosque, a court of justice, and a school.[16] If the one who graced these civilized circles with his presence was a descendant of the Prophet, so much the better. A Hadrami source describes the sequence of events following the Buginese sultan of Mempawa's success in finally drawing Sayyid Ḥusayn b. Aḥmad al-Qadrī, one of the Four Youths, from rival Matan in 1747:

> The sultan of Mempawa assembled his princes and ministers and sons, and announced to them his happiness at the coming of the sayyid, and said that it was hard to find one of the house of the Prophet in that country, and that his coming was a stroke of good fortune.
>
> A mosque and a house were built in a quarter now known as Kalah Herang. The sultan sent his son Gusti Haji with a group of soldiers in two ships to Matan. In the month of Muḥarram 1160 Sayyid Ḥusayn left [Matan]. His father-in-law the sultan [of Matan] supplied him with three sailing ships after he had spent seventeen years in Matan.

16. Legal digests from such Malay port states, which are often simply lists of rules, were largely translations from standard Shāfiʿī legal texts about transactions, the *muʿāmalāt* (Azra 1992; Liaw 1976). The Shāfiʿī school is predominant in the Indian Ocean littoral, and the Hadrami sayyid base of Tarim is one of its centers in the region. The coextension of religion and trade is not surprising if we bear in mind that medieval scholars often funded their travels by the practice of arbitrage, making a little capital go a long way, literally, as do European youths in Asia today. Sayyid Ḥusayn b. ʿAbd al-Raḥmān al-ʿAydarūs, the Lord of Mempawa, found this necessity distasteful in his own peregrinations (al-Mashhūr 1984: 510). Traders, in turn, always welcomed a moral or legal force behind contracts, which signified the lessening of risk.

> Sayyid Ḥusayn stayed with his family in his new house [in Mempawa]. He taught students who came to him from all directions, and his house became a shelter for foreigners and was sought by guests. As well, the place became a city of learning and trade. (al-Mashhūr 1984: 510)

Matan's loss was Mempawa's gain. Sayyid Ḥusayn's fame was a catalyst that extended Mempawa's reach in trade and learning. He had left Matan after seventeen years precisely because the sultan there, his father-in-law, had not fully crossed the line separating sultan from pirate. Sayyid Ḥusayn had passed judgment in Matan on a foreign trader who assaulted a woman, sentencing him to a fine and repentance, to which the sultan had agreed. When the trader left for his home country, however, the sultan's men looted and killed him and his companions at sea. The sayyid summarily severed his reputation from that of the sultan and took up Mempawa's long-standing invitation to relocate.

The Matan sultan's error lay not so much in his actions as in his timing: late in his career, after the reputations of sultan, sayyid, and state had been built. Indeed, Sayyid Ḥusayn's son, Sayyid ʿAbd al-Raḥmān, developed his own reputation as a pirate early in his career.[17]

Born in 1742, ʿAbd al-Raḥmān married the daughter of the sultan of Banjarmasin. Another wife, Utin Candera Midi, was the daughter of the sultan of Mempawa (one of the Five Opu's) and cousin of Raja Haji, the legendary Buginese warrior (Raja Haji Ahmad and Raja Ali Haji 1997: 160). After his father died in 1771 (al-Mashhūr 1984: 510), ʿAbd al-Raḥmān left Mempawa to found the settlement of Pontianak, where he and his followers "cut down giant trees in the thick jungle and built houses and a mosque" (al-Mashhūr 1984a: 504). After establishing Pontianak, he went up the Kapuas River to trade. He was blocked at Sanggau by the local chief, a battle ensued, and ʿAbd al-Raḥmān retreated to Pontianak (al-Mashhūr 1984a: 504; Raja Haji Ahmad and Raja Ali Haji 1997: 160). There, he sent word to his wife's cousin, the Buginese warrior Raja Haji.

Raja Haji responded to Sayyid ʿAbd al-Raḥmān's call for help and came with a fleet to vanquish his cousin-in-law's opponents. The military assistance he gave his young sayyid affine was part of a multigenerational series of exchanges between Buginese and sayyids that tied their families and fates together. The cycle of prestations (gifts) had begun with ʿAbd

17. Dutch sources, which characterize ʿAbd al-Raḥmān's early career as piratical, identify his mother as a non-Muslim slave; Hadrami sources identify her as a princess. She could have been both.

al-Raḥmān's father, Sayyid Ḥusayn, who had made of himself a gift to the infant Buginese settlement of Mempawa. Mempawa's sultan had reciprocated by giving his daughter's hand to Sayyid Ḥusayn's son ʿAbd al-Raḥmān in marriage. With Raja Haji's arrival in Pontianak, the cycle of exchanges intensified: his first act was to visit the grave of Sayyid Ḥusayn. After the fighting was done, Raja Haji remained for sixteen months. During this time, he and Sayyid ʿAbd al-Raḥmān traded visits, feasts, dances, jokes, palaces, and prayers; the culmination of this activity was ʿAbd al-Raḥmān's investiture as sultan of Pontianak by Raja Haji (Raja Haji Ahmad and Raja Ali Haji 1997: 163–65). The bond that developed between them was created in a process that may be called "total prestation," following Mauss (1967: 68).

> Food, women, children, possessions, charms, land, labour, services, religious offices, rank—everything is stuff to be given away and repaid. In perpetual interchange of what we may call spiritual matter, comprising men and things, these elements pass and repass between clans and individuals, ranks, sexes and generations. (Mauss 1967: 12)

Upon Raja Haji's departure, his cousin and the sayyid sultan swore that the ties that bound them would persist in their descendants and never be broken. The total social fact of their union is represented in the splicing of Buginese and sayyid genealogies. We can identify precisely where the splicing occurred by comparing the two genealogical texts we have drawn upon in this chapter: the Buginese *Precious Gift* (*Tuḥfat al-Nafīs;* Raja Ali Haji ibn Ahmad 1982; Raja Haji Ahmad and Raja Ali Haji 1997), written in Malay, and the Hadrami *Mid-day Sun (Shams al-Ẓahīra;* al-Mashhūr 1911; al-Mashhūr 1984), composed in Arabic. While systematically presenting the forward movement in genealogical time of the individual communities, each text indicates where its collateral lines merge with those of the other. We can trace this merging by juxtaposing the texts, even though they value genealogy differently. *The Precious Gift* is a voluminous set of stories attached to a smaller genealogy of the Malay and Buginese (and Hadrami sayyid) kings. The genealogy serves as introduction, table of contents, précis, and serial index of names, rolling all these elements into one critical apparatus. In the *Mid-day Sun* (the 1984 edition), the genealogy constitutes the body of the text *(matn)*, while the stories are part of the critical apparatus, in the footnotes.

Himself the product of a previous merging of Malay and Buginese lines, the author of *The Precious Gift* understood the connection between gifts and genealogies and explained it in his preface: "in it I tell the genealogy, journeys, history and reports of the Malay and Buginese kings and their descendants. And I have named it *The Precious Gift*" (Raja Haji Ahmad and Raja Ali Haji 1997: 1). Itself a gift, his genealogy/chronicle was a synecdoche that modeled and regenerated the relations between Malays and Buginese: the kinship of total prestation, in which two groups gave their genealogies to each other and to their descendants as gifts. Raja Haji Ahmad's son was in turn presented with a genealogy by the third sayyid sultan of Pontianak, which he expanded into his *Malay and Bugis Genealogies* (Raja Ali Haji 1997: 7).[18]

However, the mingling of Buginese and sayyid genealogies was not assimilation but creolization. For there remains one exception to the system of total prestation: the creole sayyid sultans maintain the practice of *kafā'a* and do not marry their daughters to their Buginese affines. Somewhere within the mingling crowd is a turnstile. When a Buginese woman married a sayyid, her Buginese kin had to be prepared to lose her female offspring, who could not return in marriage to a Buginese man. In that sense, the woman is a pure gift for which no direct return is given. That exchange is asymmetrical, and the point is paradigmatically registered in *The Precious Gift* within the first generation of sayyid-Buginese offspring in Pontianak:

> Utin Candera Midi married Pangeran Sharīf ʿAbd al-Raḥmān, who was installed as Sultan of Pontianak by the regent Raja Haji. They had two children, a son and a daughter. The son, Pangeran Sharīf Qāsim, became the second Sultan of Pontianak. The daughter, Sharīfa ʿĀ'isha, married the sayyid Shaykh bin Ḥāmid Bā ʿAbūd. (Raja Haji Ahmad and Raja Ali Haji 1997: 24)

The sayyids come to Buginese Mempawa and Pontianak bearing the precious gift of genealogy, but this gift does not include women or children. The asymmetry, after all, maintains the gift's value and keeps it precious. Only in the unusual circumstances of the twentieth century would others come to discern in the gift a poison.

These events took place in the eighteenth century and contributed to the formation of new, cosmopolitan, Muslim port societies in that period. Muslims who grew up in these places had multiple genealogies, com-

18. These genealogies were living documents, which compilers expected their descendants to extend. Their contents expanded as they passed from hand to hand as gifts and heirlooms. Plucked from their processual existence, such cumulative trails of authors and manuscripts have caused contemporary editors much confusion, as they attempt to fix definitive recensions and argue the relative merits of authors. *The Precious Gift* was begun by Raja Haji Ahmad and completed by his son Raja Ali Haji.

bining Buginese, Malay, and Hadrami ancestry, as we have seen. From the Malay Archipelago across to Malabar, Gujarat, South Arabia, and the Hejaz, they could move with relative ease in social terms. Until the advent of European steam shipping in the last quarter of the nineteenth century, they were also major shipowners in the region, whose interests and activities crisscrossed the oceanic realm.

The nineteenth century was to see this Muslim mobility curtailed. By the end of that century, European dominance in shipping was almost complete. Politically, the Dutch and the English divided the Malay Archipelago between themselves down the Strait of Melaka. The British kept the Malay Peninsula and Singapore, while the Dutch took the rest. The two parties signed this agreement in London in 1824 as part of a global swap of British and Dutch territories after the Napoleonic Wars, and tighter control of the colonial territories soon followed. By the beginning of the twentieth century, European imperial dominance of the sea, combined with the commercial opening of territory to financial investment, resulted in reorientation of Hadrami economic activity away from water onto land. New opportunities there resulted in the arrival of great numbers of Hadramis from the homeland. Many of them were single men who were not sayyid. This novel demographic development in the Hadrami diaspora in the region was to have a profound effect on the relationship between text and social action in the opening decades of the twentieth century. In the changing spirit of the age, people began to think of politics in national terms and to think of religion in ethnic ones. These trends were a result of the colonial fragmenting of the maritime, Malay, Muslim world. They essentially parochialized this world and reduced contacts between its parts, such as those now separated rather than connected by the Strait of Melaka (Ho 2002a).

The Problem of *Kafā'a*

In the early twentieth century, the Netherlands East Indies (NEI, or the Indies) was a vast, diverse archipelago unevenly colonized and on the cusp of a nationalist movement. Here, as a thoroughgoing reimagining and reconstruction of personal and regional political identities were getting under way, local Arab society appeared to withdraw into internally divisive disputes centered on genealogy. The debates seemed narrowly restricted to arcane intra-Arab differences over origins and religious obligations. They consumed a large portion of public Arab energies at a time when Indies Arab society faced other compelling challenges: oppressive colonial policies, heightened economic competition with the Chinese, and Islamic mass movements and other forward-looking initiatives in indigenous circles.[19] Why was this so?

Arabs in the Indies generally originated from Hadramawt. Two broad categories of Hadrami Arabs were recognized in the Indies: sayyids (also sharif and the feminine singular sharīfa), descendants of the prophet Muḥammad; and non-sayyids. The latter were addressed by the honorific *shaykh,* a term of respect connoting religious learning that was categorically applied to them in the Indies, especially in official circles and originated in Indian usage.

Beginning in 1905, a number of marriages between Arab sharīfas and non-sayyid men gained notoriety because they were publicly denounced by the sayyids. One such sharīfa married an Indian Muslim who claimed to be a sayyid, in Singapore; the union was annulled. Opposing *fatwā*s (nonbinding legal opinions given by Muslim jurists) were issued in these cases, giving a sharp, jurisprudential edge to a body of differences that was emerging between the Hadrami sayyids and non-sayyids.

A Singaporean reader of the Cairene journal *al-Manār* posed the following question to its editor, Muḥammad Rashīd Riḍā: "What do you say of the marriage of those who are highborn to those who are not possessed of nobility, even if some of them allege they are Hāshimīs (descendants of the prophet Muḥammad's great-grandfather Hāshim) or Muṭṭalibs (descendants of Hāshim's brother, al-Muṭṭalib) or otherwise of the rest of the Quraysh (the tribe of the prophet Muḥammad)? Would their marriage to the highborn be proper or not?" (al-Bakrī al-Yāfiʿī 1936: 244; Riḍā 1905). Riḍā replied in the affirmative, and this evinced a rejoinder from a Hadrami sayyid, ʿUmar al-ʿAṭṭās, in nearby Sumatra. The rejoinder, in the form of a *fatwā,* highlighted the issue of *kafā'a,* or "sufficiency" of a person as a suitable spouse for a sharīfa:

> Know you that upholding sufficiency *(kafā'a)* in matrimony is a duty. And it is by way of pedigree in four degrees, thusly: First: to be Arab. Non-Arabs are not equal to them. Second: to be of Quraysh. Other Arabs are not equal to them. Third: to be of the Sons of Hāshim. Others among the Quraysh are not their

19. For three decades, the common lament was that Arabs needed to unite their ranks to face external challenges. Part of the problem, of course, was that no single Arab interest or identity existed, as we shall see. John Kelly's *A Politics of Virtue* (1991) addresses a comparable debate in Indian public discourse in colonial Fiji.

equals. Fourth: the descendants of Fāṭima al-Zahrā᾿ (daughter of the Prophet), through her sons Ḥasan and Ḥusayn; others of the Hāshimīs are not their equals.

And the proof is as given in writings such as *The Gift* and *The End,* and the accounts of Muslim, where the Prophet says: "God chose from among the Arabs Kināna, and chose from Kināna Quraysh, and chose from Quraysh the sons of Hāshim." And the *ḥadīth*s which may be found regarding the virtues of the Arabs and Quraysh the descendants of Hāshim are plentiful. As says Ibn Ḥajar in *The Gift* and al-Ramlī in *The End:* "The sons of Fāṭima are not equalled by others from among the descendants of Hāshim, for one of the exceptional things about the Prophet is that the sons of his daughters are his descendants in the matter of *kafā'a* sufficiency in marriage and in other matters, such as perpetual endowment and inheritance. . . . Al-Ḥākim narrates that the Prophet said: "Every son of a mother belongs to a patriline except for the sons of Fāṭima, for I am their guardian and their patriline."

. . . Know you that nobility *(sharaf)* is of two divisions, essential (*dhātī)* and attributional *(ṣifātī)*. The scholars have deemed correct that the essential nobility of the Prophet is linked to his descendants. So, as the Prophetic essence has been set aside for him from all of existence, God has made it a repository for every praiseworthy quality. And it still runs in his folk, the purity within the repository. God has gone to great lengths in the perfection of its purity; as He said: "You have been purified greatly." Not by work do they manufacture it, nor by pious deeds, but by God's pre-existing effort upon them. As such, the effect of the Prophetic emanation *(baḍ'a)* is not known by the greatest of saints who is not of them, even if he expends the greatest effort until eternity.[20] Of this secret, God says: "Say: No reward do I ask of you except the love of those near of kin."

If you were to know this, and I were to clarify for you that the position of the Prophetic essence and its magnitude are not known, and if you know that *kafā'a* amongst the Arabs, and amongst others, is observed, and that its legality agrees with their customs, you would know that marriage with the inferior who is not her equal brings shame upon her agnates, as the scholars have explained. When a sharīfa marries one other than a descendant of the Prophet, the shame is brought upon the standing of the Prophet, and it is proven to you that such insolence is an insult to the Prophet and his descendants.

And what insult is worse than bringing shame, as the Prophet has said: "Whoever offends my family has offended me, and whoever offends me has offended God."

So, it is not permitted that a non-sayyid marry a sharīfa even if she waives the *kafā'a* and consents and her guardian does too, for the right to do so is not theirs.

20. Literally, *baḍ'a* means "part/piece." It originates from several *ḥadīth* in which the Prophet says, "Fāṭima is a part of me."

Nobility of essence is not something they gained which they can give away, but belongs to the Prophet and all the sons of Ḥasan and Ḥusayn, and their consent is inconceivable. (al-Bakrī al-Yāfiʿī 1936: 244)

Whereas the initial unions in question were between Arab sharīfas and non-Arabs, the concept of race itself was subsumed under a scheme for identifying persons that was at once more encompassing and more precise than race: genealogy. As a boundary concept for evaluating suitability in marriage, genealogy went beyond race to erect a whole hierarchy of comparisons. *Kafāʾa* was the operating concept for making these comparisons and dictated their consequences for marriage and group reproduction. Its bald assertion amounted to a theory that ranked different sorts of Muslims. While explicitly based on a genealogical rather than racial concept, it was inevitable that the idea would be seen as a mirror, within the subject Muslim population, of the race hierarchies that organized life under European rule.

The call for *kafāʾa* struck a number of discordant notes. It fell on the ears of émigré Hadrami Arabs, who considered themselves both modern and Muslim and who followed the Egyptian reformists Muḥammad ʿAbduh and Muḥammad Rashīd Riḍā with interest. To them, the image of *Homo hierarchicus* presented in the *fatwā* on *kafāʾa* represented a step in the wrong direction. Egalitarianism in civic life was the counterpart of equality before God. Being self-made, commercial men who profited from intimate association with the indigenous populace, they subscribed to notions of free association and equal opportunity, religious standing through personal piety, success through individual effort, and the possibility of their sons' transforming themselves and their social position through education.[21] This orientation may be seen in a statement by their intellectual spokesman, Aḥmad al-Sūrkatī, a black Sudanese teacher with impeccable credentials from a Meccan education, on the question of *kafāʾa* in marriage:

Verily, most of the people of religions are agreed, without dissent, that the origin of all peoples is one. And that no one is superior to another by the essence of his blood and flesh. Rather, they are superior by virtue of [personal] attributes and deeds and good upbringing. Just like different fruits taken from one tree, they are preferred [one over the other] for sweetness of taste, largeness of size and lack

21. The "pass" and "quarter" regulations that restricted the movement of Foreign Orientals, *vreemde oosterlingen,* and confined their residence to racial ghettos were still in effect at this time (de Jonge 1997).

of rot. So too are people superior by virtue of knowledge and works and moral character.

The seed which is taken from a small tree will produce a large tree possessing great fruit as a result of good cultivation and effort, surpassing its original in sweetness and grace. In like wise, the seed taken from a great big tree of the same type, its fruit will be small, not sweet, and rotten if it is cultivated badly and effort is not expended upon it.

So too is the situation of the sons of Adam, of the son of every great man. For the son of the generous, learned, superior, morally upright man could be doltish, cowardly, vile and corrupt if his upbringing is bad. And the son of one who is idiotic, foolish, vile and cowardly could be generous, brave, excellent, learned and upright if his upbringing is excellent. So, there is no place for conceit on account of descent from one who is generous, learned or one of the Prophets. (Reproduced in al-Bakrī al-Yāfiʿī 1936: 265)

Although the messages of al-ʿAṭṭās and al-Sūrkatī on origin, rank, and value are opposed, they are conveyed in commensurable terms. Al-ʿAṭṭās's formulation of hierarchy in *kafāʾa* draws consequences from connections to different branches of the Prophet's genealogy—the ascendants and descendants that fringe Prophetic irruption and are differentially implicated in its patrilineal transmission. The imagery of branching threw down a discursive challenge that was taken up by al-Sūrkatī, who made the imagery explicit, and contestably so, in the form of a tree. As a living entity whose states of being and products are variable, a tree provides ample cover for arguments that move beyond its nest of stems and branches, an architecture that seems congenitally suited to housing hierarchy. While the arboreal imagery employed by the disputants expressed a genealogical imagination at work, al-Sūrkatī used it to argue against rendering that imagination as inhibition in social and sexual practice. Whether sayyid scholars agreed with his conclusions or not, they would have appreciated his allusion to a line attributed to the Prophet: "I am a tree and Fāṭima is its ovule and ʿAlī its pollen and Ḥasan and Ḥusayn are its fruits and the beloved of my house are its leaves and all of them are in heaven truly truly" (al-Mashhūr 1911:88). This *ḥadīth* had been invoked by the sayyid mufti of Tarim, ʿAbd al-Raḥmān b. Muḥammad al-Mashhūr, to cap his newly composed genealogy of the Hadrami sayyids, *The Luminescent, Encompassing Mid-day Sun,* written in 1890 to help young creole sayyids in the Indies keep faith with their origins (al-Mashhūr 1911: 83; Ho 1997).

The tree refused to go away in broader discussions of the proper relation between Arab origin and religious obligation, revealing the persistence of genealogical habits of mind.[22] In 1918, the Javanese editor of the Islamic newspaper *Oetoesan Islam* admonished the Arab community in an editorial:

> In an article titled 'Manoesia' [Humanity], the place of *bangsa* and *agama* were laid out by using the analogy of a tree and its branches.[23] God, it claims, made many kinds of human beings: Arabs, Dutchmen, Javanese, Bengalis, Chinese and so on. However, as Islam was the greatest *Pokok* [Tree] to emerge from the Arab lands, more than any other bangsa, it was the Arabs' duty to advance Islam: "Because people in any one of those countries are only like the branches of the Arab people. It has become apparent, that because the tree has weakened so have the branches." (Quoted in Mandal 1994: 187)

Sharing in the arboreal imagery, this modernist Javanese view confirmed the genealogical conception of Islamic origins to be one that had struck roots in this part of the world as well. The question was how to prune the tree, conceptually. If Islam emerged from among the Arabs, it also emerged from a very small branch of that people, indeed from one individual. The revelation received by that individual, and the example of his life, constitute the legal and spiritual source guide for Muslims. The religion, and its Prophet, had plenty to say about family life, including that of his own family.[24] Al-ʿAṭṭās's *fatwā* drew on many of the Prophet's sayings to form an opinion on a matter that involved a member of that family. The sayings which he chose, the specific selection of *ḥadīth,* themselves constituted a composite tradition: that of the Hadrami sayyids, who had

22. Preceding and informing the Hadrami canon, such habits of mind are old in Islamic history and traceable in its historiography. The nexus of Arab identity and religious duty is expressed by the founder of a school of Islamic law, Aḥmad b. Ḥanbal: "To love the Arabs is belief *(īmān)*, and to hate the Arabs is hypocrisy *(nifāq)*" (Donner 1998: 110). While genealogical forms of legitimation long predated Islam, the construction of a total Arab genealogy and the elaboration of a whole genealogical literature were novel, and they implied religious duty from the outset: "Subject peoples . . . did challenge the legitimacy of rule by the 'rude' Arabian conquerors . . . this resentment emerged in literary form during the second century A.H. as the Shuʿūbīya movement. The development of the Arab genealogical literature was, in a sense, a counterpart or response to this . . . their rule was legitimate because, as the people to whom the Prophet had been sent and in whose language the Qurʾān had been revealed, they were the rightful heirs of the Prophet, whose mission was, after all, universal" (Donner 1998: 109).

23. *Bangsa* means "race," and *agama* means "religion." See Milner (1992) for a discussion of the term *bangsa,* which in this period was less determinate than its current sense of race.

24. Madelung's *Succession to Muhammad* (1997) discusses the Prophet's family in unusual detail.

evolved a missionary, diasporic discourse oriented toward genealogy as telos. In *The Irrigating Fount,* al-Shillī had assembled many of those *ḥadīth* in a focused narrative which now stood as a canonical text that fused genealogical with religious purpose.[25] The text had only recently been published and printed, in Cairo in 1901, four years before the debate on *kafā'a* erupted in the Malay Archipelago (al-Shillī 1901). It became an active participant in the debate. Al-ʿAṭṭās drew copiously from it in his *fatwā*; a few examples follow.

Al-Shillī's text was especially authoritative because it "pruned the tree" with legal instruments honed in *ḥadīth* disputation. Selection of individual *ḥadīth*s is one primary mode of such disputation, as we have noted earlier. If one wanted to take al-Shillī's position on *kafā'a* in a debate, the supporting Prophetic quotations were readily available in his book. Of the Prophet's ascendants from among the Arabs, "God chose from the offspring of Abraham Ismāʿīl;[26] and chose from the Sons of Ismāʿīl the Sons of Kināna; and chose from the Sons of Kināna Quraysh; and chose from Quraysh the Sons of Hāshim; and chose me from the Sons of Hāshim" (al-Shillī 1982: 30). In al-ʿAṭṭās's *fatwā* above, "God chose from among the Arabs Kināna, and chose from Kināna Quraysh, and chose from Quraysh the sons of Hāshim."

The Prophet had no male issue yet is the eponymous ancestor of a patriline: "Every son of a mother has a patriline except the two sons of Fāṭima, for I am their guardian and their patriline" (al-Shillī 1982: 42). In al-ʿAṭṭās's *fatwā*, "Every son of a mother belongs to a patriline except for the sons of Fāṭima, for I am their guardian and their patriline."

The transmission of Prophetic precedence—whether one conceived it as light, essence, substance, or Prophetic bequest—followed the customary patrilineal channels described by Islamic law on common matters such as perpetual endowments and inheritance: "Our colleagues have said that one of the exceptional things about the Prophet is that the sons of his daughters are descended from him, a true and efficacious descent, in this world and the next. . . . this has been considered to apply in legal judgments such as perpetual trust, inheritance and *kafā'a* sufficiency in marriage. Thus a non-sayyid Hāshimī does not suffice a Sharīfa [in marriage]" (al-Shillī 1982: 48). In al-ʿAṭṭās's *fatwā*, "The sons of Fāṭima are

25. For comparative views on other social purposes of genealogy, see Bloch 1983, Messick 1989, Shryock 1997, R. T. Smith 1988, and Valeri 1990.

26. In this phrase, Arab genealogy meets its Jewish sibling, with the Arabs descending from Ishmael and the Jews descending from his half-brother Isaac.

not equalled by others from among the descendants of Hāshim, for one of the exceptional things about the Prophet is that the sons of his daughters are his descendants in the matter of *kafā'a* sufficiency in marriage and in other matters, such as perpetual endowment and inheritance."

And finally, the Prophet said the following on the significance of indecorous behavior toward his descendants: "Whoever offends my family has offended me, and whoever offends me has offended God the Exalted" (al-Shillī 1982: 25). This *ḥadīth* is reproduced in al-ʿAṭṭās's *fatwā*, "Whoever offends my family has offended me, and whoever offends me has offended God."

The canonical status of al-Shillī's *The Irrigating Fount* is perhaps best attested to by those who were wont to oppose the sayyids: they studied and quoted from it.[27] I have met such persons, now old men, who partook in the disputes; they know the book well. Al-Bakrī's anti-sayyid *Political History of Hadramawt* ends his short account of their settling in Hadramawt with an attack on al-Shillī's text:

> The ʿAlawīs consolidated their position . . . and got people to believe in their spiritual power and authority, striking deep roots in the Hadrami folk. Some of them began building cupolas to their dead (God have Mercy on them), and enjoined people to sanctify those graves and seek intercession through them, and make sacrifices and give votive offerings at the graves. Thus the Hadramis sanctified the Bā ʿAlawīs, living and dead, and sought blessings from them . . . seeking the dispelling of sickness, forgiveness of sins, protection against mishaps . . .
>
> Not only that, they began authoring works which poisoned the minds of people with superstitious stories and priestly prayers, at the forefront of which was the book *The Irrigating Fount*. They were not satisfied with just this, but wanted to possess and rule, and played important roles in politics. We will deal with this later. (al-Bakrī al-Yāfiʿī 1956: 78)

In 1914, the Islamic Association for Reform and Guidance (Jamʿiyyat al-Iṣlāh wa-l-Irshād al-Islāmiyya; henceforth, Irshādīs) was formed to oppose the sayyids, and to establish schools and newspapers.[28] Al-Bakri was an early graduate of one of these schools, taught in them, and furthered his education in Cairo. The sayyids later formed their own association, The ʿAlawī Bond (al-Rābiṭa al-ʿAlawīyya; henceforth, ʿAlawīs). Through

27. These quotations appear, complete with page citations to *The Irrigating Fount,* in memoranda from anti-sayyids to colonial authorities. The memoranda are collected in colonial files documenting Arab political movements in the region, such as the IORL, R/20/A series.

28. For a perspective that emphasizes education over polemic, see Mobini-Kesheh 1999.

their schools, newspapers, and representations to colonial and international Islamic authorities, the two organizations campaigned bitterly against each other until the Second World War. In small compass, this was how the conflict between sayyids and non-sayyid Hadrami Arabs in the Indies began and proceeded. Scholarly accounts of the debate (Bujra 1967; Knysh 1997; Noer 1973) have generally taken it to be another instance of a struggle between a tradition-minded elite and a modern reformist movement. This view is close to those of contemporary onlookers, such as Hadji Agus Salim, a leading figure:

> The feeling of the Irsjad people toward the discriminatory claim of the Ba ʿAlwi is in fact similar to that of the Indonesians vis-à-vis the Dutch government which refers to any Dutchman as mijnheer (i.e. Mr.) or mevrouw (i.e. Mrs.) and to the Indonesian just as inlander (i.e. native). . . . The present existing differences between Al-Irsjad and the Ba ʿAlwi can therefore be likened to the struggle between aristocracy and democracy. The attitude of Al-Irsjad is quite in agreement with Islam, with nature and with the change of time. (Noer 1973)

The argument has even been taken a step further: some scholars view this conflict as a class conflict, between a feudal class and a rising bourgeoisie, and thus believe that it set the stage for the subsequent socialist revolution in South Yemen half a century later (Dāʾūd and Bā Ṣurra 1989).

If the struggle was indeed between aristocracy and democracy, between past and present, a number of questions arise: in what way did the sayyids constitute an aristocracy and their opponents constitute democrats? Were the sayyids aristocrats in the polyethnic colonies of the NEI, where they were subject to onerous restrictions? Were they aristocrats abroad in the same way that they were in the homeland? What were they trying to conserve? Why did similar struggles not take place in the homeland and elsewhere in the Hadrami diaspora, such as East Africa?

Differential Geographies: Creole Worlds in Nation-States

The Arab debate over *kafāʾa* in turn-of-the-century Indies appeared restricted to a narrow segment of colonial society. Yet between Singapore, Cairo, Palembang, and Java, it arose in the context of an expansive geography in which different colonial regimes, systems of law, religious authorities, cohorts of elites, and generations of immigrants—in essence, different sorts of societies—were brought into argument with one another. What made that coming together possible was the novel medium of print journalism.[29] What made it compelling was the ascendance, in these scattered locales, of one conspicuous elite possessed of its own, older technology for traversing distance and duration: the genealogy of the Hadrami sayyids. While the new arena of print journalism created a common public sphere that made debate possible, the disputes arose because of differences between Hadrami genealogical practices in Malay and Javanese locales.

As in the case of Mempawa, Hadrami sayyids such as the Four Youths were potential catalysts in connecting provincial Malay port towns with the larger networks of the Indian Ocean. That potential was commonly imagined in the form of a genealogy with religious luminescence. At the beginning of the twentieth century, the transnational space inhabited by this genealogy was governed by another diasporic power: the British empire. British officials, priding themselves on the art of ruling in someone else's name, left Malay sultans with sovereignty over "custom" and "religion" and promptly proceeded to refashion these spheres in their own image. They built an administration for the supervision of religious practice (Roff 1998; Yegar 1979), and Hadrami sayyids were well positioned to man these stations.[30]

When the Singapore Muslim wrote to Riḍā in Cairo in 1905 on the question of *kafā'a,* he sought to avoid a social and legal establishment that stood ready to make good on its rulings.[31] He wrote from a place where a public debate on the issue could not take root. *Kafā'a* was normal practice in Malay areas where creole sayyids were preeminent, as we have seen. Singapore was one such place. Local-born creole sayyids had overwhelming numerical majorities in these areas, as the Malay Towns section of figure 16 demonstrates, and sex ratios were close to one, so the restrictions of *kafā'a* posed neither social nor ideological problems.

29. Some scholars have compiled names of Arabic newspapers from the early twentieth century (Mobini-Kesheh 1996; Roff 1972; al-Zayn 1995), and innovative studies based on them are emerging (Haikal 1987; Ibrahim 1985; Mandal 1994). See the works of Benedict Anderson (1991) and Eickelman and Piscatori (1996) on the roles of print capitalism in such contexts.

30. See Mohammad Redzuan's article (Mohammad Redzuan Othman 1997) for a discussion complete with names and locales throughout British Malaya.

31. Although Hadrami sayyids were prominent as judges and advisors, they were subject to the British legal system like everyone else except the sultans. In an intriguing case, the controversial sayyid scholar and merchant Muḥammad b. ʿAqīl stood in the dock (Roff 2002).

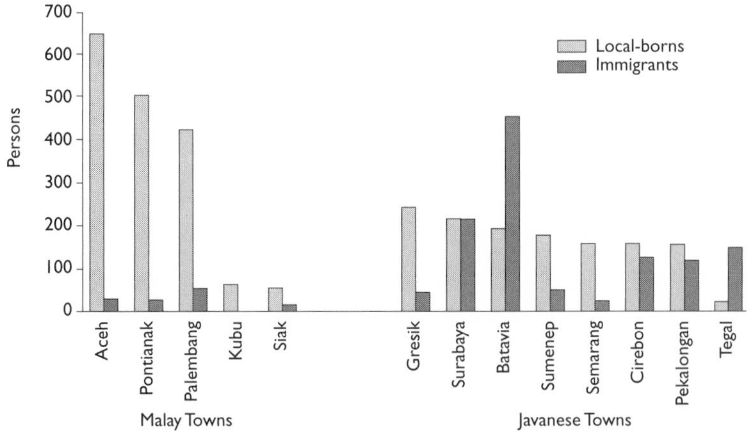

FIGURE 16. Ratios of local-born to immigrant male Hadramis in the Netherlands East Indies, 1886. Numbers from van den Berg 1989: 68–69.

Java was where *kafā'a* became a strenuously contested issue.[32] From the last quarter of the nineteenth century on, a dramatic upsurge of European and Asian immigration into Southeast Asia saw the arrival there of Hadramis who were not sayyids. Most of them took up residence in the booming commercial towns on the north coast of Java. In new centers such as Batavia and Tegal they formed the majority, while in the better-established towns of Surabaya and Cirebon their numbers were balanced by those of local-born creoles, the majority of whom were sayyids. Only in fading settlements like Gresik and Sumenep did the latter retain a majority. Male-to-female sex ratios within the census category of Arab reached five to one in immigrant centers like Tegal, and were still two to one in medial towns like Cirebon. It was in the uneven demographic landscape of Arab settlement in Java (see Javanese Towns in figure 16), where creoles and immigrants dominated different locales and a large number of non-sayyid male Arab immigrants arrived single, that *kafā'a* in marriage proved to be irksome and invidious.

Unlike the early sayyid immigrants, who eased into indigenous soci-

32. My understanding of the complex dynamics of Indies Arab identity in this era has been opened up by the dissertation of Sumit Mandal (1994). Mandal argues that a distinct Arab identity precipitated out of hybridity in this era, as part of a larger movement of racialization in the colonial polity.

ety at privileged levels, these new arrivals entered local society as petty peddlers in an era dominated by big capital and as third-class immigrants in a newly racializing colonial society. Upon arrival, they were directed to Arab ghettos within urban centers. From there, they fanned out into the Javanese countryside as itinerant peddlers, working lines of credit spooling out of financial capitals. Because they were the spearhead of monetary expansion into the interior—because they walked circuits linking financial centers with agricultural hinterlands—and were accountable to its strict time structure of demands, Javanese peasants soon came to view them as exploitative opportunists.[33] Hitherto, images of Arabs had been inextricably interwoven with near-mythical accounts of the establishment of Islam on Java by warrior-saints. From the clashing of swords to the clamor of creditors, Javanese stereotypes of Arabs devolved from local culture heroes to petty foreign exploiters.

The debasement of Arab coin must have been keenly felt in sayyid circles, as the sayyids came to be rejected as spouses by Javanese aristocrats and were sought out by nouveau riche climbers instead. While these developments contributed to incipient tensions between sayyids and non-sayyids, the roots of the full-blown conflicts over *kafā'a* and genealogy lie in their divergent responses to the racializing trend of late-colonial Java.

Hybrid but Separate: Creole Continuity

In the liberal era of private capital, colonial authorities came under the scrutiny of metropolitan constituencies and applied themselves as caretakers of native society with new gusto. Restrictions on "Foreign Orientals" became more oppressive, and creole Arabs and Chinese constantly petitioned to change their legal status to "Native" (inlander).[34] Even as

33. The commodification of Javanese agricultural production began in earnest only in the third decade of the nineteenth century, under Van den Bosch's "cultivation system." The system relied on local feudal extraction of agricultural products for sale as commodities abroad to realize monopsony profits for the Dutch state (Multatuli 1982 [1876]). As monetary exchanges were meant to be only a marginal portion of peasant production (in theory) and income (in practice), peasants quickly became ensnared in debt as itinerant Arab (and Chinese) peddlers introduced opportunities for consuming on credit. The damage such dealings did to Arab reputations was immense (Hurgronje 1906; Mukherjee 1995; van den Berg 1989).

34. Concerned as the Dutch were with physically policing these racial boundaries, their policy made no distinctions between creole, local-born Dutch, Arab, or Chinese persons, on the one hand, and the fresh immigrant, on the other (although population censuses

official racism increased, unprecedented numbers of immigrants arrived; among the Dutch and Chinese, unprecedented proportions of them were women. These new arrivals formed the bases of newly self-sustaining communities of pure ("totok") Dutch and Chinese, as distinct from creoles ("peranakan"). Creole Dutch society had been in retreat throughout the nineteenth century, as the metropolitan center reasserted control.[35] Local-born creoles were put at a disadvantage as Dutch education became more important in employment. Postings in the colonies became sojourns that began and ended in the homeland. The dismantling of creole Chinese power came later and more abruptly, when the opium farms—massive economic and political concerns dominating Javanese Chinese society—were taken out of their hands in the last decade of the century (Rush 1990; Skinner 1996). In this period, however, wealthy creole Arabs were coming into their own, converting large landholdings into income-generating housing stock. Their financial clout enabled them to support important Javanese initiatives, such as Tirtoadisoerjo's pioneering journal, *Medan Prijaji* (Mandal 1994: 169).

Racialization at home in the Indies and nationalism abroad meant that Foreign Orientals in the colonies played up their links with "national homelands" to local advantage. Japanese were granted European status in the last decade of the century, in recognition of Japan's new international standing. Creole Chinese, who were Malayophonic and read no Chinese, began educating themselves in the Confucian classics by reading Dutch sinologists (Kwee 1969). Denied education by the Dutch, they formed their own schools with examiners coming from China, and these schools inspired Arabs to do likewise. Chinese reform meant doing away with customs the Chinese had learned in the Indies from their native grandmothers, such as visiting graves of Muslim saints. In Arab circles, links were cultivated with the Ottomans, in the belief that Sultan ʿAbd al-Ḥamīd II's pan-Islamic efforts would give them leverage in the European colonies (Mandal 1997). However, this association with a rather dis-

---

were aware of the distinction). This blind spot is glaring, as the distinction between local-born and immigrant was basic to all three communities; they even shared the same euphemism for the raw immigrant: *sinkheh,* the Chinese word, which literally means "new guest" in its Hokkien form; Hokkiens formed the historical core of creole Chinese society. The word was common in Eurasian Indo circles and is used in Hadramawt even today as a pejorative of endearment.

35. The process by which creole Dutch practices and aesthetics became a source of shame rather than pride can be seen through the fine eye of Jean Taylor (1983).

tant overlord was neither rewarding politically nor satisfying spiritually. Unlike other immigrants, Arabs did not yet have a race-based national movement to identify with,[36] and they did not have women from the homeland challenging creole accommodations.[37] These may be reasons why the pervasive late-colonial themes of race and nation—and the position of women in it all—were transposed into a distinctly religious key in Arab circles.

The obverse of strengthened links with "national homelands" was cultural critiques of immigrant groups by their respective custodians. Indeed, all emergent ethnic/regional groupings in the NEI and British Malaya, indigenous as well as immigrant, were subject to such critiques.[38] Creoles in polyethnic, commercial, colonial—"Westernizing"—towns in the coastal Straits Settlements and North Java were all taken to task by standard-bearers of cultural purity for their hybrid manners in speech and dress. Creole Arabs were subjected to such critiques from Palembang and Hadramawt; Malays, from Riau; the Dutch, from Holland; the Chinese, from Batavia and China; and the Javanese, from Solo and Yogyakarta. Everywhere, late-colonial polyethnic empires were molting to reveal nation-states growing within, and each person sought his or her own cover.

In the context of creole responses to nationalist mobilizations, the ʿAlawī and Irshādī positions on *kafāʾa* can be seen as two different defenses of hybridity drawing on two different loci of historical experience in the archipelago. Insisting on *kafāʾa,* ʿAlawīs understood hybridity as creolization, in which both hierarchy and difference were structurally

36. In the Middle East, the distinct possibility was in the air that sharifians might have a big role to play once the Ottomans had been dismembered by the European powers. This role could amount to national leadership of "the Arabs" ringed within their peninsula, as British policy through the eyes of a T. E. Lawrence would have it, or to leadership of the entire Muslim world, which was a more commodious dream of personalities as diverse as the Cairene reformer Muḥammad Rashīd Riḍā, Sharif Ḥusayn of Mecca, Imam Yaḥyā of Yemen, and Sayyid Muḥammad bin ʿAqīl, the controversial, itinerant Hadrami proponent of a Shia sharifian cause. That dream survives on the national airwaves of the Hashemite Kingdom of Jordan, pushing fitfully beyond its narrow *pied à terre.*

37. Immigrant European women came into a situation that was already racially charged, and as individuals, they drew their own conclusions. From the perspective of plantation Sumatra a few decades later, Ann Laura Stoler (1989) argues that they cannot be saddled with the blame of importing racist attitudes; the timing bears her out. An exception must be made of the wife of Stamford Raffles; Olivia, first lady of Batavian society at the beginning of the nineteenth century, viewed her creole sisters in native dress with contempt.

38. Migrations within the archipelago played an important role in the formation of a new Indonesian national consciousness (B. Anderson 1991). A suggestive alternate pregeography to Indonesian nationalism, located in the wider Muslim world, has been put forward by Michael Laffan (2003).

maintained in asymmetrical marriage exchanges. Genealogy provided a sublime form of identity that could hold both pure Prophetic essence and creole human substance without contradiction. Opposed to *kafā'a*, Irshādīs opted instead for a model of hybridity that assimilated all Muslims into an ethnically and genealogically neutral melting pot, religiously conceived in accordance with the oft-quoted Qur'anic shibboleth "We have made you peoples and tribes that you may know one another; truly, the most noble of you by God are the most devout" (49:13).[39]

39. The opposition of genealogical origin and individual piety as bases of mundane status within a religious community is a fundamental issue in the genesis of Islam (Donner 1998, ch. 3). The matter sharpened over leadership of the post-Prophetic Islamic community. The range of opinion can be described schematically and schismatically: Khārijīs rejected social origin for piety; Sunnīs espoused leadership of a member of the Prophet's tribe, the Quraysh; and Shī'īs would only accept leadership by a descendant of the Prophet. In Donner's judgment, "All that really mattered in determining a person's standing, in the Qur'ān's view, was his Belief and pious action. Its rejection of genealogical legitimation was thus complete and virtually absolute" (Donner 1998: 106). Madelung, arguing from a reading of the same Book, concludes otherwise: "The Qur'ān advises the faithful to settle some matters by consultation, but not the succession to prophets. That, according to the Qur'ān, is settled by divine election, and God usually chooses their successors, whether they become prophets or not, from their own kin" (Madelung 1997: 17). God knows what He means, but the quarreling twins of devoutness and descent remain the state of the art today.

CONCLUSION TO PART II

Local Cosmopolitans

In this second part of our study, "Genealogical Travel," we have followed the travels of Hadramis abroad through their texts. These texts focus mainly on the Hadrami sayyids, combining their genealogies with other textual genres such as mysticism, history, and law. As genealogies, they are, at base, collections of names. The Hadrami canon that evolved in the diaspora thus articulated a universalizing narrative of Prophetic mission in a language of names. As we have seen, these names circulated through many lines of descent and many territories across the Indian Ocean. Their genealogies represent mobile and expansive naming practices that construct an asymmetrical relation between a transregional social entity—the Hadrami diaspora—and local ones—the Muslim populations of port towns. Names become a medium in which exchanges between parties are given value, or nominalized, and boundaries between them are redrawn. As chapter 5 shows, the genealogies of the Hadrami diaspora are traveling texts that enable persons to travel transculturally.

Such transcultural travel transforms persons. Throughout the diaspora, the names given to offspring draw from a relatively small and constant stock that is recognizably and typically Hadrami. As well, religious affiliation remains constant. Other attributes, however—such as phenotype, mother tongue, and cuisine—change. At the point of articulation between transregional and local social entities, creole communities and networks are created through marriage relations between migrant Hadrami men and local women. Here, names are again at play, now not as narratives of origin but of alliance, usurpation, and gift giving. Genealogies can also act as gifts, as we saw in chapter 6. Such gifts accompany Hadramis' marriages with local women abroad in the diaspora. Through such marriages, Hadramis and their offspring became Swahilis, Gujaratis, Malabaris, Malay, Buginese, Javanese, and Filipinos. They became natives everywhere. The depth and breadth of this indigenization has even given rise to new genres of texts, encyclopedic works attempting to track the spread: massive genealogies (al-Mashhūr 1984), a four-volume compendium of diasporic families (Bā Maṭraf 1984), a five-volume one of poets (al-Saqqāf 1984). Such works have risen to the challenge presented by diasporic natives, many of whom remained itinerant across the oceanic space, for reasons of trade, study, family, pilgrimage, and politics. Throughout this space, a Hadrami could travel and stay with relatives, who might be Arab uncles married to foreign, local aunties. Many men had wives in each port. With frequent divorces and marriages, an individual man often had, over time, children from more than the four wives allowed him at a single moment by religious law. When husbands were absent (absences as long as decades were common), wives of Hadramis often lived with their fathers and patrilineal kin. The uxorilocal marriage traditions across the Indian Ocean—in Swahili East Africa, the South Arabian coast, the southwest Malabar coast of India, and West Sumatra—enabled the creation of dispersed families, with half-siblings, offspring of the same father, living in separate countries and speaking different languages. In the arc of coasts around the Indian Ocean, then, a skein of networks arose in which people socialized with distant foreigners as kinsmen and as Muslims. The Hadrami diaspora brought together hitherto-separated peoples in single families and in a single religion. In each place, members of such families were both locals and cosmopolitans.

As naming practices and as gifts, genealogies incorporate both universal religious values and particular kinship relations. In providing collective representations for both realms, Hadrami genealogies are not only linear instruments that point back to origins. They have evolved to become, in theory and in practice, complex languages of cosmopolitanism in which the foreign and the local negotiate coexistence in vital ways. This negotiation is ongoing today in numerous places. Throughout the Indian Ocean world, the genealogies underwrite the existence of persons whom I call local cosmopolitans.

As we have seen in cases from India and Southeast Asia, such local cosmopolitans progressed from being religious adepts in sixteenth-century Gujarat to rulers of states in the Malay world of the eighteenth century. Other places—such as Muslim Mindanao during the fifteenth century, the Comoros Islands in East Africa during the seventeenth century, and

Perlis in Malaya from the twentieth century until the present—have had Hadrami sultans. By virtue of a rotating election of sultans, the Raja of Perlis, Tuanku Syed Sirajudin of the Jamal al-Layl line of Hadrami sayyids, is today the King of Malaysia (Yang diPertuan Agung). As king, this descendant of the Arab prophet Muḥammad stands as the symbolic constitutional guarantor of the territorial sovereignty of Malays over the country. In less exalted but more mobile positions, Hadrami sayyids have recently served as foreign ministers of Indonesia, such as Ali Alatas and Alwi Shihab; Syed Hamid Albar continues to serve as their counterpart in Malaysia, at the time of this writing. Having names that circulate beyond nations, local cosmopolitans are able to remain comfortably within many of them.

In the opening chapter of this book, we introduced the idea of the grave as a dense object that combines the elements of place, person, name, and text. The grave is a semiotic complex that enacts a passage from silence to vocalization. This initial motion begins a dynamic of signification that launches the dead and silent person within the earth into discourse. The local cosmopolitans who populate the Hadrami diaspora around the Indian Ocean participate in this field of signification and contribute to its dynamism. The diaspora multiplied tremendously the numbers of persons and texts, and the range of places they circulated through. Canonical works such as those of ʿAbd al-Qādir al-ʾAydarūs and al-Shillī articulated discourses of mobility that recruited the many new persons and places of the diaspora into a dynamic of signification whose initial moment is located at the grave. While the tombs of the founders of the ʿAlawī Way in Tarim initiate this dynamic, the graves of their descendants in numerous places across the ocean reproduce and expand the process, creating new origins for new migrants in new destinations to return to. In this way, new communities of local cosmopolitans were created in the Indian Ocean over centuries. Such communities were in communication and aware of one another's existence, even if they did not often see each other. By the late nineteenth century, the discourses of mobility that coursed through this society of the absent had created a stable if virtual moral geography that, by its own lights, cast a religious cover of universal proportions over a world of different places and peoples.

That stability was not to last, however. As the twentieth century began, new discourses of religion centered on places like Cairo were to become very mobile as well. *Al-Manār,* the reformist journal edited by Muḥammad Rashīd Riḍā in Cairo, was avidly read on the Islamic frontiers of the Middle East, in places like Yemen, India, the Dutch East Indies, and British Malaya (al-ʿAmrī 1987). It had columns devoted to questions and answers from readers in these places. The Hadrami debate over *kafāʾa* in colonial Southeast Asia had been sparked by such a column. Participation by diasporic Hadramis in this new, international public sphere of print journalism revealed the existence of geographical visions alternative to that of the canonical sayyid ʿAlawī Way. In the debates pursued in the pages of *al-Manār* and the Arab journals it inspired in colonial Southeast Asia, a relativization of geographical consciousness began to emerge. In canonical discourse, a return to Hadramawt was a return to ancestral origins, a pilgrimage. But there were always many reasons for returns, and these reasons were not always represented in canonical discourse.

Canonical texts have their limitations. To understand these texts and their limitations, we have to extend our analysis beyond them, to other texts and to the terrain of field ethnography. In doing so, we gain a different view of the geography of diaspora. Mobility may be considered in terms of deliberate movements projected ahead, as trajectories with specific directions and intentions. Such trajectories are projects. The concluding part of this study of mobility looks at movements to the diasporic homeland as projects of return. Pilgrimage is a project, and there are others as well.

PART THREE

Returns

CHAPTER 7

Return as Pilgrimage

In downtown Singapore, ten minutes' walk toward the sea from the gleaming, golden skyscrapers of the ministry of finance and the central bank, lies the grave of the Hadrami sayyid Ḥabīb Nūḥ al-Ḥabshī. The building that houses the grave is shaped more like a Hindu *chandi* than a Muslim saint's tomb; it is a rectangular structure rising many dozens of steps above the ground. The tomb within is covered by the green cloth of Islam and surrounded by golden yellow drapes, the color of Malay royalty. Pilgrims and supplicants from all ethnic groups—Malays, Hadrami Arabs, Chinese, and especially Indians—come to visit and sit quietly a while. On the walls are framed genealogies, pointing to Ḥabīb Nūḥ's siblings in Penang, Singapore's predecessor port city at the northern end of the Strait of Melaka, and to ascendants in Hadramawt. The line from Singapore to Penang reaches west to other port cities, which, until two generations ago, were Crown Colonies of Britain's empire of free trade: Colombo, Bombay, and Aden. Along this old trunk route of world trade, and along the smaller branches that feed into it, are older ports settled by Hadramis and housing tombs like Ḥabīb Nūḥ's. Indeed, we can visualize the diaspora of Hadramis as a distribution of graves across the Indian Ocean.

Yet the diversity of the visitors to these graves, as at Ḥabīb Nūḥ's in Singapore, mean that this diaspora cannot be understood in singular ethnic terms. Not all pilgrims come seeking their ancestors or origins. Like the British diaspora, which in its incarnation as an imperial power proclaimed its protection of free trade and the law for all comers in the nineteenth century, leading Hadrami figures often stood for causes larger than

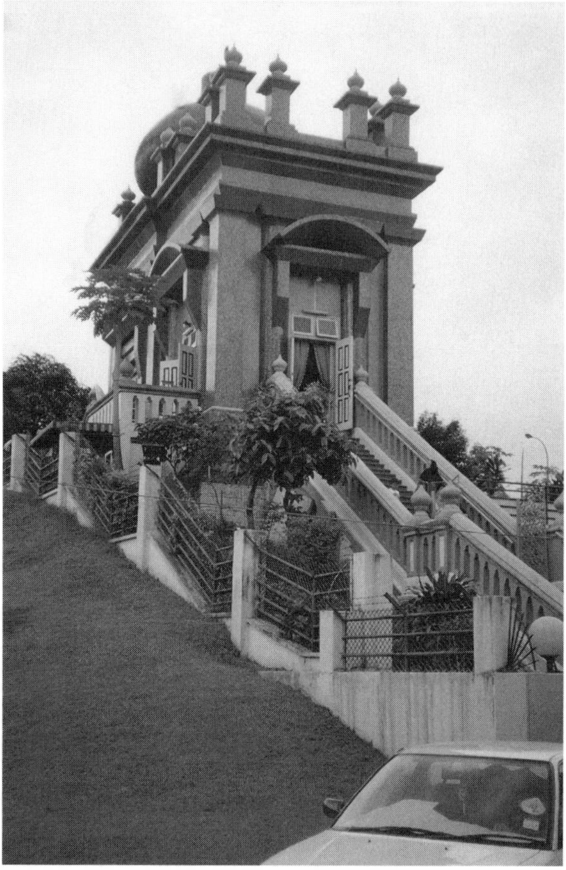

FIGURE 17. Steps to Ḥabīb Nūḥ al-Ḥabshī's Indian-style shrine, Singapore. Photo by the author.

those of their own communities. Liberal state and universal religion come together in one corner of Ḥabīb Nūḥ's tomb, where the Singapore government has placed a locked steel safe with a slot to receive the votive offerings of pilgrims in publicly accountable fashion. Many parties participate, and distribution has to be fair. The port cities of the Indian Ocean were such plural societies. In chapter 4, we saw the sayyid Zayn al-ʿAydarūs leading Surat in prayer at the easing of a naval blockade that had gripped the entire city in crisis. In chapter 5, we saw how the traveling genealogies of the Hadrami sayyids had to bear the universal Light of Islamic prophethood and lent mystical shape to ecumenical Islamic society ex-

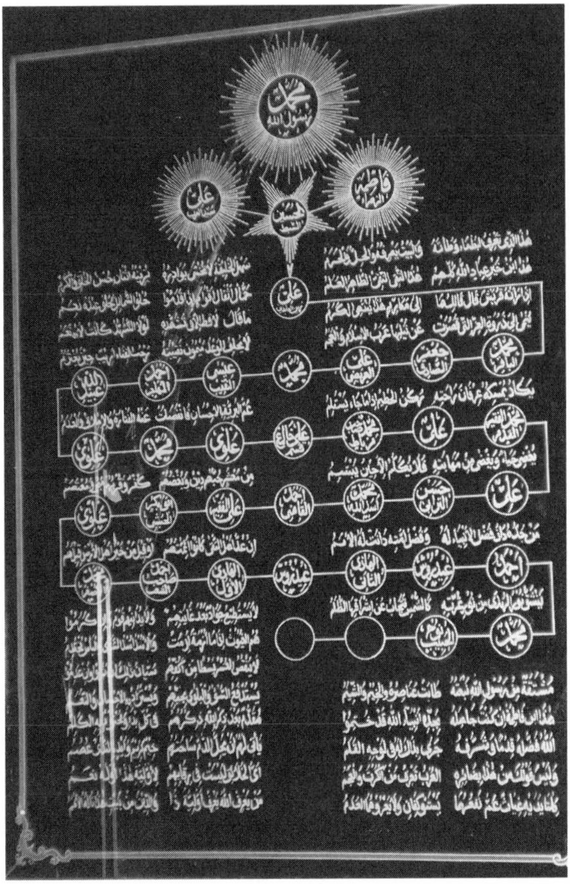

FIGURE 18. Lineal genealogy beside the tomb of Ḥabīb Nūḥ al-Ḥabshī, linking him to ascendants in Hadramawt and to Prophet Muḥammad. Photo by the author.

panding across the Indian Ocean. And in chapter 6, those genealogies became intertwined with Bugis and Malay ones, in moral exchanges that created creole communities and transcultural families. As the diaspora moved, the genealogies evolved.

Those genealogies have two important dimensions: while they enable the tracing of origins, they also allow communities of diverse origins to articulate with each other in new relations of mutuality and moral engagement, such as in shared family and shared religion. This duality involves cohabitation of closed and open aspects, or, in the more specific terms of kinship, of patrilineal and matrilateral ties. Gender asymmetry is central to this cohabitation, as we saw in chapter 6: holding the two sides together successfully turns on controlling women's choices in marriage. The theory to support such control appeared in canonical texts written abroad, such as al-Shillī's legally inflected genealogy/biography, *The Irrigating Fount*. At stake in this duality of closedness and openness was not a static tension but a dynamic of signification, which maintained discursive control over an expanding sphere of exchange rather than reject or throttle it. A diaspora, in this sense, provides characteristic ways of marking the movements of individuals, of presiding over the comings and goings of numerous persons across space, time, and culture.

Our examination of the evolving canon in diaspora noted a shift from figural to literal genealogies, embodied in the difference between ʿAbd al-Qādir al-ʿAydarūs's mystical *The Travelling Light* and al-Shillī's legalistic *The Irrigating Fount*. The move is again one from openness to closedness, but as the diaspora expands, so does what the enclosure contains. The different literary sensibilities of ʿAbd al-Qādir al-ʿAydarūs and al-Shillī, demonstrated in the way each handles genealogy, color their descriptions of the homeland Tarim as well. Both call for visiting the graves of Tarim, but while ʿAbd al-Qādir al-ʿAydarūs's account is short, mythological, and folkloric (al-ʿAydarūs 1985: 76), al-Shillī's is positivistic, systematic, and prescriptive (al-Shillī 1901: 148–49). In a section devoted to the mosques, cemeteries, hills, and wadis of Tarim, al-Shillī encourages a return to the town by embedding in his description a manual for visiting its graves. He instructs the reader to visit the grave of the First Jurist before anyone else's. He proceeds to detail a list of graves to visit, in less than a page. But his manual then stops abruptly, for he says that those far away will not benefit from his instruction, while those living there could easily find a reliable guide.

Like the diaspora, society in the homeland is also plural, composed of different groups and categories of persons, engaged in relations of exchange. In his book, al-Shillī has a non-sayyid, a Bā Ḥarmī shaykh, say that without first visiting the First Jurist's grave, a pilgrimage is not valid. Just as Hadrami sayyids entered into exchanges with Indians in Surat and Bugis in Pontianak, in the new polities of the diaspora, so too in the homeland did they engage with other townsmen—tribals, farmers, and builders—in relations of exchange. From afar, the density of such exchanges makes them opaque, and al-Shillī abandons his effort at representing them. Furthermore, as we have seen, al-Shillī narrowed the scope of genealogy, refocusing it along the Prophetic patriline and allowing numerous lateral ties to fall away.

In this chapter, we return to Aḥmad al-Junayd, whom we left at the end of chapter 3, and examine this resolute localist's project of place making: restoring the houses, mosques, and graves of the ancestors. As part of that project, al-Junayd also wrote a manual for visiting the graves of Tarim. As one of the reliable locals, like those recommended by al-Shillī, he sought not to provide a description for visitors from far away but to create a text that could guide pilgrims in and around those graves. The text was a manual, a guide to proper action, and was part of his project to make Tarim a place of return. Here, we see genealogy acquiring a bending power, curving the journeys of persons back to the graves of Tarim. That power builds on the genealogical canon that developed in the diaspora, even borrowing from and extending the manual that al-Shillī had begun but abandoned. Al-Junayd's manual makes return a performance of pilgrimage to the graves of Tarim. As we have come to expect from al-Junayd, the stakes are large. After all, he wanted his brother back from Singapore for good. The poetics of pilgrimage brings together people who, in the course of the return, become a community. It concretizes such a community in a visit to the grave, in which the living call out the names of the dead, following the manual, and exchange greetings with them. As a place where mobile texts and mobile persons meet, the grave becomes a site where the resolute localist finds much work to be done and meaning to be invested. Considering al-Shillī's emphasis on the closed aspect of genealogy, what seems surprising here is that in the heart of the homeland, at the graves of Tarim, the open aspect of genealogy gains prominence again, in al-Junayd's manual. This prominence is less surprising if we recall that Hadramawt was initially a destination, rather than an origin, for the sayyids. In his concern with revivifying the traces of the ancestors, al-Junayd preserves something of that sense of Tarim as a diasporic destination. As we have seen in the travels of part I, much transcultural work needs to be done in the diaspora. It turns out that the same is true of the homeland as well, for within it, native status, *aṣāla,* is endlessly relative, layered, and deferred. In al-Junayd's manual for visiting the graves of Tarim, that transcultural work is again of a genealogical sort but now in a different, performative register: genealogy becomes pilgrimage. In pilgrimage, genealogy opens up the graveyard by expanding its space into an itinerary of ritual stations, and thereby increases its interpretive possibilities. Recognition of that interpretive amplification sensitizes one to the social complexities of the homeland

and reveals it to be no less plural and complex than the diaspora, as we shall see.

Visiting the Graves of Tarim

The graveyards of Tarim are three: Zanbal, al-Furayṭ, and Akdar. At the edge of town, just within the old town wall, they lie on either side of a road that is also a wadi bed.[1] The floods, when they come, pass through this major channel to water the gardens surrounding the town. It is well known that the water arrives in seven timed surges over a number of hours, due to the specific distribution of branches feeding this main channel upstream. What is unknowable is whether the rains will come at all. It is along the sides of this artery, by the graves, that men stand during prayers for rain *(ṣalāt al-istisqā')*, led by religious leaders of the town. In 1993 and 1994, they said such prayers during an extended drought. People say that such prayers will not work if men's hearts are not clean, if they harbor ill will toward each other. The prayers enjoin the townsfolk to concentrate not on what divides them but on what they have in common. The location of the prayer for rains is apt for this purpose. The gathering of the living is reflected in the society of the dead beside them. The men praying for water all have ancestors here who share the earth waiting for eternal relief. The two societies meet and mingle on such portentous occasions, and do so regularly. Every Friday, some individuals visit the graves. Every year, on the fourteenth of the month of Shaʿbān, after the largest annual pilgrimage, to the tomb of the prophet Hūd, visits are organized to the graves of Tarim, and visitors place sweet-scented basil at the headstones. As with prayer, such visits have leaders who head, guide, and chant. These leaders are normally the preeminent sayyid scholars of Tarim. The itinerary and liturgy of such visits among the ancestral remains trace out specific ways in which dead and living, sayyid and non-sayyid, relate to one another in one grave society, one town, one religion, and one history.

A number of manuals for the visit have been written and are incorporated into the diasporic texts, as we have seen(al-ʿAydarūs 1985; al-Ḥaddād n.d.; al-Shillī 1982; Kharid 1985). But the most popular one in use today is the *Salve for the Sickly in Organizing Visits to Tarim's Ceme-*

1. This layout is illustrated in von Wissman's early 1:25,000 map of Tarim (Van der Meulen 1932, jacket insert).

tery,[2] which Aḥmad al-Junayd wrote in the nineteenth century out of concern for the traces of the ancestors. It exists in many manuscript recensions produced for personal use. One version that I consulted had a colophon indicating that the owner was licensed in its use by a teacher.[3] While such authentications of transmission are common, in this case the evidence of transmission is crucial to the nature of the text. By itself, the volume is of no use. One needs a guide who has prior knowledge of the graveyard and who will walk the visitor through both text and cemetery, pointing to the referents on the ground. Without such a guide, entering the graveyard with the manual is like coming upon a strange town with a map consisting only of an alphabetical list of street names. Aḥmad al-Junayd was urged by his contemporaries to write the manual because he had frequently accompanied his teacher the sayyid ʿAbd al-Raḥmān b. ʿAbd Allāh Bā Faraj around the graveyards of Tarim and had been shown the graves of the famous pious. When the teacher died, al-Junayd's community wanted to preserve his great knowledge of the tombs. Aḥmad was able to write down that knowledge and to pass it on as a guided tour. In this sense, the knowledge exists in the inseparable conjunction of teacher and text and is reproduced as a performance in real space and time—as educational tourism in the city of the dead. Some of the tombs had multiple inhabitants, and Aḥmad pointed them out as well. The cemetery provides another reason for thinking of knowledge as personal contact and for representing it in genealogical form. Let us now consider the knowledge that is inculcated through the itinerary of the text. We follow the recension of ʿAbd al-Raḥmān al-Mashhūr, whose abridgment of his teacher Aḥmad al-Junayd's *Salve* is the version commonly used. This recension, the *Gift of the Generous Intimate for Visiting Tarim's Saints,* is the slimmer version that is hand-copied and taken round the tour.[4]

The manual begins with a direct prescription:

It behooves the visitor to begin at (the grave of) the First of the cemetery, our master the First Jurist, and say: Greetings to you, Oh Saints of God! Greetings to you, Oh Best of God! Greetings to you, Oh Elect of God! Greetings and the mercy of God be upon you! . . . Greetings to you, Oh Folk of the Graves, may

2. The manual's Arabic title is *Marham al-saqīm fī tartīb ziyārat turbat Tarīm* (al-Junayd n.d.).

3. The license is an *ijāza*.

4. The Arabic title of this version is *Minḥat al-ʿazīz al-karīm fī ziyārat awliyāʾ Tarīm* (al-Mashhūr n.d.).

you receive what you have been promised, and God willing we will follow. We ask God for us and for you health.[5] Oh God, make enter among them spirit from you and greetings from us. Greetings to you, Oh Folk of "There is no god but God"[6] (repeated a number of times with variation). . . . Greetings to you, our brothers of the Muslims and the believers. May God bless you, the ancient and the recent . . . tame your wildnesses . . . be merciful to your absence . . . record your virtues . . . forgive your transgressions . . .

The visit to the graves is opened at the first station, the grave of the First Jurist *(al-Faqīh al-Muqaddam)* Muḥammad b. ʿAlī. We met him in chapter 2. He is the unique first point where Prophetic descent and organized Sufism come together in Hadramawt. The scholarly etymologies agree that the attribution of precedence in his title refers directly to his position as the first figure in the graveyard to be visited on such occasions. Yet the sense of the "Paramount Jurist" is buttressed by his other title, the Greatest Teacher *(al-Ustādh al-Aʿẓam),* and underscores his orthodoxy, as an exponent of religious law. This stamp is important because of the First Jurist's hand in introducing Sufism to Hadramawt; the law and Sufism have often been pitted against each other in Islamic history (al-Ḥibshī 1976; Memon 1976). The First Jurist received the investiture (*taḥkīm)* from a courier dispatched by the Maghrebian saint of Telemcen, Abū Madyan Shuʿayb, in the thirteenth century; on his shoulders was placed the mantle *(khirqa*) of Abū Madyan. His contemporary al-Shaykh Saʿīd bin ʿĪsā al-ʿAmūdī, of Dawʿan at the western end of Hadramawt, also received the investiture of Abū Madyan. Opinions differ about whether the First Jurist or al-ʿAmūdī first received the investiture directly from the courier and passed it on to the other. The First Jurist was the first to denounce violence and the use of arms, breaking his sword over his knee. This action inaugurates the sayyid tradition of pacifist Sufism and became a major plank in sayyids' self-identification as independent arbiters of the peace between armed tribes. Al-ʿAmūdī himself is visited in a popular annual pilgrimage, but his descendants carry arms and ruled parts of the western end of the wadi intermittently over centuries.[7]

5. This line, and part of the preceding one, are *ḥadīth,* which the Prophet reportedly taught his followers to say when they went to the cemeteries (Ibn Taymiyya 1998: 176–77).

6. This line—"*Lā ilāha illā Allāh*"—is part of the Muslim declaration of faith.

7. Rivalry between the al-ʿAmūdīs and the sayyids is a theme that runs through Hadrami history until the twentieth century. The issue goes beyond the scope of this book, but a skeletal account would include al-ʿAmūdī's alliance with the northern Qāsimī imams in the eighteenth century and with Irshādīs in the twentieth.

The descent line of the Hadrami sayyids begins to branch at the First Jurist. Most sayyid descendants are his progeny, while a small minority revert to his father's brother, who is known as the "Uncle of the Jurist (*ʿAmm al-Faqīh*). Significantly, visits to the graves of Tarim begin with the grave of the First Jurist rather than with that of his great-grandfather ʿAlī the Endower of Qasam (d. 1135 C.E.), who was the first sayyid buried in Tarim. While genealogical descent is one ordering modality of a visit to the graves, the Sufi complex initiated by the First Jurist organizes the orthopraxy of religion itself in Hadramawt. Visits to the graves are thus also construed as visits by Sufi initiates to their masters. In this sense, a visit is merely an extension of calls made to teachers for instruction while they were alive and is an affirmation of the perduring pedagogical relation. Correspondingly, the "First" to be visited is also the "Greatest Teacher." Indeed, as we will see in the next chapter, pilgrimages to the tombs of saints are combined with and assimilated into visits with living scholars, in return journeys of creoles to the homeland. The educational tourism of the visit to Tarim's graves is one moment in an ongoing didactic process of ambitious proportions. This school began with the First Jurist (d. 1255), eight generations or three hundred years after the advent of his ancestor Aḥmad b. ʿĪsā the Migrant (d. 956) in Hadramawt, the first sayyid to settle there and arguably the progenitor of the largest Hadrami tribe.

At the First Jurist's grave, the visit opens with two exchanges between the living and the dead. All of the living, regardless of social affiliation, stand in one rank, as a moiety facing all of the dead, as their opposite. First is the exchange of greetings. The greetings to the dead are a call for their presence. The question of whether they reply is the subject of much discussion; the old texts are replete with instances in which they do. Second is the repetition of the first line of the Muslim declaration of faith, "There is no god but God" *(Lā ilāha illā Allāh)*, as a gift to the souls of the departed. The declaration is named by the onomatopoeia *tahlīl*, and its repetition bestows merit upon the dead. Pious, wealthy Hadramis leave trusts in their wills specifically for the annual performance of the *tahlīl*, for the sake of their own souls, and as gifts to their deceased relatives, followers, servants, and slaves. The endowment pays for the coffee and incense used on such occasions. The arrangement is one pious act that endures after death—a pious son praying for one's soul, as the Prophet said.

At the cemetery, the dead are accorded powers in various degrees, typically thaumaturgic in nature: thus the title of Aḥmad al-Junayd's manual, *Salve for the Sickly.* The hagiographies of many of those lying in this graveyard reveal that requests asked of them will be answered, and in the course of the visit, requests are made. In parallel with the pedagogical ambition, the visit is also one moment in an ongoing process of votive exchanges that brings together living and dead in a relation of supplicant to saint.

The pedagogical and votive aims of the visit are pursued within a poetic structure whose performance is scripted in the manual. The iterative process of its movement enables us to highlight the formal elements of that structure by way of a summary. The linear motion of the ritual through written and performed time is marked at various points by paradigmatic figures, of whom the first and the prototype is the prophet Muḥammad. The plots where these figures lie buried or are invoked are the major stations of the visit; between them are minor ones. These figures are surrounded by associates, followers, and dependents in a circle, as it were. Across the historical and performative times that separate them, the major figures are brought into paradigmatic consociation by ritual invocations shared only by them. These utterances create a resonance between the figures, raising them above the smaller individuals who surround and separate them and creating landmarks on the ritual terrain. Between these landmark figures, movement takes on a linear appearance. In the early part of the text, the progress is genealogical, chain-linking fathers and sons in a single, unbroken, vertical line of patrilineal descent. Subsequent parts abandon the genealogical line, and the linearity takes form in corporeal movement on the ground, as visitors move down rows of graves, enfilading laterally. In this phase, successive stations in the textual itinerary are guided by locations on the ground. Here, the order of the sequence does not imply generational or hierarchical precedence but is simply an accident of burial location. Each station, however, reiterates both the linear and circular elements in the form of mini-genealogies and collateral lines of the residents of the plots, and through evocation of an orbit of kinsmen, associates, teachers, and followers. In the course of the visit, visitors may invoke individuals a number of times by name, as they are emplaced in related genealogies and overlapping clusters of associations. Repetition of their names within different groups reinforces familiarity and creates a sense of sociability among the dead. The overall effect is of an imbricated series of spirals, formed by the liturgical dynamic of vertical, circular, and lateral elements. The resulting movement of bodies, voices, and minds across the graveyard, analogous to that of a slow-moving tornado, if an image is desired, actualizes a commingling of persons and groups, dead and alive, in the shared time and space of the visit to the graveyard. Visitors come to meet persons, and at their resting places, greet them and theirs by name. Together, the living and the dead are referred to as "the folk of this noble presencing *(ḥaḍra)*."[8] The virtual collectivity enacted is not an amorphous amalgam; it is constituted in relations of generational precedence, hierarchical rank, filiation and agnation, tutelage, attachment, service, sepulchral distance, and so on.

The tombs of the ancestors are metonyms of relics that are consubstantial with them. Positioned on the earth of the grave, visitors stand in the presence of those they visit, in enfleurage, by a tactile logic of contiguity expressed in ʿAbd Allāh al-ʿAydarūs's formulation: "their places are directly in contact with their clothes; their clothes cover their bodies; their bodies clothe their souls, and their souls adorn the presence of their God . . . the fragrance of souls we find in their clothes" (al-Ḥaddād n.d.: 71). The graveyard is a reliquary of the traces of the ancestors, which Aḥmad al-Junayd's choreography in his manual brings alive for the moving reciter. The number of names in the manual runs in the hundreds, and with classificatory extensions added, its scope is infinite: the family of so-and-so, root and branch; the family's neighbors; the folk of Jerusalem; all the scholars; all the saints; all Muslims. Even people not buried in Tarim can be incorporated. The poetic structure organizes them in a coherent fashion that, with familiarity, can even be memorized. This is less difficult than at first blush, as the organizing categories, families, and even individuals are already known from everyday social life, and from the regular rituals that texture it.

Recalling the pedagogical and votive aims of the visit, the manual has, coordinate with the form, messages conveyed in its contents. Two things predominate in the contents: history, and a cure. The history is of the arrival of the prophet Muḥammad's mission in Hadramawt and its deposition in Tarim, specifically in Tarim's preeminent graveyard, Zanbal, the resting place of the Prophet's descendants. Their tombstones stand erect as witnesses, marks in the engraving of that history. They make the mission locally present and available to the folk of Tarim, if they seek it. What is available is a cure for this world and the next, salve and salvation. One takes in the history with the cure.

Like the canonical texts we have read in their diasporic contexts, the contents of this history are shaped by the form of their presentation. The

8. On *ḥaḍra,* see chapter 2.

TABLE 2. Who's Who: Engraving History

Year of Death	Name	Significance
622	**I. Prophet Muḥammad**	Prophet of Islam, ancestor of all sayyids
	Prophet Hūd and other prophets	
956	Aḥmad b. ʿĪsā the Migrant	Founding ancestor of sayyid line in Hadramawt
	ʿAlawī b. ʿUbayd Allāh	Eponymous ancestor of all Hadrami sayyids
1135	ʿAlī Endower of Qasam	First sayyid buried in Tarim; founder of Qasam town near Tarim and investor in its productive date palms
1161	Muḥammad Principal of Mirbāṭ	The ancestor in whom all Hadrami sayyid genealogical ascent lines meet
1255	**II. The First Jurist**	Initiator of sayyid, Sufi ʿAlawī Way
1416	**III. ʿAbd al-Raḥmān al-Saqqāf**	Originator of ritual forms that mark the beginning of the institutionalized ʿAlawī Sufi complex
1430	**IV. ʿUmar al-Muḥḍār**	Originator of geographical form (sanctified landscape); first leader of a formal sayyid association
1451	Muḥammad b. ʿAlī Kharid	Author of first major sayyid genealogy
1461	ʿAbd Allāh al-ʿAydarūs	"Sultan of Notables"; progenitor of al-ʿAydarūs lineage, the lineage most famous abroad and with the greatest number of sovereign settlements at home
1490	al-Shaykh ʿAlī b. Abī Bakr al-Sakrān	First sayyid author of biographies
1513	Abū Bakr al-ʿAydarūs the Adeni	Saint of Aden; founder of first translocation of the sayyid Sufi complex outside Tarim

Year of Death	Name	Significance
1561	Aḥmad b. Ḥusayn al-ʿAydarūs	Founder of the first sovereign settlement under a sayyid (*manṣab*ates)
	\	
1584	Shaykh Bū Bakr bin Sālim	Founder of the ʿAynāt *manṣab*ate; reorganized Hūd pilgrimage. Father of al-Ḥusayn, who brought Yāfiʿī mercenaries to repel the northern Qāsimī imams
	\	
1720	**V. ʿAbd Allāh al-Ḥaddād**	Distinguished saint of Tarim and author of widely used books and liturgies
	\	
	Ḥasan Ṣāliḥ al-Baḥr	Associate of the three men below who repelled Yāfiʿīs from Hadramawt
	Ṭāhir b. Ḥusayn bin Ṭāhir	The only person to attempt to establish a sayyid state (imamate) with arms
	ʿAbd Allāh b. Ḥusayn Bilfaqīh	One of "the Seven ʿAbd Allāhs"
1858	Aḥmad b. ʿAlī al-Junayd	Author of the manual for visiting the Tarim graveyard, *Salve for the Sickly*
	\	
1902	ʿAbd al-Raḥmān al-Mashhūr	Author of an abridged version of al-Junayd's manual; author of the "total" sayyid genealogy *The Luminescent, Encompassing Mid-day Sun*

NOTE: The central column contains names invoked in al-Mashhūr's liturgy *Gift of the Generous Intimate for Visiting the Tombs of Tarim's Saints.* The grave of the First Jurist (II) is the first station of the visit to the graves. Here, visitors read the Fātiḥa chapter of the Qurʾan for the souls of the people in this table. The names numbered I to V are ritually elevated in the liturgy. I have added information that does not appear in the manual: the year of death and the person's historical significance. Vertical lines between names denote unbroken genealogical progression, whereas slashes indicate jumps in the genealogy, moving sideways to collateral lines and downward to descendants.

pilgrimage itself is the message. As such, our reading of that history is compelled to follow the paths traced around the graves of Tarim by al-Junayd's incantatory text, and by the pilgrims who lend its written words their bodies and voices. Let us see how form and content inform each other along the way.

Who's Who: Engraving History

At the grave of the First Jurist, al-Junayd's manual says to sit and recite the Yāsīn verse from the Qur'an and the opening verse, the *Fātiḥa,* while leaving open the choice of other verses. After this recitation, the prayer for the Prophet, the *taṣliyya* of presencing, is enjoined. The *Fātiḥa* is then read for three major groups: first, prophets and descendants of the prophet Muḥammad, in chronological order down to the early twentieth century; second, the shaykhly lineages of Hadramawt, families that have some historical religious fame and standing but are not descended from the Prophet; third, a global Muslim community comprising the founders of legal schools in Islamic law, famous Sufi figures, and others.

The order of the three *Fātiḥa*s at the first station initiates the spiral patterns that are subsequently recapitulated at each unit station. There is an emphatic vertical axis—a lineal genealogy—surrounded by a circle of followers. At the first station, the axis is the line of the prophet Muḥammad (first *Fātiḥa*), followed by the circle of local followers (second *Fātiḥa*) and then the maximal circle of the global community of Muslims (third *Fātiḥa*). This order also anticipates the overall sequence of the entire visit. First, the visit works its way through the cemetery of the sayyids, Zanbal; then it moves on to that of the shaykhs, al-Furayṭ; and in closing, it invokes all Muslims in a grand finale of benedictions. Considered within the total poetic structure of the visit, then, the three *Fātiḥa*s of the first station are a part that can stand for the whole, a synecdoche for the cadaveral and living body of Muslims of Tarim and the world, headed by the prophet Muḥammad and his descendants. At this signal point, within the poetic representation is the content of a history lesson, a message elaborated in detail. We have seen something of this message in chapter 2, in the formation of the ʿAlawī Way in the homeland and the routes thereto. Here we pick up that thread again, now on its own narrative terms and its preferred stage, the graves of Tarim. Table 2 highlights the key personages in the discussion to follow.

The First Fātiḥa

> First, the Fātiḥa for his Presence our Sayyid (master) the Prophet of God Muḥammad son of 'Abd Allāh, God's prayers be upon him, and upon the Prophet of God Hūd, and all the Prophets and Messengers all of them, and upon their companions and followers until the Day of Reckoning.

The first *Fātiḥa* opens with Prophet Muḥammad (I in table 2) and Prophet Hūd. It mentions the first four caliphs after Muḥammad, as well as members of his family: his daughter Fāṭima and her sons Ḥasan and Ḥusayn, his wives Khadīja and 'Ā'isha, his uncles 'Abbās and Hamza, and 'Abbās's son 'Abd Allāh. Broader categories—of Prophet Muḥammad's wives, descendants, all scholars, and all saints—are invoked. The litany then moves in a direct unilinear progression of the sons of Ḥusayn (Muḥammad's grandson) until Aḥmad b. 'Īsā the Migrant, the ancestor of all Hadrami sayyids. The parsimonious chain-linking of his descent from Ḥusayn, without collaterals, asserts the truth and force of his extraction. Reaching the Migrant in the progression recalls his circle of brothers, sons, and grandsons. The descent lines of his sons and grandsons went extinct except for that of the grandson 'Alawī b. 'Ubayd Allāh, the eponymous ancestor of the sayyids of Hadramawt. Thus, this lineage group is also known as the Folk of Father 'Alawī *(Āl Bā 'Alawī)*, or 'Alawīs *('Alawīyyūn)*.

Past 'Alawī, the genealogical recitation proceeds with no break to 'Alī the Endower of Qasam. As we have seen, 'Alī the Endower reputedly founded the settlement of Qasam by investing 20,000 dinārs in planting date palms, bringing value to the land. The Endower of Qasam is the first sayyid to be buried in Tarim, and his burial initiated their presence there. Historically, he stands for the settlement of the sayyids in Tarim. The Endower's son is known as Muḥammad Principal of Mirbāṭ, a town on the Indian Ocean coast, where he is buried. All living Hadrami sayyids are descendants of Muḥammad the Principal of Mirbāṭ; their lines of ascent meet in him.

The domiciling of the sayyids in Hadramawt took three centuries from the time of the Migrant's arrival, finally being fixed only with the First Jurist (II in table 2), the eighth-generation lineal descendant of the Migrant, seventeen generations following the prophet Muḥammad. The manual for visiting the graves scrupulously recounts all the generations from the Prophet to the First Jurist with no omissions, until it reaches Abū Bakr al-'Aydarūs the Adeni (see table 2).

Four generations past the First Jurist, his lineal descendant ʿAbd al-Raḥmān al-Saqqāf (III in table 2) is the next major figure in the litany. He stands at the beginning of a new phase in the history of the ʿAlawī Way: the development of an institutional complex of Sufi practices, comprising ritual, geographical, and textual elements. Al-Saqqāf initiated rituals still practiced today. His son, ʿUmar al-Muḥḍār (IV in table 2) is linked to significant places on the ritual landscape: Umar's Rock, the first station at the pilgrimage to the prophet Hūd's tomb, by the perpetual stream; and al-Muḥḍār's mosque, where the fasting month of Ramaḍān is brought to conclusion.

Another figure, ʿAbd al-Raḥmān al-Khaṭīb (d. 1451), appears a number of times in the manual, though he is not represented in table 2. We have met him in chapter 2, as the author of the *Garden of the Heart Essences, Apothecary for Incurable Maladies* (subsequently renamed the *Transparent Essence*), the foundational compilation of Hadrami Sufi biographies upon which subsequent canonical authors, such as ʿAbd al-Qādir al-ʿAydarūs and al-Shillī, drew copiously. While al-Khaṭīb was not a sayyid, his text, along with al-Muḥḍār's places and al-Saqqāf's rituals, brought together the institutional complex of the ʿAlawī Way in the mid-fifteenth century.

A cluster of significant figures in the manual is the ʿAydarūses, some of whom we have met. ʿAbd Allāh al-ʿAydarūs, a grandson of al-Saqqāf who was raised by his uncle al-Muḥḍār, appears as the Sultan of Notables in the manual. He was nicknamed al-ʿAydarūs by his grandfather and fostered the lineage of that name, which became famous away from Tarim, in surrounding regions and in Aden, India, and elsewhere. The Saint of Aden, Abū Bakr al-ʿAydarūs the Adeni, is called out here, as is Aḥmad b. Ḥusayn al-ʿAydarūs (d. 1561), who founded the first settlement in Hadramawt under a form of sayyid sovereign rule *(manṣab)*, while his brothers prospered in India. A number of *manṣab*ates subsequently developed around Tarim under the leadership of other ʿAydarūses, in plantation settlements such as Thibī, Būr, Tāriba, and al-Ḥazm that were funded by remittances from India. This usage of the term *manṣab* is not found elsewhere in the Arabic-speaking world and may be an adoption of Indian usage. As a result of these linked expansions abroad and at home, the ʿAydarūs family became the grandest of the sayyid lineages. The family's eponymous ancestor ʿAbd Allāh al-ʿAydarūs, father of the Adeni, is thus invoked with the honorific Sultan of Notables in the graveyard manual.

Other major figures in the manual have similar transregional presences. Shaykh Bū Bakr bin Sālim, who appears in table 2 after the ʿAydarūses, is not buried in Tarim, like the Adeni. From the family base at ʿAynāt, a town forty minutes today by car from Tarim, the lineage of Shaykh Bū Bakr has had a transregional presence beyond Hadramawt since the late sixteenth century. In 1584, Shaykh Bū Bakr deputed ʿAlī Harhara, one of his students, to the region of Yāfiʿ near Aden to spread the ʿAlawī Way. Links between Shaykh Bū Bakr and the Yāfiʿīs have been strong since then, in a relation of spiritual clientage. In the seventeenth century, the Shaykh Bū Bakrs obtained Yāfiʿī assistance in expelling the northern Zaydi Qāsimī occupiers from Hadramawt; this was achieved in 1704. Besides creating alliances with the Yāfiʿīs, Shaykh Bū Bakr's son al-Ḥusayn was famous for his campaign against tobacco, as we saw in chapter 3. Abroad, Muslim sultans in the Comoro Islands in East Africa belonged to branch lineages of Shaykh Bū Bakr, as does the Raja of Perlis, who is now (2005) King of Malaysia. Before the advent of socialism in South Yemen, the Shaykh Bū Bakr lineage maintained an open kitchen as a public institution to host visitors and celebrate calendrical events. The family received annual votive offerings of coffee from the Yāfiʿīs and money from endowments in India for the upkeep of the kitchen. Shaykh Bū Bakr himself composed various litanies and Sufi works, as well as specific traditions that are practiced in Hadramawt today. For instance, he initiated the tradition of praying the five obligatory prayers all at once after noon on the last Friday of the fasting month of Ramaḍān. Shaykh Bū Bakr first started this tradition within his own family, but as his reputation grew, the practice spread, and people came from towns such as Sayʾūn, Tarim, and Qasam for these special prayers at ʿAynāt.[9]

A more purely religious figure, ʿAbd Allāh al-Ḥaddād (V in table 2) was a relatively late saint of Tarim, living through the occupation of the northern Qāsimī imams; he died in 1720, a decade and a half after their expulsion. He was blind from an early age and is well known for his writings, which were among the first Hadrami printed texts (al-Ḥaddād 1876, 1891, 1895, 1927) and are today translated into Malay (al-Ḥaddād 1981, 1995 [1985]; Al-Husaini 1999), English (al-Ḥaddad 1991; al-Ḥaddad 1992), and French (al-Ḥaddād 2002, 2004).

The last major grouping of sayyids invoked at the first *Fātiḥa* in the manual are the associates of Aḥmad al-Junayd, from the late eighteenth and early nineteenth centuries. They were united in expelling the Yāfiʿīs from Hadramawt, who were associated with Shaykh Bū Bakr and came

9. These prayers are referred to as the "five obligations," *khamsa furūḍ*. The practice is not based on the primary sources of Islamic law, and a parallel is drawn to the Prophet's extra-Qurʾanic pronouncements *(ḥadīth)* by naming the practice *Sunnat al Walī,* or Tradition of the Saint.

to dominate the region in the century after the expulsion of the Qāsimīs (bin Hāshim 1948; al-Kindī 1991; al-Mashhūr 1984: 229 ff.). Ṭāhir b. Ḥusayn b. Ṭāhir issued a call to arms and declared himself imam, the leader of an Islamic state. He drew, though not explicitly, on the northern, Zaydi model of a religiously guided descendant of the Prophet unsheathing his sword in a stand against oppression and injustice (Zayd 1981). The move broke with the pacifist tradition of his ancestor the First Jurist and was controversial. The experiment was short-lived, and Ṭāhir subsequently removed to the coast at al-Shiḥr, where he was an exile of sorts. His brother ʿAbd Allāh was one of seven scholarly contemporaries all named ʿAbd Allāh, who supported Ṭāhir. They came to be called the Seven ʿAbd Allāhs; ʿAbd Allāh b. Ḥusayn's grave at al-Masīla near Tarīm is visited annually. As an outgrowth of their histories, the lineages of Shaykh Bū Bakr of ʿAynāt and the bin Yaḥyās (of whom the Ṭāhirs are a branch) of al-Masīla are the only sayyids who are recognized as arms bearing.

The first *Fātiḥa* ends with the names of Aḥmad al-Junayd and his student ʿAbd al-Raḥmān al-Mashhūr, respectively the author and popularizer of the manual itself. Unlike the graves it visits, the manual is not a relic. Rather, like the genealogy within it, the text is a living process that develops and grows. In writing and editing it, al-Junayd and al-Mashhūr created a vehicle for their own perpetuation, as ancestors. In the end, they themselves were inducted into the liturgical genealogy by subsequent manuscript copyists of the manual.

As this account of the first *Fātiḥa* indicates, the names chanted in what at first blush appears to be a genealogical liturgy move seamlessly between religious and historical registers as well. At the grave of the First Jurist, and beginning with the prophet Muḥammad himself, these names of a Prophetic genealogy trace out known geographies and histories, abroad and at home, down to recent times, finally including the manual's authors, and their associates, at the end of the nineteenth century. They had created a political movement to rid Tarim of the Yāfiʿī interlopers who caused Aḥmad al-Junayd such misery and ultimately caused his brother ʿUmar to disavow returning to Tarim for good, choosing the security of Singapore instead.

The Second Fātiḥa

At the end of the first *Fātiḥa,* which is for the ʿAlawīs, the liturgy invokes recitations for a class of persons collectively known as *shaykhs*. *Shaykh* is a generic term in Arabic meaning "chief, elder, leader"; in the Sufistic context of Hadrami social history, it functions as an honorific, connoting a teacher and mentor to an initiate. Unlike the first *Fātiḥa,* the second has no overarching ordering principle such as genealogy or chronology. Rather, it is a list of religious notables, the majority of whom are considered indigenous to Hadramawt. These notables came from South Arabian groups that had been famous since pre-Islamic times, such as the tribes of Kinda, Madhḥij, and Banī Hilāl. A few families such as the al-ʿAmūdīs trace clandestine histories emerging in glorious origins, such as descent from ministers of the Abbasid empire (conventionally considered the high-water mark of Islamic civilization), which had to be concealed for fear of pursuit after a defeat. They have family names, like most Hadramis, and the names have a categorical stability spanning the past five hundred years, since at least the sixteenth century. The al-Khaṭībs, for example, have delivered the weekly Friday sermon at the congregational mosque in Tarim from those times until today. In Singapore, the most senior religious authority among Hadramis in recent years was an al-Khaṭīb, Shaykh ʿUmar, until his death in 1998. The word *Khaṭīb* itself means preacher.

Beyond ancient or clandestine origins, the shaykhly families historiographically trace descent to the first ancestor who had religious distinction and fame. ʿAbd al-Raḥmān al-Khaṭīb's *Transparent Essence,* the compendium of Sufi biographies which became the founding text of the sayyid ʿAlawī Way, is the primary source for the ancestral "firsts" of the shaykh families as well. The Bā Faḍls began with Sālim b. Faḍl Bā Faḍl, in the twelfth century (d. 1185). In some accounts, he left Hadramawt at a time when the light of knowledge there was flickering and spent forty years abroad in Iraq studying (al-Ḥāmid 1968: 473). He finally returned with a camel-load of books and revived religious scholarship. He was so successful that in his time, Tarim had three hundred scholars, all students of his and all of them muftis. One of these students was the First Jurist (al-Ḥāmid 1968: 720). Shaykh Sālim b. Faḍl Bā Faḍl heads the liturgy of the shaykhs in the grave manual. The positions of the First Jurist and Shaykh Sālim Bā Faḍl as liturgical heads of their respective cemetery groups in the manual puts them in a relation of equivalence and connection, a notion that purified sayyid genealogical representations, such as those of al-Shillī, lose sight of. In Tarim in the early 1990s, the head of the Jurisprudential Opinions Council *(Majlis al-Iftāʾ)* was a Bā Faḍl: Shaykh Faḍl Bā Faḍl, a legist with a twinkle in his eye who was born in the Dutch East Indies and repatriated to Tarim for schooling as a boy. Another member of this family, Shaykh Ruḥayyim b. ʿAbd Allāh Bā Faḍl, was the teacher and informant of the preeminent British scholar of Hadramawt, R. B. Serjeant. He authored numerous accounts of pilgrimages to sites in the region (Ruḥayyim Bā Faḍl n.d.-a, n.d.-b, n.d.-c, n.d.-d, n.d.-e).

In recorded history, many of the shaykhly families, such as the Bā Marwāns, had religious reputations before the proliferation of sayyid scholars and saints around the fifteenth century. For example, the shaykh ʿAlī b. Aḥmad Bā Marwān was the teacher of the First Jurist, and he became angry when his student broke his sword and took up the mantle of the Maghrebian saint Abū Madyan. He appears early in the *Fātiḥa* for the shaykhs in the manual, as does another teacher of the First Jurist, Muḥammad b. Aḥmad b. Abī al-Ḥubb (Bā Wazīr 1961: 126). The invocation of Bā Marwān and Abī al-Ḥubb at the second *Fātiḥa* foreshadows their positions in the visit. After the visit to Zanbal, the sayyid graveyard, pilgrims are to visit the graveyard of al-Furayṭ, where the shaykhs are buried. Here, the tombs of Bā Faḍl, Bā Marwān, and Abī al-Ḥubb are the first three stations visitors encounter. Engaged in the continuous biographical process of teaching and learning, shaykhs and sayyids are found as teachers and students to each other. Some sources say that Shaykh Sālim Bā Faḍl was a student of the sayyid Muḥammad Principal of Mirbāṭ (al-Ḥāmid 1968: 702; al-Shillī 1982), while others do not (al-Khaṭīb n.d.; Bā Wazīr 1961: 118). Shaykhly families can decline in religious standing if they stop producing scholars of note. The Bā Rashīds are an example. They were known for the Bā Rashīd mosque, one of the oldest in Tarim, which was already standing when the Endower of Qasam and his family of the Prophet's descendants began settling there in 1127. Aḥmad b. Muḥammad Bā Rashīd was a rich man who built five mosques; he was also considered a saint. He is known as the Trader of This World and the Next. The biographies of the early sayyid saints are replete with references to the indigenous shaykhs. The mother of ʿAbd al-Raḥmān al-Saqqāf (who established basic rituals of the ʿAlawī Way; III in table 2) was the daughter of the shaykhly Trader of This World and the Next (al-Ḥāmid 1968: 757). Al-Saqqāf's teacher was another shaykh, Muḥammad b. Abī Bakr Bā ʿAbbād (Bā Wazīr 1961: 134). Another Bā ʿAbbad, ʿAbd Allāh b. Muḥammad, a teacher of the First Jurist, practiced ascesis at the tomb of the prophet Hūd before the sayyids; because of his precedence, his descendants continue to be the custodians of the land of the prophet Hūd's tomb complex today, in association with the bin Kūb Tamīmī bedouin who live in the vicinity. Other shaykhly lineages have always been of lower standing, such as the Bā Ḥarmī and Bā Gharīb lineages. They specialize in teaching children the basics of reading and memorizing the Qur'an.

The Third Fātiḥa

Upon completion of the second *Fātiḥa,* a third is read for the souls of Muslims elsewhere, those not buried in Tarim nor otherwise associated with it. These begin with the founders of the four orthodox schools of Sunni Islam, the jurists al-Shāfiʿī, Malik, Aḥmad, and Abū Ḥanīfa. Next come the luminaries of Sufism, such as Abū Madyan Shuʿayb, ʿAbd al-Qādir al-Jīlānī, and al-Ḥasan al-Shādhilī. Although Abū Madyan is credited with being the master of the First Jurist, his location here reflects the social perspective of the manual and the visit, which gazes out from the locale of Tarim and its spiritual leadership. Positioning the jurists before the Sufis affirms the orthodoxy of the visiting congregation, as does positioning the invocation of Muḥammad al-Ghazālī (d. 1111) after those for both groups; al-Ghazālī is credited with effecting a reconciliation of law and mysticism. In the same vein, the name of Ibn al-ʿArabī is absent, despite his formative historical and doctrinal influence, for he is a controversial figure. Pilgrimages to the graves of Tarim shun controversy; they seek harmony instead.

The third *Fātiḥa* completes the first station of the visit. As a self-contained cycle within the liturgy that models the whole visit, it ends with prayers for the general desiderata:

God raise their rank in heaven and preserve us with their protection and extend to us their assistance and benefit us through their grace in this world and the next, with their eminence and their secrets. God forgive the sins . . . make easy the required, sort out the affairs of the Muslims. Choose for us what's good, in contentment and submission. Grant us success, wherever and to whomever He desires; freedom from all sickness. . . . Give us sustenance as He did the followers of the prophet Muḥammad, grant us the imitation of his deeds, let us be formed by his character, grant us what he gifted to the pious ones. We give thanks to God. May He lengthen our lives in good health; give us sustenance and a believing and obedient wife and good, blessed, pious descendants; a legitimate, healthful, ample livelihood, and complete belief. And make this true for our parents and children and shaykhs and whomever has claims upon us; and whomever leaves us testaments of prayers; and all Muslims. May God grant these prayers, and help the ʿAlawī sayyids and all Muslims, and settle their affairs; may He revivify the signs of religion and the traces of the law of the Lord Messenger, and make the successors follow their pious predecessors, purely for the sake of God. And this through the intercession of the Great Prophet and all the Folk of This Noble Presencing.

At this point, the manual instructs the visitor to gather together his supplications, seek forgiveness, and direct the prayers for the dead. So ends the first station. The manual then moves on to the other stations of the visit, stopping at the graves of those named in the first and second *Fātiḥa*s. A summary of the itinerary has been given in the earlier discussion on the poetic structure of the visit. It remains to note that the manual does not encompass the entire necropolis of Tarim. Only the cemeteries of the sayyids and shaykhs, Zanbal and al-Furayṭ, are visited in the liturgy. The other social categories—tribals and townsmen who are neither sayyids nor shaykhs—are left out of the manual. Their families visit them at the conclusion of the visit prescribed in it. The pedagogical and votive aims of the visit mean that only those who are thought to confer benefit, whose presence counts, are sought out. These are persons who have significance in the view of Hadrami history embedded within the manual.

Despite all that it contains, the manual for visiting the graves of Tarim is a compact volume of a mere forty-five hundred words, approximately. As liturgy, it serves as a mnemonic, an aid to ambulating recitation rather than a text to be studied indoors while sitting still; thus, it is small and portable.[10] Its parsimony belies the richness of its content, which is evoked but not explicated. For that purpose, it relies on other books of reference, which provide exhaustive and detailed elucidation. The manual cites these references by invoking their authors. Al-Khaṭīb, the author of the *Transparent Essence,* for example, is recalled among other al-Khaṭībs, at two stations, as "ʿAbd al-Rahman b. Muhammad, Author of the *Essence.*" Other authors receive mention among their kinsmen and associates. For bibliophiles, within the manual is found a genealogy not only of persons but one of texts as well. In the murmur of citation within recitation, the manual signals its membership within a wider historiographical tradition of Hadrami literature, which encompasses distinct genres of biography, hagiography, chronicle, genealogy, and law. In part II of this book, "Genealogical Travel," we have seen something of how these genres combined to form a distinct, hybrid canon that took shape in the movement of a

10. The difference between vocalized recitation *(qirāʾa)* and silent reading *(iṭṭilāʿ)* in Islamic literary culture is significant; Messick (1993) treats the topic theoretically and ethnographically. Comparative and historical studies attest to the vitality—even primacy—of orality within traditions that seem to be dominated by texts (Graham 1987; Svenbro 1993).

specific, Hadrami diaspora. Yet these genres are general in Arabic/Islamic literature and partake of broader Islamic discourses from which they were never isolated. The specifics of Hadrami lineages and places are always suffused with the more general history and imagery of Islam, and thus retain a vital openness. How the specific and the general coexist in any situation is never obvious but can at moments be perceived if one looks closely or listens carefully.

A Light Like Rain: Graves of Tarim, Gardens of Paradise, Genealogies of Diaspora

In ʿAbd al-Raḥmān al-Khaṭīb's fifteenth-century *Garden of Heart Essences/ Transparent Essence* is an account by a sayyid, ʿAbd Allāh b. Aḥmad b. Abī ʿAlawī, who said:

> In the year I went for the pilgrimage in Mecca, I met some Syrians.[11] We were chatting, and one of them asked me: "Do you know the Red Hill, the one in Tarim?" I told him "Yes." He said: "Our great ones say that it is found in some of the books that under it is one of the gardens of Paradise."[12]

The account connects with another story widely recounted in Tarim, which has the prophet Muḥammad's cousin and son-in-law, ʿAlī b. Abī Ṭālib, asking a man if he was from Hadramawt. When the man replied in the affirmative, ʿAlī said, "In it is the Red Hill." This hill is identified by Hadramis as al-Furayṭ, which overlooks the graveyard of the shaykhs by that name. ʿAlī holds a special position among Yemenis, for he was sent to Yemen by the Prophet to claim their allegiance for the new religion of Islam (Ibn Hishām 1955: 649). ʿAlī is also the progenitor of all the descendants of the prophet Muḥammad, through his marriage to the Prophet's daughter Fāṭima; the Prophet had no surviving male issue. These accounts bring an otherwise obscure corner of the Arabian Peninsula within the sweep of Prophetic history and allow its participation in the cosmic events of Mecca-Medina. They make of the hill of al-Furayṭ in

11. In the hagiography of Prophet Muḥammad, the learned Christian monk Baḥīrā, whom the Meccans encounter on a trading expedition to Syria led by ʿAlī's father, Abū Ṭālib, authenticates the prophethood of Muḥammad. Baḥīrā recognizes the seal of prophethood between Muḥammad's shoulders, as well as other features that correspond to descriptions in his book, a repository of knowledge handed down through generations of monks who lived in his cell (al-Ṭabarī 1988: 44–46).

12. A similar account is attributed to ʿAbd al-Raḥmān al-Saqqāf (al-ʿAydarūs 1985: 76).

Tarim a relic of that history. When wealthy Hadramis die abroad in East Africa, they leave a provision in their wills for importing a tombstone carved from a bit of this hill, with its unmistakable red coloring, from Tarim and erecting it over their graves. In death they will reside under this tombstone and hope that "under it is one of the gardens of Paradise."

In al-Khaṭīb's *Garden* is a subsequent account, by a shaykh, Muḥammad b. ʿAlī al-Zubaydī, of what he saw at the graves of Tarim:

> When I returned from the pilgrimage to Mecca, I came to Tarim to visit its pious ones. So I entered the graveyard of the ʿAlawīs at the time of the Sacrifice. When I was upon it, I saw a light which appeared like rain, descending upon al-Furayṭ, then encircling the graves, and finally encompassing the town.

This image condenses a number of the elements that are brought together in the visit to the graves. Although the graves can be visited at any time, the formal annual visit takes place on the fourteenth of the month of Shaʿbān. This day is two weeks after the twenty-seventh of Rajab, which is celebrated as the day the Prophet made his night journey to Jerusalem and ascended the seven heavens. It also follows immediately upon the return of pilgrims from the annual pilgrimage to the tomb of the prophet Hūd. The people to whom Hūd had been sent did not heed his message, so God sent down great winds which destroyed them (Qur'an 11, Hūd). Two weeks later, the fasting month of Ramaḍān begins, when God first sent down the revelations to His messenger Muḥammad. The organized visit to the graveyards of Tarim thus takes place in a period of intense interaction between sky and earth. Poised between the two, the rituals of this month engage associations already present in Islamic discourse, and draw them together in a directed narrative that is locally performed. As a Semitic religion, Islam is the "sky religion" (*al-dīn al-samāwī*); "Semitic" is a cognate of the Arabic *samāwī,* an adjectival derivative of "sky." Its religious law, the *sharīʿa,* has etymological roots with the sense of "road (leading to water)" (Chittick 1994: 129). Believers who observe its precepts have the chance to reside eternally in paradise, which is described as a garden.

The element that connects the images of sky, water, and garden is rain. In the southern Arabian Peninsula, rain is indisputably the direct, visible source of the flood and well waters on which agriculture depends. If it comes, it is borne on the monsoon winds blowing inland from the Indian Ocean, some time in the summer. The rains embody and are apprehended as a direct, vertical, linear relation between sky and earth. As a flood in the wadi bed, rain expresses its power in the directed linearity of the flow, which washes away everything in its path. It is for rain that Hadramis hold prayers during the pilgrimage to Hūd's tomb.[13] It is also for rain that they hold their prayers by the graveyards of Tarim, beside the main watercourse. Such activities at the sites of tombs activate relations between elements that are nascent in the discursive imagery of Islam.[14] The first biographical anthology of Hadrami sayyids, *The Blaze* (*al-Ghurar,* in reference to the white forehead of a horse), by the sayyid Muḥammad b. ʿAlī Kharid (1985:104), quotes a poem that puts the matter succinctly:

Within al-Furayṭ, Zanbal, Akdar and the watercourse
Innumerable are they
—sufi, saint and jurist—
precepting the waterway[15]

The word I have translated as "precepting" is *sh-r-ʿ*, a root verb whose derivations mean both "to legislate" and "to irrigate," with a more abstract, underlying sense of "to direct." The poem suggests that the Sufis, saints, and jurists buried in the cemeteries of al-Furayṭ, Zanbal, and Akdar have the power to make water flow in the waterway. This power is that of the rainmaker. Who is the rainmaker? Al-Khaṭīb's *Garden* suggests the answer in a number of ways. The rain falls on al-Furayṭ, which is the location of the cemetery of the shaykhs, above one of the gardens of paradise; the shaykhs were already there when the sayyids arrived in Tarim. It is the shaykhs who draw water from the sky and circulate it around the town. The person who perceived the light as rain falling on al-Furayṭ is a shaykh.

Yet the imagery of light, and of Abrahamic sacrifice linked to Jerusalem

13. The question of whether rain descends on the tombs of prophets is much discussed in the polemical literature. Ibn Taymiyya recounts that ʿĀʾisha, Prophet Muḥammad's favorite wife, once exposed his grave so that rain might fall, but to no avail, even though God's mercy does descend upon his grave, in Ibn Taymiyya's opinion (Ibn Taymiyya 1998: 197).

14. For example, in the chapter "The Heights" (al-Aʿrāf) of the Qurʾan, the following line appears eight lines before mention of the prophets Hūd and Ṣāliḥ, who are associated with Hadramawt: "It is He Who sendeth the Winds like heralds of glad tidings, going before His Mercy: when they have carried the heavy-laden clouds, We drive them to a land that is dead, make rain to descend thereon, and produce every kind of harvest therewith, thus shall We raise up the dead: perchance ye may remember (Qurʾan 7:57, Abdullah Yusuf Ali's translation). Etymologically, the name of Hadramawt is sometimes derived from *ḥadara mawt,* making it a land in which "death was present."

15. In Arabic, these lines are *wasaṭ al-Furayṭ wa-Zanbal wa-Akdar wa-masāyil / kam fīhim ṣūfī walī wa-faqīh sh-r-ʿ masāyil (Kharid 1985: 104).*

and Mecca, has everything to do with the prophets and their descendants (Combs-Schilling 1989; Rubin 1975; Schimmel 1985). The prophet Muḥammad's father, ʿAbd Allāh, underwent a trial in which he was almost killed in sacrifice by his father; immediately after ʿAbd Allāh's death was averted, he married the Prophet's mother, Āmina, who conceived the Prophet. The earliest Prophetic biographies contain reports of women who propositioned ʿAbd Allāh before he consummated his union with Āmina (al-Ṭabarī 1988; Ibn Hishām 1955: 69). He refused them, but after lying with Āmina, returned to them to take up their offers. They rejected him, because he no longer had the light he previously possessed: Āmina had taken it away. One of these women, another of his wives, explained that "when he passed her he had between his eyes something like the white blaze on a horse's forehead, that she invited him in the hope that he would lie with her, but that he refused and went in to Āmina bt. Wahb and lay with her, as a result of which she conceived the Messenger of God" (al-Ṭabarī 1988: 6). The imagery of light, and its association with the prophet Muḥammad, underwent extensive doctrinal elaboration at the hands of mystical thinkers such as Ibn al-ʿArabī, and it shows up in the titles of Hadrami books, such as Kharid's *The Blaze,* and in the white gowns, turbans, and tombs of descendants of the Prophet. On the axis that joins Prophetic seed and Light turns the renaming of al-Khaṭīb's book. The title he chose named effects and loci (garden, apothecary), while the title it was eventually given named causes and sources (the transparent essence, the grace of the sayyids of Tarim).[16] In the image recounted by al-Zubaydī above, of light falling like rain, cause and effect are united.

The unification was achieved by the interpolation of Prophetic genealogy. The ability to bring rain and to divine water for wells is a persistent theme in sayyid hagiography. It is especially prominent in accounts of sayyids moving away from Tarim in the Arabian Peninsula, either to found new settlements on the frontiers of religion or to make pilgrimages. The most famous and probably earliest instance is that of ʿAbd Allāh Bā ʿAlawī (d. 1331). He lived before the convergence of streams that created the ʿAlawī Way in the fifteenth century and is not known for rituals, special places, or written works. His hagiography is replete instead with the operations of grace as events. He visited Mecca twice and both times brought rain to the parched town, conducting the prayers for rain (al-

16. Al-Khaṭīb chose the title *Garden of the Heart Essences, Apothecary for Incurable Maladies.* Later the book was retitled *The Transparent Essence, Recounting the Marvels of the Sayyids of Tarim, and Their Contemporaries in It of the Greatest, Gnostic Saints.*

Khaṭīb n.d.; al-Shillī 1982: 403 ff.; Bā Wazīr 1961). Sayyid founders of settlements in Mashhad and Sayʾūn in later centuries divined wells where they settled (al-ʿAṭṭās n.d.; al-Kindī 1991).

In the emergence of the ʿAlawī Way from the fifteenth century on, Prophetic genealogy came to provide a master narrative that brought together previously independent domains of ritual, place, and text. These domains combined to form an institutional complex that, while inseparable from the descendants of the Prophet, enabled participation by others. To borrow Peter Brown's terms, persons like Aḥmad al-Junayd were "impresarios" who "coined a public language" of the saints that developed and persisted over centuries (Brown 1981: 48–49). In this language, lexical elements such as sky, rain, grave, water, irrigation, law, learning, and cure were brought into syntagmatic relation in the chain-linking of genealogy. Genealogy enabled performative texts such as Aḥmad al-Junayd's manual for visiting the graves of Tarim to activate the necropolis of the cemetery, opening it up to commerce with the living and engagement with history. With his *Salve for the Sickly,* visitors exchange visits, greetings, and votive requests with the dead, and in doing so, they relate to the dead as interlocutors with whom they interact in the same space and time: one does not simply go to the graveyards of Tarim; one goes to meet specific persons. In geographical and genealogical space, ancestors, the prophets Hūd and Muḥammad, and their descendants are not strangers but locals and intimates. In focusing his attention on them, al-Junayd was able to avoid the outside world, whose mediating circuits he was so suspicious of. Instead, value and blessings are obtained right at home, along the straight and narrow of religious rectitude and lineal descent. Intercession by the saints does not constitute mediation in the fraught ways we discussed in chapter 3, "A Resolute Localism." They simply make accessible divine grace, which flows downward like rain.

Even so, the linearity of the genealogies and the inexorability of their emanation are more apparent than real. The genealogies do not live in timeless self-sufficiency; they are products of and subject to histories in which their discursive forms and human contents change considerably. The first two *Fātiḥas* of al-Junayd's *Salve* give us an idea of the content of these histories. Between al-Khaṭīb's fifteenth-century *Garden/Apothecary/Essence* and al-Junayd's nineteenth-century *Salve/Gift* are four centuries and as many countries. In this time, the concepts, representations, and human content of the genealogies underwent tremendous development. In al-Khaṭīb's *Garden,* genealogy made a modest and circumscribed showing, appearing mostly as part of a person's name, or as acknowledgment of a general precedence accorded Prophetic descent. The interest of the book was that of the enthusiast; it lay in savoring the particulars of each story of the saints rather than in an overarching narrative structure. The book strictly organized the stories, as a sequence of numbers, not the persons. Persons were simply lumped into gross groups, generations. The ratio of four generations to five hundred stories indicates the relative emphasis. In contrast, by the time al-Junayd's *Salve* was written and copied, genealogy had become an elaborate and specialized knowledge, which could organize hundreds of names in a compact manual. Its maturity as a science allowed Aḥmad al-Junayd to wield it with economy and precision.

Historical development is not everything. Location too is important. Unlike the diasporic texts, which came to concentrate on the sayyids, or on their relations with non-Hadrami nobility abroad, al-Junayd's manual represents a broader profile of Hadrami society in Hadramawt. It was written for Tarim and for the various categories of persons living in it. In the conduct of their lives, disparate groups of people had plenty to do with each other. Thus, while the manual amply represents the lineal genealogies, it also engraves lateral exchanges between unrelated categories of persons, and enacts these exchanges in the visit. In return to Tarim as pilgrimage, the homeland expands from being a pure point of sayyidly origin to a diverse one of many families with different histories and other beginnings. Prophetic precedence in the pilgrimage does not so much exclude others as lead and gather all. The point was to get along, to have hearts that were clean and wadis that were watered. That was the point of collective prayers at the cemetery, beside the flood path, the prayers for rain.

CHAPTER 8

Repatriation

Fraught Returns

We have seen how the imperative of asymmetrical marriages, as set forth in the legalized genealogical vision of al-Shillī and practiced by sayyid communities in Malay port towns, led to the rapid accumulation of descendants under a patrilineal cover in the diaspora. Such persons were creoles whose mothers or grandmothers were Malay, Javanese, Buginese, Indian, or Chinese, rather than Arab. The patrilineal genealogies were not restricted to particular phenotypes, languages, or cultures; they were commodious enough to accommodate all in the matrilateral dimension. The genealogies enabled the Hadrami diaspora to travel transculturally. At the same time, the lines of descent—the path of fathers—charted a way back to origins. The textual canon of genealogies contained a discourse of mobility that, from places such as Surat and Mecca, pointed a way back to Hadramawt, and especially to Tarim, as both genealogical and geographical origin. Within this discourse, returns were valued. While daughters were required to return to origins in a genealogical sense, in marriage, sons were encouraged to return in a geographical sense, as part of the journey of education and inculcation of the moral virtues. While genealogical returns for daughters were couched in the legal language of *kafā'a* in marriage, the geographical returns of sons partook of the language of pilgrimage. Indeed, viewed from India and Southeast Asia, Hadramawt was on the route to Mecca, and both locations could be taken in on one journey.

Such at least were the intentions of patriarchs, and their views are the ones that the canonical texts reflect. While the texts encourage mobility, the reasons for movement in discourse are few and pious. The canon fosters travel but within narrow moral channels. The textual sources we explored in the previous part do not tell us all the reasons for itineraries nor the difficulties involved. People have many reasons for travel, and these reasons do not necessarily bear any relation to the pious ones celebrated in the texts. What is it like to move about in a space whose contours have already been mapped within the matrices of morality? How does genealogical belonging enable or constrain one's actions? For answers to such questions, this chapter looks to the personal accounts of people we meet on their journeys. Some of these accounts are written travelogues *(riḥla)* from the late nineteenth and early twentieth centuries. Others emerge from dialogues I had with Hadrami creoles repatriated to the homeland from abroad.

In the twentieth century, returns to origins were fraught, in the Hadrami diaspora as elsewhere. In colonial Southeast Asia, the debates over *kafā'a* and the rivalry between the schools and curricula of the ʿAlawīs and the Irshādīs reflected profound disagreements over the nature of origins and the meaning of return. Such disagreements first emerged abroad in the diaspora at the beginning of the twentieth century, but they showed up in the homeland as the century progressed. Major political developments there, such as the entry of colonial rule in the 1930s, the onset of socialist government in the 1970s, and that government's collapse in the last decade of the twentieth century were ineluctably wrapped up in the question of returns, and were enormously complicated for being so. It could scarcely have been otherwise in the society of the absent, which inhabited a space far larger than the lot left to it by the vicissitudes of modern national politics.

This chapter explores the difficulties of return from the perspective of individuals. Creoles born abroad are *muwallad,* which literally means "born" and is correctly part of a construct, such as *muwallad Jāwā,* "born of Java." Since the late nineteenth century, we have had records—in poetry, family history, travelogues—of *muwallad*s returning to Hadramawt. By looking at this literature, we can build a bridge between the view of diasporic geography in the canon and the experiences of individuals in their own lives.

Passport Problems

The first *muwallad* I met in Yemen was an Indonesian Hadrami in Aden. I was on a research trip in the early 1990s, and one day a man approached me in Crater, in the heart of Aden, and addressed me in Malay. I am from Malaysia, and I suppose it must show in some way. We had tea, and he proceeded to tell me what he was doing in that corner of the world. ʿAlī was from Indonesia and had ended up here in Yemen by accident. He really wanted to be in Australia, he had decided. He had been there five times, following his father, who was in "the Australia business." He and his father used to enter Australia from eastern Indonesia by boat, smuggling in goods, spending a couple of months there, and then returning with other goods. The venture was somewhat risky, but they did well. On their last trip, he met an Australian girl, who took him home to stay with her family for a few weeks. When his father found out, he was very angry and stopped taking him along. Soon after, his mother had to travel to Hadramawt to see her sister, who was seriously ill, so he accompanied her. That was five years ago. "So why haven't you returned?" I asked, somewhat surprised. He replied that he had stayed in Hadramawt for a few months until his money ran out, and he "couldn't take it anymore," so he ran off to Aden, staying with a relative there until he found a job in a restaurant.

> You see, I am a Sayyid, a descendant of the Prophet, like my namesake ʿAlī al-ʿAṭṭās, the foreign minister of Indonesia, and couldn't take just any job in Hadramawt. I couldn't stand being dependent on my relatives, unable to move. When they started talking of marrying me to a local girl, my cousin, I got scared and took off to Aden. Otherwise, I would have been really stuck. Here, thank God, I found a job in a restaurant, and stay upstairs at night. I have friends here, other Indonesians, and we hang out together. I will take you to meet them.

I met ʿAlī and his friends later for drinks, and most of them turned out to be refugees from Kuwait. They had worked there before and had come to Yemen as a result of the Gulf War. The conversation soon turned to passports. Some had Indonesian passports that had expired, and others had Yemeni ones. All wanted to return to the Gulf, but how? Those with Yemeni passports cursed their stupidity. They had come to Yemen to get Yemeni documents before going to work in Kuwait, thinking that this would make things easier. Yemeni passports had been easy to get. One did not have to be born in the country to obtain a passport but merely to prove genealogical descent from a Yemeni émigré. For Hadramis, that was easy, especially given that the official name on the passport took the form of a genealogy, albeit a short one going back only four generations. With Yemeni passports, Indonesians could easily find work in the Gulf before the Gulf War. Now, with the clampdown on Yemenis in Kuwait and Saudi Arabia, the situation had reversed. The thing to do was to return to Indonesia to get a passport from there. But no one had the money to do so. One of the Indonesians Abū Bakr, planned to go to Tanzania to get a passport. He had relatives in Dar es Salaam who would help him, and plane tickets going there were cheaper than those to Indonesia. He could even go by boat.

"You all have relatives here, can't they help you out with a loan or something?" I asked. There was laughter all round.

> You don't understand, my friend, these people are not like us. They are Arabs. Don't you know? You study history. Three days, you are welcome and fed, *ahlan wa-sahlan* ["welcome"]. After that, it's *maʿa al-salāma, selamat jalan, sayonara* ["so long" in Arabic, Malay, and Japanese]. Bedouin, the desert, it's dry. Have you seen the movie with ʿUmar Sharīf in it? There is a killing in the beginning . . . it is over water. See, it's dry. There's no rain here, no trees. There's nothing to keep the sun away. That's our biggest problem here, the sun.

ʿAlī took me aside later and told me to be careful of Abū Bakr: he would cheat me, as he had done the others. Right on cue, the next day, Abū Bakr came to me at the hotel. He told me he had a wife and a baby daughter in the Philippines. They had returned there from Kuwait before the war, and he was anxious to see them. A boat was leaving for Africa in two days. The captain, a friend of his, had agreed to take him on as a stowaway, and he needed some money for expenses. Would I help him out? He had an uncle in Say'ūn who was very fond of him. I should go to him when I arrived in Hadramawt, and he would reimburse me and furthermore help me in my research, for he was in the government, put there by the socialist party. His tribe was strong, they were everywhere—in Africa, Indonesia, Hadramawt. Even here, in Aden, he lived in a house that was a *waqf,* endowed by one of them who had made his money in Java, for people of their tribe who were in Aden in transit. I could stay there if I wanted, instead of wasting money on the hotel. What was I to believe? The truth I wanted to know, as that was for my notebooks. Certainly, this story had interesting elements: the family's geographical connections, the family *waqf* as part of that structure, the operation of kinship links in the socialist government. The money was secondary, for he probably needed the twenty dollars more than I did. The transaction done, I saw no more of him, put the story down to experience, and wrote nothing in my books.

I told ʿAlī none of this when I saw him later. He reiterated his warning. He had been saving money to return to Indonesia and had almost collected enough when Abū Bakr swindled him of a chunk of it. But never mind, ʿAlī's family was going to send him a ticket and a new passport from

Indonesia. Not all the fingers of your hand are equally long, you see, and not all people are alike. All he wanted from me was friendship, *al-gharīb li-l-gharīb nasīb:* to the stranger, another stranger is kin. On subsequent trips to Aden, I would always visit with ʿAlī, who continued patiently to await his plane ticket.

For all the time he spent in Aden, ʿAlī certainly did not feel at home there. In the city, he felt in suspension, between Hadramawt, where his father wanted him to be, and Australia, which was his own first choice. Journeying with his mother to Hadramawt had not been a homecoming to a place of origin. Hadramawt was one destination among others but one in which he could have been stuck. His running away was a refusal to marry his cousin, a refusal to return to genealogical and geographical origins. He thereby lost the support of his family and was left to his own devices. Either way, inside or outside of genealogy, he would have been stuck. But at least in Aden, the coffeeshops, clubs, cinemas, and beaches were good diversions.

For ʿAlī and his friends, Aden was a place of transit. His friends had come here for their passports and had been expelled back here because of those passports. Their situation was not comfortable but not completely hopeless either. The chance would come to try for the Gulf again, starting from another place with another passport. Funnily enough, Indonesia actually looked like the best bet the next time around. They all wanted to go back there to start the process again. Going to granddad's village in Hadramawt was the last thing on their minds.

Hadramawt: Home or Halfway House?

Whether one feels comfortable or happy in a place is affected by many things: the ability to make a living, how one gets along with kin, the color of one's skin, the experience of the place, even the sun. A place, experienced as a totality, determines one's well-being in numerous ways. *Muwallads* are extremely sensitive to this fact, having grown up elsewhere and finding themselves in a new place often not by choice. If dissatisfied, they easily and naturally think of changing the whole environment and moving elsewhere, voting with their feet. Indeed, the ability to move is itself part of being comfortable in a place.

Many *muwallads*, especially those who were brought to Hadramawt in their teens or after, expressly do not like being there and constantly talk of leaving. They are strangers at home because home is not where their hearts are. It is, rather, an alien and unpleasant place into which they have been inscribed, first of all by their very names. They may remain for decades, marry and have children, yet never fully come to terms with the place. They often say the people in Hadramawt are hard-hearted (in Malay, *keras hati*).

For these reasons, *muwallad*s come and go a lot, and don't stay long if they can help it. Often caught between the requirements of kin, their own desires, and the current status of their passports and pockets, their movements appear erratic. Their relativist attitude toward places in general, and this place in particular, Hadramawt, puts them at odds with locals and migrants who originate from here. The latter, usually male, may remain forty years abroad without ever returning, despite having a wife and offspring at home. Nevertheless, Hadramawt, as home to such men, has an absolute value: the intention to return is ever present. People from Hadramawt constantly think of their movements in relation to the homeland. Concomitantly, these movements are subject to moral criteria and moralizing commentary. Hadramawt natives are far away, suffering privation, for the sake of others back home; they return to be with their family and ancestors for an authentically religious life. The *muwallad,* however, has other things to worry about. He has neither the existential commitment nor the memories of the migrant. His starting point in life is not Hadramawt but Mombasa, Pontianak, Singapore.

*Muwallad*s often string together narratives of their experiences in Hadramawt in terms of their movements, as an itinerary. At the same time, these experiences are shaped by how others view those movements. As a direct product of migration to the outside world, the *muwallad*'s reputation precedes him, so to speak: it is colored by locals' perceptions of that outside world and its relation to the homeland. Those perceptions are shaped by the weight of the diasporic canon. We have seen how the canon transformed the geography of the Indian Ocean into a map of moral signs. That map was inculcated into moral selves in the diaspora, especially in persons who took religious learning seriously and engaged in the ʿAlawī pathway. Those who did not embrace the spiritual path ran the risk of going feral, assimilating into the local societies of their mothers abroad, and being lost to the society of diasporic Hadramawt. The debate over *kafāʾa* turned on this issue. Was assimilation into local society abroad an abandonment of Prophetic obligation, Hadrami society, or religion itself? The debate reflected anxieties about the dissolution of internal boundaries in the diaspora. In the homeland, people had such anxieties about the diaspora itself. *Mu-*

wallads returning to Hadramawt from the diaspora were often followed by a shadow that was not easily dispersed. Were they still Hadramis, after all?

In the travel writings of such persons, the moral map of diasporic geography becomes instantiated in the itineraries of individuals. Let us briefly examine three such works.

Travelogues

THE JOURNEY OUTWARD

The *Maqāma dham al-dunyā,* by Aḥmad b. Muḥammad al-Muḥḍār (d. 1887), is a work of rhyming prose that disparages the world (al-Muḥḍār 1984). The term *dunyā* equates a number of things: it stands for the world outside Hadramawt, for the corrupt material world opposed to the hereafter, and is a synonym of money in Hadrami parlance. In his writing, al-Muḥḍār depicts the worldly and base nature of the lands to which Hadramis migrated, the *mahjar,* via his journey away from a homeland stricken by famine. He leaves home and family for the coast, and there, at the edge of Hadramawt, he asks for advice on where to go, where gather women and sons, hoards of gold and silver, branded horses, and well-tilled land. The expression is a giveaway, for in the Qurʾan (III: 14), these items are the possessions of the world, the *dunyā,* which men covet; from these things, one does better to return to God.

Our author, however, has just begun his journey. He continues and finds himself in Surat, India, a fertile and graceful land of rain and trees. One day in the moonlight he comes upon a shadowy figure, a woman wearing a shawl, carrying a stick, unshyly surrounded by companions, and spitting as she goes along. He is entranced and wants marriage, but her price is heavy. She wants five treasures: his sense of shame, his manliness, his mind, his ancestry, and his religion. The symbolism is rather unsubtle; she is the *dunyā* he has been searching for, over land and sea. She taunts him, "What are the likes of you doing here? Your land is sought by pilgrims, your ancestors the earliest, who cared not for the world nor its trappings. Why don't you follow them and go home?" But he is not to be shaken off so easily. He wants to be considered one of the locals. So he gives her his sense of shame, and they write it on a piece of paper. The next morning, after dawn prayers, he looks for her in vain. She has gone to Hyderabad, he is told.

So he goes to Nāṣir al-Dawla, walking among Banyans and other infidels, a place of drink and fornication, where Islam is weak. He is told by the ruler to be as one of them if he wants to fill his pockets; otherwise he has no business being there. He meets the woman again, and the crowd tells him to give her all the five treasures. He gives her the second, his manliness. Again she disappears. He is told she's gone to Java, a sweet land without harshness. So he goes, first to Singapore, a place famous for business; she has just gone to Batavia. Batavia, Semarang, Tegal, Cheribon, Surabaya—she leads him through the trading towns of north Java, well known to Hadramis; places where they don't hold to the Friday congregation, and thought revolves around prices. He finally catches up with the woman; she still demands all five treasures. He remonstrates with her, and no one comes to his aid nor respects the rights of the stranger; their women's clothes are scandalous. These people are lost to religion and ancestry. He is in too deep by now. Two treasures are with her, and he still has not the *dunyā*. How can he face going home? He gives over his ancestry; never mind, this treasure is preserved in the books at home.

The plot is predictable. He follows her to Cairo and Istanbul, where he finally manages to wrench back his treasures, barely saved from losing the most precious of them all, his religion.

THE RETURN JOURNEY

If al-Muḥḍār's travels outside Hadramawt are motivated by worldly concerns, ʿAbd Allāh b. Muḥammad Bā Kathīr al-Kindī's travel to Hadramawt, which he describes in *Journey of the Strong Desires (Riḥlat al-ʿashwāq al-qawiyya)*, stems from concerns that are the perfect opposite (Bā Kathīr al-Kindī 1985). A *muwallad* of Zanzibar who has studied in Mecca and visited Indonesia, Egypt, and southern Africa, Bā Kathīr al-Kindī conceives a strong desire to visit Hadramawt, the homeland of the ʿAlawī sayyids and the origin of his beloved teacher's teachers *(mashāyikh)* and predecessors *(aslāf)*.[1] His teacher grants him leave, and writes to the leading shaykhs there, the Sufi axes *(quṭb*s*)*, on his behalf. On arriving in al-Shiḥr in 1896, he visits Shaykh Sālim b. Muḥammad Bā Wazīr, a

1. A comparable figure from East Africa, the sayyid Aḥmad bin Sumayṭ, is now the subject of a fine full-length monograph by Anne Bang (2004). His book *al-Nafḥa al-shadhiyya* is known for its detailed descriptions of his travels. Bang locates his career in both the ʿAlawī Way and the colonial society of East Africa.

venerable old man one hundred fourteen years old, who grants him licenses *(ijāza)*, including one for the chant *(dhikr)* "prayer and peace be upon you, oh my sayyid Prophet of God" *(al-ṣalā wa-l-salām ʿalayk yā Sayyidī yā Rasūl Allāh)*, which was granted Shaykh Sālim by the Prophet himself, without intermediary. The shaykh also reveals to him the provenance of his name, Bā Kathīr: his eponymous ancestor had many sons, all of whom were saints, so he was called *Abū Kathīr*, "father of many."

ʿAbd Allāh's itinerary in Hadramawt consists of visits with the great Sufi shaykhs of Hadramawt, meeting the living in their houses and the deceased at their tombs. In the course of this journey, he learns his true genealogy, which was lost because his father had died when he was young, and his grandfather had died when his father was young. Here in Hadramawt this genealogical orphan has his origins first revealed to him, by a *quṭb*, through esoteric illumination, *kashf*. His ancestor had been the judge of Tarim in the time of ʿAbd Allāh b. ʿAlawī al-Ḥaddād (d. 1720), one of the most venerated Hadrami saints (al-Mashhūr 1984: 568). This ancestry is later confirmed by the historian Sālim b. Muḥammad al-Kindī (al-Kindī 1991) through exoteric *(ẓāhir)* devices, triangulating upon his identity by asking for his name (which he knows for five generations), the names of the original emigrant and of a relative who stayed behind, and a genealogical tree.

The return journey of this *muwallad* to Hadramawt deepens his ancestral and religious identity. He is perhaps an ideal *muwallad*, morally, whose encounter with the homeland is felicitous and beneficial because it is driven by purity of purpose.

Despite the varied topography of these two journeys, their itineraries form a neat and simple narrative with little room for surprise. They are made to conform to a strict moral standard, which constrains the geographical imagination into an essentially bipolar form. The migratory life is a two-way street: one way leads to purity of religion and ancestry; the other, to contamination. The choice is brutally simple. Who dares contradict it? Although the geographical destinations vary, the moral ones do not. The fortune hunter in the first *riḥla* ends up not marrying the material world (and producing *muwallads*), while the pious *muwallad* in the second reinscribes his very identity by insinuating it into the tombs, domes, books, and chants of the homeland. While he arrived knowing his name only up to the fourth ancestor, he leaves knowing the full thing to the source, which is the meeting point of genealogy and religious distinction.

U-TURNS

Although human situations and actions—including those of *muwallads*—are replete with ambiguity and hesitation, these aspects can hardly be expressed in a literature so beholden to the moral standard. Yet occasionally, such things do seep through. In the following biography (al-Junayd 1994: 185 ff.), one gets a glimpse of a moral problem and a perhaps imperfect response by a morally upstanding *muwallad*. Its representation is possible only because the moral geography itself is not completely bipolar. The sayyid ʿAbd al-Raḥmān al-Junayd was born in Singapore in the mid-nineteenth century. He studied in Mecca as a youth and then plunged into business in Singapore, augmenting the fortunes of his already-well-off family. He visited Hadramawt at the age of thirty-four, where he contracted a marriage. His moral comportment pleased the leading citizens. He bought land, a well, and date trees and planned the building of a large house in Tarim. He remained four years, returned to Singapore, and then came again after two years with his family, the family of Muḥammad, his *ʿadīl* (a man married to the sister of one's wife), slaves, and horses. He used to have a scholar come weekly to give lectures and would play host with desserts and sweet, cool drinks. He became a respected figure in Tarim.

Only three years later, after moving into his grand new house with his family, he decided to move to Mecca with them and the family of Muḥammad. The group had just begun to settle into life in Mecca when ʿAbd al-Raḥmān again insisted on moving, this time back to Hadramawt. Muḥammad was upset by his instability. He reasoned with ʿAbd al-Raḥmān to wait just one more year so that their sons, who were to come of age then, would get the chance to carry out the pilgrimage. ʿAbd al-Raḥmān refused. A nephew weighed in on Muḥammad's side, pointing out that Mecca is the best of places and that the sons might not have another chance to complete the pilgrimage. ʿAbd al-Raḥmān burst out, "Ya ʿUmar! From the time I arrived till today, I have seen the moral character of my sons change from what they were in Tarim. They have remaining only one-quarter of the good morals they had in Tarim. We had better go back with what they have left of good character, that this and their good nature may return" (al-Junayd 1994: 189). To this outburst ʿUmar could not reply, so they returned. The moral climate is better in Tarim than in Mecca, asserted ʿAbd al-Raḥmān. Yet the author adds, tellingly, that the sons never were able to come back for the pilgrimage to Mecca. The erratic movements of this *muwallad*, though explained by good moral reasons (he was, after all, an ancestor), ultimately led to neglect of the pilgrimage. What other forces and feelings led to his hesitations and his U-turns, the erratic movement that shades his image, we cannot know. The strict moral code allows for their expression only as an argument about the relative merits of Tarim and Mecca.

Beyond the Text: Repatriation as Lived

In the 1990s, many *muwallads* lived in Hadramawt, having been repatriated from their places of birth. In their personal narratives, the tradition of repatriation from diaspora is experienced as displacement instead of homecoming. While Tarim is indeed the homeland of the diaspora, it most decidedly is not home to many members of that diaspora. Their origins rather are in Kenya, Malaysia, Sri Lanka, and elsewhere.

CAR TROUBLE

Muḥsin was at the *bunshar* again. This time, the spring in his car had snapped. Before that, a sharp rock had caused the tire to puncture (or "*bunshar*"); before that, the shock absorbers were the problem. To own a vehicle like Muḥsin's was to spend afternoons at the *bunshar*, at the welder, or at the scrap yards that hold bits of deceased vehicles to be scavenged. He was talking to the mechanic about how to get a replacement spring. The parts stores had no stock, not even "*Taiwanī*" ones. *Taiwanī* parts were cheaper than *aṣlī* ones, original ones from Japan. *Taiwanī* things were fakes or imitations made to look like the real thing; they might very well do the job—until they broke down. *Taiwanī* parts could not be original, by definition, because there were no *Taiwanī* cars. Broken-down cars, cheap electronic goods with fake brand names, and all manner of imported appliances with missing parts were so common in Hadramawt that the term *Taiwanī* became popular. Thus, apart from *Taiwanī* rotors and distributors, there were *Taiwanī* friends, *Taiwanī* doctors, even *Taiwanī* Muslims.

With no new spring available in Tarim, either *Taiwanī* or *aṣlī*, Muḥsin thought he might find one in the scrap yards in Say'ūn. He could hitch a ride with an uncle sometime that week and look for one. But when he arrived in Say'ūn, he found that no springs were available in all of Hadramawt, as far as the salesman knew. Muḥsin was discussing his options now, back at the *bunshar*. The mechanic thought that a spring might be available at a shop he knew in Ṣanʿāʾ, the capital city. That shop dealt with a different make of car, but the spring could be modified at the blacksmith's to fit Muḥsin's car. Did he know anyone going to Ṣanʿāʾ who would be willing to bring back the spring? Muḥsin knew a distant cousin who might be going there within the next couple of weeks. His cousin could get the part then.

Despite the contortions involved in procuring a car part, Muḥsin's plan for future employment was to buy a minivan to transport tourists around Yemen. Meanwhile, he was stuck in Tarim, waiting for his cousin to return with the spring so that he could take it to Sayʾūn to be banged into shape at a discount price through the negotiations of an uncle. The process could take weeks.

As Muḥsin's experience shows, substantial networking and stamina are necessary to maintain a car in working order in Hadramawt. The place is not easy to travel through. Roads are few and very rocky. Even on the main roads, speed bumps offer great entertainment to inhabitants of small villages. One does not want to take off without spare car parts, and usually one does not want to take off alone. A great deal of coordinated effort may be necessary to get going, and many people are asked many favors just to get one disabled vehicle running again. No one can do it alone. People do things for you. You do things for them. If people decline their favors, a person can get stuck.

Muḥsin was feeling a bit stuck. Like many *muwallad*s, he preferred other places to Tarim. He never liked to stay in one place, and he got along with tourists. This did not make him well regarded in Tarim. Despite being a sayyid, he carried a questionable reputation; he had come recently from Kenya, he ate in the local restaurant instead of in a proper home, and he talked to people whom he shouldn't talk to. His hope was that he might make enough money from his future tourist business to go back to Kenya. He would have a long wait, though, because he didn't have the resources or connections or visas or mode of transportation to get there and live there. He had, in a sense, gone feral. He was in constant dispute with one uncle. And he always had car trouble. If he was a Hadrami sayyid, then he was a *Taiwanī* one, he'd often say before bursting out in laughter.

The dry immobility of life in Tarim is a remarkable contrast to the illustrious history of diaspora in the Indian Ocean that I have been describing. Is this tangible "stuckness" also part of the diasporic experience? For many, it is.

Those who feel stuck are stuck in places that are not home to them. Consider the situation of Yūsuf.

YŪSUF

> I came here four years ago. I used to live in Mombasa with my cousin's family. My father lived in another town with one of his wives. I used to go to the disco a lot, on Fridays, Saturdays, and Wednesdays. Wednesday was ladies' night, and they got a discount. With a partner, you can spend a thousand shillings easily there. I played a lot and didn't do anything with my life. There was plenty of ganja (soft drugs). When my dad found out, he was very angry. We were just playing cat and mouse, my dad and me. He said if you want to be on good terms with me, you better go Hadramawt. I said OK, no problem. I came with my mum and elder brother. There is too much problem in Kenya, too much. Since 1989, there was tribal war. Army was just going round, getting people. One day, they come to our house, right to the door, and ask if you have big son. When they saw us this half-caste color, they leave me. If I was black man, they would have beat me. Later, my father's third wife and her children came. My dad brought them and left. We all stay in the same house. My mum is divorced from my dad, seven children, and is very unhappy here, even though she was born here. She went as a child to Africa during the *majāʿa* [famine]. She still has a stepbrother here and goes to stay with him often.

Yūsuf, his elder brother, and a half-brother work with the oil companies when the companies have jobs. Between jobs, their only alternative is to work in house construction, but they'd rather not because, unlike the locals, they can't stand the sun. Yūsuf likes working in the oil camps because many *muwallads* work there; the oil companies like *muwallads* because they speak English and like to joke around. The *muwallads* also help them deal with the local hires, who speak only Arabic. Yūsuf doesn't like to come back to Tarim even on vacations, because he doesn't like living in the town. His relatives constantly complain about "this and that"—about how he gives them a bad name, for example, by wearing jeans and T-shirts rather than the local sarong. So when he's back, he spends his time at the *qāt* market chewing and chatting with friends. This activity bothers his relatives even more, but what can he do? He can't just stay home drinking tea all day while on vacation, listening to Michael Jackson and thinking about Saturday nights in Mombasa.

Yūsuf wants to save up money so that he can go back to Kenya with a minibus and earn a living with it there. But he is far from achieving that goal because he alone has to support his mother and his stepmother and her children, who are younger. His elder brother is unreliable because he is married to a local woman who is demanding, and also because he chews too much *qāt*. His half-brother used to chip in but went to Saudi Arabia, had problems getting a sponsor and visa, and is back in Kenya waiting for a new passport. "It's just snakes and ladders for him," says Yūsuf. His father has written once since the family came to Tarim and has never sent money. Yūsuf plans to marry an African woman of Arab origin. That is better than marrying a local Arab woman because she knows his sisters, and they get along. When he is away working, she can stay home with his sisters for months without problems, unlike his brother's local Arab wife, who runs away to her parents every time he's gone. Also, if you have Arab relatives (i.e., in-laws), they will talk and cause you much headache, he says. He hopes his marriage will make his father and half-brothers in Saudi Arabia realize that he cannot shoulder all the responsibilities and make them do something about the situation.

ZAYNAB, YŪSUF'S HALF-SISTER

Yūsuf's half-sister, Zaynab, came to Tarim three years ago with her mother and sister and brothers. Her father had brought them, telling them only that he wanted them to see his country. When they arrived, he said they would stay. They would marry Yemeni men and settle down.

She is incredulous that some women are as young as fourteen when they marry here. Even stranger, they are happy to do so; they can then have nice clothes and gold to wear and go to parties. She is upset that marriage is all that her friends look forward to. She had been studying for her "O"-levels before she came and was concerned about how she could continue her studies. She went to school for a few months in Tarim and then stopped. Although she had learned to read and write Arabic, she had been in a class with children much younger than herself. She didn't like this arrangement and decided to read and learn at home. She was serious about learning. She wanted to do something. At her work, her employers don't train her at all. She does her job, and that's all. She and her mother and siblings are waiting for father to return from Kenya so that they can tell him they want to leave. If she goes back to Kenya, she can complete her training. If she stays here, she doesn't know what will happen. Her aunts don't even want her to work. They are not supposed to go out much, and everything is forbidden, *ḥarām*. Who tells them this?

It is the neighbors. Everything is *ḥarām*. They tell us that we shouldn't go out, go here, go there, but we do anyway. We go to the vegetable *sūq*, where it's mostly men. The neighbors say *ḥarām*. But we need good fruits and vegetables; there isn't much here, not like Kenya, so we must choose ourselves. It's also my brother, although he's not my real brother. He's my brother from my father's first wife. He didn't used to be like this—he didn't used to pressure us—but since we've come here he tells us not to do this and not to do that. My brother's Arab wife, she doesn't like us. She doesn't like the way we are, and she eats alone when she comes over here. She talks about us in her home and tells things to my brother. He's not our real brother though. He didn't used to do that, but his wife's mother complains to him and tells him we shouldn't do this or do that and gives us a hard time. He didn't used to be like that.

Their house is near some big old houses built by people from Singapore. Tourists come by frequently, and Zaynab and her family have made friends with some of them and corresponded. One friend in Canada was about to send her a ticket fully paid so that she could go there and study, but her mother wouldn't let her go. She said she was ready to pack her bags and leave anyway, but her mother said that she (the mother) would be the one to suffer if Zaynab disobeyed. What kind of woman begets such a daughter, who runs away by herself to the infidels? Zaynab didn't want her mother to pay for her strong will.

ʿĀʾISHA

ʿĀʾisha came to Tarim from Malaysia at fifteen, with her sister and father, after her mother died. Her mother was Chinese, and her father Hadrami. They stayed in her grandfather's house, a big, scary place with fifty rooms and a huge gate. The house had so many rooms she had to trace her daily paths on the floor with a marking pen. Living in Tarim was hard for her at first because she was not allowed outside at all, and if so, the car windows had to be curtained. She felt she could not breathe. She and her sister would make one of the servants take them out at night after everyone was asleep. They would walk up to the mountain and breathe the air. Sometimes they saw bedouin weddings, with men and women dancing together. Although they could sneak out in the dark, the gate squeaked, so during the day they oiled it. When people saw them subsequently, they would tell their father and he would yell. But he was okay because he knew the situation was hard for them and that they weren't used to the ways of their adopted home. After a while, they got smart and would wear a sarong, shirt, and headdress when they went out at night, so that people who saw them would think they were men. They had no more problems after that! Unlike their neighbors, they looked out the windows with their faces showing when street festivities like camel races took place. Their neighbors did not like this behavior, but their father let them watch, so they did. The men outside watched them instead of the camels. Once, when their house was being repaired, an architect came. He came, saw her, and later asked to marry her. She jumped at the chance to get out. He was a cousin. Her life changed dramatically after her marriage. She lived in the Gulf for some years when her husband worked there, and she spent time in Europe when her husband went there for training. She comes back to Tarim once in a while to see to her mother-in-law. When here, she makes sure the old lady eats well by going to the market herself to choose the vegetables. Her driver takes her there and pops into the market to buy the food while she waits in the car. He brings the items to her, and if the choice is bad, she makes him exchange them.

Harm and *Ḥarām*

The moral conceptions so clearly articulated in the literature are sometimes hard to distinguish from prejudice when encountered in the daily life of *muwallad*s among kin, neighbors, and others. They have consequences for the itineraries, lives, and well-being of *muwallad*s. Some—the young, dependent, or female—are apt to have their lives greatly shaped by them, while others—adult, independent, or male—may be less touched. What is puzzling is the persistence of prejudice against *muwallad*s in a society so fundamentally and continuously shaped by migration. Perhaps *muwallads*' cheerful disregard for time-honored local ways, coupled with their easy familiarity with the paraphernalia of modern life, present a contradictory complex that challenges local self-conceptions of the superiority of their ancestry and homeland. The anxiety is, after all, similar to that which the powerful but ungodly Christians, the *naṣāra,* bring about.

The *muwallad*s whose stories appear here are neither exceptionally good people nor exceptionally bad ones, in the local scheme of things. Although Yūsuf used to live it up in Kenya and chews *qāt* now, he came to Tarim because he concurred with his father's judgment, and he now bears the burden of supporting two of his father's seven wives and ex-wives, and their families. Zaynab, though she goes to the men's *sūq* and talks to foreigners, is concerned about her education. ʿĀʾisha, for all her youthful indiscretions, regularly returns to see to the old lady's comfort, despite disliking the lack of chairs and abundance of flies.

Yet there are many who would maintain that Yūsuf simply wants to go back to Kenya to resume his *ḥarām* activities, just as you can see him chewing *qāt* in the coffeeshops. Maybe Zaynab wants to run off to Canada because she's shameless, just as she is when she goes to the *sūq*. For those so concerned, the movements of these *muwallad*s, on the large and small scale, are all of a piece. This moralized space has no place for the simple sensuous desire, as felt by ʿĀʾisha, to climb an escarpment in order to breathe, an act that is valued elsewhere. Little room exists for dialogue, as we see in the argument between the two brothers-in-law over whether to stay in Mecca or return to Tarim, which cannot develop.

The moral discourse concedes no ground. It cannot be modified by seeing the other's point of view. Thus, to find a solution, one must create an interstitial space, through the use of partitions to break up the ubiquitous, homogenized, moralized space. The house of an understanding father is such a refuge. Where two women want the choice of good vegetables on the spot, she with car and driver is the one who can do so without being judged.

Perhaps the main shortcoming of *muwallad*s is the lack of skill in or attention to playing with such partitions to create comfortable niches for themselves. Without such management, one's movements are exposed and seen to be what they are—erratic. Many *muwallad*s, constantly told that their actions are *ḥarām,* and harmed by such accusations, simply want to leave. They focus on getting out as much as on fitting in, and in so doing, they go for the grossest partition of all, that between the homeland and the *dunyā*. Thus do they fall on the wrong side of the divide and, unwittingly, confirm all the local stereotypes of themselves.

Repatriation as Project

In the late nineteenth century, tens of thousands of Hadramis ventured to Southeast Asia to participate in the booming colonial economies there. Precisely in this period did the figure of the *muwallad* arise as a problem in Hadrami literature. The advent of steamships was equally convenient for exporting produce and transporting *muwallad*s home. Concern about the unwholesome effect of commerce with the diaspora on the current generation, down to young people's dress and speech (al-Mashhūr 1911: 83), drove the judge Muḥsin b. ʿAlawī al-Saqqāf (d. 1873), who heard disputes from the *Jāwa* lands (al-Saqqāf 1993) and composed poems disparaging the region (al-Saqqāf n.d.), to write his book *Familiarizing the Descendants with the Virtuous Lives of the Ancestors (Taʿrīf al-khalaf bi-siyar al-salaf).*

This effort was continued by his student, ʿAbd al-Raḥmān b. Muḥammad al-Mashhūr, mufti of Tarim, in his compilation of a new kind of genealogy in 1890, the *Luminescent, Encompassing Mid-day Sun (Shams al-ẓahīra al-ḍāḥiya al-munīra;* al-Mashhūr 1911, 1984; al-Saqqāf al-ʿAlawī 1964). This book was innovative because it combined four distinct elements:

1. It set out a comprehensive scheme of descent from the prophet Muḥammad.
2. Within this scheme, it located the major, named family subgroups, such as al-ʿAṭṭās and al-ʿAydarūs, and explained the origins of the family names, so that each living individual sayyid, who inevitably has a family name but may not know his exact genealogy, can be located within this larger scheme.
3. It included information about outstanding ancestors within each family and jumped straight from them to individuals living close to the time of composition (unlike a strict *silsila,* "chain," which links descent through every generation).
4. It mentioned the places to which family members migrated, with particular emphasis on the Southeast Asian lands.

These features aimed to bind young sayyids to their origins and to remind them of the ascetic glories of their fathers, even as they were tempted by the degenerate ways of the wealthy East Indies far from the stony graves of their ancestors. They could not hide from the high "Mid-day Sun" of their heritage.

This biographically and geographically expanded genealogy was an instrument for the long arm of moral discipline. The book had subsequent transmigratory reincarnations abroad: as a lithograph print in the classical manuscript style, published in Hyderabad in 1911 (al-Mashhūr 1911); as a complex of tables and charts checked and cross-linked with abiding passion (al-Saqqāf 1964), compiled in Solo 1946 and published in Jakarta; as a reference volume with copious additional historical footnotes on Hadramis abroad and multiple indices, published in Jedda (al-Mashhūr 1984). Through these reincarnations, the book acquired pedagogical accessories that enhanced its educative purposes. A compact, mass-produced volume suitable as a gift to a young person, it was a synopsis of the author's seven-volume, centralized manuscript genealogy of all Hadrami sayyids, which is still maintained by the al-Mashhūr family in Tarim today. The charts were checked in 1959 against the fifteen-volume genealogy in Indonesia maintained by the Perpetual Office for the Compilation and Control of the Genealogy of the ʿAlawī Sayyids (itself transferred from the Tarim original in 1922).

The *Mid-day Sun* reminds one of that other product of a mobile society: the ninth-century *Genealogies of the Nobles* (*Ansāb al-ashrāf*) of al-Balādhurī (1997). This distinguished predecessor, itself a hybrid text, emerged in the geographically medial and ethnically plural zone of Iraq after a period of intense migration out of the Arabian Peninsula. It is an encyclopedic history that combines fragments of biography, tribal oral history, and poetry within a genealogical scheme and recasts the complex history of Islamic expansion in non-Arab lands in the genealogical vision of an Arab aristocracy (Duri 1983).[2]

The concern for *muwallad* morals was echoed in Dutch colonial studies. The anxieties of fathers, whether colonizer or colonized, often meet in the recalcitrance of their offspring, as the piquant observation below illustrates:

> The Arabs who wish to give their children a more careful education send or take them to Hadthramut . . . beyond the enervating surroundings of the Javanese or Malays, at any rate for a few years. Moreover, Hadthramut appears to be a country specially suited to the education of youth. All the children of the well-to-do classes, at least in the towns, go to school there, and when they leave it, have no other distraction but study and the practices of religion. The ordinary amusements of European cafes, and their accessories, are absolutely unknown in Hadthramut: thus one is obliged to lead an austere and orderly life there. What is more, I know of Arabs who have sent their sons to Hadthramut because of tendencies to become worthless fellows, just as, in Europe, individuals of this character are sent to school in the country. They cost less there, and have no opportunity of giving themselves up to debauchery. (van den Berg 1887: 59–60)

Nouveau riche, émigré parents with a touch of anomie in new countries everywhere are wont to worry about the moral fiber of their offspring, unfortified as these youth are by the experience of want. The concern gains

2. The expanded genealogical vision of Arab conquerors was not necessarily accepted by non-Arabs on the Islamic frontier. Mottahedeh argues that Iranian elites were wedded to territorial conceptions instead and that "the assimilation of the two ruling classes . . . took place because both classes accepted a mixed territorial and genealogical self-definition" (Mottahedeh 1976: 180).

significance, however, in a cultural tradition in which the words and deeds of ancestors not only serve as moral exemplars (witness the *riḥla* of Bā Kathīr al-Kindī) but attain the status of religious law, as in the precedent of the prophet Muḥammad, progenitor of arguably the largest Hadrami tribe. Thus, in the Hadrami diaspora, while the pleasures and the pitfalls of *mahjar* life provided material for a literary sport of sorts, more pragmatic minds sought to establish firmer means through which they could reap the rewards of the bountiful world outside while mitigating its deleterious effects on their progeny. They made the repatriation of their offspring into a project.

In 1886, a group of wealthy Hadramis in Singapore, the jewel of the diaspora, established an endowment to found a new school in Hadramawt, the famed Ribāṭ of Tarim, independent of the mosques and study corners in which teaching and learning occurred in a relatively disorganized fashion, with students of different levels mixed together (Bilfaqīh 1961; Sulaymān 1994a). The group constituted a board of trustees in Singapore, set up a committee for pedagogy, and enacted rules and regulations in the European fashion current in the colonies. A number of houses in Singapore were donated as endowment for the cause, and the rents from them went to the upkeep of students who would reside in the school. The idea was innovative in Hadramawt: Ribāṭ was to be a boarding school, the "school in the country," and indeed, many *muwallads* were to pass through its hallowed halls.

Similar concerns motivated Shaykh b. ʿAbd al-Raḥmān al-Kāf, the most fabulously wealthy of all Hadrami migrants abroad. In his will, he directed that his children and grandchildren in Singapore be repatriated to Hadramawt for "education and instruction in manners" while they were minors, before they could assume the inheritance held by their guardians.[3]

As it turns out, these measures taken by the fathers were done with great foresight. By the 1930s, when the British began to administer Hadramawt, colonial administrators found within the ranks of the *muwallads* influential and powerful men who could speak their language, literally and metaphorically—men who were equally used to conducting big business over little cups of tea. On the coast, such fellows were the ruling Quʿayṭī sultans, born and raised in British India, while inland, they were the rich and public-spirited *muwallads* like Abū Bakr b. Shaykh al-Kāf, the Singapore-born son of the testator mentioned above, whose enthusiastic partnership made possible the high heroisms that accompanied British entry into Hadramawt proper, as we shall see in the next chapter.

3. IORL, R/20/A/3874, "Will of Shaykh al-Kaff" (1910).

Javanese Days

Gone is the golden age of Hadrami migration to the non-Arab lands, the *ayyām Jāwā*: languid, sepia-tinted Javanese days, when Southeast Asia was *jannat al-dunyā*, "heaven on earth," and Aden was *nusf Lundun*, "half London." In those days, the *muwallads* were an elite and dynamic element, scions of noble and wealthy families; they were clever devils who ran pharmacies, tuned in to radio broadcasts in the ether, opened cinemas and roads, fraternized with the English, and even ruled over whole swaths of territory. It was a time when creolized, diasporic Asian communities flourished in the lands around the Indian Ocean, feeding off the second tier of colonial capitalist economies.

In those days, a number of *muwallads* plotted their own returns to the homeland. Flush with seemingly endless resources from Singapore and Java, friendly with English officials, and belonging to influential families in Hadramawt, they conceived fantastical projects of return. Elite elements in the diasporic society of Hadramawt were in search of a state strong enough to protect them wherever they were. The British empire, which ruled over the main countries of the Hadrami diaspora—in East Africa, southern Arabia, India, and Malaya—seemed a natural candidate for the job.

Hadramawt was the last piece of land grasped by the British empire. It came under colonial administration in 1937, very late in the imperial day. What interest the British could have had in this corner of the Arabian Peninsula remains something of a puzzle. From the point of view of Hadrami *muwallads* born in the diaspora, however, British presence had certain advantages. Between diaspora and homeland was a very long route that remained to be secured. Even the journey from the Hadrami coast to the interior entailed passing through the jurisdictions of tribes and sultans jealous of their prerogatives. Despite the diasporic successes of Hadrami families across the Indian Ocean, Hadramis were really at home only in the towns: port cities in the diaspora and urban, agricultural centers in the homeland. Between these points, their word carried little weight.

In the 1930s, it seemed possible to some Hadramis that this state of affairs could be ameliorated. The initiative came from abroad. In this moment, the classic relation between homeland and diaspora seemed about to reverse. To Hadrami creoles born abroad and repatriated home, the British appeared to be a solution of sorts.

CHAPTER 9

The View from the Verandah

Tarim, its measure like its rhyme is ʿaẓīm (great). . . . A town in Hadramawt. The most temperate air of God's lands is to be found there, and the best earth, and the sweetest water. It is ancient, it is said that it was very prosperous in the old days. But now it has become very weak.

ʿAbd al-Qādir b. Shaykh al-ʿAydarūs (1985: 73)

Tarīm. 16° 02' N, 49° 00' E; alt. 2,200 feet. Population 15,000. Kathīri State, Eastern Aden Protectorate.

The second town of the Kathīri state, a centre of religious teaching, is built on a slope at the foot of cliffs on the north side of the Wadi Hadhramaut, and a small stream, the Kheilah, runs through it. It is surrounded on all sides by the Āl Tamim, who are a Quʿaiti tribe. The walls, pierced by five gates and defended by twenty-five forts, enclose an area sufficient to hold over 2,000 houses and extensive gardens. ʿAidid is a wealthy suburb. All the houses are mud-built, but rich Seiyids with East Indian connexions own imposing mansions, fitted up with such modern conveniences as electric light and fans, telephones, ice-plants, and bathrooms and shower-baths with running water (photo, 206). Mosques are said to number 300, the elegant balconied minaret of one being the tallest in the Hadhramaut (photo, 191).

Gazetteer of Inland Towns, Naval Intelligence Division
(H. Scott et al. 1946: 582–83)

The Last Colony

The theme of mobility lies at the heart of this book, and we have seen how the Hadrami diasporic canon couched returns in the language of pilgrimage and moralized movement. In earlier centuries, the mobility of Hadramis throughout the Indian Ocean was wide-ranging and untrammeled; the diaspora had a reputation and renown that gave its members relatively easy entry into many places. All this changed in the twentieth century. At the century's end, in the previous chapter, we met individuals who were stuck in places not of their choosing, whether because of family reasons, lack of money, or passport problems. The technology had improved, but people were less mobile. What had changed?

In the last three decades of the nineteenth century, which we can conveniently date from the opening of the Suez Canal in 1869, the industrializing nation-states of Europe began to wrap their expanding ambitions in the mantle of classical empires. With British prime minister Disraeli's flair for drama, Queen Victoria became Empress of India, a unified Germany acquired a kaiser, the French Third Republic declined to be left out, and the scramble for new African and Asian markets and supplies was joined. The period is best remembered for a dramatic proliferation of territorial colonies acquired in short order. As European claims jostled one another across continents and oceans, the world came to seem very small. Yet it was now small not only because there was not enough of it but also because steamships, telegrams, and newspapers telescoped the time necessary to cross it. The exhilarating modernity of the belle époque and a sense of accelerated participation in an interconnected, universal concourse were shot through with the monopolistic rivalries of the new nation-empires. The world was both more free and less so.

In the Indian Ocean, even as European capital and non-European labor poured into colonial destinations in liberal measures, native sovereignties were being reconfigured within a tightening imperial embrace. In the Dutch East Indies, while brutal wars of conquest expanded the domain of direct colonial rule outward from Java to places such as Aceh, Bali, and Lombok, its internal space was reduced by partitions, pass-and-quarter regulations restricting the movements of diasporic "Foreign Orientals" such as Arabs and Chinese. In India, the British disposed of some native "princely states" or tucked them in under others, which were thereby enhanced; all states were in turn hemmed in by the exercise of imperial power from without. After the Indian Mutiny of 1857–58, in which dispossessed rajas participated, Britain affirmed the sovereignty of native

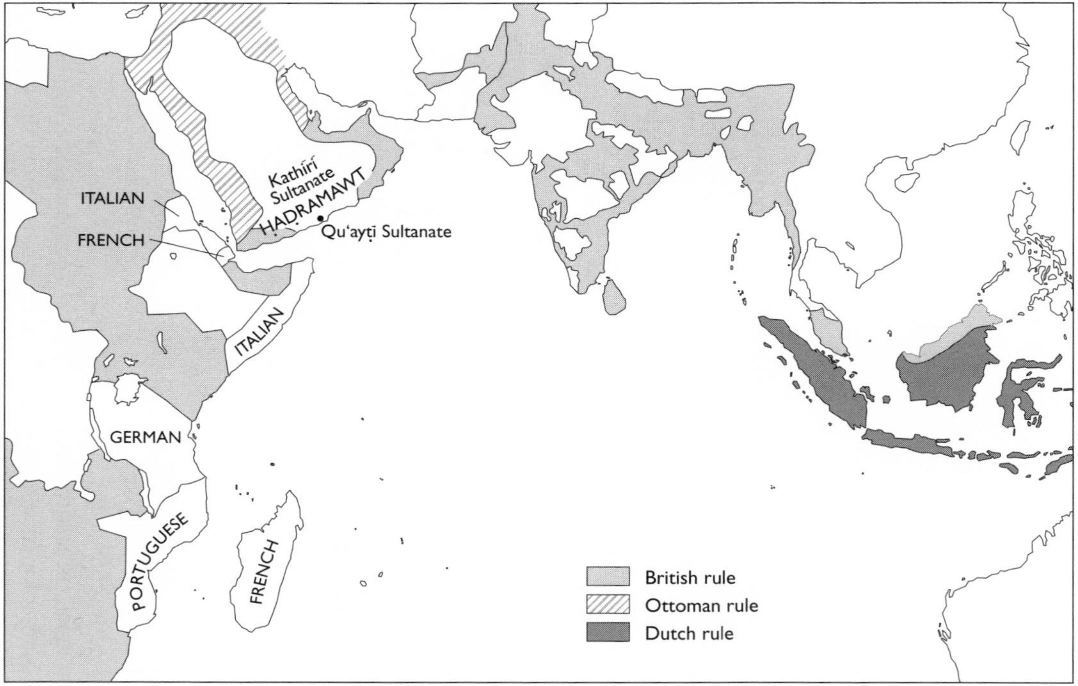

MAP 4. Diaspora in imperial space, 1914

princes by royal proclamation, and similar arrangements of indirect rule were carried to British Malaya and Africa in subsequent decades, with the help of personnel from India. Native sovereignty was conceptualized as a bundle whose parts could be divided and portioned out (Alexandrowicz 1967; Keene 2002; Maine 1888). All ceded the sovereign conduct of foreign affairs to the British suzerain, retaining a diminished bundle of jurisdictions within the domestic sphere. In this domain of native states, chiefdoms, and tribes—now having only an internal legal personality—rights were recognized as inhering in collectivities; as a result, claims were advanced in the collective terms of indigenous nation and culture.

As such terms developed representational forms and gained sociopolitical mass, diasporic persons who straddled the widening gap between internal and external found themselves having to decide where they belonged, if indeed the choice was theirs to make. Creoles were becoming anomalous; everywhere, races were forming. Rulers whom we have met around the Indian Ocean, more often as foreigners, had to become natives. Descendants of Alexander the Great and the prophet Muhammad became Malays, in order that they represent that race. Overall, the resulting constitutional forms resembled Chinese boxes or Russian dolls, with smaller chiefs, sovereigns, and their populations folding into and being subject to the gatekeeping powers of larger ones. In experiential terms, these constitutional forms of divided sovereignty felt like the naval blockades of gunboat diplomacy, which had played such a large role in their shaping. Those caught inside could not leave, while others stranded outside could not return. Diasporic circuits of travel and return became troublesome, if not suspect. Conceptually, the naval blockades and constitutions of indirect rule in this period of "new imperialism" were self-conscious exercises in developing modes of control from afar and without contact, as distinct from the older forms of direct occupation by European colonial settlers or army garrisons (Ho 2004). Even as their presence weighed more heavily on the colonies, with the creation of bureaucratic states under the sign of native sovereigns, the imperial powers seemed to be preparing for their own eventual departure. Strangely enough, that was what they had often said.

At the same time that imperial authorities were setting up such controls, the means of communication and transportation were rapidly increasing in speed and volume, and falling in price. Across the Indian Ocean, British and Dutch shippers had largely defeated and supplanted most other national carriers and were widely relied on for ferrying passengers, pilgrims, and products. Where the Portuguese had failed to dominate movement across the ocean using a coercive strategy of warships and passes, the British had succeeded with a commercial one, by making British bottoms cheaper and faster than anyone else's. By the early twentieth century, dependence on British shipping was almost complete.

As economic costs fell, political controls increased. Passage and blockade worked in tandem to create a system of imperial channeling, which ramified across the ocean: free movement for the approved, interdiction of the troublesome, and surveillance of the suspect. For non-Europeans whose diasporas moved across the Indian Ocean region—which was now densely interpenetrated by the competitively evolving claims and controls of multiple European powers on land and of multiple British administrative departments at sea—any business involving travel or transportation became increasingly complicated. Depending on person, place, papers, time, and circumstance, one could be waved on with a smile or rudely stopped. One was constantly passed off from one hand to another, and not always in rational or predictable ways. Steamship companies, in particular, felt the tension between their private profits and the policing of passengers that states sought to impose on them, making them "sheriff's deputies" (Torpey 2000: 9–10).[1] Lines of control were not obvious, but the nature of bureaucracy and the dynamics of interimperial rivalry virtually guaranteed that problems would occur, and during the First World War, civilian traffic was suspended.

Across the Indian Ocean, the Hadrami diaspora overlapped with imperial powers in many places. Both parties were very mobile affairs and traveled the same routes, often in the same vessels. But diasporas were now being simultaneously contained within and pushed out of the Chinese boxes of subordinate sultanates and nations, channeled along intersecting lines of private and public control when traveling abroad, and at times displaced by the shifting boundaries of interimperial rivalry. Under such circumstances, returns were no longer simply recurring aspects of diasporic life, reflecting the internal life cycles of diasporic families. In the period between the two world wars, as diasporic Hadramis became

1. In 1921, for example, the British company "Maclaine and Watson, esteemed," requested permission to sail with passengers between Batavia and al-Mukallā, direct. It undertook to perform customs inspection, check for arms, and board only passengers with passports from the British consul in Batavia. By telegram to his superiors at the Foreign Office, who passed it on to the Colonial Office, which in turn forwarded it to Aden, the Batavia consul recommended that permission be denied, even though he supported the request. The question was one of "practicability" (PRO, FO371/6256, E7372/487/91).

enmeshed in the expanding rivalries of imperial powers around a shrinking ocean, their own rivalries became entangled with those of the great powers as well. As the stakes rose, returns became ambitious political projects, which eventually put their stamp on the writing of history.

In 1937, the British empire colonized the Hadrami homeland, establishing indirect rule with the installation of a Resident Advisor by treaty. The homeland was the last colony acquired by Britain in its long imperial history, and its story, surprisingly, can also be told as a story of diasporic returns. In this chapter, we revisit the events of this final colonization and their telling by the principal actors, English and Hadrami. The world in which diasporic return became imperial colonization is not entirely different from that of today, and the historical controversies it gave rise to among diasporic Hadramis continue to inform debates in the present.

Bungalows by the Sea

Looking up from the expanse of water to the fronds of the palm trees from my perch on the verandah, finishing up the last bits of curry, rice, achar, shrimp chips, and chili sambal at the end of a long lunch, I found myself at home in the town of Tarim. It was late spring, not long after I had arrived to spend a year or two, maybe more, and I had finally begun to eat well and settle down. Today I had an invitation to lunch at a bungalow in the suburbs of Tarim, up the road past the cemeteries, in the middle of acres of date palms. The floods had recently hit town in their unpredictable way, rushing past the cemeteries along the wadi bed, which doubles as a road on normal days. The waters spill out of the wadis north of town and course through channels along its perimeter, swirling around the roots of palm trees and flooding gardens, passing through trenches under garden walls, moving on to the next set of gardens, and so on before finally disgorging south of town to join the giant floods that sweep everything before them in the main wadi Hadramawt. On such days, young boys and grown men are content to sit under the sun and watch the broad, open waters for hours on end. The mood of the flow changes—now angry, now calm and firm, sometimes positively serene. And then there are the surprises—a dead goat bobbing along, a classroom chair sailing by—confirming that school is out, if one hadn't guessed it. Many years may pass before one gets to see such a sight again, not to mention an impromptu holiday.

Where I was, the scene was different. The verandah was cool and shaded by the palm trees, and the water was calm, hemmed in by bunds carefully laid out to trap it. I could have been in a paddy field back in Malaysia or a holiday bungalow there by the sea, contemplating unusually fat and hairy coconut trees. The only incongruity was the high wall surrounding bungalow and garden, which created a large, private compound and spoiled the view from both directions.

In their journey around Tarim and beyond it, the floods pass through a number of such compounds, running unchecked through channels under the walls. On normal days, only kids and cats have that privilege. In the bungalows and villas set within those compounds, I imagined other families and other guests were enjoying their *rijsttafel* lunches, afternoon tea, and siestas, on other verandahs perhaps, taking in the sight and scent of water, lots of it. The suburbs of Tarim are the creation of these floods sent by God, and of their careful channeling by men. The title deeds of some of the villas mention not just house and garden but the *mamarr* too, the water channels that run between them.

One day a number of years ago, a channel running under a wall had been blocked. An absent-minded carpenter had dumped pieces of wood and furniture there. When water came, it could not break through the barrier, so it veered off to the old town instead. The houses there are very different from those in the suburbs. They are not raised high on a podium of stones, nor are they separated from each other by acres of land. They are mud-brick creations that cluster together for strength and lack of space. When the flood entered the old town, the waters rose quickly and ate into a number of these mud houses, which collapsed. An old man lost his life. Some locals said that the tragedy was not the carpenter's fault but the World Bank's, whose agricultural project had interfered with the watercourses. The huge floods come in a twenty-five-year cycle, and the foreign experts had not been here long enough to know that fact. The old town, which is ancient, was not built to face the floods. In fact, its houses were built without faces at all. One never gets a good view of a house, as the streets are narrow. And good manners demand that one shouldn't look, even if one could. And just in case, entrances to doorways are shielded by small walls: the interiors are never exposed, and neither are comings and goings through the doors. In the old town, the houses present a flat and impassive front, suggesting nothing of the divisions and diversions within them. One thing they never have is a verandah. It would be unthinkable.

The houses in the suburbs are different. Some were built in the late nineteenth century, like the one commissioned by the *muwallad* ʿAbd al-

Raḥmān in his hesitations between Singapore and Mecca. Most of the houses date from the 1930s. They were built by *muwallads* repatriated from Singapore and Java, and they mirror the hybrid architectural fashions current there: "Straits colonial" or "Anglo-Straits" style (Yeang 1992: 146), in reference to the Straits Settlements, which are the English Crown Colonies on the Strait of Melaka. Some of these new-style houses in Hadramawt are bungalows, while others are absolute mansions.

Bungalows in British India and Malaya were stand-alone, detached structures, usually single storied, placed in suburbs outside the cities (King 1984: 37).[2] They combined elements of English classicism with features of Bengali huts and Malay houses. The most distinctive feature of this hybridization was the verandah, an intermediate space between interior and exterior that quickly became the favorite spot for most activities: working, smoking, lounging, sleeping. Though the verandah worked like other elements of tropical architecture to maximize the flow of cool air—featuring opposing doors, interior air wells, and jack roofs—some scholars insist on its Spanish or Portuguese origins. In King's estimation,

> Its importance is not simply a matter of "style"; it is a feature which has frequently characterized the dwellings of people who have moved from their normal habitat in temperate zones to hotter climates where the houses which they constructed have been adapted to meet cultural expectations established in their countries of origin. (King 1984: 265)

Palm Trees and Swimming Pools

If King's argument is right, it goes some way toward explaining what those verandahs were doing in the suburbs of Tarim. Two of the biggest complaints of *muwallads* about Hadramawt are that it is hot and that it is dry. Repatriated from the Malay Peninsula to Arabia, they indeed moved to a hotter climate. Verandahs borrowed from the colonials in their coun-

2. The European spaces outside the cities had been set up as military cantonments in the nineteenth century but evolved into residential quarters for civilian officials and foreign merchants. Public Works Department engineers built offices, churches, bungalows, and other structures from pattern books and templates such as those of John Loudon and H. Goodwin. The buildings exude the new confidence of the British in nineteenth-century India, expressed in a classical language of built form derived from eighteenth-century English derivations of Palladio's interpretation of the classical spirit (Ware 1756). The rapidly erected classical buildings that housed the British in nineteenth-century India announced that they would be there forever.

FIGURE 19. Swimming pool, Tarim. Photo by the author.

try of origin certainly suited *muwallad*s in style and function in Tarim. Add water to verandah, and one no longer feels so hot and so dry. Some of the bungalows and mansions in Tarim's suburbs added water by building swimming pools, right in the house, flanked by generous verandahs, or in front of it under palm trees. Van der Meulen, a Malay- and Arabic-speaking Dutch official who served in the Dutch East Indies and Jedda, told of his swim at the Tarim home of a Singapore-born *muwallad,* Sayyid Abū Bakr b. Shaykh al-Kāf, on a pioneering visit in 1931: "The temperature of the water is so warm that swimming itself cools one but little, though standing afterwards with wet body in the dry evening breeze certainly does" (Van der Meulen 1932: 132–33). Artificial pools were definitely more reliable than natural floods. Van der Meulen's facility with Malay gained him acceptance in Hadramawt among the repatriated *muwallad*s, allowing for an unusually intimate view of the society of the swimming pool. How the pleasures of such novel places are integrated into *muwallad* lives in the ancestral homeland is suggested in his account:

Swimming by moonlight is an unexpected luxury and a particular pleasure to us in this country. On one side, close to the swimming-pool, there is a space for the *ṣalāt*, where a niche in the wall indicates the *qibla* (the *qibla* is the direction in which Mecca lies); on the other side there is a summer pavilion. Everything has a wash of light, delicate colour; the lines of the walls and roofs are edged with fine figures and borders, and one is inclined to forget that the material of which they are made is plain, brown mud. We spend quite a long time together with the young people on brotherly terms. They let themselves go now that no elders are present. Swimming and diving competitions are held with great gusto, until the time comes for the *ṣalāt el-ʿishāʾ* (the late evening ritual prayer), which is performed with suitable solemnity. (Van der Meulen 1932: 133)

Nūra, the polished quicklime that Aḥmad al-Junayd used on gravestones to suggest the traces of the ancestors, now found new uses, as a waterproof lining for swimming pools. European travelers like van der Meulen never failed to comment on these marvels encountered in a remote corner of Arabia, nor to enjoy them, hosted by wealthy *muwallad*s from Southeast Asia (W. H. Ingrams 1942a: 206; Johnston 1964: 92). For me, they were ready reprieves from the rigors of fieldwork. One of those houses had been converted to a public hotel by the socialist government and was always good for a swim. I especially liked the frogs in the pool and the exuberant bougainvillea nearby, flaunting their extravagant pinks and oranges. I felt at home there long before knowing why.

The surprising scene conjured by van der Meulen in Tarim—swimming and diving with gusto one moment, solemnly praying the next—is not alien to youths brought up in the Malay Archipelago and sent to Arabia. Haji Yusuf Rawa, the charismatic leader of the leading Islamist party in Malaysia, PAS (Partai Se-Islam Malaysia), treasured a similar image from his time in Mecca. Haji Yusuf was educated at the Penang Free School in British Malaya, sang English songs round the campfire as a Boy Scout, and aspired to be a lawyer in the colonial government. After completing his Junior Cambridge exams, he was sent by his father to visit relatives in Mecca and perform the pilgrimage. Upon completing it, his mind turned toward his English school home in Penang and the upcoming Senior Cambridge exams. But his relatives informed him that his father wished him to remain in Mecca, learn Arabic, and continue his studies there. They would hold his passport. A playful teenager of sixteen or seventeen, he was shocked and dismayed at this turn in his life. The event that stands out in his memory from this period is an occasion when heavy rains caused a flood in the vicinity of the *Kaʿba*, around which pilgrims circumambulate. While the Arabs looked on agape, the Javanese and Malay boys had a gala time swimming around the *Kaʿba* and taking dives off its entrance, getting up to their old tricks from the rivers back home. This frolicking led to taunts from the Arab youth, and fights broke out (Mujahid Yusof Rawa 2001: 16–26).[3]

Had some of the *muwallads*, who had been sent back to a homeland that was not theirs but their grandfathers', found a way to make their predicament tolerable? Were the swimming pools under the palm trees their private way of reconciling their personal origins with those of their entombed and entextualized ancestors—making the best of a difficult situation by combining both origins in one architectural meld, so to speak? Did a virtual Singapore now exist in a very real Tarim? The thought was intriguing.

Certainly, the bungalows and mansions that *muwallads* built for themselves in Tarim were different. Unlike the impassive houses in the old town, these new ones in the suburbs had elaborate façades. Windows could be topped by pediments, pointed or curved, and might have ornaments such as swags and festoons embroidered in mud plaster. On mansions, severely straight roof lines could be graced by a balustrade, with the dentilation beneath them that was so beloved of the Straits Settlements banks and government offices, making buildings at once imposing and approachable. Doric and Ionic pillars and pilasters are in liberal supply but lack the firmness of articulation necessary to set a mood. Instead, the fluting can be a little wide and aggressive, especially in the larger mansions. In the mud-brick buildings of Hadramawt, thick walls carry the weight, and columns seldom do real work on the outside, physically or emotionally. Instead, on these large façades, monotonous rhythms of windows and pilasters are broken up now and then by galleries with twin pillars, modest verandahs flush with the wall.

But by the standards of the old town, verandahs are always immodest, whether or not they jut out. It takes a certain kind of person, and a certain kind of self-confidence, to inhabit houses with those verandahs and those façades. Verandahs always invite guesses about the shapes of the interior. These houses are not shy about proclaiming those shapes. They are often symmetrical, for example. A curved central stairway leading up to a raised principal story may reinforce a hint of Palladian inspiration, and a portico topped by a triangular pediment may rise over the central doorway, conveying an unmistakable sense of verticality. One

3. Posters of the great flood of 1941 still delight Southeast Asian pilgrims and others in Mecca today, and they are widely sold in the markets frequented by these groups, such as Pasar Seng. I am grateful to Dadi Darmadi for sharing this observation, which he made in 2004.

of these buildings, now the Qaṣr al-Qubba Hotel, presents such a front to the visitor. Plumped within the central pediment over the portico is a rather cheeky gold crown. Behind it, in the raised center of the building, is the small dome that gives the hotel its name, the Cupola Castle Hotel. This hotel was where I went swimming in a pool under the palm trees.

Visitors ascending the stairs of such a building would appropriately be impressed with their hosts, as the latter stood at the entrance above, looking down with arms outstretched in greeting. In the 1930s, important Europeans, often colonial officials, ascended such stairs in houses in the suburbs of Tarim and were greeted by *muwallads* sent home from Singapore and elsewhere. W. Harold Ingrams, the English official who introduced British colonial administration to Hadramawt in 1937, and his wife, Doreen, were greeted and hosted by members of the al-Kāf family of Hadrami sayyids in such mansions in both Tarim and Singapore. They initially visited Tarim in 1934 and were hosted by the al-Kāfs. The family hosted them again in Singapore in 1939, when they toured the model colony of British Malaya to take lessons in indirect rule and to drum up support in the diaspora for colonial rule at home as war was breaking out. Ingrams was so impressed with his hosts that he settled on one of them, Sayyid Abū Bakr b. Shaykh al-Kāf, a Singapore-born *muwallad* repatriated to Tarim, as his partner in creating a colonial order in interior Hadramawt. Van der Meulen had earlier swum in Abū Bakr's pool; the sayyid seemed a natural choice. Sayyid Abū Bakr had his own reasons for returning the compliment.

Roads

Like my friend Muḥsin the *muwallad* of the previous chapter, whose car in Hadramawt kept breaking down, Sayyid Abū Bakr was feeling stuck. This was in the late 1920s. In compliance with the wishes of his father, Shaykh al-Kāf—who founded the family fortunes on rental houses in Singapore and willed that anyone who wanted to inherit them would have to spend his youth in Hadramawt—Sayyid Abū Bakr had repatriated to Tarim from his birthplace, Singapore, when he was thirteen.[4] He returned

4. Abū Bakr was born in Singapore in 1886 (Ṣafar 1304 A.H.; see Ruḥayyim Bā Faḍl n.d.-f: 2; W. H. Ingrams 1942a: 262).

to Singapore only once thereafter, for a brief trip. Sayyid Abū Bakr was a very rich man. He received a huge income from Singapore. Every Thursday, he distributed bags of food to the poor in Tarim. The al-Kāfs owned many of the grand new houses in the suburbs, as well as the palm gardens surrounding them. Actually, the lands were owned in perpetuity by mosque endowments and rented out for mere shillings over many years. But the rights to such rentals were transferable, and obtaining them required a lot of money. The swimming pools were fed by diesel pumps, Lister pumps from England and Deutz's from Germany. An engineer was brought in from Japan to help with them. Telephones connected these houses via a small private network, which included the sultan's palace. Sayyid Abū Bakr paid for a modern dispensary and for an Indian doctor he imported to serve the local population. With his brothers, he underwrote the budget of the Kathīrī sultanate that ruled over Tarim. The al-Kāfs had recently built a wall around the town that met at the slopes of a hill topped by a fort. Anything Sayyid Abū Bakr did, he did on a big scale.

So when Sayyid Abū Bakr felt stuck, he did not go talking to relatives looking for spare parts for a car, as my friend Muḥsin did in the 1990s. He built himself a road, all the way from Tarim to the coastal port of al-Shiḥr, a hundred miles away. Up impossible passes and across rock-strewn plateaus. Through inhospitable bedouin country. When construction of the last stretch of the road to the coast met with obstructions, he started planning an alternative route—an air connection—and invited van der Meulen's traveling companion, the German geographer von Wissman, who drew the earliest scientific maps of Hadramawt, to make surveys for an airport near Tarim.

Sayyid Abū Bakr was not alone in feeling stuck in Tarim. Most of interior Hadramawt felt the same way. The problem was that two sultanates were at odds with each other: the Kathīrīs in the interior and the Quʿayṭīs on the coast. The goods imported by merchants and bought by the population were taxed a number of times on the journey inland from the coast, as they traveled through the alternating jurisdictions of the sultanates.[5] The British had helped the Quʿayṭīs become the sole state on the coast.

5. The unsatisfactory arrangement persisted until the sultanates fell when the British left in 1967. In 1965, visitors heard complaints that luxury goods were taxed at 20 percent at the Quʿayṭī port of al-Mukallā and again at 15 percent at Say'ūn by the Kathīrīs, after being hauled over a hundred miles into the interior on the backs of camels (Zabbāl 1965: 70–71).

They had been Yāfiʿī-Hadrami commanders in the army of the Nizam of Hyderabad in India. The Muslim Nizam was one of the last and most powerful Indian rulers to resist British rule; he ensured his independence by recruiting thousands of Hadrami Arab mercenaries, rewarding them with extensive revenue fiefs on the Mughal model. Some of them had fought the British earlier on the side of the last indigenous power on the west coast, the Marathas. When the Marathas finally lost in 1818, the Arabs were disbanded. Some returned to Arabia, but most remained in India. At the British victory in Nagpur in 1817, Arabs born in Hadramawt were deported home, but those who had been born in India, the *muwallads*, could not be disposed of. The Nizam of Hyderabad offered to take them, and the British assented (Khalidi 1997: 72). While the Hadrami mercenaries were at times a thorn in the side of the imperial administration in India, they had, with the Nizam's other forces, stood by the British in their hour of need during the Indian Mutiny of 1857. In the 1860s, at the behest of the Nizam's chief minister, Britain had helped the Quʿayṭīs establish their sultanate on the Hadrami coast with arms and loans. In doing so, the British turned someone who could be a good friend and a bad enemy into a permanent ally. In one stroke, they exported a potential problem from India and imported a sovereign native ally into Hadramawt, making the Quʿayṭī's repatriation their project. What was set up on the Hadrami coast in Arabia was a "princely state" along Indian lines, independent but bound to the British by a treaty of "subsidiary alliance." In India, such treaties were coveted by the "little kingdoms," freezing into place fluid politics and making dynasties good for the next hundred and fifty years (Jeffrey 1978: 8–9).

The Kathīrī sultan was also a commander in the Nizam of Hyderabad's army. But he rebuilt his sultanate in Hadramawt without British help and allied himself with the Ottomans instead. From the time the Ottomans sent a steam warship to Hadramawt in a show of force in 1867, at the invitation of the Kathīrīs and a hundred and fifty Hadrami sayyid notables, the British made the Quʿayṭīs sovereign over the Hadrami coast and left the Kathīrīs, sayyids, and others politically stranded inland, with their only outlet to the sea under Quʿayṭī and thus British sufferance. British-Ottoman rivalry on the South Arabian coast in the nineteenth century echoed the old competition between Portuguese and Ottomans in the sixteenth century. Rivals within Hadrami circles then availed themselves of both powers (bin Hāshim 1948; Serjeant 1974 [1963]); the nineteenth century was no different. The Kathīrīs abandoned the Ottomans and came around to the British only at the end of the First World War, when their

Ottoman patrons were defeated along with their German allies. Under the Treaty of Aden, which the Kathīrīs signed in 1918, all communications with the British had to go through the Quʿayṭīs. In effect, the Kathīrīs were kept the junior party, and their vital access to the diaspora and the outside world—people, goods, letters, guns, and petitions to the British—remained at the pleasure of the Quʿayṭīs. Schematically, the Kathīrī and its neighbors in the interior were encapsulated by the Quʿayṭī on the coast, which itself was encapsulated by Britannia's rule over the waves, and over Hyderabad. These were the nested Chinese boxes of indirect rule. They allowed Britain to exercise control from the outside, without laying claim to or taking responsibility for the country of Hadramawt itself. This state of affairs continued until the eve of the Second World War, when a new round of treaties was signed, binding both states even more tightly to the British bosom and seeing off Italian advances.

In the context of Kathīrī encapsulation, Abū Bakr's road was an attempt to break out of an impasse, to force the issue in a concrete manner. In the late 1920s, he recruited a road builder with experience from the Sudan, furnished him with a crew, and began at the most difficult end, going up an impossible wadi wall near Tarim. The corners were so sharp the cars had to go up backward. The gradient was so steep that rocks had to be wedged under the tires. From Tarim, the road reached out to the port of al-Shiḥr on the coast, under the Quʿayṭī sultan's jurisdiction. Abū Bakr had the sultan's agreement but not his blessings. Between Tarim and al-Shiḥr were a number of bedouin tribes that were not well disposed toward either town or their masters. Their respective positions can be imagined in the following way, in terms of cars.

The Quʿayṭī sultan owned three cars in al-Shiḥr; a grand total of seven or eight cars were in working order on the coast.[6] The sultan preferred to spend his time back in Hyderabad in India and had little interest in motoring to the Hadrami interior. The bedouin made a good living transporting goods by camel to the interior from the coast. In the 1930s, some eighty-five thousand camel trips made the journey annually, and cameleers had little interest in seeing cars or lorries compete with them. In the interior, the situation was reversed, as it were. Of the main towns there, Shibām boasted three cars; Say'ūn, thirteen; and Tarim, a whopping sixty. Every single one of these cars had been imported by sea, carried from the

6. The transportation statistics are from W. H. Ingrams's 1936 report on his 1934 reconnaissance in Hadramawt (W. H. Ingrams 1936), which set out the basis for colonial rule over Hadramawt beginning in 1937.

coast in parts on camels—twelve camels per car—and reassembled inland. The sayyids of Tarim had done very well for themselves in colonial Southeast Asia.

Now, however, the interior towns, foremost among them Tarim, demanded unfettered access to the coast, and to the great diaspora beyond it, beyond the coast's sultan and his petty squabbles with his rivals. Many in the interior, like Sayyid Abū Bakr, were *muwallad*s who had been born abroad in the diaspora, in places like East Africa, India, Malaya, and Singapore. Thus, they were British subjects with rights to British protection and travel passes. The quirks of the local political arrangement between coast and interior in Hadramawt were not consonant with the *muwallads*' status as subjects of the world empire that straddled the continents and ruled the waves. While their sixty cars in Tarim were a measure of the greatness of British rule in Malaya, their inability to drive those cars to the British satrapy at al-Shiḥr was a measure of the weakness of British rule in Hadramawt. When Sayyid Abū Bakr decided that something had to be done, he spent large amounts of his money from Singapore to get those cars from Tarim to the coast, back toward Singapore, as it were.

Sayyid Abū Bakr's efforts are described in the book *Journey to the Two Garrisons, al-Shiḥr and al-Mukallā,* by the sayyid Muḥammad bin Hāshim (bin Hāshim 1931). In 1930, word came to Tarim that Sayyid Abū Bakr's brother ʿAbd al-Raḥmān b. Shaykh al-Kāf was journeying from Singapore to al-Shiḥr by ship, along with other al-Kāfs. Sayyid Abū Bakr decided to travel by car to the coast to meet his brother, and he invited some friends along for the ride. Some twenty showed up, among them the author of the *Journey,* bin Hāshim. A Hadrami sayyid who had spent many years in Java teaching in sayyid schools, bin Hāshim was familiar with cars and other modern conveniences. He later authored an official history of the Kathīrī sultanate (bin Hāshim 1948). His *Journey* was to be an official record not only of Abū Bakr's trip to the coast but of his road-building venture as well. The text is a *riḥla,* a travel account faithful to the genre in Arabic literature. As we have seen in earlier examples, the narrative traces the itinerary of the journey, describing boon companionship, sights along the way, people met, difficulties encountered, some poetry. The vividness of the account is enhanced by many photographs, which were a novelty at this time. Given the contentious nature of the road and journey, the pictures play the role of evidence as well.

A journey, especially one such as this pioneering trip by car to the coast, is an adventure. The fun cannot be spoiled by officialese. Therefore, bin Hāshim tactfully keeps pronouncements under control within the footnotes. There, unobtrusively, he informs us that the road is three hundred kilometers long and that Sayyid Abū Bakr had spent a great deal of his own money to build it, on account of God and the well-being of future generations.[7] In building the road, he had also established public watering places along the way, the sort of continuing good works (*ʿamal jārī*) that earn the benefactor merit in the afterlife. As the journey progresses, bin Hāshim mentions the tribes whose areas they pass through, such as the al-Jābrī and the Maʿʿāra. In the footnotes, he reproduces treaties of protection given by tribal representatives to Sayyid Abū Bakr for safe passage of motor traffic on his road, including the names of all chiefs of subsections who have pledged their word. In the treaties, the sayyid wisely allays their concerns about loss of their livelihood as cameleers. Passing through the territories of the sultanates, bin Hāshim provides their histories, acknowledging their sovereignty. Approaching the coast, he presents in the footnotes a lengthy correspondence between the Quʿayṭī sultan and Sayyid Abū Bakr, documenting the sultan's consent to the road. He also sets out with barely suppressed venom all eleven points of the 1918 Treaty of Aden, which made the Quʿayṭīs gatekeepers to the coast. This treaty was the document that had sealed the Kathīrī towns up in the interior, as punishment for siding with the Ottomans during the First World War. Bin Hāshim presents the road as a great attempt at a *nahḍa,* a "renaissance," in a place where ways of doing things have remained unchanged for thousands of years, such as the use of camels for transport. More subtly, he also describes an attempt to rectify an egregious political impediment to the free mobility of Hadramawt's diaspora in their homeland, imposed by the British in the 1918 settlement.

Sayyid Abū Bakr's road was a political project that faced insurmountable obstacles. That fact was clear to most observers. Bin Hāshim's *Journey* was a political tract that attempted to open up a diplomatic solution. In the treaties, histories, and correspondence documented in its footnotes, the *Journey* sets out the positions of the interested parties in terms acceptable to them, acknowledging their rights and obligations. No one party really is at fault. The problems happen in the interstices.

In the hills of Hadramawt live the grand Arab tribes of Quḍāʿa, Nuwwaḥ, Nahd, Kinda, Ḥimyar, Madhḥij and others. Among them remains blood and revenge. This causes the lack of a strong, settled government in the country, built on a sound ba-

7. Ingrams estimates that Sayyid Abū Bakr spent $180,000 on the road (W. H. Ingrams 1936: 90, 1942a: 251).

sis. The country is in commotion and the land disturbed. If large garrisons are erected on it the state's treasury would be weakened in financing them. If few garrisons are erected, the people would not celebrate because not all the country would submit and be brought to heel. This is the current situation. (bin Hāshim 1931: 27, n 1)

Bin Hāshim's statement has a classical ring to it. He associates the tribal names with original Arab, pre-Islamic kingdoms. He presents the inability of government to bring them to heel as a compliment, playing to the tribes' self-regard. Governments come and go, but these grand old tribes remain on the land forever (Dresch 1989). The sultanates are not at fault either, for the country is not rich enough to support strong states. The situation is not a case of corrupt rule. The author's use of classical language is diplomacy at work because it allows each party to assume its place with neither finger-pointing nor pretense that all is well. A problem exists. All parties are equally responsible and equally respectable. But no solution is at hand. The situation depicted is one of incompleteness; it will take a party yet unnamed to complete the circle and resolve the situation.

In classical terms, that figure would be a sayyid, a descendant of the Prophet. As a figure with a noble provenance associated with the common good of religion, a sayyid can act as a disinterested outsider, a mediator, and craft a solution.[8] Is Sayyid Abū Bakr al-Kāf that figure? Perhaps. The book is dedicated to him. He has been hard at work for the common good. The classical sayyid in Hadramawt is also a Sufi mystic. He is able to draw upon resources far away and unseen, and he can be in two places at once. Sayyid Abū Bakr's reach extends from Tarim to Singapore, whence comes his abundant gold. Bin Hāshim calls the al-Kāf sayyids "kings of gold," who are a great favor bestowed upon Hadramawt (bin Hāshim 1931: 25, n. 1). His reach extends to al-Shiḥr, where he has procured from the sultan the palace with the exotic name of al-Bāgh, Hindi (originally Persian) for "garden," a terminus where work can be carried out to complete the road.[9] In al-Shiḥr, too, the sultan's chief minister is now a sayyid, another descendant of the Prophet who is thus an agnate of Sayyid Abū Bakr, who may aid him in his work. To complete the cir-

8. The figure of the mediator is a staple of anthropology (Caton 1990; Dresch 1989; Evans-Pritchard 1949; Gellner 1969). In pragmatic colonial eyes, he had a useful if conservative and antimodern role to play: to maintain order where the long arm of government has not yet reached (W. H. Ingrams 1936: 40).

9. Seen from India, the etymology is a little less lofty. The Anglo-Indian term *Company Bāgh* means "the usual phrase for the public garden of a station" (Hobson-Jobson 1994 (1903): 462, entry for John Company).

cle, bin Hāshim's book is published by the al-Kāf sayyids of Tarim. The mystic and mediator is a virtuoso skilled at representing his work.

But there are cards the sayyid does not have. The Quʿayṭī sultan's troops brought in from India, for example. The all-important European ships of Rotterdam Lloyd, Netherland M.V.S., and Blue Funnel Line, which call eight times a year at the Hadrami ports on their journey between Rotterdam and Singapore. The aeroplanes that would fly to and from the airport the sayyid dreams of building near Tarim. Who holds these cards? The same hand that dealt out the problems in the first place? That wrote the 1918 Treaty of Aden? Aden, Hyderabad, and Singapore—the absent places whose names feature so prominently in this apparently local *Journey to the Two Garrisons* within Hadramawt—are key nodes of the Hadrami diaspora. Hadrami protagonists in this story come from there. But these places also fall under the jurisdiction of the great British empire, whom the Arabs address in correspondence as "Ruler of the Waves."[10] Is the journey from Tarim to the coast a call out to sea to invite the Ruler of the Waves onto shore? To assume some moral obligation perhaps? In the colonization of Hadramawt, which began in 1937, diaspora and empire did a delicate dance. It all had to do with the roads.

The colonial administration of Hadramawt began in 1937 with the enactment of a new treaty, in which the Quʿayṭī sultan accepted a British Resident Advisor along Malayan lines. Following the Malayan formula, the sultan's word held on Muslim religion and custom; on everything else, it was the Advisor's.[11] The Kathīrīs signed two years later, and a shiny new colony was minted right when the Second World War began: the Eastern Aden Protectorate. This area was the last bit of land colonized by the British, at the end of almost half a millennium of expansion (Johnston 1963: 35; Morris 1980: 317). The timing is puzzling, as independence was already in the air worldwide, Woodrow Wilson's Fourteen Points shadowed British action everywhere, and what Elizabeth Monroe calls "the decline of British nerve" was in full evidence, as were its reasons (Monroe 1964: 131–50). From 1936 to 1939, these reasons included full-scale Arab rebellion in Palestine, with guerilla compatriots pouring in from Syria and highly visible, international congresses to publicize their cause

10. For example, see PRO, FO371/5237: 135.

11. The Malayan formulation was Islamic religion and Malay custom, but in Arabia, the British resisted making a cognate distinction between Islamic religion and Arab custom. The original Muslim race was touchy on the matter, and the British treaty writers did not want any trouble.

in Syria and Cairo, attended by delegates from India, China, Yugoslavia, and Arab America (Monroe 1964: 122–23). Further afield, the British Indian government had been devolving power in a democratic direction for over two decades, with the Minto-Morley and Montagu-Chelmsford reforms, in attempts to stay ahead of the nationalists and retain the initiative. Attempts to reverse decades of a laissez-faire policy toward the princely states remained the domain of political officers, who dragged their feet, siding with their native wards (Copland 1978; Manor 1978: 313). In China, nationalists had forced embarrassing retreats from Western concessions. More to the point, the British public and its politicians had just spent over a decade disgorging themselves of Iraq, saved by Churchill, Lawrence "of Arabia" (in a second, redemptive Arabian performance), and the new air force, and they were in no mood to lose any more blood or treasure shooting brown men. In addition, imperial rivals such as Italy and Germany were crying foul from the sidelines.

Collaboration or Clarification?

> You speak to me continually of the British Government and British Policy. . . . But I see five governments where you see one, and the same number of policies. There is a policy, first of your Foreign Office; second of your Army; third of your Navy; fourth of your protectorate in Egypt; fifth of your Government in India. Each of these British Governments seems to me to act upon an Arab policy of its own.
>
> Sharif Ḥusayn of Mecca to
> Lt. Col. C. E. Wilson (Westrate 1992: 26)

> The affairs of the Middle East are . . . the joint concern of the Foreign Office, the India Office, and the War Office; three of the strongest departments, each with a tradition. In each are officials with experience and knowledge, who write admirable minutes in criticism of the others' recommendations.
>
> T. E. Lawrence (Westrate 1992: 204)

The customary geostrategic reasons for British colonization of Hadramawt are not hard to find. The new "forward policy" was initiated in 1934 at the end of three decades of expansion in Arabia by three states: the Saudis, the Ḥamīd al-Dīn imams of North Yemen, and the British in Egypt, Palestine, Transjordan, Iraq, the Persian Gulf, and the Aden Protectorate. In the process, other potentates such as the Ottoman overlords, the Rashīdīs of Ḥāʾil, and the Idrīsī of ʿAṣīr had been squeezed out. The British had had a hand in every one of these maneuvers. In the southwest corner of Arabia, now only the Saudis, the Yemenis, and the British were left standing. In 1934, their mutual borders were stabilized by treaties, which were to hold for decades. In that year, the Yemeni imam acknowledged that his northern territories of ʿAṣīr and Najrān would be under Saudi control. In the south, he sued for peace with the British and withdrew his troops from a number of villages along their border. While the new weakness of the Yemeni imam enabled the British to strengthen their hold on Hadramawt, the enhanced strength and closer proximity of Saudi Arabia now encouraged them to do so. Italian designs on Ethiopia, coupled with Italy's influence in Yemen, introduced another important consideration. In the runup to the Second World War, Italy and its colonies in the Mediterranean and Gulf of Aden threatened to disrupt British naval passage between England and India, and indeed British ships had to revert to the long route around Africa in the course of the war.

At the same time, the air force was growing in importance to Britain. Airplanes, with their ability to control whole swaths of land, had helped extricate British troops from Iraq in the early 1920s. From that success, the air force had bid for and successfully taken over the defense and governance of Aden and its protectorate in 1927, from the army. Air power necessitated political footwork on the ground. In contrast to army and artillery, aircraft were effective over longer distances and demanded a forward policy, some have claimed (Gavin 1975); Britain had to strengthen regional rulers and its alliances with them. Whether air power indeed demanded a forward policy, or enabled one, of a peculiar sort, is not clear. On a transregional scale, the development of an air route between South Africa and India called for securing points on the southern coast of Arabia because the planes had short ranges. The air force had been given control of Aden and its protectorate with the arrival of twelve bombers in Aden. In consequence, political officers were hired and sent out into the countryside to secure landing grounds and enhanced treaties with sultans. Within the region, any place was now only a few hours away by air, rather than weeks through difficult country without roads.

These are the good reasons for direct British interference in sultanates of the region. But they do not account for the actions of men on the ground who went beyond their orders, the passion with which they acted, and the lengths to which they went in explaining their actions. The colonization of Hadramawt was remarkable not for the amount of blood it spilled but for the amount of ink. W. Harold Ingrams, the British political officer who had been called from Zanzibar for the undertaking, had been told to sign treaties with three sultans. After a few weeks in Hadramawt, he came back with treaties with some fourteen hundred independent sovereigns (at times he would claim two thousand). He had a lot of explaining to do. Ingrams wrote four monographs about Hadramawt and his work there (W. H. Ingrams 1936, 1940, 1942a, 1942b), and his wife, Doreen, wrote two (D. Ingrams 1949, 1970). Thirty years after his first monograph, just a year before eventual British withdrawal, he was still adjusting his explanations:

> But I am sufficiently grateful for the encouragement I had from Sir Bernard Reilly; that, and the fact that I disregarded official policy were probably the two things which helped me most to avoid trouble . . . There was no question here of running a district as I had done in Zanzibar and Pemba, with the certainty of security and the comfortable feeling of law and order at one's back. One had to learn the systems which made life in anarchic conditions possible—the methods of truce-making, the weeks and months sitting cross-legged on the floor and arguing with independent-minded indignant tribesmen who sat with their rifles in their laps and had no doubt whatever that they were the kings of their particular castles or caves or shelters, and you a stranger guest if you played the game their way. Sometimes they would shoot at you if they felt you were an intruder on their territory, but at 200 yards one could feel reasonably safe. (W. H. Ingrams 1966b: 15)

What is puzzling here is the quality of the British men and women responsible for the late expansion into Aden's protectorate hinterland. In the 1930s, British officers in southern Arabia exceeded their orders, made treaties without authority, dressed in native Arab getup, eschewed starched tunics, and spent inordinate amounts of time sitting on floors scheming with Arab cronies. They seemed more like the romantic adventurists of empire in eighteenth-century India, who finagled and grabbed large chunks of land seemingly with as much charm as arms, than like the bureaucratic administrators who followed them in the nineteenth and twentieth centuries and incrementally spread administrative capillaries throughout those chunks of land.[12] And this in an empire of democratic accountability, departments and jurisdictions, regular reports, telegraphic instructions, and stable salaries, staffed by sober "examination men" of the exalted Indian Civil Service.

12. Indeed, they appeared so to the urbane Charles Johnston, one of the last British governors of Aden (1960–63): "The men who carried it out in the field—Belhaven, Ingrams and others—are in fact the last breakers of new ground in our long imperial tradition; and for violent energy and eccentric individualism some of them seem more akin to the pioneers of our eighteenth-century Empire than to officials of their own generation" (Johnston 1964: 35).

Moreover, through an active press, colonial administrators were subject to the scrutiny of oppositionist politicians and home populations weary of the imperial burden. Just what did they think they were doing?

Historical interpretations of British action in the Middle East in the years between the two world wars are bedeviled by such odd juxtapositions of the eighteenth and twentieth centuries. In the Anglo-Arab labyrinth, systematic interpretations cut of the whole cloth of romanticism, imperial *realpolitik,* or enduring Orientalist categories of knowledge do not satisfactorily capture the mix of action, intention, and self-representation spilling out of the autobiographies and histories of the period. In the British colonization of Hadramawt, similar observations were being made on the Arab side, juxtaposing antiquity and modernity. The twentieth-century swimming pools and cars of the *muwallads* in the ancient homeland of Tarim, cut off from progressive Singapore by the medieval feuds of bedouin in Hadramawt, constitute such juxtapositions, as eloquently expressed in bin Hāshim's *Journey* and other writings of the 1930s published in the Southeast Asian diaspora.[13] In the act of colonization, parallel developments on the British and Arab sides converged. This coming together sharpens a line of interpretation we have been developing in this book. We have seen the movement of a diaspora draw together world regions. Here, it is an empire doing so. In the interwar years, empire and diaspora could not escape becoming entangled with each other across the Indian Ocean. We chart the course of that entanglement in the following pages.

In British imperial circles, the temporal dissonance one senses in the interwar years was generated by a conjunction, as it were, of different world regions in Arabia. In the British Middle East of the First World War, policies and personnel from different parts of the empire met and competed (Westrate 1992: 79–101).[14] The British Government of India,

13. These writings include the first modern history of Hadramawt, al-Bakrī's *Political History of Hadramawt* (al-Bakrī al-Yāfi'ī 1936), written by a Java-born creole and published in Cairo; and the numerous newspapers published in the Dutch East Indies in Arabic and Malay, such as *al-Mishkā, al-Murshid, Pewarta Arab, al-Hudā, al-'Arab, al-Sha'b al-Ḥaḍramī,* and *al-Ḥisāb.*

14. Halfway between India and the Mediterranean, Aden's position within imperial administration was always a bone of contention between the Indian and British governments. During the First World War, the Indian government relinquished authority over Aden to the War Office while retaining control of the settlement itself; the hinterland Protectorate went to the Foreign Office, "and for the next twenty years it drifted uncomfortably and uncertainly in the rock-strewn waters of administrative reorganisation, before being placed firmly under the control of the Colonial Office in 1937. During the intervening period it was the subject of incessant bureaucratic wrangling between different departments of Government" (Gavin 1975: 252–53).

which was responsible for Iraq, the Persian Gulf, and Aden, was a mature imperial government with established administrative and racial hierarchies. Within its orbit, nationalism was a subversive and dangerous idea to be suppressed, usually as the crime of "sedition." Viewed from the commanding heights of the Government of India, nationalism represented a dagger poised at the heart of empire. Viewed from Britain's Arab Bureau in Cairo, however, nationalism was a good thing, which would help the British take over or free parts of the Ottoman empire, secure the sea and air routes to India (via Baghdad), and ensure strategic access to the Persian oil needed by the navy's warships. The "good old Turk" stopped being good when he took the side of the Germans. Nationalism was an irresistible tide that one would do better to ride than counter, and Lawrence of Arabia would show how it was to be done.

While parts of India had been in British hands since the eighteenth century, the "penetration of Arabia" was still in its infancy in 1904, when D. G. Hogarth published his summation of European knowledge of Arabia under this title. Oxford archaeologist turned imperial mastermind, as director of the Arab Bureau in Cairo, Hogarth was to inspire T. E. Lawrence, H. St.-John Philby, D. van der Meulen, Ingrams, Freya Stark, and others to write, in the 1930s, of their Arabian travels and conquests in the grand old mode of geographical exploration (Franey 2003; Phillips 1997; Pratt 1992). Thus, in British Arabia, canons of classics and colonial saints of different provenances fed into British thinking from different directions, giving rise to conflicting views. Progressive, forward-looking opinion in India sought to run ahead of the nationalists and loosen control from a position of strength. Its counterpart in Cairo sought to get behind nationalists and then tighten control from an initial position of weakness. War had brought them all together in Arabia, quickening the pace of communications, tightening up the roads, and throwing separate imperial departments and jurisdictions into the same pot. The sense of temporal dissonance in the British Middle East was a result of extraordinarily high and developed channels of mobility within the empire at the end of World War I. This dissonance found expression in an oddly simple question of geography: did Hadramawt—and the Aden Protectorate more generally—belong in the Middle East or in India?

This contest between Cairo and Delhi in the Middle East over the question of colonial expansion in a nationalist age was resolved in a novel way in South Arabia: it was given a Malayan solution. As we have seen, when the Quʿayṭī sultanate was set up by the British, it was essentially an Indian princely state, legally independent but in other ways dependent upon the British. The logic of the "princely state"—indirect rule—was different from that of the "provinces" in India, as the latter were directly ruled by a central government in Delhi under the sovereignty of the British Crown. Two different ruling logics partitioned India into separate geographical spaces. In Indian terms, Hadramawt was a princely state, ruled indirectly. Malaya, in contrast, was a strange beast. In the Federated Malay States, the two ruling logics coexisted on the same strip of land, on the west coast of the peninsula.[15] Malaya was ruled by native sultans with Resident Advisors, but at the same time these independent treaty states were rigorously bound together by modern primary industry and a central administration under a British Resident-General in a political federation (Fisher 1991: 467).[16] A federation along these or similar lines became the new model envisaged for Hadramawt, and subsequently for all of British South Arabia. Thus, when the government of Hadramawt was reorganized in the 1937 and 1939 treaties, Hadramawt essentially jumped categories in terms of British colonial departments: from that of the Indian princely state to that of the Federated Malay States—sovereign native entities in a federal association run by a British administrative machinery subordinate to its own centralized, British executive. For urban Hadrami society, in the homeland and the diaspora, this shift was less a colonization of the homeland by an external entity than an internal reorganization of part of the British empire in the Indian Ocean.

As long as that reorganization did not take place, diasporic Hadrami society was divided among sovereigns and imperial jurisdictions: an Indian-style princely state in the Quʿayṭī sultanate on the Hadrami coast, an unreliable treaty partner in the Kathīrīs; settlements directly ruled by the British Crown in Aden, Bombay, Colombo, Singapore, Malacca, and Penang; communities under Dutch sovereignty in the Dutch East Indies; military command in Jedda, Aden, and Singapore at various times; Italian rule in Italian Somaliland; German rule in German East Africa; Ottoman imperial administration in parts of the Middle East before the First World

15. I thank Sugata Bose for sharing this insight with me. He makes the India-Malaya comparison in chapter 2 of his forthcoming *Empire and Culture on the Indian Ocean Rim* (Bose forthcoming). The chapter argues that the reorganization of British India after the Mutiny of 1857–58 put a new emphasis on the princely state, thereby creating a new model of sovereignty, which was then exported to British colonies around the Indian Ocean.

16. In African terms, derived from the Indian ones, the different logics of rule were the separate "rule of difference" over the customary chiefdoms of the Bantustans and that of civic rights in the cities (Mamdani 1996; see Fisher 1991 and Low 1978 for comparisons between India and other parts of the empire).

War; and so on. For individuals, this proliferation of statelike entities with overlapping claims on diasporic Hadramis produced difficulties—but opportunities as well—of movement, residence, evasion, and adjudication. At the level of interstate relations, it produced a nightmare of jurisdictional jumbles. Were the affairs of a deceased pilgrim in Mecca, born in Hadramawt and resident in Batavia, subject to Dutch, English, Turkish, or Islamic legal jurisdiction, for example? Colonial files, such as the one entitled "Disposal of Effects of British Subjects Who Die in the Hejaz," teem with exchanges of letters agitating over such jumbles.[17]

Diasporic life presented questions to Hadrami Arabs similar to those presented by Arab nationalism to the British: was one to resist the waves or to ride them? The colonization of Hadramawt late in the imperial day met with surprisingly muted international reaction and economical military action because a successful partnership was struck, for a while, between some Arabs and some Englishmen, who were able to agree that the questions and problems they faced were not only similar but were in fact the same.[18] This coming together developed as Arab and Englishman traveled along the same roads, in similar vehicles, and met one another at the same stops. Empire and diaspora were both very mobile affairs and thus understood each other very well. In seventeenth-century Surat, the East India Company needed help from Hadrami sayyids in order to rent houses. In the nineteenth century, when Stamford Raffles wanted to establish his free-trade port in Singapore, he enlisted the help of those who already were conducting big business in the region, enticing Hadramis from nearby Palembang, the home port of an extensive Arab merchant sailing fleet. Subsequently, as the British achieved "paramountcy" around the Indian Ocean in the closing decades of the nineteenth century, they in effect ruled

17. See the file IORL, R/20/A/3477.

18. The Hadrami Arabic journal *al-Murshid*, newly launched in Surabaya in the Dutch East Indies by Muḥammad ʿAbbūd al-ʿAmūdī, observed in the opening article of its first issue that Hadramis abroad read news of the homeland no differently from that of Spain and Germany—that is, with detachment and with concern only for their own villages. The people of Tarim, Sayʾūn, Shibām, and Dawʿan took news of the colonization of Hadramawt with indifference because only the Āl Jābir—not their own towns—had been bombed in the process. *Al-Murshid* expressed exasperation at the lack of "what is called public opinion" among Hadramis, unlike the situation in other nations, and called for the voices of Hadrami persons of consequence to be heard ("Ḥaḍramawt," *al-Murshid* Year 1 Issue 1, 2 August 1937: 2–3). The paucity of Hadrami expressions of nationalism does not sit well in the literature on colonialism and nationalism. The apparent anomaly is easier to understand if we compare the Hadramis' situation with that of other diasporas that prospered under the wings of other people's imperial states, such as the Genoese (Arrighi 1994: 96–126; Braudel 1992: 157–74).

the Hadrami diaspora, even without ruling the homeland itself. Thus, we may see attempts to involve the British in the homeland not so much as collaboration as getting the British to live up to their obligations and to clarify matters. A succession of diasporic requests for regular banking, postal, transport, and consular facilities—to domesticate and normalize the imperial space of the ocean—was steadily rebuffed by British authorities concerned with security instead. Episodes of pan-Islamic panic coursing through British officialdom in Arabia and South and Southeast Asia, such as fear of Muslim support for the Ottoman declaration of *jihād* during the First World War and the subsequent search for a universal caliph, dissuaded officials from allowing a liberal flow of civilian business across the ocean. However, from the point of view of the diaspora, and of its predominantly merchant and city interests, if the homeland was already encapsulated by the British empire, why should it not reap the benefits of the much-vaunted imperial peace? This question vexed many Hadramis after the First World War, as wartime restrictions on movement across the ocean continued to be enforced on certain categories of diasporic Hadramis, while the 1918 treaty put new impediments in place in the homeland by installing the Quʿayṭī sultan as sole gatekeeper on the coast.

An exchange of views between British officials in Batavia and Aden, in response to a request to transport passengers between Java and Hadramawt, shows what diasporic Hadramis were up against, as civilians suspected of divided loyalties across the lines of divided native sovereignty and interimperial rivalry during the First World War. In a 1916 telegram to the Foreign Office in London, the British consul-general in Dutch Batavia asked for instructions on a suitable response:

> Agent Netherland Steamship Co. here enquires whether Arabs wishing proceed Mukalla can be landed there or at Aden in batches of 100 up to maximum of 600 and what if any formalities are required regarding conveyance of these nominally Turkish subjects. Intercourse between bonafide Makala Arabs there and their native place should I think be encouraged and I could if necessary control bonafides.[19]

This query was forwarded from the Secretary of State to the Viceroy in India, across departmental jurisdictions, and handed down to the Viceroy's subordinate in Aden, the Political Resident, for an informed response. He replied as follows:

19. PRO, FO371/2781, "Hadramawt Arabs Proceeding from Batavia to Mukalla," Consul-General Batavia to Foreign Office, October 1916.

The reason for this sudden exodus from Batavia is unknown, and this precludes my doing justice to the query. Prima facie not advisable to allow direct communication between Batavia and Makalla by foreign steamship qua possible landing of contraband. Hadramawt people not nominally Turkish subjects, and if they claim to be so their passage at this time into country within our sphere is objectionable. Makalla Sultan would certainly like to check entry of these people into Makalla, as he is closely engaged in coping with sedition fostered by Turkish agents and their advent would hamper him. As regards bona fides of Makalla people, Sultan is best judge, and he might prefer they be returned home via Aden. I am referring matter to him.

Consultations between the India Office and the Foreign Office resulted in instructions to the consul in Batavia to strike a balance between blockade and free passage, channeling passengers through Aden for control. An apparently innocuous request for diasporic return was ineluctably swept up in much grander concerns:

Inhabitants of the Hadramawt are not Turkish subjects, and all Arabs desiring to proceed from Java to that region must land at Aden first. Confidential: can you explain this sudden exodus? We know that Turkish commander at Lahej has been intriguing actively in the Hadramawt, and the whole movement may be connected with pan-Islamic propaganda in the DEI [Dutch East Indies].[20]

Transdiasporic Initiatives: The Question of Reform

> It is obvious that the leaders of the Sayyid party use different means in dealing with the English authorities to those which they employ with the officials of the Dutch Indies or the Government of Hadramaut. They spread the rumour in Hadramaut that the Irshad converted the Arabs to Christianity and that Surkati was not circumcised; they tried to intimidate the Indian Government by denouncing the Irshad people as Bolsheviks; for England, they accused it of anti-English agitation and pro-Turkish intrigues.
>
> B. Schrieke, Advisor, Bureau for Native and Arab Affairs, Netherlands East Indies, to Prof. T. W. Arnold, Advisor, British Indian Government[21]

20. Lahej is a town, settlement, and sultanate just north of Aden in Yemen. This passage comes from PRO, FO371/2781, Foreign Office to Consul-General Batavia, December 1916, parenthetical comments added.

21. PRO, FO371/5235.

> The telegrams are a perfect babel of conflicting suggestions and views, which interweave and intertwine from man to man and place to place in an almost inexplicable tangle.
>
> Mark Sykes (Westrate 1992: 24)

In the course of the First World War, British authorities drew an absolute distinction between "good" and "bad" Arabs. Good Arabs had sided with the British and were major landlords in Singapore, religious bureaucrats in Malaya, businessmen in Batavia, sultans in British southern Arabia, and enthusiasts of T. E. Lawrence's pro-sharif policy in Arabia. Bad Arabs had sided with the Ottomans and were pan-Islamic caliphate agitators in Java, India, and Ceylon; Turkish agents in British southern Arabia; Italian ones in Ethiopia and Somalia; and fundraisers for the Yemeni imam among wealthy, diasporic Hadramis in Singapore and Java. In colonial sociology, good Arabs were the Quʿayṭī sultans and the sayyids, who possessed great wealth tied up in the British colonies of Hyderabad and Singapore. Sayyids, as descendants of the prophet Muḥammad, could be counted upon to support their agnates the sharifs, whom the British were busy installing on thrones in Transjordan and Iraq after the war. Bad Arabs were the Kathīrī sultans, their tribal kin and allies among the notables, and self-made men from the lower orders of Hadrami society, many of whom had grown rich outside of British colonies and control, such as in the Dutch East Indies.[22] They were suspected of supporting the Saudis, rivals to the British-backed sharifs. Dutch favors were often the reverse of British ones, for the Dutch were ever apprehensive of sayyid influence over the native Muslim masses (Hurgronje 1906; Mandal 1997). For over two decades after the First World War, and through the Second, the British continued to punish those they disfavored, denying them travel documents, monitoring and interdicting them along all the shipping routes when they did not, and keeping them subservient to favored Arabs, like the Quʿayṭīs who controlled Kathīrī access to the Hadrami coast.

Such policies, maintained over decades across the ocean from Arabia through India to the Malay Archipelago, shaped the internal politics of

22. Tribal kin included bin ʿAbdāt, bin Ṭālib, Bi-l-Fās, and Bā Jaray tribal sections of the Shanāfir confederation. Allies among the notables included the al-ʿAmūdī Shaykhs of Wadi Dawʿan, as well as tribal groups of the region such as the Bi-l-Ḥamr, Bā Ṣahī, Bā Qabṣ, and al-Māḍī. Men in the so-called lower orders included bin Sunkar, Manqūsh, and Bā Ḥashwān.

Hadrami society throughout the diaspora. British favor itself became a crucial object of Hadrami politics. In this, sayyids held the advantage. British officials, from their dealings with Malay states in the nineteenth century, in which sayyids played key advisory and diplomatic roles (Ho 2002a; Mohammad Redzuan Othman 1997), had come to rely on a number of elite sayyid individuals for intelligence while promoting them within the new colonial religious bureaucracy; this relationship of trust continued into the twentieth century.[23] These personages were not shy about pressing their colonial advantage to the detriment of their rivals within internal Hadrami conflicts, making external British favor and disfavor a factor within Hadrami circles.

As internal and external politics fed off each other after the First World War and through the interwar period, conflicts within the large internal space of Hadrami society, in the homeland and abroad, took on the appearance of a systematic and growing division between two groups. While the Dutch East Indies, Saudi Arabia, Italian Ethiopia, and the Hadrami interior—all outside of British rule—provided countries where British disfavor did not matter, travel and communications among these places unavoidably passed through British hands. Suitably intimidated, those disfavored by the British protested their innocence and repeatedly petitioned for relief from undeserved official opprobrium. The eminent Dutch scholar B. Schrieke, then a colonial official in Java, sought to enlighten his British counterparts on behalf of the disfavored, explaining that the British were needlessly frittering away the loyalty of "progressive" Arabs of consequence. The point was debated within British officialdom, and while adjustments were made here and there, the British continued to hold established sayyid and sultanic allies in regard as pillars of establishment order and to tar the rest as potential troublemakers who needed watching. Progressives they might be, but the new Indies money of self-made Hadrami men smelled like the new education of Bengali baboos: they were all in much too much of a rush. They were, after all, not aristocrats (Cannadine 2001) nor even noble bedouin, for that matter (Tidrick 1989 [1981]).

Instead of rushing, what was called for was "reform": considered, delib-

23. Among the names that appear repeatedly in the colonial files are ʿAlī b. Aḥmad bin Shihāb, advisor to the British Consul-General in Batavia; ʿAlawī b. Ṭāhir al-Ḥaddād, mufti of Johor, the Malay princely state whose sultan had been raised up to sovereign status by the British; and Muḥammad bin ʿAqīl, gem trader, scholar, and member of the Muslim Advisory Board in Singapore (Roff 2002).

erate, steady action in the English spirit of improvement. A series of reform acts in nineteenth-century England had successfully extended the franchise with minimal social upheaval. British-initiated "reforms" in Indian government were now devolving power downward. Reformist natives were not thrown in jail or banished; revolutionaries were. Should we be surprised, then, that in the interwar years, Hadramis of all political shades and social stripes under the British penumbra claimed that what they were doing was just that, "reform," and nothing more, even as they pursued incompatible objectives and interests rapidly clustering around opposed poles?

These rivals were the Irshādī and ʿAlawī-sayyid movements, whose origins we have traced to different diasporic experiences in the Malay Archipelago. The "new men," new sorts of immigrant Hadramis without the privileges of sayyid status, were calling for an ethic of universal Muslim assimilation, seeking to reverse the venerable sayyid history of asymmetric marriages that had created elite, Arab-native creole communities. While the dispute originated in the mixed demographic map of Java, it had spread to Singapore and across the Malay Archipelago with the expanding circulation of print media, helped along by Cairene impulses. British partisanship in what seemed at the outset an internal Hadrami or Muslim affair guaranteed that the dispute would grow, and persist, especially in areas beyond the long arm of Britain's imperial grasp. Right as the First World War broke out, this diasporic Hadrami dispute gained new institutional form, in the founding of the Irshād, shorthand for the Islamic Association for Reform and Guidance, in Dutch Java in 1914.[24] Opponents to the Irshād also adopted the banner of reform, holding the Hadrami Reform Congress in Singapore in 1928 under sayyid auspices (al-Mu'tamar al-Iṣlāḥī al-Ḥaḍramī n.d.).The objectives that each side hoped to achieve under the common label of reform are not immediately self-evident. Nevertheless, recent historians of Hadramawt, seeking to restore agency to non-Westerners, have taken the Hadramis at their word, taking reform as their object of study. They have examined Hadrami associational life to gauge how much it looked like the West, how that similarity was the influence of the diaspora, and how early it happened (Boxberger 2002; Freitag 2003). But reform is what the British claimed they were doing, so everyone under their thumb followed suit, as a safe

24. The institutional development of the Irshād within the Dutch East Indies has now been studied by Mobini-Kesheh, and interested readers may consult her excellent work (Mobini-Kesheh 1999).

banner under which to proceed. What different parties wanted done—with, to, or against each other—was camouflaged rather than revealed by agreed vocabulary.

Attempts to measure self-advertised Hadrami projects of reform between the wars by the standard, familiar criteria of modernism, civil society, and the like extend that camouflage: the more they seem like Western projects, the more inscrutable they become. Sayyid Abū Bakr b. Shaykh al-Kāf's road-building project between Tarim and al-Shiḥr certainly was one of these. As bin Hāshim's book shows, a road is not a self-contained thing; it engages numerous parties. What is important is not to judge individual projects in isolation as the first modern, progressive ventures but to understand how numerous parties interact with each other in any project and seek advantage and position within an ongoing relationship. In this perspective, I take reform to refer to ambitious projects that sought to recast relations between categories of Hadramis, with an eye to assistance from larger powers. It is only in this expanded sense that Sayyid Abū Bakr al-Kāf's road was an effort at reform.

The construction of that road, in the late 1920s, stands at the midpoint of a much larger al-Kāf project, which spanned the two world wars. In space, it spanned the al-Kāfs' efforts in Tarim and al-Shiḥr, connecting the interior with the coast, and moved across the ocean to Singapore. Already in 1915, along with other notables of Tarim, mainly sayyids, the al-Kāfs had founded the Society of Righteousness, Jamʿiyyat al-Ḥaqq. Not unlike the merchants of the Italian city-states of the *quattrocento,* the hundred and twenty-seven members of al-Ḥaqq were a monied elite who stepped into the business of government and reorganized the state along commercial lines, keeping written records of members, constitutional rules, minutes of meetings, decisions, elections, and accounts (Jamʿiyyat al-Ḥaqq n.d.). Abū Bakr bin Shaykh al-Kāf's brother ʿAbd al-Raḥmān b. Shaykh al-Kāf was elected president, and a cousin, Ḥasan b. ʿAbd Allāh al-Kāf, was elected treasurer. Meetings were often held in their houses. The society took over fiscal responsibility for Tarim from its Kathīrī sultan, organizing municipal taxes, paying slave soldiers, constructing a new city wall, building a school, and so on. On the coast a few years later, in the port of al-Shiḥr, the al-Kāfs became revenue farmers in 1919, undertaking to pay the Quʿayṭī sultan an annual sum of sixty thousand dollars in exchange for the right to collect customs, usufruct of farmlands, and other privileges. The dramatic expansion of al-Kāf influence caused alarm in some circles. One detractor, the sayyid ʿAlī b. Aḥmad bin Shihāb, was a regular informant of the British consul in Dutch Batavia, and he reported these developments to the consul in ominous terms.[25] The bin Shihāb family of sayyid notables, possessed of extensive landholdings in Java, were counterparts of the al-Kāfs in Dammūn, a town that abutted Tarim, and were rivals for influence. To ʿAlī bin Shihāb, it was clear that the al-Kāfs were constructing a net of influence within existing state structures inland and on the coast. He tried to inveigle the British into containing them by representing them as a threat to the Quʿayṭī sultan, but the Quʿayṭī differed and the British demurred. Monopoly farms like those of the al-Kāfs were nothing new; they had provided the bulk of colonial state revenue in Dutch and British Southeast Asia (Rush 1990; Trocki 1990, 1999). As in the Malay Archipelago, the British had attained overlordship of India a century earlier with the help of multifaceted merchants with fingers in every pie including the state, whom Subrahmahnyam and Bayly have styled as "portfolio capitalists" (Subrahmahnyam 1990), "*Banias*" who were quite easily contained or disposed of once they had outlived their usefulness (Subramanian 1983, 1996). The Quʿayṭī sultans were themselves such figures in Hyderabad, having progressed through the nineteenth century from commanding revenue fiefs in exchange for military service to moneylending.

By 1928, however, the al-Kāf project had developed to the point that even British eyebrows were raised. To everyone's amazement, it had unified the squabbling sultanates of the interior and the coast, and it even seemed poised to become a national Hadrami movement stretching across the diaspora to British Singapore and the Dutch East Indies. A conference in al-Shiḥr in 1927 had resulted in the al-Shiḥr Agreement, a surprising document that created novel joint military-security arrangements between the rival Quʿayṭī and Kathīrī sultanates.[26] An unprecedented instrument of internal security to hold over the population was also created: anyone seeking to leave Hadramawt had to possess a passport, which one could obtain only from a board composed of a representative of each of the sultanates and a sayyid.[27] The board could also jail troublemakers and have their properties confiscated. Relatives of troublemakers were li-

25. See PRO, FO 371/6256; IORL, R/20/A/1409.

26. PRO, FO967/17, XC 12097, Batavia despatch No. 41, Confidential of April 11th 1928, and No. 44, April 18th 1928, Crosby to Chamberlain. My discussion of the al-Shiḥr agreement and its immediate consequences draws from this file, especially these two dispatches and their enclosures, unless otherwise noted.

27. PRO, FO967/17, XC 12097, "Proclamation by sultans Ṣāliḥ b. Ghālib al-Quʿayṭī, ʿAli b. Manṣūr; ʿAbd Allāh b. Muḥsin b. Ghālib," 5 October 1927.

able as well. Such measures controlled not only the domestic population but its diasporic counterpart too.

In a more positive vein, plans called for forming a Council of Representatives to work for education and the general prosperity of Hadramawt. The Quʿayṭī sultan explained that the council would be composed of "Syeds (Sayyids), rich men and elders of the Hadramout," but would be broadened into "a nationalist union with the aid of which each and everyone of Hadramout can express their opinions and submit their claims."[28] A delegate would be sent to the Dutch and British colonies in the Malay Archipelago to explain the new arrangements to Hadramis there and to secure their participation. The person chosen for this task was Shaykh al-Ṭayyib al-Sāsī, who was not Hadrami but had been editor of the journal *al-Qibla* in Mecca, which supported Sharif Ḥusayn and his kingship.[29] With Sharif Ḥusayn's 1924 defeat by the Saudis, al-Sāsī was now employed by Abū Bakr al-Kāf in al-Mukallā and was available to travel to Southeast Asia to organize a society in the diaspora to support the Council of Representatives in Hadramawt.

In Singapore, al-Sāsī was met by ʿAbd al-Raḥmān b. Shaykh al-Kāf, now Justice of the Peace, who had been founding president of al-Ḥaqq in Tarim a dozen years earlier. ʿAbd al-Raḥmān hosted a conference in Singapore, the Hadrami Reform Congress, to endorse the al-Shiḥr Agreement and follow up on its resolutions. Minutes were kept, elections held, and proposals announced (al-Mu'tamar al-Iṣlāḥī al-Ḥaḍramī n.d.). These actions were of a piece with the commercial spirit of the Society of Righteousness, which had taken over the municipal finance of Tarim in 1915, and included the formation of a national trading company in the diaspora by subscription, some of whose profits would support education and welfare in the homeland; the abolishment of double taxation in customs; and a demand for the sultanates to publish annual government budgets. At both ends of the diaspora, the al-Kāfs were creating entities that took on municipal and national casts—organizations with published rules, budgets, and membership lists—and that called for their local and national states to do the same. They were doing precisely what British political agents on the ground were calling for in the princely states in India to forestall the coming popular deluge—reform,

28. PRO, FO967/17, XC 12097, "Sultan Ṣāliḥ b. Ghālib al-Quʿayṭī to the people of Ḥaḍramawt resident in Malaysia," 10th November 1927.

29. *Al-Qibla* was an organ funded and equipped by Britain's Arab Bureau in Cairo (Westrate 1992: 111).

modernization, and bureaucratically benevolent autocracy. But they were doing it a bit too early, and without official English tutors.[30] With colonial officers sitting in Dutch Batavia, British Singapore, and Indian Aden, but not in Arab Tarim or al-Shiḥr, imperial managers could not quite see the full shape of the amorphous, diasporic society of Hadramawt and did not quite know what to do with native initiatives in state formation or reformation emerging out of that society. It was, after all, a society of the absent.

Mr. Crosby, British consul-general in Dutch Batavia, feared that a nationalist movement was in the making, fomented by literate elite sayyids like the al-Kāfs. A new sayyid organization, al-Rābiṭa al-ʿAlawiyya, was being established in the Dutch East Indies and was registering sayyids throughout the archipelago, fitting them into their comprehensive genealogical register brought from Tarim in 1922. With the advent of a national representative council for a diaspora, a comprehensive genealogy began to look, lo and behold, like an unusual and unusually practical foundation for an electoral roll. In India, Malaya, and other colonies, the tug-of-war between nominated and elected seats for natives and foreign Asiatics within legislative and representative councils was precisely the focus for colonial politics at this time. Others, like Mr. Onraet, acting director of Political Intelligence, Singapore, remained sanguine, confident that "rich Arabs like the Alkaffs at Singapore, who have given hostages to fortune in the shape of substantial possessions in the Straits Settlements, would not dare to incur the displeasure of the British authorities by intriguing against the established order of things."[31] Contrary to appearances, these rich Arabs were not quite the overeducated and overexcited Bengali baboos clamoring for a greater say in Indian affairs. Their published positions were not so much nationalist tracts as constitutional articles of friendly societies, like those registered under the Societies Ordinance of 1890 in colonial Malaya and Singapore. This draconian law declared all civil associations illegal until they submitted written rules, budgets, and membership lists for approval and registration. Instead of being seditious, al-Kāf initiatives such as the Singapore Hadrami Reform Congress seemed concerned rather with hewing to the

30. In India itself, no lower-level criticism of the laissez-faire policy of Minto and Burton was heard through the 1920s; such criticism was first articulated in Wingate's secret note of 1934 (Copland 1978: 296).

31. PRO, FO967/17, XC 12097, Batavia despatch No. 41, Confidential of April 11th 1928, Crosby to Chamberlain.

letter of the law, thereby enabling the state to see them with its own eyes.[32]

In the event, the British nipped the initiative in the bud through the instrument of the Quʿayṭī sultan sitting in princely Hyderabad, who turned around and repudiated the al-Shiḥr Agreement, ejected its instigators from the port of al-Mukallā, and roundly denounced the whole affair as half-baked sedition cooked up in his absence. No further measures were necessary in Onraet's tight little Singapore.

However, in the Dutch East Indies, away from British oversight, strong reactions were generated in proportion to the huge ambitions of the project announced by the al-Shiḥr and Singapore conferences of 1927–28. In the Dutch colony, the old ʿAlawī-Irshādī rivalry flared up anew, and it raged on with new vehemence for the better part of a decade. The imposition of drastic new security arrangements to control mobility between diaspora and homeland, iconified by the new requirement of a passport issued by sultanic and sayyidly authorities, was particularly galling. In response, non-sayyids in the Dutch East Indies began applying for Dutch passports and British visas for travel to the homeland. To top it off, they affixed "Sayyid" to their names on these documents, making it hard for colonial authorities to discriminate on the basis of categorical distinctions. The British consul-general in Batavia reported many such requests through the 1930s, particularly for young boys aged four and up who were being repatriated for schooling, like the creole *muwallads* of our previous chapter. One thirteen-year-old from the Javanese town of Pekalongan, who had a Dutch passport under the name Sayyid Abdullah b. Salim b. Hamid al-Jaʿayd, applied to the consul-general for a visa to Hadramawt for education. Because the consul-general recognized that the family name was not a sayyid one, he surmised that the father must be an Irshādī; when challenged, "His father, though admitting that he was not a Seyyid, said he liked the idea of his son being called a Seyyid."(!) Sayyids protested such attempts to "steal" the title.[33]

As such incidents accumulated, questions about what the honorific Sayyid meant and who was entitled to it incited philological exercises that ran the gamut of sources from the Qur'an and the canon of sayyid texts like *The Irrigating Fount* to Egyptian newspapers and Dutch and English

32. The al-Kāfs were rather attached to their English solicitors, Allen and Gledhill, according to Michael Gilsenan, who is preparing a study of Arab family and English law in colonial Singapore (Gilsenan n.d.: 18).

33. IORL, R/20/A/3413, "Use of title 'Seiyid' in official documents" (1931).

reference works like the *Encyclopedia Britannica*. Arguments were recited in public lectures, such as one by Umar Hubeis at the Irshād Congress of May 1931. Hubeis's comments were published in Chinese newspapers like the *Siang Po;* Malay ones like *Bintang Timoer;* pamphlets translated into English, Dutch, Arabic, and Malay (Lujnatoen Nashir Watta'lief 1931); and confidential representations to the Dutch and British authorities. In these documents, competing, multiple translations, equivalents, and oppositions were created between Egyptian usage, Hejazi custom, Hadrami sociology, Javanese hierarchy, English class prejudice, and radical Bolshevist tendencies. While a direct aim of these arguments was to influence colonial passport policy, an indirect one had even more profound consequences, raising questions about sayyid origins; sayyids' roles in Hadrami society, native Malay society, and colonial Java and Singapore; and their standing in the wider worlds of Islam.

Out of these contentious debates about the Hadrami past and its relation to a sociologically variegated present arose a new historiography—including new Irshādī works such as al-Bakri's 1936 *Political History of Hadramawt*—that engaged classics of the sayyid canon such as al-Shillī's influential *The Irrigating Fount*. Who, after all, were these sayyids? Why could we not marry their daughters? Why did they sit on sultanic boards in Hadramawt and issue or deny passports needed by everyone else? What after all was in the name Sayyid? Did the Egyptians not use it to honor and humor every man on the street? The historiographic contretemps proved persistent and resurfaced at critical junctures in Hadrami history, both at the beginning of socialist rule and upon its demise.

More immediately, however, representations to authorities in the early 1930s instigated a back-and-forth of queries and counterqueries among officials in London, Cairo, Jedda, Aden, Delhi, Batavia, and Singapore. These exchanges generated more questions than answers, especially about the homeland Hadramawt, where no colonial official sat to field queries. The homeland became the absent center around which all these questions revolved. It became a vacuum of knowledge, a place about which the omnipresent Ruler of the Waves heard a lot but that it could not see.

To help it see, Sayyid ʿAlawī b. Ṭāhir al-Ḥaddād, the Hadrami-born mufti of Johor in Malaya, sent a memorandum to the British consul-general in Batavia to persuade the British to intervene in the issue of the sayyid title.[34]

34. PRO, FO371/16849; IORL, R/20/A/3413, "Use of title 'Seiyid' in official documents" (1931).

In addition to having high legal standing, al-Ḥaddād was a major scholar of Hadrami history (n.d.-a, n.d.-b, n.d.-c, 1940, 1971), and he could marshall impressive material to make his case. He tied the controversy over the title to the much larger question of social order in the homeland, thereby raising the stakes. He did so by floating a sociological theory of tribal societies that, curiously enough, anticipated the influential segmentary lineage schemes of the British anthropologists E. E. Evans-Pritchard and Ernest Gellner.[35] Al-Ḥaddād explained that while sultanic governments controlled towns in Hadramawt, the countryside eluded their grasp. Away from the towns, independent tribes jealously guarded their lands, life, and property against all others. Members of each tribe resided within their sovereign tribal lands, and no residential mixing was possible. The sayyids were unusual because they alone could associate with all: their residences were found within all tribal territories. They were unarmed and did not threaten any tribe. As such, they were uniquely placed to maintain the peace, as mediators. Their settlements and graves were sanctuaries specially set apart from tribal violence, and enabled universal participation in markets and pilgrimages.

On a journey, al-Ḥaddād continued, a caravan being plundered had only to call out that a sayyid was with them, and it would receive safe passage. In short, sayyids made public life possible out of the welter of private tribal jurisdictions. From this elegant structural theory, al-Ḥaddād reasoned that if the Irshādīs were allowed to call themselves sayyids, the category would lose its value. Bedouin would no longer respect anyone who claimed to be a sayyid, sayyids would no longer be able to function as peacemakers, and the existing rivalries across Hadramawt, which he set out in detail, would escalate into open warfare. While the self-serving intent of al-Ḥaddād's memo was clear to officials, his linking of the rivalries across the landscape to British elevation of the Quʿayṭī and Kathīrī sultanates in 1918 at the expense of other established, sovereign entities accorded with their understanding of the colonial politics of indirect rule, and made al-Ḥaddād's argument plausible. Theoretical elegance itself was seductive, and when seasoned with names that officials had pondered in

35. Evans-Pritchard's *Sanusi of Cyrenaica* (1949), which showed how an outsider built a sayyid-Sufi order in the interstices between tribal lineages, subsequently providing leadership and structure for mobilization against the Italians in anticolonial resistance, was a political intervention that provided arguments leading to the creation under U.N. auspices of independent Libya under a Sanussi sayyid as king (Pelt 1970: 5–30). I thank Paul Dresch for this reference.

their files, proved irresistible. Al-Ḥaddād's memo became the subject of much intercolonial correspondence.

The memo arrived at a time when officials were reevaluating the place of Hadramawt in the British scheme of things. The sentiment was becoming common among officials that "the status of Hadramis has given rise to constant trouble."[36] Some felt that precisely because the diaspora straddled different state jurisdictions, incorporation of the homeland itself would simplify matters, extending British sovereignty throughout the diaspora over the persons of Hadramis, by designating them British Protected Persons no matter where they were found.[37] With incorporation in mind, the British Resident at Aden, Bernard Reilly, made a historic tour of the Hadrami interior by air in 1933, at which time he took special care to assess al-Ḥaddād's thesis. Reilly concluded that al-Ḥaddād was alarmist, but nevertheless requested that Irshādīs be denied entrance to Hadramawt and be referred to him.[38]

While al-Ḥaddād may have been exaggerating, the al-Kāf project, the al-Shiḥr and Singapore conferences it sponsored, and the renewed disputes between Irshādīs and sayyids all signaled that Hadrami society was on the move in the contemporary world. Whether initiated by sultans, sayyids, or Irshādīs, moves were afoot to create new organizational structures in both homeland and diaspora—and most alarmingly, to connect the two. Disputes between Irshādīs and sayyids were disagreements about the bases of these organizations and about who would dominate them. The Hadrami scene, in both diaspora and homeland, began to look like the Indian one, usually assumed to be the most advanced of colonies. There, new classes of "public men" were noisily creating new movements and organizational vehicles, in the process arguing as much among themselves as with their British masters.[39] In the Hadrami case, the organizational dynamism had the further potential of cutting across imperial boundaries, as it was internal to a diaspora that already did so. This dy-

36. PRO, FO371/16008.

37. The idea of designating all Hadramis British Protected Persons was first floated during the First World War and led to the 1918 treaty binding the Hadrami sultanates more closely to Britannia's bosom, extending her territorial assertions from Aden all the way across to Oman (IORL, R/20/11416). The seesaw of British claims—now to Hadrami persons, now to lands—reflected the complexities of colonizing a diasporic society, wherein relations between land and people were by no means obvious. In the event, the British kept claiming more and more.

38. PRO, FO371/16849.

39. Bayly's category of the "public man," modeled on late nineteenth-century Indian men of letters like Bhartendu Harishchandra, hero of the Hindi movement, provides a useful way

namism threatened to expose fundamental disjunctions in British modes of imperial rule, such as the difference between India and Arabia.

In Arabia, Britain was in an expansionist mode in the early twentieth century, seeking to ride the waves of Arab nationalism on the backs of "natural leaders" of the natives, like the Sharifs of Mecca. Peninsulawide, this ambition was expressed in T. E. Lawrence's concept of drawing a ring around Arabia, sealing Arab aspirations off from the advances of other European powers and keeping them within subnational containers under the sorts of natural leaders exemplified by the sharifs. In India, in contrast, the British were gingerly maintaining an orderly retreat. Comparatively, then, the new Hadrami initiatives represented an Indian sort of native social dynamism, now threatening to break through Lawrence's ring around Arabia. The comparison is not merely theoretical but necessary because the density of intercolonial correspondence and mobility of people, news, and ideas within empire forced regions into argument with one another. Mobility was now part of the material reality, which one ignored at one's peril. Within the colonial files, bourgeoning with titles such as "National status of natives of the Hadhramaut," British officials themselves were increasingly questioning "our dog-in-the-manger policy," which precisely names a stubborn attempt to lock out all that is streaming in from abroad.[40] The semipermanent blockade of the Hadrami interior—the Chinese boxes of indirect rule that enabled control from the outside without taking responsibility for the inside—was becoming harder to maintain. Natives in the Hadrami diaspora, whether Irshādī or sayyid, clearly had designs on their homeland and would sooner or later do something about it. The question was no longer how to stop them from doing so. Rather it was now which of these two dynamic groups, who among the new "public men," would be a less unhealthy influence on the townsmen and tribesmen of Hadramawt, and a suitable native partner to collaborate with? And how was that to be arranged? While the Quʿayṭī sultan was reliable, he was mostly absent in Hyderabad and was hardly interested in cultivating

of thinking about individuals who were among the most powerful shapers of colonial public opinion. Literate in both the European and indigenous traditions, such persons "had put together a powerful and flexible range of communications which informed them about a newly emerging India while maintaining their stake in regional society" (Bayly 1996: 350).

40. IORL, R/20/A/3397; other examples include R/20/A/1416, "Status of the Arabs from the Hadhramaut"; and R/20/A/3539, "Hadramaut status." For a typical comment on the "dog-in-the-manger" policy, see G. W. Rendel, 8 November 1932, file comments in PRO, FO371/16008.

influence among the populace, unlike the dynamic new "public men" among the Irshādīs and sayyids. Unless British officialdom could bestir its portly self to seize the initiative, others would do so. Meanwhile, Hadramawt and its Aden master—suspended as they were between India and Arabia, civil and military government, and Colonial and Foreign offices—drifted in a haze of official indirection and indecision.

This neglect provided the man on the spot, Bernard Reilly, Resident of Aden, a measure of freedom to settle Hadramawt's perennially ambiguous position by binding it to Aden as part of Aden's protectorate. Hadramawt presented a special sort of problem to Reilly. Hadramis in the British and Dutch colonies of Southeast Asia seemed bitterly divided over arcane religious matters. The disputes threatened to spill over into the homeland, where consequences could be drastic. While officials were familiar with the Irshādī-Sayyid dispute, receiving a stream of petitions from Southeast Asia like al-Ḥaddād's, they had no way of assessing how the rivalry articulated with groups and movements in the homeland. As in the diaspora, things were definitely astir in the Hadramawt. But in the varied landscape of tribes, priests, castes, slaves, townsmen, merchants, "new men," and returnees from abroad, calibrating who was rival to whom, and who thick with whom, was not easy to do from the outside. The Irshādīs, with their proliferating modern schools in the Dutch East Indies spreading Cairene ideas, would not be a good thing for Hadramawt.[41] The sayyids, for their part, were pillars of colonial society in Singapore and Malaya, but in Hadramawt they seemed to have united the two rival sultanates, and were organizing the possible germ of a national movement in both diaspora and homeland. Al-Ḥaddād's memo, which described the sayyids as indispensable peacemakers because of their unique ability for intercourse with all tribes, also contained an unspoken threat: that structural position gave the sayyids the capacity to stir up those tribes as well. The potential for trouble was serious, and to make a determination, officials had to "go in." Going in presented a problem, however, for it meant taking over yet more new land, in a fresh colonial adventure liable to undermine Britain's vociferous opposition to nearby moves by its rivals, such as Mussolini's menacing (and eventual conquest in 1935) of Ethiopia. Whatever the compet-

41. After the Indian Mutiny, it became a commonplace among colonial officials that the British "possess in a very high degree the power of acquiring the sympathy and confidence of any primitive races with which they are brought into contact," but they "succeed less well once the full tide of education has set in" (Lord Cromer, quoted in Monroe 1964: 144).

ing claims over Hadramawt were, and whatever their merits, officials had to go in themselves to avoid being dragged in by others. London would not appreciate such incompetence. But on what basis could they go in?

Angels Should Be Invisible: The Roads Again

> In the *broad daylight of the 'forties and 'fifties of the twentieth century,* vast areas of the Protectorate were brought for the first time under beneficent British control. This control was loose and indirect in character, but no less effective for that. The process was camouflaged by the fact that these areas had long been coloured red on the map. . . . For this reason, the assertion of British authority, although a revolutionary development, had not the appearance of being so. Seen in perspective, however, *it is an extraordinary, little-publicised achievement* of high-minded European Imperialism; perhaps, historically speaking, *its last foray in the world.*
>
> Sir Charles Hepburn Johnston (1963: 34–35, emphasis added)

> We have come to the Hadhramaut not to rule but to advise and advise discreetly in the background. Trouble enough has been caused in the Empire by those "heaven-born" ones who are not sufficiently "heaven-born" to realize that angels should be invisible.
>
> W. Harold Ingrams (1940)

In the colonies, the man on the spot was charged with accomplishing plenty and given precious little. While the Aden hinterland did not count for much in imperial priorities, missteps there could have wide repercussions. Rewards were small, but the possibility of incurring the wrath of superiors large. In a twentieth-century world of telegrams, steamships, newspapers with photographs, and the League of Nations, many eyes were watching, and the man on the spot could quickly find himself put on the spot. The mythic District Officer was no longer master of all he surveyed, but rather a bureaucrat accountable at any moment it seemed to world opinion. Brewing problems needed to be dealt with preemptively, nipped in the bud before they overwhelmed. While metropolitan authorities were slow to approve such decisive action, they were reliably quick in casting blame if inaction allowed things to get out of hand. The man on the spot was often in a fix. One way out of such an impasse was to combine initial stealth with a viable propaganda line to provide both cover and rationale as necessary. A good line was one that satisfied the most constituencies while offending the fewest.

In initiating his "forward policy" in the Aden Protectorate, where few Englishmen had tread, Reilly settled on "peace on the roads" as his banner. Though the motto sounded relatively benign and innocuous, it allowed wide scope for action. There was even a certain ring to it. To an international audience, "peace on the roads" was less encumbered than "colony" or "mandate" ideologically. It was not one party commandeering the lands of others, but rather securing communications between them in the interests of all. It was sensible and unambitious enough that it could be unilaterally declared from the bottom up out in the colony rather than top down from the League of Nations. Open roads harkened back to Britain's high liberal moment of the mid-nineteenth century, when free trade rather than territorial rule was her cause. To London, it "could easily be represented as the absolute minimum that a progressive government could require in the territories for which it was responsible" (Gavin 1975: 297). To Yemen, "peace on the roads" underscored an assurance that Reilly had given the imam: when signing the Yemeni-British peace treaty in 1934, the imam had cast aspersions on England's ability to protect merchants traveling on her side of the border, unlike the security that British subjects enjoyed throughout Yemen. To Hadramis like Abū Bakr al-Kāf, such security was exactly what he needed to complete his half-finished road. Best of all, the idea was practical. To Reilly himself, peace on the roads could be pursued with materials already at hand—the twelve air-force bombers parked at Aden—and he could hire a couple of new political officers on the ground.[42] The combination of air power and political groundwork had already proven to be efficacious and economical in Iraq. The machines now available to Reilly were in fact No. 8 Squadron brought from Iraq, along with the speedy armored cars that worked in tandem with them along desert flats (Clayton 1986: 150; Towle 1989: 9, 27–34).

42. Reilly made the case for the hires in a letter to the Secretary of State, 9 November 1933, stressing the need for security on the roads: "The lack of security for travellers through the Protectorate has been a frequent reproach to us and a constant source of the complaint on the part of the Imam of the Yemen. . . . Flagrant outrages on the roads have at times led to Residency interference by the imposition of fines enforced when necessary by punitive air action, but this is a remedy which can be applied only sparingly. Preventions are preferable to punishment, and an important duty for Political Officers from Aden should be the periodic inspection of tribal measures for safeguarding the roads. . . . Closer supervision

The only problem was that unlike the situation in Iraq, which had already erupted in revolt, peace on the roads had to be achieved even more cheaply by Aden, which had not. Lord Belhaven, who as a young man was sent into the western half of the Aden Protectorate as a political officer to secure roads under the authority of native chiefs, was alive to his quandary:

> An order, a declaration of purpose, was promulgated by the Government of Aden, that all main routes in the protected territory must henceforth be free and safe. One would have thought that the Colonial Office . . . would have made the most comprehensive study of this question of the security of inland trade. . . . The officials concerned may have conferred endlessly—I do not know. If they did, if they gave the matter the thought and study it required, then their labours were those of the proverbial mountain which produced a mouse. The mouse was me . . . I, with orders to live as much as possible in the Protectorate, was appointed Political Officer for an area of roughly fifty thousand square miles. . . .
>
> . . . Before me British officers had travelled with strong escorts. Colonel Jacobs, the Political Agent in 1904, had always the support of Indian troops. . . . But inherent in the vague orders I received—to raise small bodies of police here and there, to make the roads safe—lay a sharp difference between my position among the Arabs and that of my predecessors—I travelled where I listed, a disturbing influence in the affairs of the tribes, the declared enemy of brigands, calling all good men to help or at the least to stand aside and not hinder us: "For the road," we swore, "shall be Tariq Allāh, the Road of God, free and safe to all who pass by." (Belhaven 1955: 112, 124)

Belhaven spent much time with Arabs on the ground and tried to get his way with words as sweet as the tea he was offered, then with bluff and bluster, and finally, when all else failed, with bombs from airplanes. This was one combination of twentieth-century means with eighteenth-century men, an observation we puzzled over earlier. It was difficult country, and a large one to boot, some fifty thousand square miles. When used, air bombing worked, but the security Belhaven achieved was sporadic and could not hold. Political arrangements were more lasting, but conditions had to be right to even attempt them. In the western part of the

---

in this respect might obviate the need for punitive bombing. These are essential objects of Residency policy; apart from them, general intervention in tribal quarrels and feuds is undesirable, as too much interference by British Officers might involve us in the beginning of the direct administration that we wish to avoid" (Ingrams Papers Box XI, St. Antony's College, Oxford).

Aden Protectorate, the means Reilly had at his disposal were not sufficient to the ends of complete pacification (Dresch 2000: 37–39).

Things were different in the eastern part of the Aden Protectorate, whose most important component was Hadramawt. Pacification was more successful there, and the relatively stable security conditions that resulted allowed for the growth of government institutions: customs revenue; a standing police force; health, education, and public-works departments; and courts of law. Success hinged on finding suitable local collaborators, who had the means to get things done, and whose word carried weight. The political officer sent into Hadramawt was W. Harold Ingrams, brought in from Zanzibar where he had been a district officer. Ingrams's handiwork stood in contrast to that of Belhaven, who wrote:

> This is my story and Ingrams, in studied understatement, has written his. To me, the peace he had made had shown that peace was possible in South-West Arabia, without occupation by military forces, which otherwise I would not have believed; for although I could make roads safe here and there under the shadow of the R.A.F.'s [Royal Air Force's] protecting wings, the security I created lay on shifting foundations. (Belhaven 1955: 203–204)

Why was Ingrams's story different?

In his report from his first trip into Hadramawt, Ingrams had identified factors that would ease the government's way in (W. H. Ingrams 1936). They hinged on the importance of the outside world to Hadramawt. He noted that the rulers of Hadramawt, including the current Quʿayṭī sultans, had often been outsiders; the British were no different. While the sultans maintained order in the towns, other historical outsiders, the sayyids, were indispensable in places beyond the sultans' urban reach, holding sway through moral suasion and force of personality. The final chapters of the report were devoted to the Hadrami diaspora abroad. Some 20 to 30 percent of the population lived abroad, and Ingrams reckoned that this figure must be one of the highest national proportions in the world. The large invisibles component of the current account, some 630,000 pounds sterling, was "not to be neglected" (W. H. Ingrams 1936: 142). He surmised that the large diasporic population wanted Hadramawt to have the peace and good government that it enjoyed in European colonies and could well pay for it. A combination of circumstances and individuals, these factors were pieces of a "jig-saw puzzle" from which a successful system of government could be assembled (W. H. Ingrams 1940: 91).

On his first trip in 1934, Ingrams had identified one person who shared Reilly's vision of peace on the roads, and who saw in the British government a morally worthy custodian for the roads.[43] Ingrams tells the story of Sayyid Abū Bakr b. Shaykh al-Kāf, who returned to his birthplace, Singapore, for a short visit after having left it for Hadramawt at the age of thirteen. There, the British government had planned to demolish a mosque to make way for a road and then to build a replacement mosque elsewhere. But when advised that consecrated mosque ground could not be violated, the government relented and took its road elsewhere. Such a government, which did not press its considerable advantage, could be trusted with Hadramawt, concluded Abū Bakr al-Kāf, in Ingrams's telling (W. H. Ingrams 1942a: 262).

When Ingrams returned to Hadramawt in 1936 with a mandate to make treaties with two or three sultanates, he took on Abū Bakr al-Kāf as his partner in treaty making. Al-Kāf provided cars, cash, and counsel for visits and deal making with all manner of "sovereigns," some of whom had jurisdiction over only a couple of houses. In building his road, al-Kāf had already begun making a number of such treaties himself, as bin Hāshim's book demonstrates. Within a few weeks, Ingrams claimed he had made peace treaties with fourteen hundred independent parties. In this whirlwind of activity, the road was no longer simply a means but had become the end as well. One group, the al-Jābrī, had violated its own promises by shooting at a road crew; when the group refused to pay the fine decreed by Ingrams, its members were bombed from the air. This event proved to be an object lesson for the rest of Hadramawt. The treaties stuck for three years and were later renewed for ten. The combination of centralized bombing from the air with separate treaties on the ground brought the country under the sway of the British. Ingrams became Resident Advisor to a strengthened and refurbished Quʿayṭī sultanate, and set about creating an administration for Hadramawt, structuring a federation of the two major sultanates, Quʿayṭī and Kathīrī. In this way, the

43. The secret political intelligence summaries reveal that Ingrams had been preceded by Lieutenant-Colonel Boscawen, in 1930. Boscawen called the al-Kāfs "virtual rulers of Tarim," and was repeatedly told of their wish and that of the Kathīrī sultan to develop road communications and a commercial air service, which they "were obviously able to pay for." He identified Sayyid Abū Bakr al-Kāf as the wealthy and influential head of the family in Tarim and noted that the "senior member of the family," Sayyid ʿAbd al-Raḥmān al-Kāf, would return from Singapore in a few months. This was the reason for the journey recorded in bin Hāshim's book. (See the reproduction of Political Intelligence Summary No. 168 for the week ending 29th March 1930, attachment, in Jarman 2002: 178–80.)

FIGURE 20. Queen Elizabeth II knighting Sayyid Abū Bakr al-Kāf, Order of the British Empire. He knelt before no one but his Maker, so a special stool was found. Photo courtesy of John Shipman.

road became not only means and end, but also provided constitutional form for a federal state as well:

> As the administrations grow stronger I am confident that cooperation and coordination will become more real and that some services will become truly federal, with a federal administration rather like that exhibited in embryo in respect of the Al Kaf road, a road serving both States which is separately administered by a Board on which both States and the Al Kaf Seiyids are represented. (W. H. Ingrams 1940: 47)

In the al-Kāf road, Ingrams found the ingredients of the new kind of government that Reilly wanted to establish: a federal, stable concern like the Federated Malay States, with the natives providing startup funds, that could pay its own way and be run by reliable collaborators who could bring their less enthusiastic countrymen on board. The al-Kāf road had been built without government money, was potentially usable by many, and would produce tolls to pay for its maintenance and generate revenue; both traditional elites and common people had stakes in its success. In

1939, it returned a tidy profit of 6,000 rupees, rising to 7,155 rupees a year later. This "flourishing little concern" was happily administered by a board now chaired by the First Political Officer, Ingrams.[44]

For his part, Abū Bakr al-Kāf could not have been displeased that the ambitious al-Kāf project to integrate interior and coast, which in 1928 had been scuttled by the authorities, was now being promoted by no less than an officer of the British Crown, W. Harold Ingrams, as his own grand achievement. As a result of Ingrams's success in establishing indirect British rule in Hadramawt, Abū Bakr al-Kāf's word carried ever-greater weight, and some saw him as the virtual ruler of interior Hadramawt.[45] As if acting to script, Ingrams followed up on his successful achievement of rapprochement between the Hadrami interior and the coast with a trip to the diaspora in the Malay Archipelago, just as the al-Kāf emissary al-Ṭayyib al-Sāsī had done a decade before, to drum up support for the new arrangements at home (W. H. Ingrams 1940). In Singapore, as in Tarim, Ingrams enjoyed al-Kāf hospitality, with a mansion on the lofty Mount Washington at his disposal, complete with car (W. H. Ingrams 1940: 22).

Colonial Creole

The success of Ingrams's and Abū Bakr al-Kāf's joint creation, a colonial creole, was driven as much by a mutuality of fantasies as of interests. For al-Kāf, the vision was of a secure route between Singapore and Tarim that was connected by steamships and motor cars, easing the way of pilgrims and traders, terminated by bungalows with swimming pools at both ends. For Ingrams, the fantastical image was of some two thousand fractious sovereign Arab microstates, deaf to the blandishments of modern na-

44. IORL, R20/C/243, "Al-Kaff Road."

45. The journal *al-Murshid,* published in Dutch Surabaya, interpreted news from international Arabic sources in this manner: "The news shows that the Hadrami lands are now divided into regions under the two governments and under the government of al-Kāf (or The Society of Righteousness in Tarim) (see *al-Rābiṭa al-ʿArabiyya* number 30, and the second issue of *al-Salām*)" ("Ḥaḍramawt," *al-Murshid* Year 1 Issue 1, 2 August 1937: 2–3). Almost a decade later, the Resident Advisor in al-Mukallā was to complain that Abū Bakr al-Kāf "has become so accustomed to being the uncrowned King of the Wadi that he unconsciously resents any diminution of his powers, which is bound to occur as the local States—his own creations—gradually progress" (IORL, R20/C/1475, British Agent Al-Mukallā to Chief Secretary Aden, 7 September 1946).

FIGURE 21. Verandah of the sultan's palace by the sea, al-Mukallā. Photo by the author.

tionalism and pledged instead to Britain in friendship and common interest. They would be franchisees of British empire, the large business firm that everyone wanted to associate with.[46] For al-Kāf, the means were the modern machinery, published state budgets, and open roads of British liberalism, summed up in the glory and safety of the King's Way. For Ingrams, the means were restraint of tribal violence and promotion of honor through treaties of passage crafted by traditional mediators; the open roads of sayyid peacemaking could be summed up in the glory and safety of *Ṭarīq Allāh,* "God's road." Arm in arm, religious diaspora and liberal empire traveled down the same road for a glorious if brief three years, just before the Second World War swept away all illusions, whether shared or jealously guarded. Regardless, this partnership set the pattern for the

46. Taking his cue from Lawrence, Ingrams wrote, "In 1928 Lawrence wrote to D. G. Pearson, 'I think there's a great future for the British Empire as a voluntary association: and I'd like it to have Treaty States on a big scale attached to it. We've lots of treaty states now from Nepal onwards. Let's have Egypt and Iraq, at least, to add to them. We are so big a firm that we can offer unique advantages to smaller businesses to associate with us, if we can get out attractive terms of association.' One small business which wanted to associate with us was the Hadhramaut." (Ingrams 1966a: 8)

coming of government to Hadramawt. In the 1960s, the ethnographer Abdalla Bujra noted that a "modern" sayyid was the one who hosted and counseled the colonial district officer and who held in his hands the power to authorize or deny passports to those seeking work abroad (Bujra 1971: 145–63). This privilege was, of course, first claimed by sultans and sayyids in the al-Shiḥr agreement of 1927, which was ratified in Singapore the following year.

The view from the verandah, whether seen from Singapore or from Tarim, took in great distances, encompassing roads traveled and untraveled, and could be shared no matter who did the looking. It was a view of mobility untrammeled, a fantasy shared equally by imperial officers and diasporic *muwallad*s, and only for their friends. In the 1930s, such fantasies had to be shared to be realized. They became the stuff of propaganda. In his writings, Ingrams assumes the very English mantle of Lawrence of Arabia, fancying himself an Arab sayyid with all the powers and manners appertaining to the station. Just as Lawrence was *Ṣadīq al-ʿArab,* "Friend of the Arabs," Ingrams would be *Ṣadīq Ḥaḍramawt,* "Friend of Hadramawt" (though to his colleagues, "headline Harold" seemed more appropriate [Dresch 2000: 229]). In the writings of bin Hāshim, Abū Bakr al-Kāf assumes the role of the great modernizer and reformer, bringing the Arab renaissance already in progress in Cairo and Singapore back to an apparently unchanging homeland. The idea of "reform," associated through these writings with the al-Kāf name as with that of Ingrams, a propaganda device honed to fit into many conflicting demands simultaneously, was so well faceted that it still provides grist for the historiographic mill.

CHAPTER 10

Evictions

> Whether migration is controlled by those who send, by those who go, or by those who receive, it mirrors the world as it is at the time.
>
> K. Davis (1974: 96, quoted in Zolberg 1982)

For over a century, since the 1870s, the rivalries of Great Powers—first the newly industrial European nation-empires, then the Cold War protagonists—have churned the world. Through this period, the unbundling (from the Indian Mutiny of 1857 to the First World War), bundling (from the Second World War to 1989), and re-unbundling (from 1989 to the present) of sovereignties at the state level has been accompanied by similar processes lower down the hierarchy of power and its representation, drawing and redrawing the boundaries of social collectivities. The leveling of society by government, in which a multitude of local sovereignties and powers had been eviscerated by the late nineteenth century in Europe (de Tocqueville 1955; Tilly 1990), was played out again in the colonies (Batatu 1978; Dodge 2003). A scholarly division of labor, with political scientists taking the top, anthropologists taking the bottom, and historians wavering between the two, has made it difficult for us to see how the different levels of state and society interconnected—or became disconnected. Nevertheless, it was perhaps inevitable that an old diasporic society such as that of Hadramawt, in the course of its journeys, would continually trip over the multifarious lines of state control being assembled and reassembled within countries and across the ocean in the past century. The stories of this diaspora connect with other stories, and all can profit if they can be shared. In this final chapter, it remains to show how the concerns of the Hadrami homeland, now sequestered within national and local containers, continue to be disputed in terms that little acknowledge the parochial status to which Hadramawt has been consigned, in a world of nation-states. Whereas the previous chapter told one story of colonization as that of diasporic return, the coming-of-age of the new nations out of imperial tutelage in the past century can also be told as one of evictions. And the story of those evictions can be recounted in a language of names, which is perhaps a fitting way to end our account of genealogy and mobility across the Indian Ocean.

"Englishry"

While the writings of colonial officials such as Harold Ingrams evince the best of intentions, the countries they passed through continue to pay for the half-fulfilled expectations generated by those intentions to this day. Unable to undo the histories of those intentions, these countries are condemned to seek their fulfillment as best they can. The intentions as stated were usually good government, first, then democratic rule. Europe had both and would bequeath them to the colonies. Colonialism was building good government, and teaching the natives to run it so that they could rule themselves, democratically, at some unspecified future date. Since the end of the First World War, the voluminous writings of colonial officials have told a remarkably consistent story, and an emphatically moral one.

Good government was administration by bureaucracy, which was sustained through taxes paid by the governed. In Europe, this new moral economy had been initiated through the instrument of tax farming and the private gathering of public taxes, and its further advance entailed what Max Weber called the "leveling of social differences" (Weber 1978: 983). "Levelers" in the English civil war of the mid-seventeenth century had been advocates of a concept we now understand as equal citizenship rights (Pease 1915; Sharp 1998). They had many sympathizers in the professional parliamentarian "new model army" commanded by generals rather than aristocrats. In a broader sense, Europeans understood *leveling* to mean dissolving local hierarchies and reciprocities, dispensing with intermediaries such as the nobility. Freed from obligations to their immediate masters, populations became yoked to a larger one, giving the centralizing state direct access to society as a resource to be mobilized (Tilly 1990).

Emancipation freed up populations for new kinds of labor, taxation, and conscription. "Masterless men" swelled the ranks of nations, which grew to fit the ambitions of states that accorded them rights as individuals and as citizens, rather than as members of assorted groups and estates. France exemplified this pattern best; the Revolution merely capped a process of disintermediation that was most conspicuous under the rule of Louis XIV (de Tocqueville 1955). In England, the process was less advanced; less centralized administration through local appointees, such as justices of the peace, remained adequate and was cheaper.

Out in the colonies, the leveling of social differences was consciously pursued, but incompletely so, especially under the British. After conquest, colonial pacification often shaded into an extended project of social leveling that sidelined obstreperous nobles and chiefs, who protested the loss of their customary authority and privileges; but regular administration set up a smaller number of them or their sons again as notables, burnishing their old status with new administrative authority. Ingrams lovingly drew up plans for a school for the sons of chiefs, which was built in Aden. The students of these schools were to be, as it were, the progeny of the Malayan marriage of Indian princely state and centralized British rule, a consensual coupling of old and new ruling classes that resonated with an English sense of how England herself had avoided violent revolution after the mid-seventeenth century. The arrangement created a new, leaner stratum of modernized notables by refurbishing old family materials. John Stuart Mill had puzzled over the question of how to imbue English "examination men" of a meritocratic Indian Civil Service, sourced from all social classes, with the aristocratic virtues necessary to exercising power with grace and care for their native charges (Mill 1867); Anglo-educated sons of native nobles provided one natural alternative.

In the barely defined territory of Britain's Aden Protectorate, which stretched from Aden to Oman, the egalitarian imperatives of social leveling combined with the inegalitarian instruments of bureaucratized notables to form the modern state. This very odd and very English combination of *Homo aequalis* with *Homo hierarchicus,* which had worked so well in England herself, imparted a schizophrenic quality to the modern state of the Aden Protectorate. That quality was to persist through subsequent reincarnations of the state, in its colonial, postcolonial, socialist, and postsocialist guises, periodically taking the form of violent convulsions that sought to evict undeserving elites and wipe the slate clean. Diasporic returns, which had become entwined with the lineaments of an oceanic imperial state, now became caught up in its colonial, territorial adjunct being set up in the homeland. This transformation of the homeland forms the latest chapter in the history of the old diaspora of Hadramawt, and the parting chapter of this book. A contradictory cohabitation of equality and hierarchy, manifested as periods of state development and social leveling punctuated by episodes of eviction, forms its main theme. In the homeland, as abroad, the diaspora is no longer exempt from the communalist politics of the colonies that became the nation-states of today.

In this chapter, the odd combination of old and new social categories within the new British colonies of the Middle East and their successor states echoes the combination of eighteenth- and twentieth-century colonial styles I noted in the previous chapter. It seemed like magic at the time, the exploits of a Lawrence or an Ingrams—magic the empire needed to sustain the interest of its home population. It was the magic of a balancing trick that was no longer possible in England herself—nor in India—but that might be sustained a little longer in the Middle East:

> When the English acquired some power in the Middle East they found a traditional society which seemed to offer the possibility of dominance with a good conscience. . . . This power over the Arabs was acquired at a time when the English class system appeared to be in danger from the newly organized working class. The illusion of social consensus, of familyhood, had become increasingly difficult to sustain. Perhaps it was consoling to find a corner of the earth where the old balancing trick could still be performed, where political illusions long cherished could be cherished a little longer. The English working man might be showing distressing signs of getting above himself, but the unreconstructed Bedouin seemed ready to settle for equality before God without worrying about equality before man. (Tidrick 1989 [1981]: 215)

When Ingrams and Abū Bakr al-Kāf set out to remake Hadramawt after the peace treaties were signed in 1936–37, that balancing act still seemed possible. The combination of an efficient centralized bureaucracy and notables as administrators had proved itself in Malaya. It had even led to the creation of a novel postcolony in Iraq in 1932, an independent state under a sharifian sovereign satisfactorily amenable to British requests. Sure of their models, Ingrams and Abū Bakr al-Kāf proceeded in confidence in Hadramawt. The colonial files of the 1940s bulge with reports of disputes that arose as local elites used to receiving taxes were made to pay them to the new Government (represented by sultanic officials) instead. Questions about the sumptuary privileges they enjoyed added insult to injury. In November 1942, for example, in the sanctuary-town of ʿAynāt headed by the sayyid *manṣab* of the Shaykh Bū Bakr lineage, a certain Tufan got it into his head that he was now a subject of the British government rather than of the sayyid *manṣab* and refused to perform his ritual duty of waving the fan at a sayyid wedding. The newly arrived sultanic official *(qā'im)* gave him shelter in his house.[1] Shaykh Bū Bakr sayyids impressed upon the official that the duty of fanning had reposed in Tufan's family "from father to son," and when some local inhabitants confirmed this, the neophyte official obliged Tufan to comply. Subsequent orders from his superiors, however, instructed that Tufan did not have to fan if he did not want to.[2] Once colonial authorities got involved, the *manṣab* no longer had the last word.

Sayyid Abū Bakr al-Kāf's letterhead appears regularly in the files, his words by turns counseling, cajoling, and threatening his peers. He ordered a blockade on the settlement of Suwayrī near Tarim, controlled by the bin Shamlān Tamīmī tribe, when the tribesmen did not pay taxes on their date harvest.[3] The ban extended to the coastal ports, and because the bin Shamlān were dependent on diasporic links in Java, they capitulated. The al-Kāfs and other Tarim families had land in Suwayrī subject to bin Shamlān control, and colonial assistance was a novel advantage in this regard, shifting an old balance in their favor. In Iraq, special shaykhs recognized by the British were given the power to ban bedouin from markets (Dodge 2003: 84), and Sayyid Abū Bakr al-Kāf was evidently accorded this privilege.

To the *manṣabs*, who claimed sovereignty over sanctuary settlements *(ḥawṭa)* like ʿAynāt and complained about the garrisoning of troops and imposition of taxes, Abū Bakr al-Kāf helpfully suggested that they petition to become Crown Colonies like Singapore, as that move would give them security and freedom of action, as well as tax-free status. Crown Colonies, directly subject to the British monarch, were proper imperial spaces whose natives enjoyed *pukka* civic rights, in contrast to the colonial places of princely states, whose subjects were buried within the Chinese boxes of native rule and enjoyed little legal recourse. The al-Kāfs, who traversed the empire with such ease, knew what they were talking about; what they did not know, their English lawyers in Singapore did. The miniscule size of sayyid-led *manṣab*ates made the idea something of a joke, and in the eyes of colonial officials, they were an anachronism in

1. A *qā'im* is the equivalent of "district officer" in administrative terminology borrowed from colonial Iraq.

2. IORL, R/20/C/1432, "Einat Affairs," Qaim Einat to acting F.A.R.A. Seiyun, 27 November 1942, and subsequent correspondence.

3. IORL, R/20/C/1672, "Report on Suweiri."

the modern era of "organized government." Yet the constitutional thinking was serious enough.[4] In 1946, within a decade of British entry, the ʿAydarūs *mansab*s of the *ḥawṭa*s of Būr, al-Rayḍa, Tāriba, and al-Ḥazm petitioned to be made Crown Colonies—"we having seen the prospects and happiness which our brothers resident in British Colonies enjoy"—in order to bypass the depredations of local officials of the sultanates.[5] The Resident Advisor in al-Mukallā, impatient with the compromises his predecessor, Ingrams, had made in earlier days, was inclined to press ahead in bringing the *manṣab*s under the authority of the sultans, the matter being "a critical issue between the Old and the New Orders in the Hadhramaut and the time for dissimulation is past."[6] His superior in Aden counseled caution and diplomacy: "It is unnecessary for me to remind you of the power and influence they possess for good or evil and you will recollect that but for the support of the Al Kaf family, in particular Seiyid Bubakr, we should never have been able to negotiate an Agreement with the Kathīrī Sultanate."[7] On balance, sayyids were brought around as the taxes paid by the elders among them came to pay for the salaries of younger ones who were inducted into the bureaucracy.

Tribal chiefs were somewhat easier to deal with. The office of the Resident Advisor in al-Mukallā drew up lists of chiefs in their various grades (three, plus a "special/distinguished" category), and made them regular payments. In their embrace by the new bureaucracy, these haughty microsovereigns were subtly transformed into administrators of sorts, even as their chiefly claims were recognized through the payments they received.

On this landscape of sayyids and chiefs becoming administrators were overlaid other layers of bureaucracy—district officers, school teachers, and so on. Underneath this activity, the "leveling of the governed" proceeded

4. The *manṣab*s insisted that they were not part of the augmented colonial Kathīrī and Quʿayṭī states, making reference to the terms of the 1937 treaty, into which respect for the rights of the sayyids was written; but this was only in the Arabic version, not the English one. Given the perfidy of Albion, it is not surprising that the translation gap takes on an interpretive life of its own in subsequent historiography (Dāʾūd 1989).

5. They had also seen the British storm the town of al-Ghurfa nearby just months before, led by the bin ʿAbdāts, millionaires from Java who espoused Irshādī principles and insisted that they too were sovereigns independent of any sultan (bin ʿAbdāt n.d.; Dāʾūd 1989; W. H. Ingrams 1942a). See IORL, R/20/C/1475, Al-ʿAydarūs *manṣab*s to Acting Resident Adviser al-Mukallā, 23 June 1946.

6. IORL, R/20/C/1475, British Agent al-Mukallā to Chief Secretary Aden, 7 September 1946.

7. IORL, R/20/C/1475, Chief Secretary Aden to British Agent al-Mukallā, 6 September 1946.

(Weber 1978: 985). Hadramis, with all these officials now in charge of them, began to behave as if they were individuals with rights they could demand from officialdom, no matter their own tribal chiefs and sayyid *manṣab*s. The best of colonial intentions inculcated the highest of native expectations. When these expectations were fulfilled, genuine goodwill could be generated; when they were not, blame was not far to seek; neither was violence. Much turned on perceptions.

Perceptions vacillated because policy did so. This dynamic instability had begun even before colonial administration of Hadrami territory. As imperial Britain exerted control of steamship movements across the Indian Ocean from the First World War onward, the British dealt inconsistently with Hadramis as individuals and as members of social collectivities. While visas, passports, and tickets were issued to individuals and gave them specific rights and expectations, officials insisted on identifying those individuals with specific groups or categories. Were they British Protected Persons with claims on the British government, or Turkish or Dutch subjects without? Were they sayyids, who could generally be relied on to support establishment order, or seditious Irshādīs, pan-Islamists, or Turco-German-Italian sympathizers? Should British Protected Persons who were possibly members of suspected seditious groups be allowed to exercise their formal rights to travel and protection, be blocked, or—in a costly compromise—be individually monitored? Could or should suspect groups such as the Irshādīs be categorically denied papers to exit Batavia, or should authorities evaluate them individually, perhaps allowing them to travel as British subjects or private fare-paying passengers, but deny them entry into al-Mukallā, the Hadrami port under a native sultan's sovereignty? The vacillation in policy over travel between places that Britain did not even rule—at times treating travelers as individuals and at times as members of groups—continued into places Britain did rule, imparting to its colonies a curious, unstable shape. Moreover, the materiality of travel—involving points of exit, entry, and transit, as well as companies, vessels, and routes—when combined with the multiple jurisdictions of divided sovereignties, allowed officials to operate notionally within the rules but with wholly unpredictable outcomes for individual passengers.

British policies in most of their Old World colonies were shadowed by a chronic debate: should natives be governed as individuals or as groups?[8]

8. For a recent, sustained analysis of this issue in Iraq, see Dodge 2003: 83–101. The Iraqi comparison is particularly germane because equipment and organizational forms

Should property be held individually by alienable title or collectively as tribal commons? Should natives be represented by elected politicians or dealt with through chiefs? Was modern education necessary, or should custom be preserved? Some officials, whom we can call rationalists, wanted for colonial subjects what Europeans wanted for themselves. Rationalists were modern descendants of the English levelers, intent on remaking the world in the liberal English image. Other officials, who wanted for colonial subjects to avoid what Europeans had gone through, we can call romantics. Rationalists promised the many; romantics rewarded the few. While rationalists championed the underdog and sought to give access regardless of background, romantics would select their friends for perquisites. In constitutional debates after the Second World War about the shape of the future independent states, rationalists typically argued for unions, whereas romantics preferred federations. Unions contained abstract citizens and centralized bureaucracies; federations were "jigsaw puzzles," in Ingrams's terms—mosaics of races, regions, and royal families. Policy swung between the two, sometimes in response to election results in Britain. Through the vacillation between rationalists and romantics, the bureaucracy kept expanding, leveling the governed while conferring new forms of authority on the governing. While the governed became more and more alike, the governing classes were reinvented, gaining in distinction. Palaces were built for tribal chiefs, whom the British elevated to sultans. Later, when the revolution arrived, the people would evict the sultans and expand the bureaucracy in their own name.

In European terms, colonial state and society were not being reshaped in the same ways; they were put on divergent paths. While in Europe the expansion of bureaucracy was followed by the extension of suffrage, as the category of the individual became a social reality, the colonies mostly got the bureaucracy, without the vote. Colonial subjects saw Europeans enjoying individual civil rights that the colonized did not have and increasingly chafed for the self-rule that promised to bring the social equa-

---

were imported from there to Hadramawt, sometimes via Transjordan. India was the original colonial testing ground for such debates. The question of rights arose there in debates over the colonial organization of land tenure and revenue. The *ryotwari* system championed by Thomas Munro and implemented in South India vested rights in individuals, whereas the village-based *mahalwari* system advocated by Holt Mackenzie in the North-West Provinces vested rights in groups (Baden-Powell 1892; Stokes 1959, 1978). The Iraqi debates were directly informed by Indian models and legal codes. I have benefited greatly from discussions with Stanley Tambiah on this matter.

tion into balance. After independence, postcolonial governments proved no better at bridging the gap between state and society. The former British colony of South Arabia was replaced by a Marxist state, which was eventually renamed for the people, as the People's Democratic Republic of Yemen. Yet even as that new state promulgated the most egalitarian laws in the Arab world, with the adoption of Tunisian personal status codes, and was ruled by a politburo elected via party congresses assembled from the bottom up, various factions sought to infiltrate the center of government. The gap between state rhetoric and practice, between the shapes of state and society, would periodically be expressed as violent factional fallouts within the central politburo. Regionally based factions were the clearest ones, but other kinds of loyalties were always operative and suspected. On a daily basis, individuals continued to claim their rations and jobs and education as equal citizens of the socialist state. Anything beyond that had to be sought via well-placed persons one knew through common participation in particular social collectivities.

In his ethnography of the Hadrami town of Ḥurayḍa in the 1960s, Abdalla Bujra described with great clarity the dual process of leveling and reinvention, and the confusion and distrust it bred. Locally in Ḥurayḍa, the old ruling alliance between sayyids and tribes had been dissolved by the interposition of the centralized state, and junior members of these social categories sought positions in the new administrative structures of rule.

> People were accepted into the Sultan's administration on the basis of their loyalty to the Sultan and of their education. Thus townsmen (generally Sadah [sayyids]) from the Sultan's town went into the administration, whilst loyal tribesmen from the Sultan's tribe and ex-slaves were taken into the army and the police . . . the traditional pattern in which the Sadah dominated the Sultan's judiciary and administration, whilst loyal tribesmen monopolized the army and police forces, continued in force. Thus it was not an accident that the first Wazir to hold office under the new Government was a Saiyid. . . . [9] the head of the army and the police at the capital, the Governor, and the D.A. . . . are all members of loyal tribes that had been traditionally working for the Sultans. (Bujra 1971: 127–28)

9. The wazir was the chief minister. In Iraq under British-mandate rule in the 1920s, nine out of thirteen premiers were sayyids (Batatu 1978: 176). The British had "a somewhat exaggerated view of the influence" of the local sayyids on the population, in Batatu's estimation (177) and employed them in the cities as a counterweight to the sayyid they had brought in from the Hejaz as monarch. In the countryside, the tribal chiefs played a similar balancing role.

The old dominant social categories of tribesman and sayyid had been disembedded both from preexisting locales and from diasporic networks, and they were now being reincarnated within the new and expanded, Hadramawt-wide institutions of state rule that the colonial administration was building for an aggrandized native sultan. Bujra writes of Ingrams, who had engineered this transformation:

> Afterwards he wrote of this policy that: "the reasons we succeeded in building up an indigenous administration . . . were that we believed them (the Ḥaḍramis) inherently capable of doing the job and had no reason to think we thought ourselves superior." The result has been that the Quaʾity State has no written constitution, and that the administration has been characterized by improvisation, uncertainty, and confusion. . . . In this kind of situation, then, the ability to influence the decisions of officials through personal contact becomes a main source of power for people outside the formal political structure. (Bujra 1971: 127)

While more power was concentrated in the administration than before, the lines and loci of authority and influence within it became opaque. A new theoretical equality between individual subjects accompanied the expansion of administration, but migration of old categories of elites to new, translocal state structures created the sense that things were not what they were supposed to be. Influence in the new state was garnered through personal contacts, and these contacts were easiest pursued by mutual participation within the old social categories, such as those of sayyid and tribesman, that were now expanding within the colonial-sultanic government. The continued salience of such categories in the new structures of rule meant that one could never be certain whether actions stemmed from bureaucratic, personal, or group considerations. As the bureaucracy continued to roll over more and more of social life, the reappearance of the old categories within new administrative circles engendered widespread distrust. Influential persons were not always bureaucrats; they were likely to be the younger generations of old families of notables. British officials were aware of such developments under their watch. As the British Resident in al-Mukallā volunteered to his superior in Aden,

> You may be interested to know that the Mansab of Hautat Al Ahmed bin Zein said the following in a speech there during the ʿId: "The power is now in the hands of the Seiyids, thanks to God; the State Secretary, Saiun, the Naibs, the Qadhi and most of the senior Officials are Seiyids."[10]

10. IORL, R/20/C/1475, British Agent al-Mukallā to Chief Secretary Aden, 10 September 1946.

Bujra reports from Ḥurayḍa that the local council, which occupied the lowest rung of administration in the provincial settlements, was run by the "traditional authorities" (Bujra 1971: 140). These authorities were sayyids, who, having influence among other sayyids much higher up in the bureaucracy, such as the chief minister, needed their local clients and allies less and less.

Under colonial rule, the lives of the governed were subject to even greater government control and more sets of influential persons than before, but from a smaller pool of elites. To those left out of this new dispensation, the simple call of nationalism became ever more attractive, promising a radical leveling and equality of all, as patriots. Ethnographies from the 1950s and 1960s noted the demoralization of local tribal powers, who could no longer tax and protect within their customary domains, and commented on the dependence of a new generation of sayyids on influence with government officials rather than local clients (Bujra 1971; Hartley 1961). Their sons went away to schools in Aden, Iraq, Syria, and Egypt, to return as Arab nationalists (bin ʿAqīl 1949). Throughout the colonial period, bedouin uprisings continued away from the towns (ʿAlī and al-Mallāḥī 1989; al-Khanbashī 1989). At the end of that period, a year before independence, Ingrams reflected on how his beloved Hadrami wards could have turned into virulently anti-British nationalists. He recalled an early difference of opinion over the risks of introducing colonial rule into Hadramawt, at a time when Palestine was in the throes of full-scale revolt:

> The great problem was how far one could go in guiding the Arabs towards peace and a better life without interfering with their independence. Chief advocate of the non-interference policy was Maurice Lake, the Political Secretary, whose immediate subordinate I had become on arrival in April 1934. . . . When I maintained it was possible to do a good deal more without interfering with their independence and stirring up the nationalism with which the Fertile Crescent was already aflame, he shook his head. "You may be right," he said, "but the nature of the Colonial Office is such that it cannot stop. It has to go on and on. It won't work with Arabs." That conversation took place in January 1935, just after I had returned and was trying to secure his support for help to the Hadhramaut . . . At that time I had not appreciated how difficult it was to maintain a policy which could prevent "Englishry" asserting itself. (Ingrams 1966b: 16–17)[11]

11. In the footnotes, Ingrams strikes a rueful note: "When I was a child, I was resentful when I found there was a particularly unpleasant powder concealed beneath a spoonful of jam and I hoped there was no powder in the jam I was able to give the Hadhramis . . . . I fear Maurice Lake was right and that our 'Englishry' does make us 'go on and on'" (Ingrams 1966b: 16–17, footnote).

"Englishry," the leveling of society while raising its "natural leaders"—along with its historical consequence in the colonies, rising nationalist sentiment—was a condition that Hadramawt shared with other colonies, where its diaspora resided. In the aftermath of decolonization, the identification of the new states with single nations made the creole, transnational commitments of diasporic communities untenable. The new, independent nation-states broke the diasporas straddling them into two: citizens and aliens.

From Cosmopolitan to Minority

> It appears, in the East, that when you do not have Jews you have Hadhramis or Chinese and all are alike in their exclusiveness.
>
> W. Harold Ingrams (1942a: 43)

> The so-called pariah communities of "foreign" traders that are found in so many of the new states—the Lebanese in West Africa, the Indians in East Africa, the Chinese in Southeast Asia and, in a somewhat different way, the Marwaris in South India—live in an altogether different social universe . . . than do the settled agricultural groups.
>
> Clifford Geertz (1973: 268)

> Recent experience confirms the special vulnerability of certain types of minorities to designation as target groups. Very prominent among them are the trading diasporas scattered throughout the Third World, the contemporary successors of Jews and Armenians. Among the victims to date are not only Indians in East Africa and Chinese in Southeast Asia, but also a variety of black diaspora groups scattered among African countries, such as Ibos in northern Nigeria, Hausas in Ghana, Togolese and Dahomeyans in Ivory Coast.
>
> Aristide Zolberg (1982: 33)

The world inhabited by the Hadrami diaspora disappeared after the Second World War. One of its enduring verities, the British empire, within which diasporic families like those of the al-Kāfs had made themselves comfortable, was soon to be no more. Native states and colonies, which had been nurturing self-consciously indigenous nations and cultures within, now came into their own, as independent states. The nested hierarchies of indirect rule flattened out as fledgling national cultures asserted their sovereignty, filling up the space of the only Chinese box that was now allowed to remain, the nation-state. As native state sovereignties were bundled up and made whole again, their insides began to look like the outside they now inhabited: the interstate system of the United Nations, which represented a sudden expansion of the Westphalian compact among nations recognizing each other as equals, as states (Philpott 2001). All were now civilized, and empires were no longer needed to give unending tutorials in good government. Big or small, all states were equivalent, and so each had or desired its own national army, navy, language, anthem, flag, flower, costume, soccer team, currency, passport. Desires for national mascots reflected desires for national majorities; minority rights were not written into U.N.-sponsored international law but were presumed covered by universalist declarations of human rights. Once again, good intentions did not fulfill the expectations they generated: only colonies, not peoples or tribes, received recognition as independent new states (Philpott 2001: 36). The ensuing Herculean politics of matching majorities with state power generated refugees, genocides, and sullen minorities (Isaacs 1975; Malkki 1995; Rae 2002; Zolberg 1982, 1983). Electoral politics, if anything, paradoxically kept majorities insecure and chronically mobilized.

Diasporas were now anomalous: everyone had to become a citizen of a state. In prison terminology, this was the equivalent of a universal lockdown. The opposite was also true: it was to be an age of evictions as well. The naval blockade of old, which had caught people short on both sides, within and without, was now a permanent, global institution, effected through almost two hundred nation-states. Within the U.S.-dominated half of this world, capital and goods were ideally allowed free passage, but people could not reside wherever they wished. A comparable realm took shape in the Soviet half as well, with states apportioning the favor of mobility in differential ways. Exit, in particular, became mostly impossible. The hyphen in the nation-state replaced the hyphen in the hybrid: the Javanese-Hadrami, the creole *muwallad,* was being dismantled, as it were. In this new, culturally relativist world of equally valid states, persons had to choose one nation to belong to. Jews, Hadramis, and Chinese were precipitated out of many of the new nations in which their old, creole diasporas had long been settled. Now perceived as being exclusivist by the likes of Ingrams and their nativist, majoritarian apprentices, they had to prove that they were assimilable—or be excluded. Unending cycles of diasporic travel and return were no longer permissible. It was as if diasporic travel and residence had been a game of musical chairs, and the music had stopped—for good, apparently. Party over. Diasporic persons became minorities within the new nations. Some were then expelled to homelands they had never known; others became permanently stateless.

In the decades after the Second World War, the new, independent governments constricted or banned remittances to Hadramawt from East Africa, India, and Indonesia (Dresch 2000: 60; Lekon 1997: 272–74). Places like Uganda and Zanzibar took more drastic measures, evicting Hadramis as foreigners along with others. In the runup to decolonization, newspaper wars between rival factions in Zanzibar had done representational violence to a long-term process of creolization, localization, and achievement of elite status, producing a racialized caricature of Africans and Arabs locked in mortal combat over slave exploitation (Glassman 2000). Diasporic Hadramis who fled Idi Amin's Uganda headed for Kenya; some caught mercy flights to Aden provided by the South Yemeni government, while others remained with relatives in Kenya, a marginalized Muslim minority hugging the coast where their ancestors had landed. In India, the princely state of Hyderabad held out after national independence, proclaiming its sovereign status. Hyderabad had remained the most powerful of the princely states under British rule, in part because the ruling Nizam had managed to maintain his own troops, led by fief holders such as the Hadrami sultans. When the newly constituted central state of independent India seized Hyderabad from the Nizam in 1948, seven thousand Arabs, many of them Hadramis, were deported to Aden (Khalidi 1997: 80–81). A Hadrami, General Sayyid Aḥmad al-ʿAydarūs, was the person who officially surrendered Hyderabad. Back in Hadramawt, the sayyid *manṣab* of ʿAynāt, who was accustomed to receiving income from pious endowments in Hyderabad for maintaining his open kitchen, was reduced to petitioning the British for help in regaining the endowments and reinstating payouts from the Indian government. The petitions continued into the 1950s, in vain.

Elsewhere, as in independent Malaysia, diasporic Hadramis hunkered down on the other side of the hyphen, some to become archlocals, as Malay nationalists. The alternative to assimilation was minority status, which was an unappealing condition in a nationalist state with a dominant majority. Half a century was to pass before a discussion of the place of Hadrami Arabs in the new Southeast Asian nations could take place. In 2005, a conference was held under the broad umbrella of the International Islamic University of Malaysia, with hats tipped to the sovereign

FIGURE 22. Uncertain times. Hadramis who were evicted from Kuwait after the first Gulf War, outside a government office at al-Mukallā. Photo by the author.

indigenous nation-states; it was gingerly entitled "The Arab Hadramis in Southeast Asia: Identity Maintenance or Assimilation?" The conference was opened by Syed Hamid Albar, the Malaysian foreign minister of Hadrami sayyid origin. More confidence was shown in Indonesia, where in 2003 the national archives organized a conference with the Yemen embassy entitled "Arab's Legacy in Indonesia: Yemenis-Indonesian Mestizo Culture." The keynote speaker was an Indonesian Hadrami sayyid, Prof. Dr. Said Agil Al Munawar, in his capacity as Indonesia's minister of religion. Singapore, where Muslims, Malays, and Hadramis were all minorities, was a decade ahead of Malaysia and Indonesia in this regard, its newspapers having hosted a spirited debate in the early 1990s about whether Hadramis were Malays (Alatas 1997: 28–29), in the wake of government proposals to set aside special seats in parliament for minorities.

In the young Republic of Indonesia, matters were more mixed and muddled after independence in 1949. Some Hadramis went back to Hadramawt, some continued on to other Arab countries, and many stayed put. The writing had been on the wall decades before. In the 1930s, as

ʿAlawīs and Irshādīs were squabbling, a younger generation of Hadramis born in the Dutch East Indies had looked ahead, with the restless *muwallad* A. R. Baswedan pointing the way. They formed the Indonesian Arab Association (subsequently to become the Partai Arab Indonesia, PAI), throwing their lot in with the Indonesian nationalists.[12] They did so just in time, for after Indonesia became an independent country, Hadrami Arabs and others formerly classed by the Dutch as "Foreign Orientals" who remained in the country wanted to become Indonesian nationals. An ocean away, their siblings and cousins living in Hadramawt and studying in Aden, Cairo, Baghdad, and Damascus started thinking of themselves as Arab nationalists. Families were now separated by nations.

Socialist Leveling in South Yemen

Back in the homeland, national independence was granted in 1967, and Hadramawt became part of the new country eventually called the People's Democratic Republic of Yemen. Educated sons of chiefs and sayyids, now nationalists as members of the National Front, became governors and mayors. However, within two years, a new "corrective line" radicalized government and forced them out. Radicalization meant that the incomplete process of leveling begun in the colonial period was to be carried further, to now include the nationalization of private land

12. Baswedan's close friends and fellow journalists Liem Koen Hian and Tjoa Tjie Liang championed a linked movement among the creole Chinese (in the Partai Tionghoa Indonesia, PTI), urging them to stand with their indigenous mothers' peoples (Suryadinata 2005: 88–94). These nationalist parties were spawned from within the descent-based cateogories of Dutch rule by the Indonesian nationalist party (Persatuan Bangsa Indonesia, PBI). Across racial lines, young nationalist *muwallads* like Baswedan and Tjoa Tjie Liang cultivated shared enthusiasms, working together in the newspapers *Sin Tit Po* (edited by Lim Koen Hian), *Soeara Oemoem* (organ of PBI), and *Matahari* (edited by Kwee Hing Tjiat) and sharing living quarters in Semarang. As a local-born *muwallad,* Baswedan eloquently expressed feelings of social distance from Hadramis born in the homeland in his article "Peranakan Arab dan Totoknya" (*Matahari* 1 August 1934), while his close association with like-minded Chinese *muwallads* are attested to in letters from Tjoa Tjie Liang to him, recounting their shared experiences working and living together in short-lived journals and modest rented houses (Suratmin 1984–85, appendix C). Baswedan was to rue the unhappy fate of his Chinese friends in independent Indonesia, exemplified by Tjoa's having to change his name (to Anang Satyawardaya) under suspicion of national disloyalty, like other Chinese. I am grateful to Dr. Ahmad Samhari Baswedan for sharing with me his wide knowledge of the cultural politics of Indonesian nationhood and his fond understanding of his father's life.

and houses under the banner of socialism. Some families had only recently repatriated wealth from the newly independent states, seeking stability in real estate in the homeland; many were sayyids, and they were the hardest hit. Confiscation of private property set off fresh waves of emigration through the 1970s, now to the booming petro-economies of Saudi Arabia and the Persian Gulf states. Leading personalities in towns and sizable villages, whether sayyids, tribal leaders, traders, or officials, headed the exodus. The state was now officially Marxist, and the poles of debate were between Soviet and Chinese tendencies. In this decade, especially under the lead of President Sālim Rubayiʿ ʿAlī (nicknamed "*Sālmīn*," as in "*Viet-min*"), militias orchestrated Maoist-style peasant confrontations with landlords, to sunder what remained from precolonial days of reciprocal obligations tying local groups to each other. The "Chinese line" was in the ascendant within the party and took inspiration from China's Cultural Revolution. Peasants were organized into popular militias *(mīlīshiyāt shaʿbiyya)* and mobilized in "uprisings" *(intifāḍāt)* to denounce feudal landlords, bourgeoisie, and priests. In Hadramawt, it is often said that those militias were not composed of locals but of outsiders bused in from elsewhere. This was not always the case.

Pilgrimages, like that to Tarim's graves, which enact social reciprocities and emplot them in overlapping genealogical histories, were sharply attenuated. Some, like the pilgrimage at al-Qaṭn, lost all religious significance and reverted to being annual markets (Knysh 1997: 211). Tearing down town walls, such as that built by the al-Kāfs in Tarim, was a favorite activity for consciousness raising. Local social categories were translated into generic Marxist ones in identifying class enemies: tribal chiefs were "feudalist" *(iqṭāʿī)*, and sayyids were "priestly" *(kahnūtī)*. At other times, they were all lumped together as "bourgeoisie," from big to small, with those receiving income from abroad topping the list. A common refrain was "No priests, no bourgeoisie, no voice above the voice of the party." At the other end of the scale, the oppressed were the stratum that had been ground down, the "pulverized class" *(al-ṭabaqa al-masḥūqa)*, like powdered residue at the base of a mill, or between mortar and pestle. Such was the language of leveling. Gathering distrust of the old social categories through colonial days now gained expression in violent action.

The period was known for excesses. On 30 November 1973, for instance, schoolchildren lined up on the street outside the town of Shibam in Hadramawt, cheering and clapping in anticipation of the motorcade of the president, Sālmīn. As the cars approached, they raised a storm of dust, and as they passed by, the crowd saw things bumping along behind the vehicles; these objects turned out to be bodies of men dragged along with ropes, most of them sayyids. Many in the audience became sick and remained ill for days. Old and young men of chiefly and sayyidly families left Hadramawt in droves, some to Aden, most abroad. The stratum of "modernized notables" created in the colonial period went north into exile in the neighboring countries of the Arabian Peninsula, just as Tories had gone from the United States to Canada two centuries earlier. They were not evicted all at once; they departed as each cycle of central mobilization and populist uprising identified, targeted, and dispossessed ever-lower levels of the "bourgeoisie." Each time a political falling out took place in Aden, a change of leadership in the provinces ensued: thus, local control descended into the hands of ever-lower orders, it was said. A wave of exilic migrations from Tarim in the early 1970s was even named for one of the militia leaders of the uprisings, *tanaqqulāt Khamīs Ḥamdūn*. In such ways, the leveling of social differences that had begun under colonial rule was carried further under socialist government. The intermediate category of modernized notables standing between citizens and state, now eviscerated and in exile, was replaced by cadres *(kawādir)* of the ruling Yemeni Socialist Party. On this flattened social landscape, absolutist methods of state surveillance imported from Europe were applied at the fine level of individuals, with the help of the East German *Stasi*. Needless to say, relations between homeland and diaspora were severely curtailed.

A decade later, when asked what had been achieved after ten years of socialism, one wit replied, "We've made the Mahris speak Arabic, made the Hadramis think they're Yemeni, and made the people ask for a lower salary."[13] In this caricature of egalitarian national development, Hadramis forget about the diaspora, tie themselves to the territorial nation instead, and sacrifice for the public good. Most working adults became employees of the state, tied to a Chinese sort of "iron rice bowl," which was secure if modest.

13. This quip is attributed to Fayṣal "al-Nuʿayrī" al-ʿAṭṭās, a young sayyid socialist who fomented revolt against the Hadrami sultans upon decolonization. The Mahrīs, who live in the region of Mahra between Hadramawt and Oman, are a linguistic minority who speak a non-Arabic, Hamitic language.

Openings and Closings: Diasporic Place and Pace

In tracing the trajectory of the ʿAlawī pathway, the first two sections of this book, "Burial" and "Genealogical Travel," followed the evolution of a social category—the ʿAlawī, or Hadrami sayyid—over a long period. Over the course of half a millennium, the Indian Ocean provided a series of openings that allowed persons of this category entry and provided them a wide field of endeavor. On this stage, we followed the course of long-term processes as they produced the rise of new polities, the spread of ecumenical Islam, the emergence of transcultural marriage and kinship relations, and the development of a genealogical canon of texts. Such processes create patterns that become visible only over long periods of time, and in that sense, they are slow. The long incubation and the degree to which the category of sayyid has become embedded—in different ways—in societies in the Indian Ocean region give it a stability and a resilience that is easier to perceive than to understand. The slow pace of this embedding helps explain why the category *sayyid* is a venerable one—in the minds of people; in books, charts, and grave sites; and in how persons dress, carry themselves, and treat others.

Yet the past century has been anything but slow. It has, rather, been hectic—hectic not because of modernism or the pace of communications or technological change or economic growth but because the many places inhabited by this category have changed hands many times within a short space of time. The opening of colonies to external capital and labor in the late nineteenth century, the disruptions of wars and revolution, the spectacular growth of new industries such as oil, the collapse of international regimes of political order, such as the retrenchment of European empires and the later dismantling of Cold War structures—coupled with the national succession struggles ignited in their wakes—have brought in their train major changes in the dynamics of migration. Whole countries and regions have opened and closed their doors and hearts wholesale to summary categories of persons in quick succession. The pace of events has been rapid—rapid in relation to the time frame involved, typically multiple decades, in making real-estate investments, setting up religious endowments, raising a family and building a career, committing to educational languages and systems, and indeed to whole countries. The pace has been rapid because the leveling of social differences under colonial administration paved the way for new kinds of political events, such as media campaigns and mob riots that target whole categories of persons—what Tambiah calls "leveling crowds"—all at once

(Tambiah 1996). Such events and their aftermath serve as switches that close social spaces and opportunities to some and open them to others. This is the politics of communalism, in which old social categories, with their various religious, linguistic, regional, or ethnic affiliations, are reduced to single dimensions and become enmassed, physically colliding objects positioned along narrow lines of competition for administrative favor. They become subject to a faster, almost mechanical pace of politics. Yet they retain something of their older character. While Hadrami sayyids could become sultanic tax farmers, millionaire landlords, and colonial collaborators, as the al-Kāfs did in the 1930s, they could also be charismatic or respected divines or jurists, like the ʿAydarūses and al-Ḥabshīs, who presided over schools, courts of law, pilgrimage destinations, and *manṣab*ates and who shunned controversy in the interests of dignity. These sorts of sayyids, who exemplified the virtues of the old category, were not always happy with the faster pace of the twentieth century and its modern men like the al-Kāfs.

Politics of the communalist sort also created categories of persons where none existed before. The Irshādīs, who emerged in the first half of the twentieth century to challenge the sayyids, were a characteristic artifact of divisive British policies that generated communal rivalries in their colonies. Somewhere between al-Shiḥr and Singapore, the exercise of British disfavor had unwittingly encouraged the emergence of a new category of Hadramis who were determined to organize themselves, persons whose shared discontent stemmed from unequal treatment by the authorities. The Dutch advisor on native affairs, B. Shrieke, had alerted his British counterpart to the risk of such unhappiness. The sociological composition of the Irshādīs—Kathīrī tribalists, Cairene modernists, Islamic reformists, and successful businessmen—has never been properly understood, precisely because they were the residue of administrative action, a residue that became surprisingly indignant, active, and vocal. Areas under British influence, such as the coastal Quʿayṭī sultanate, India, Malaya, and Singapore, became closed to the Irshādīs, so the Irshādīs gravitated toward areas that did remain open to them: the Dutch East Indies, the Hadrami interior, Italian Ethiopia, Saudi Arabia. Today, those who went to the Arab lands rather than colonial Southeast Asia, who threw their lot in with the Saudis two generations ago, are the cream of the new Hadrami diaspora, resident in Arabian countries a desert drive away from Hadramawt. Among them, al-ʿAmūdī, Buqshān, bin Maḥfūẓ, and bin Lādin are the best-known family names; these families own the biggest trading, banking, and construction conglomerates in the realm and are purveyors to the Saudi court; extending beyond the kingdom, the al-ʿAmūdīs reportedly control close to 40 percent of the industrial base of Ethiopia, under the wing of their holding company, MIDROC. Some of them, who were opposed to sharifians and sayyids and disfavored by the British as Irshādīs in the early days, went on to cultivate a very different way of combining wealth, influence, and piety in the Kingdom of Saudi Arabia. By a twist of history, in the socialist period they were to be joined by those the British did favor, the modernized notables who went into exile in successive waves.

For Hadrami families with little history of diasporic experience, socialist rule brought enhanced life chances through external travel and training. Sons and even daughters of peasants, artisans, officials, and bedouin were educated in national schools and sent to Eastern-bloc countries such as Cuba, East Germany, Hungary, Azerbaijan, and the Soviet Union. They returned as doctors, opticians, pharmacists, engineers, naval officers, pilots, philosophers, historians, and other professionals and professors. In the 1980s and 1990s, such persons could be found in the main towns of the country, some joined by their Eastern European wives. The sight of local women in cotton print skirts, sometimes astride a motorbike, was not unusual. The materialization of this category of persons, who experienced the external world through higher education in the Western socialist countries rather than through diasporic residence in the old Indian Ocean ones or neighboring Arab countries, lasted for all of two decades. Their ranks were not replenished in the 1990s, as the socialist bloc crumbled. Instead, after the unification of Yemen at the beginning of that decade, they faced the threat of eviction from their jobs and homes.

We can view the internal politics of diasporic Hadramis in each period as a landscape of places that closed or opened up to different categories of persons, as internal divisions became intertwined with external rivalries. Even as the path of education and promotion in the sphere of international socialism closed down, another path opened up. With the unification of Yemen in 1990 and the weakening of socialist control, a range of restrictions on internal social life in the south was lifted.[14] One dramatic result was a surge in organized religious activity and the emer-

14. For an analysis of periods and possibilities for democratic openness in Yemen, see Carapico 1998.

FIGURE 23. Graves of socialist martyrs upended by the northern Yemeni army on the road south to Aden, May–July 1994. Photo by B. Haykel and the author.

gence of a divide between *"ṣūfī"* and *"salafī,"* among others. Individuals are happy to identify with these labels because they are distinct from terms of abuse such as "grave worshippers" *(qubūriyyīn)*, "bearded ones" *(Abū laḥya)*, "horned ones" *(Abū qarn)*, fundamentalists *(uṣūliyyīn)*, and Wahhabis. Across the Middle East in the 1980s, religion had emerged as a renewed platform for mass politics, supplanting the tired ideologies of nationalism and socialism. Hadramis readily associate the term *Sufi* with the sayyid ʿAlawī Way. *Salafī,* literally "someone inclined to predecessors," derives from an orientation associated with Muḥammad b. ʿAbd al-Wahhāb and references the prophet Muḥammad and his Companions as exemplary predecessors and guides to comportment and faith. In Hadramawt, the identification of *salafī* with Wahhabi goes back to the destruction of the tombs of ʿAlawī saints in the first decade of the nineteenth century, when the combination of Saudi state and Wahhabi doctrine made its first dramatic showing in such acts of demolition around the Arabian Peninsula. While antagonisms between groups known as Sufis and Wahhabis/*salafī*s have expanded beyond the peninsula since then, embracing various regional constituencies, in the Hadramawt the historical and geographical referents are clear.

What *salafī* refers to in recent times is less clear. During the Cold War, the northern Yemeni government nurtured a *salafī* movement along its border with the South, as a fifth column to subvert the southern socialist government. Within the borders of the socialist state itself, any sort of politics with religious overtones had been suppressed. In the early 1970s, Sufis were the target, associated with sayyids as a priestly elite in the ancien régime. Subsequently, state attention turned to *salafīs* instead, suspected of collaboration with the North. With the unification of North and South Yemen in 1990, differences between Sufis and *salafīs* emerged as one of the most visible and contentious arenas of conflict in Hadramawt, and across the South more generally. The relaxation of border controls and internal surveillance had opened the country to a host of external parties. As Hadramawt, with its large and diverse diaspora, became the object of different projects of return, emergent differences within it became inscribed more categorically as a Sufi-*salafī* rift and became intractable, fueled by external support.

The combination of rival states and rival social movements in Hadramawt in the 1990s resembled the diasporic conflicts of the 1930s. Rivalries between states played out internally with the bestowal of state favor or disfavor on specific groups. As we have noted, internal Hadrami rivalries became coupled with external ones. In the early twentieth century, imperial British disfavor had all but guaranteed the growth of the Irshādī movement within the diaspora; in the late 1980s, socialist-state disfavor provided a similar impulse to *salafīs* in the homeland. Like the earlier Irshādīs, today's *salafīs* do not easily fit into long-standing social categories. While state disfavor clearly provided a strong impulse, the social and institutional shapes fill out as rivalries gather momentum. After the unification of Yemen in 1990, these rivalries played out in an efflorescence of new schools and mosques (which became stops on new lecture circuits for preachers from afar), cassette recordings of the speeches of popular speakers, shops selling those cassettes, and the publication of many new books and pamphlets. Much of this activity was funded by migrants in Saudi Arabia. In addition, *salafīs* received a boost through support from a network of schools based in the North, the *Maʿāhid ʿIlmiyya,* which received funding from the government. After unification in 1990, such schools were established in towns throughout the South, where they attracted the children of farmers, minor officials, and others who, in a previous generation, would have enjoyed the benefits of socialist education. Northern *salafīs* had links to the government through the Iṣlāḥ party, a sometime ally of the ruling General People's Congress. Iṣlāh itself was conspicuously multifaceted, articulating with tribal, military, and *salafī* constituencies through its various leaders.[15]

The *salafīs*' rivals are easier to identify, being persons from the established sayyid families. In the 1990s, sayyids refurbished and reorganized schools that had been neglected during the decades of socialist rule, such as the Ribāṭ of Tarim. Endowment monies of the school held in trust accounts in Singapore became available once again. A new religious school and university were built, thanks to new diasporic contributions.

As in the old rivalry between ʿAlawīs and Irshādīs, which resulted in the competitive construction of schools across the Malay Archipelago (and less formal tutorial arrangements in the homeland), education is a major site of contention in Hadramawt today. The religious orientations and social loyalties of the future are being shaped in the schools of the present, as an anxious postsocialist generation of students casts about for a clear trajectory of personal and vocational advancement. Students have a choice of textbooks, schools, teachers, and mentors with decidedly different orientations, orientations that may influence the course of their lives for decades to come. The biographies of those teachers are important. They connect past to future and give a sense of the stakes. Let me offer three brief examples.[16]

One of these teachers is influential in a wadi adjoining Tarim. He is descended from a line of local tribal leaders and lives in a fort in one of their tribal settlements surrounding Tarim. As a boy, he was fascinated by the clear distinctions in grammar he overheard from a class in the local mosque. He asked to join the class but was rebuked by the teacher, a sayyid, who said, "No, why don't you just take some bullets and a gun and go shoot and kill? *Ḥarām* for a tribal to study."[17] This sayyid teacher subsequently went to Java, where he had a change of heart, and after his return, opened

15. Dresch and Haykel chart an instructive course through the thicket of rhetoric, personalities, collectivities, ideas, and interests (Dresch and Haykel 1995).

16. Knysh, who conducted fieldwork in Hadramawt in both the socialist and postsocialist periods, provides one example from a visit in 1999 in an article on the "resurgence of sufism in Yemen" in the 1990s (Knysh 2001).

17. Interestingly, Shaykh Muqbil al-Wādiʿī, about twenty years younger than this Hadrami teacher of tribal origin and perhaps the most influential *salafī* teacher in North Yemen until his death in 2001, also told of being refused entry to mosque lessons—at the Great Mosque of al-Hādī Yaḥyā in Ṣaʿda—by a sayyid teacher because of his tribal origins. Al-Wādiʿī subsequently obtained a religious education abroad, in Saudi Arabia, and returned to Yemen in 1979 after getting into trouble with the authorities there. He finally was able to achieve his educative ambition by basing his school in his home region of Wādī Dammāj east of Ṣaʿda, protected by his fellow Wādiʿī tribesmen against the prevailing Zaydī religious

his classes to all. The would-be student himself went to Java in the 1920s, where he sold cloth in markets and found opportunities to study, first with a sayyid teacher (who as an orphan had been taught by the Sudanese Irshādī leader Aḥmad al-Sūrkatī), then in Irshād schools. For two years, he studied under al-Sūrkatī himself, and later he became a teacher in Irshādī schools. He spent a few years in Singapore, where he married a woman of his clan. When he later returned to Singapore to obtain British subjecthood for his children, the government-designated chief of Arabs, a sayyid, gave his assent, but the chief of police, who was an Indian, rejected his application because he had been identified as an Irshādī. This rejection turned out to be a blessing in disguise, for when the Japanese occupied Java during the Second World War, they accused him of being an English sympathizer. He was released when he showed them his passport, which recorded that he had been refused British subject status for being an Irshādī. He later spent three years in Saudi Arabia, where he met the Saudi king and requested help with building a school in Hadramawt. He was not successful, so he returned to Hadramawt in 1960, where he has worked as a teacher ever since. His influence grew through the socialist period, and his followers took over the Friday mosque of the settlement from its sayyid imam. When the former sayyid leader of the settlement, the *manṣab,* returned from exile in the Persian Gulf, he received little attention, even though he had been treated like a sultan before, the teacher said.

Another of these teachers wields great influence in another wadi adjoining Tarim, where he preaches in the Friday mosque. Although his family is of peasant origin, his father was known for his intelligence, had acquired learning, served as a leading jurist in the colonial period, and expanded the reach of education in the wadi around his home. This area became one of the first in interior Hadramawt to manifest trade-union activity in the late colonial period. He himself was very well educated and widely read, was constantly consulted on all manner of questions, and officiated at marriages, divorces, and the like. He opposes the Sufi practices of the sayyids, rejects grave visits as superstition, and wonders at the

establishment. Al-Wādiʿī claimed that several tens of thousands of students from across Yemen and beyond passed through his *ḥadīth* institute in the 1980s and 1990s (Haykel 2002). The parallels between these two biographies are significant. Both involved an early encounter with prejudice within the local religious establishment because of social origin, subsequent access to education abroad, trouble with authorities, return and establishment of a permanent educational mission under tribal protection at home, gradual expansion of antiestablishment religious ideas, and social influence through students.

amount of money spent at major pilgrimages, noting that the sums could be put to better use feeding families or educating children. Yet he is bound to sayyids by friendship and scholarly teacher-student links going back to his father, as well as neighborly family relations from childhood involving his siblings, and he is often invited to sayyids' social functions. He seeks to keep religious orientation distinct from personal relations; indeed, for those who take care in such matters, the fundamentally formal, textual basis of religious disputes itself enables the pursuit of wide-ranging differences at very close spatial and social quarters, partially insulating long-term relationships from the corrosive effects of such differences.

The third of these influential teachers is a sayyid, who spent time in exile abroad during the socialist period. His father was a well-respected scholar who disappeared one day on his way to the mosque, leaving no trace save his shoulder shawl. It was widely believed that he had been killed by socialists. After unification, the son returned to Hadramawt and quickly established himself as one of the leading lights of the new sayyid religious firmament, reinvigorating Islam in a land where it had been suppressed under socialism. Charismatic and well traveled, he gathered enough funds to start his own school, which now has students from as far away as Indonesia. He frequently lectures in Tarim and the surrounding regions and can always be seen with his father's shawl over his shoulder. In recent years, he has taken to touring Indonesia regularly. In Java, posters of him and other sayyid divines are sold at pilgrimage centers, such as the tomb complex of Sunan Ampel in Surabaya, by the Arab quarter.

Even in these brief accounts, we can see that through the shifting course of personal migrations and regime changes of the twentieth century, the lives of individuals are modulated by the social categories into which they are born. Yet in a number of important respects, all three teachers share similar social qualities. The known histories and reputations of their families and fathers—whether they were tribal leaders, scholars, or sayyids—give them a fundamental credibility, which the trajectories of their own social commitments enhance and confirm. To have consistency in "good works" over generations is standard fare in the hagiographies, biographical dictionaries, and genealogical family histories; to have living individuals who stand at the end of one such line in a particular place—and exemplify this continuity of "good works" themselves—is rare. These are the ones who are mindful of their internal obligations to their progenitors, their *salaf* and their memories, in the first instance. This mindfulness of internal obligations is recognized through their public works, in which they help their fellow man in ways their fathers were known for.

"He taught me; his father taught my father," is a prototypical statement of such recognition: the canonical texts mimic such declarations of faith in persons. This intertwining of internal—genealogical—obligations with external, social ones produces the unusual individual in whom a community is willing to invest its trust. Such trust is in short supply in a society where the old social categories have become intercalated with the structures of state administration over six decades of Englishry. Persons who command that trust become the public figures of a diaspora that predates and circumvents the public officials of national states. Hard-nosed Hadrami businessmen, from the air-conditioned fastnesses of their company offices in Jedda and Abu Dhabi, are happy to place in their hands millions of shillings during the fasting month for disbursement to the needy, no questions asked.[18] Contributions for rival schools and mosques flow through the same channels.

As intellectuals and as social leaders seeking to establish broad platforms of participation, such teachers who possess the public trust necessarily align themselves with visions and causes larger than those of social origin. Those larger causes are conceived of and pursued as educational projects, and as such, are oriented to a much longer time frame than is the cut-and-thrust of contemporary party politics. The teachers have the credibility to speak for the future because their stories and those of their fathers are genealogically interwoven with the narrative pasts of their supporters. Such bonds may find ritual and discursive representations in what we might call communities of pilgrimage, such as those enacted at the graves of Tarim, and constituted in the circulatory rhythms of the diaspora led by the erstwhile sayyids of Hadramawt. They may also find representation in alternative communities that form around schools, such as those of present-day *salafīs* and their predecessors, the Irshādīs of old. Sayyid or *salafī* in inspiration, grave and school ground shape radically different kinds of communities, which take radically different paths toward recognizing and realizing the truths of religion and society. Thus, disputes are pursued between them without regard to boundary or scale; listening in, one cannot easily tell whether villages, wadis, towns, regions, nations, states, diasporas, or the whole of Islam are involved. One thing is clear, however: in some places, they have stopped praying at the same mosques.

18. These donations amount to tens of thousands of U.S. dollars. During the fasting month, an individual may receive such charity monies equivalent to three times the monthly salary of a government employee, from individual handouts of fifty dollars.

CONCLUDING REMARKS

Names beyond Nations

> The mystical orders did not fit into this new pattern. They had spread all over the Islamic world and could therefore not be confined to the borders of the newly founded states; what had looked cosmopolitan in earlier days looked unpatriotic now.
>
> Josef van Ess (1999: 41)

As we saw at the beginning of this book, the 1994 civil war in Yemen came with a few surprises, notably the appearance of many sayyids in the cabinet of the newly declared secessionist state. After suffering decades of property confiscation, stigmatization, eviction, and exile, Hadrami sayyids had in the late 1980s become visible in the higher echelons of socialist-state administration, and even in the governing politburo. Now, their numerical domination of the secessionist cabinet resuscitated all the old issues of trust that had plagued the colonial regime. Were they in it for self-interest, for the good of the people, or for their own agenda, like the narrow factions that had riven the socialist politburo in the past? Although the secessionist sayyids came from different parts of the country and very different backgrounds, they were easily identifiable by their family names. Though their names were not prefixed by the honorific *sayyid,* they were well known as sayyid ones.

As we have seen, Hadrami sayyid names do not stay within small locales but are distributed and recognized across the Indian Ocean. The Hadrami genealogies that comprise the names evolved as the diaspora moved, spreading a tissue of names across the ocean. In their various hybrid forms, the genealogies articulate with places, as in burials and pilgrimages to the graves of Hadrami sayyids. Each site brings together places, persons, names, and texts in architecture and rituals. At the graves of Tarim, pilgrimage recognizes and enacts relations among different categories of persons, between the living and the dead, and between those present and absent. While the relation between names engraved on headstones and persons buried in the graves is one of contiguity or metonymy, genealogy links those names to others far away and makes possible the metaphorical associations that elevate individual figures. Over centuries, the interplay of these signifying elements has produced, in port towns across the ocean, characteristic combinations of locally known families of sayyids, tombs of saints serving as pilgrimage destinations, genealogical charts displayed at those tombs and in homes, and modest collections of the canonical texts we have discussed. In combination, they serve as a ready apparatus of signs through which persons resident or sojourning may be identified as individuals, authenticated as sayyids, and recognized as their fame spreads. In their very names, these signs and their persons become the cores of new, creole communities.

This signifying apparatus developed over centuries of diasporic travel and burial beyond the jurisdiction of any one state. In the twentieth century, when imperial authorities became concerned to authenticate the identities of individuals within and between colonies for their own reasons, this sayyidly apparatus of signs stood ready to translate its operations into terms familiar to the imperial administrations. As we have noted, in the 1920s a comprehensive genealogy of the Hadrami sayyids was brought from Tarim to the Dutch East Indies; a bureaucratic organization with an office and forms was established to register and record new births from across the archipelago in the genealogy; and the idea of a diasporawide national representative council was floated. Toward the end of that decade, these measures for tightening up links within the diaspora became associated with an ambitious attempt to integrate the diasporic space politically in partnership with Britain, as we saw in the last chapter.

The most provocative of the measures, the proposal passed by the 1927 al-Shiḥr conference to require passports of all persons wishing to leave Hadramawt, had a wholly unforeseen consequence. It spurred nonsayyids to adopt the honorific *sayyid* on passports they obtained from Dutch authorities in the East Indies. This practice was opposed by sayyid elites, such as ʿAlawī b. Ṭāhir al-Ḥaddād, who made vigorous representations to the Dutch and English authorities. The ensuing contretemps rapidly widened into a geographically broad and historically far-reaching discussion of the word *sayyid* and its meanings and usages. Certainly the term could travel. At issue was whether its referent stayed stable throughout its peregrinations. Irshādīs argued that it did not. They pointed to

Egyptian and Syrian usage, which commonly used the term in polite address, like "mister" in English.[1] Going back in time, the Irshādīs quoted from canonical sayyid texts such as al-Shilli's *The Irrigating Fount* to show that the grand, early figures of the ʿAlawī sayyid tradition, such as the First Jurist, were referred to by the honorific *shaykh* rather than *sayyid*. Having established that usage was historically relative, they then argued that no one group could monopolize the term. No basis existed for preventing Irshādīs from adopting it in their passports.

That the unintended yoking of sayyid naming practices to those of imperial passports generated intense controversy is probably no coincidence. In different ways, the handling of names in both had great consequences for how persons travel, a matter of vital interest to diasporic communities. As the mobility of the Hadrami diaspora became the business of European empires in the twentieth century, the passport became a key site of articulation between these distinct but equally mobile social entities, diaspora and empire. Standing at the junction of very different but equally powerful dynamics of signification, problems over passports set in motion a train of events that was to take apart and recombine relations among names, persons, texts, and places in unexpected and at times violent ways. Sayyid naming practices—as a dynamic of signification that moves through culturally defined moments of burial, travel, and pilgrimage—enable long journeys through time and space, and across culture. Such naming practices, which have evolved into hybrid genres of genealogy, produce representational forms without which the diaspora does not exist, but dissolves into scattered places and persons who bear no relation to one another, within a few generations of emigration. Without their genealogies, sayyid families cannot travel transculturally and remain sayyids. Non-sayyid Hadramis, who do not possess such an extensive genealogical apparatus, disappear even faster in diaspora, losing their names and becoming indistinct from others around them. Without those genealogies, distance and duration defeat categorical stability.

Passports do similar work. Consider their basic media: the photograph, text, paper. The relation of photograph to face, the similarity between image and visage, engraves person onto paper and establishes a connec-

1. One important arena in which these disputes played out was in representations to colonial authorities. The sample of arguments I give here comes from representations pertaining to the issuance of passports. See IORL, R/20/A/3413, "Use of title 'Seiyid' in official documents," File no. 831 of 1931, pp.13–31.

tion of metonymy with the bearer, while the text inscribes the name of that person in the country of which he or she is thereby made a part.[2] Like the combination of gravestone and genealogy, a passport identifies the one it points to, differentiating that person from others while assimilating him or her into a category shared with others—citizen or national (Caplan 2001: 51). Without a passport, the bona fides or authentication required for travel through a U.N. world of states that acknowledge only each other cannot be established, and one remains stuck. The Indonesian *muwallad*s who were stuck in Aden after the first Gulf War knew this fact well. In such a world, individuals do not possess inter-national legal personality; only states do. Individuals can only borrow the personalities of states, by carrying their passports. Passports are loans from states to persons, for a fixed term, according them passage rather than blockade through the great big business of channeling goods and persons across spaces fully parceled out among sovereigns. Before persons, it was ships passing through ports that had to carry passports, such as those stipulated in the 1604 treaty between the Dutch and the Zamorin of Calicut (Alexandrowicz 1967: 75–77). Whether carried by persons or ships, passports are letters from one sovereign to another, identifying and authenticating the bearer, thereby allowing persons to travel through places where they do not belong, "without let or hindrance," as my Malaysian passport kindly requests. Passports do so by removing ambiguity about where their bearers do belong.[3]

Two months after the conclusion of the Yemeni civil war in 1994, much ambiguity remained. Was the sayyid majority in the secessionist cabinet

2. Jeremy Bentham proposed establishing identity the other way around, mandating that each person's name be unique and tattooed on his or her wrists, given that skin is a more secure surface for engraving than paper is (Caplan 2001: 65).

3. Erasing any ambiguity about their descent status, sayyids in contemporary Malaysia officially register the honorifics *Syed* and *Syarifa* as integral parts of their personal names, after the fashion of the Malay nobility and their titles. In republican Yemen, discretion is called for, and the egalitarian "brother"/"sister" *al-ākh/al-ukht* are the preferred terms of address in official correspondence. Sayyids in republican Indonesia also leave out the honorifics. Instead, a portable personal genealogy in the form of a passport is issued by al-Rābiṭa al-ʿAlawiyya's Perpetual Office for the Compilation and Control of the Genealogy of the ʿAlawī Sayyids. Like a passport, the document carries its own number and particulars of issuance and contains the bearer's name, date of birth, place of birth, and photograph sealed to the paper with an official stamp and plastic laminate. In addition, the document carries section and reference numbers to the master genealogical tree maintained by the office, identifying the bearer's branch location. In the pages where visas, entries, and exits are normally stamped is a genealogy from the prophet Muḥammad to the bearer: a

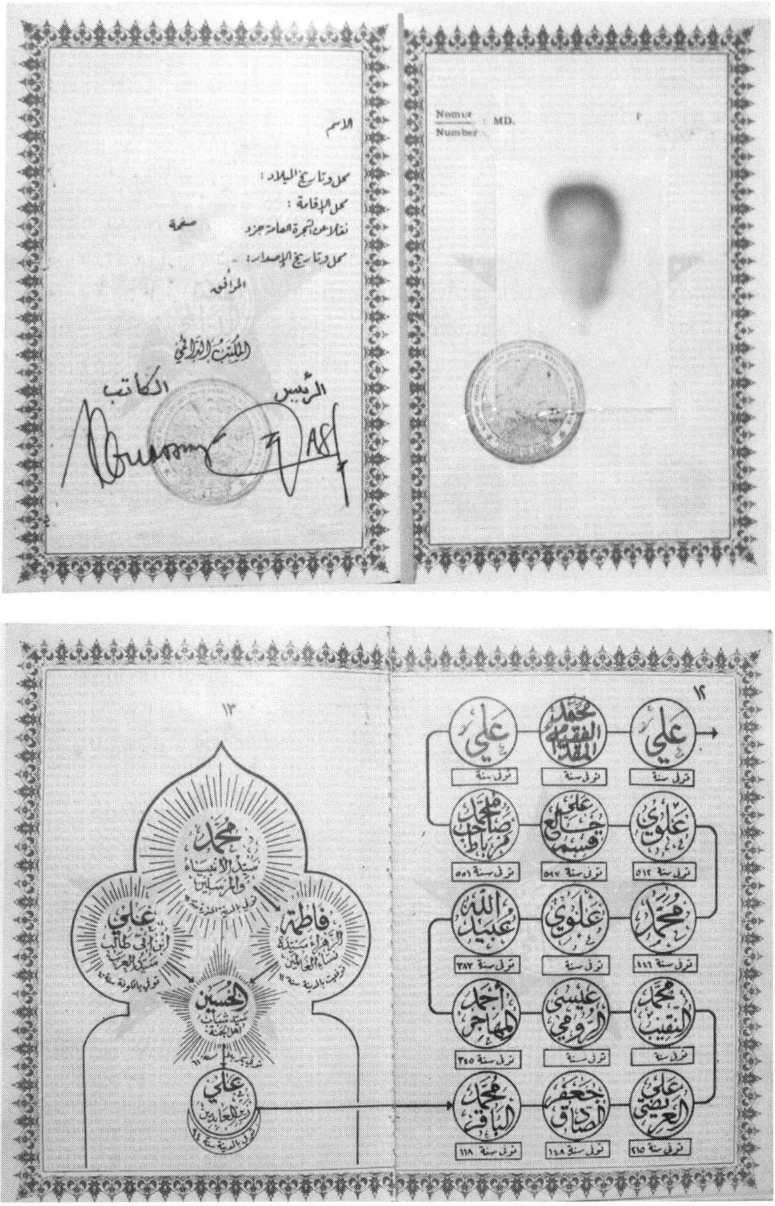

FIGURE 24. Genealogical passport issued by the Jakarta office of al-Rābiṭa al-ʿAlawiyya. A similar document is issued by its counterpart office in Medina.

FIGURE 25. A name undone. Shattered headstone at cemetery of the Adeni's tomb complex after the desecration, September 1994. Photo by B. Haykel and the author.

significant? Was this presence yet another migration of old categories of elites to new state structures where they did not belong, as had transpired in the colonial period? Were these sayyids patriots or a recidivist ancien régime faction intent on seizing its turn? The attackers of the grave of Abū Bakr al-ʿAydarūs the Adeni sought to place them right back in the old categories of sayyid and Sufi where they did belong, tying them to the Adeni's tomb and gesturing to a network of shadowy figures beyond the nation. As van Ess so aptly describes the Sufi orders in the twentieth century, "What had looked cosmopolitan in earlier days looked unpatriotic now." By their action at the grave, the desecrators sought to remove any ambiguity as to who the unpatriotic secessionist leaders were. Attacking the burial complex of person, place, text, and name, knocking down gravestones and exhuming bodies, they physically pulled apart its fundamen-

succession of stamped names with death dates—a trail of entries and exits—running through the pages. In its startlingly unique, hybrid way, this "genealogical passport" or "genealogy for travel" documents the contentious, twentieth-century intertwining of diaspora and empire and attests to the continuing hold of both genealogical and statist imaginations.

tal semiotic elements. In doing so, they activated its authenticating potential even as they were dismantling it. Two days after they were done, the international Arabic weekly *al-Wasaṭ,* published in London under Saudi ownership, got the message. *Al-Wasaṭ* featured a piece entitled "Spread out from Hadramawt to Indonesia, Malaysia and Singapore: The ʿAlawī Sayyids Stood Up to the Socialists and Are Ready to Face the Iṣlāḥ Party . . . and Ṣanʿāʾ" *(Al-Wasaṭ* 1994).[4] In the cemetery adjacent to the grave of the Adeni, row upon row of graves had had their headstones knocked over. They had all been literally leveled.

The graves in Aden are linked to the graves of Tarim, of Ahmad Ābād, and to other places, by poetic associations, as drawn in books such as *The Travelling Light,* and enacted in circuits of pilgrimage. When pulled into the contentious language of states, such associations can become suspect. Pulled into politics and viewed from a distance, the associations surrounding graves acquire an opacity which resembles the ambiguities that shadow states and provide reasons for distrust. Conversely, the ambiguities generated by states, in their inability to live up to their own norms of equality and transparency, can become identified with the semiotic operations of graves and genealogies. Distrust in one arena breeds distrust in another. The attacks on the graves, as incitements to discourse, sought to spread that distrust around. As religion was brought into politics, the movements of an old diaspora once again became ensnared in the lines being drawn between and within states.

Violence at the graves of Aden and Tarim takes place in the context of theological disputes over the structures and rituals appropriate to the graves of the dead. One side makes reference to Sufi authorities such as the eighteenth-century Hadrami sayyid ʿAbd Allāh al-Ḥaddād and the fifteenth-century Egyptian polymath Jalāl al-Dīn al-Suyūṭī; the other side invokes their *salafī*-identified detractors, the eighteenth-century Muḥammad ibn ʿAbd al-Wahhāb and his thirteenth-century inspiration, Aḥmad ibn Taymiyya.[5] But the violence also takes place within the modern his-

4. *Al-Wasaṭ* no. 136: 31–33, 5 September 1994. The magazine piece was wide-ranging, linking the defeat of the southern separatists in 1994, as sayyids, to the defeat of northern sayyids in the 1962 overthrow of the Zaydi imamate. The article reproduced a hint made by a detractor that southern sayyids might have supported the separatists, hoping to regain old positions of privilege. The piece discussed their long migration histories and commented on their penchant for maintaining their genealogies.

5. Between these two sides, Muḥammad al-Shawkānī (1947), the great "sunnifier" of Zaydī Yemen, crafted an intermediate position, which Haykel explicates with subtlety (2003: 127–38). Al-Shawkānī's own grave in Ṣanʿāʾs famous Khuzayma cemetery barely escaped be-

tory of the Hadrami diaspora, whose movements abroad and at home can no longer be disentangled from those of the states that share its world. Both diaspora and state seem geared to expectations of leveling that can look only forward, not back. The twentieth-century history of leveling had brought in its train a series of evictions. Disputes over passports in the 1930s virtually evicted the sayyids from Hadrami indigeneity in the realm of historiography. At the time of the destruction of graves, the just-concluded Yemeni civil war of 1994 had evicted separatist, socialist, southern sayyids—who were probably Sufi sympathizers as well, some would say—from Yemen. Because the southern state had inherited the British colony, the collapse of the South in this war also represented the eviction of the last vestiges of British colonialism from the country. In its aftermath, even ancestors and saints were evicted from their graves. Digging deeper still, those with very long memories thought of southern Yemen as now caught up with its northern compatriots, republicans who three decades earlier had evicted their own sayyids, the Zaydi imams. All sayyids, as offspring of the Prophet from Mecca, were really northern Arabs, descendants of ʿAdnān; true Yemenis, in contrast, were southern Arabs, sprung from the loins of Qaḥṭān, in the reckoning of really ancient genealogy. Turning our gaze forward, we can see that evictions are likely to continue to mark the twenty-first century, even as sovereignties promise to become unbundled again, and mobile states and mobile peoples return to playing musical chairs.

For their part, the graves of Tarim, needful as they are of tending by the resolute localist, and vulnerable as they are to those who would breach their walls, have become tied to communities of pilgrimage elsewhere by the genealogies and the mobilities of the old diaspora. Sharing their names with others beyond the nation, their inhabitants are no longer fully invested where they are interred and have already moved on.

---

ing flattened and paved over in favor of an officers' club in 1966: it was identified, exhumed, and relocated just before the bulldozers began their work. Other religious scholars were not so lucky and lie beneath the officers' boots (Haykel 2003: 1).

Bibliography

bin ʿAbdāt, Sālim b. ʿAbdāt b. Khālid b. ʿUmar

n.d. Ḥarakat Ibn ʿAbdāt bi-l-Ghurfa, Ḥaḍramawt, 1924–1945. Typescript.

Abir, Mordechai

1980 *Ethiopia and the Red Sea: The Rise and Decline of the Solomonic Dynasty and Muslim-European Rivalry in the Region*. London: F. Cass.

Abu-Lughod, Janet

1989 *Before European Hegemony: The World System A.D. 1250–1350*. New York: Oxford University Press.

ʿAkāsha, Muḥammad ʿAbd al-Karīm

1985 *Qiyām al-salṭana al-Quʿayṭiyya wa-l-taghalghul al-istiʿmārī fī Ḥaḍramawt 1839–1918*. ʿAmmān, al-Urdun: Dār Ibn Rushd.

Alatas, Syed Farid

1997 Hadhramaut and the Hadhrami Diaspora: Problems in Theoretical History. In *Hadrami Traders, Scholars, and Statesmen in the Indian Ocean, 1750s–1960s*. U. Freitag and W. G. Clarence-Smith, eds. Leiden: Brill.

Alexandrowicz, C. H.

1967 *An Introduction to the History of the Law of Nations in the East Indies*. Oxford: Clarendon Press.

ʿAlī, ʿAlī Ḥasan, and ʿAbd al-Raḥmān ʿAbd al-Karīm al-Mallāḥī

1989 Al-Ṣirāʿ al-Ḥumūmī al-Quʿayṭī wa-dawāfiʿuh 1867–1967. In *Wathāʾiq al-nadwa al-ʿilmiyya al-tārīkhiyya ḥawl al-muqāwama al-shaʿbiyya fī Ḥaḍramawt 1900–1963*. Muḥammad Saʿīd Dāʾūd and Ṣāliḥ ʿAlī Bā Ṣurra, eds. ʿAdan: Maṭbaʿat Jāmiʿat ʿAdan.

Ali, M. Athar

1966 *The Mughal Nobility Under Aurangzeb*. Bombay: Asia Publishing House.

1985 *The Apparatus of Empire: Awards of Ranks, Offices and Titles to the Mughal Nobility, 1574–1658*. Delhi: Oxford University Press.

al-ʿAmrī, Ḥusayn b. ʿAbd Allāh
1987 *al-Manār wa-l-Yaman, 1315–1354 H./1898–1935 M.* Damascus: Dār al-Fikr.

El Amrousi, Mohamed Mohamed
2001 Beyond Muslim Space: Jeddah, Muscat, Aden and Port Said. Ph.D. diss. University of California, Los Angeles.

Andaya, Barbara, and Leonard Andaya
1982 *A History of Malaysia.* London: Macmillan.

Andaya, Leonard Y.
1975 *The Kingdom of Johor 1641–1728.* Kuala Lumpur: Oxford University Press.

Anderson, Benedict
1991 *Imagined Communities: Reflections on the Origin and Spread of Nationalism.* London: Verso.
1998 Long-Distance Nationalism. In *The Spectre of Comparisons: Nationalism, Southeast Asia, and the World.* Benedict Anderson. London: Verso.

Appadurai, Arjun
1988 Putting Hierarchy in Its Place. *Cultural Anthropology* 3 (1): 36–49.
1996 *Modernity at Large: Cultural Dimensions of Globalization.* Minneapolis: University of Minnesota Press.

bin ʿAqīl, ʿAlī
1949 *Ḥaḍramawt.* Damascus: Maṭbaʿat Sūriyya.

Ibn al-ʿArabī, Muḥyī al-Dīn
1972 *al-Futūḥāt al-Makkiyya.* 3 vols. ʿUthmān Yaḥyā, ed. Cairo: al-Hayʾa al-Miṣriyya al-ʿĀmma li-l-Kitāb.

Aristotle
1962 *The Politics,* T. A. Sinclair, trans. Middlesex, England: Penguin.

Arrighi, Giovanni
1994 *The Long Twentieth Century: Money, Power, and the Origins of Our Times.* London: Verso.

Asad, Talal
1993 *Genealogies of Religion: Discipline and Reasons of Power in Christianity and Islam.* Baltimore: Johns Hopkins University Press.
2003 *Formations of the Secular: Christianity, Islam, Modernity.* Stanford, Calif.: Stanford University Press.

Ashtor, E.
1976 Spice Prices in the Near East in the 15th Century. *Journal of the Royal Asiatic Society* 1: 26–41.

al-ʿAṭṭās, ʿAlī b. Ḥasan b. ʿAbd Allāh
n.d. al-Maqṣad fī shawāhid al-Mashhad. Manuscript.

al-Attas, Syed Muhammad Naguib
1963 *Some Aspects of Sufism as Understood and Practised among the Malays.* Singapore: Malaysian Sociological Research Institute.
1966 *Rānīrī and the Wujūdiyyah of 17th Century Acheh.* Singapore: Malaysian Branch of the Royal Asiatic Society.

Auerbach, Erich

1959 Figura. In *Scenes from the Drama of European Literature.* Original German text published in *Neue Dantestudien,* Istanbul 1944. New York: Meridian.

Augé, Marc

1995 *Non-places: Introduction to an Anthropology of Supermodernity.* London: Verso.

al-ʿAydarūs, ʿAbd al-Qādir b. Shaykh

1985 *Ta'rīkh al-nūr al-sāfir ʿan akhbār al-qarn al-ʿāshir.* Beirut: Dār al-Kutub al-ʿIlmiyya.

al-ʿAydarūs, Abū Bakr b. ʿAbd Allāh

1970 *al-Quṭb al-kabīr al-Rifāʿī, aw al-najm al-sāʿī fī manāqib al-quṭb al-kabīr al-Rifāʿī.* Cairo: Maktabat al-Qāhira.

al-ʿAydarūs, al-ʿAydarūs ibn al-Sharīf ʿAlī

1954 *Hādhā kitāb bughyat al-āmāl fī ta'rīkh al-Ṣūmāl.* Muqdishū: Maṭbaʿat al-Idāra.

Azra, Azyumardi

1992 The Transmission of Islamic Reformism to Indonesia: Networks of Middle Eastern and Malay-Indonesian 'Ulamā' in the Seventeenth and Eighteenth Centuries. Ph.D. diss., Columbia University.

2004 *The Origins of Islamic Reformism in Southeast Asia: Networks of Malay-Indonesian and Middle Eastern 'Ulamā' in the Seventeenth and Eighteenth Centuries.* New South Wales, Australia: Allen & Unwin; Honolulu: University of Hawaiʿi Press.

Baden-Powell, B. H.

1892 *The Land-Systems of British India.* 3 vols. Oxford: Clarendon Press.

Baḥraq al-Ḥaḍramī, Muḥammad b. ʿUmar

1988 Mawāhib al-quddūs fī manāqib Ibn al-ʿAydarūs. In *al-Majmūʿa al-ʿAydarūsiyya.* Ṭāhir b. Muḥammad al-ʿAydarūs, ed. and pub.

al-Bakrī al-Yāfiʿī, Ṣalāḥ ʿAbd al-Qādir

1936 *Ta'rīkh Ḥaḍramawt al-siyāsī,* 1st ed. Vol. 2. Cairo: Muṣṭafā al-Bābī al-Ḥalabī.

1956 *Ta'rīkh Ḥaḍramawt al-siyāsī,* 2nd ed. Vol. 1. Cairo: Muṣṭafā al-Bābī al-Ḥalabī.

al-Balādhurī, Aḥmad b. Yaḥyā

1932 *Futūḥ al-buldān.* Cairo: al-Maktaba al-Tijāriyya al-Kubrā.

1936 *Ansāb al-ashrāf.* Vol. 5. Shlomo D. F. Goitein, ed. Jerusalem: University Press.

1997 *Ansāb al-ashrāf.* Maḥmūd al-Fardaws al-ʿAẓm, ed. Damascus: Dār al-Yaqẓa al-ʿArabiyya.

Bang, Anne K.

2003 *Sufis and Scholars of the Sea: Family Networks in East Africa, 1860–1925.* London: Routledge; New York: Curzon.

Barbosa, Duarte

1918 (1518) *The Book of Duarte Barbosa.* Vol. 1, Second Series no. 44. Mansel Longworth Dames, trans. London: The Hakluyt Society.

Barnes, Ruth, ed.
2005 *Textiles in the Indian Ocean.* London: Routledge; New York: Curzon.

Batatu, Hanna
1978 *The Old Social Classes and the Revolutionary Movements of Iraq.* Princeton, N.J.: Princeton University Press.

Bauman, Zygmunt
2000 *Liquid Modernity.* Oxford: Polity Press.

Bayly, C. A.
1996 *Empire and Information: Intelligence Gathering and Social Communication in India, 1780–1870.* Cambridge: Cambridge University Press.

Belhaven, Lord
1955 *The Uneven Road.* London: John Murray.

van den Berg, L. W. C.
1887 *Hadthramut and the Arab Colonies in the Indian Archipelago.* Major C. W. H. Sealy, trans. Bombay: Government Central Press.
1989 *Hadramaut dan Koloni Arab di Nusantara.* Rahayu Hidayat, trans. Jakarta: Indonesian Netherlands Cooperation in Islamic Studies.

Bilfaqīh, ʿAbd al-Ilāh b. Ḥasan
1961 *Tadhkirat al-bāḥith al-muḥtāṭ fī sh'ūn wa-ta'rīkh al-Ribāṭ.* ʿAdan: al-Fajjāla al-Jadīda.

Bilfaqīh, ʿAlawī b. Muḥammad b. Aḥmad
1994 *Min aʿqāb al-buḍʿa al-Muḥammadiyya al-ṭāhira min dhuriyyat Muḥammad b. ʿAlī Ṣāhib Mirbāṭ al-mutawaffī fī Ẓufār salṭanat ʿUmān ʿām 556 H.* al-Madīna/Tarīm, Ḥaḍramawt: Dār al-Muhājir.

Ibn Bishr, ʿUthmān b. ʿAbd Allāh
1982 *ʿUnwān al-majd fī tārīkh Najd.* Vol. 1. al-Riyāḍ: Dār al-Malik ʿAbd al-ʿAzīz.

Bloch, R. Howard
1983 *Etymologies and Genealogies: A Literary Anthropology of the French Middle Ages.* Chicago: University of Chicago Press.

Bose, Sugata
Forthcoming *Empire and Culture on the Indian Ocean Rim.* Cambridge, Mass.: Harvard University Press.

Boxberger, Linda
2002 *On the Edge of Empire: Hadhramawt, Emigration, and the Indian Ocean, 1880s–1930s.* Albany: State University of New York Press.

Boyarin, Jonathan, and Daniel Boyarin
2002 *Powers of Diaspora: Two Essays on the Relevance of Jewish Culture.* Minneapolis: University of Minnesota Press.

Braudel, Fernand
1992 *The Perspective of the World: Civilization and Capitalism, 15th–18th Century.* Berkeley: University of California Press.

Brown, C. C., trans.

1970 *Sejarah Melayu, or Malay Annals.* Kuala Lumpur: Oxford.

Brown, Peter

1981 *The Cult of the Saints: Its Rise and Function in Latin Christianity.* Chicago: University of Chicago Press.

Bujra, Abdalla

1967 Political Conflict and Stratification in Hadramaut I. *Middle Eastern Studies* 3 (4): 355–75.

1971 *The Politics of Stratification: A Study of Political Change in a South Arabian Town.* London: Oxford University Press.

Bukayr Bā Ghaythān, ʿAlī Sālim

1973 *al-Jāmiʿ fī taʾrīkh al-Jāmiʿ: Baḥth fī taʾrīkh Jāmiʿ Tarīm.*

Burton, R. F.

1966 (1856) *First Footsteps in East Africa,* new ed. G. Waterfield, ed. London: Routledge.

Cannadine, David

2001 *Ornamentalism: How the British Saw Their Empire.* Oxford: Oxford University Press.

Caplan, Jane

2001 "This or That Particular Person": Protocols of Identification in Nineteenth-Century Europe. In *Documenting Individual Identity: The Development of State Practices in the Modern World.* Jane Caplan and John Torpey, eds. Princeton, N.J.: Princeton University Press.

Carapico, Sheila

1998 *Civil Society in Yemen: The Political Economy of Activism in Modern Arabia.* Cambridge: Cambridge University Press.

Caton, Steven C.

1990 *Peaks of Yemen I Summon: Poetry as Cultural Practice in a North Yemeni Tribe.* Berkeley: University of California Press.

Chaudhuri, K. N.

1985 *Trade and Civilisation in the Indian Ocean: An Economic History from the Rise of Islam to 1750.* Cambridge: Cambridge University Press.

1990 *Asia Before Europe: Economy and Civilisation of the Indian Ocean from the Rise of Islam to 1750.* Cambridge: Cambridge University Press.

Chittick, William C.

1994 *Imaginal Worlds: Ibn al-ʿArabī and the Problem of Religious Diversity.* Albany: State University of New York Press.

Chodkiewicz, Michel

1993 *Seal of the Saints: Prophethood and Sainthood in the Doctrine of Ibn ʿArabī.* Cambridge: Islamic Texts Society.

Clayton, Anthony

1986 *The British Empire as a Superpower, 1919–39.* Houndmills, Eng.: Macmillan.

Clifford, James
1997 Traveling Cultures. In *Routes: Travel and Translation in the Late Twentieth Century.* Cambridge, Mass.: Harvard University Press.

Cohen, Robin
1997 *Global Diasporas: An Introduction.* Seattle: University of Washington Press.

Coleman, Simon, and John Eade, eds.
2004 *Reframing Pilgrimage: Cultures in Motion.* London: Routledge.

Coleman, Simon, and John Elsner, eds.
1995 *Pilgrimage: Sacred Travel and Sacred Space in the World Religions.* Cambridge, Mass.: Harvard University Press.
2003 *Pilgrim Voices: Narrative and Authorship in Christian Pilgrimage.* New York: Berghahn.

Combs-Schilling, M. E.
1989 *Sacred Performances: Islam, Sexuality and Sacrifice.* New York: Columbia University Press.

Conte, Edouard
2001 Filiations Prophétiques. Réflexions sur la Personne de Muḥammad. In *Émirs et présidents: figures de la parenté ed du politique dan le monde arabe.* Pierre Bonte, Édouard Conte, and Paul Dresch, eds. Paris: CNRS Éditions.

Copland, Ian
1978 The Other Guardians: Ideology and Performance in the Indian Political Service. In *People, Princes and Paramount Power.* Robin Jeffrey, ed. Delhi: Oxford University Press.

Corbin, Henry
1997 (1969) *Alone with the Alone: Creative Imagination in the Sūfism of Ibn ʿArabī.* Princeton, N.J.: Princeton University Press.

Cornell, Vincent J.
1996 *The Way of Abū Madyan: Doctrinal and Poetic Works of Abū Madyan Shuʿayb ibn al-Ḥusayn al-Anṣārī (c. 500/1115–16–594/1198).* Cambridge: Islamic Texts Society.
1998 *Realm of the Saint: Power and Authority in Moroccan Sufism.* Austin: University of Texas Press.

Croken, Barbara
1990 Zabid under the Rasulids of Yemen, 626–858 A.H./1229–1454 A.D. Ph.D. diss., Harvard University.

Daḥlān, Aḥmad Zaynī
1887 *Khulāṣat al-kalām fī bayān umarāʾ al-balad al-Ḥarām.* Cairo: al-Maṭbaʿa al-Khayriyya.
1950 *al-Durar al-saniyya fī-l-radd ʿalā al-Wahhābiyya.* Cairo: al-Bābī.

Dallal, Ahmad
1993 The Origins and Objectives of Islamic Revivalist Thought, 1750–1850. *Journal of the American Oriental Society* 113 (3): 341–59.

Das Gupta, Ashin

1967 *Malabar in Asian Trade, 1740–1800*. Cambridge: Cambridge University Press.

1979 *Indian Merchants and the Decline of Surat: c. 1700–1750*. Wiesbaden: Steiner.

1982 Indian Merchants and the Trade in the Indian Ocean. In *The Cambridge Economic History of India*. Vol. 1, *c. 1200–c. 1750*. Tapan Raychaudhuri and Irfan Habib, eds. Cambridge: Cambridge University Press.

Dā'ūd, Muḥammad Sa'īd

1989 Ḥarakat Ibn 'Abdāt fī-l-Ghurfa bi-Ḥaḍramawt 1924–1945. In *Wathā'iq al-nadwa al-'ilmiyya al-tārīkhiyya ḥawl al-muqāwama al-sha'biyya fī Ḥaḍramawt 1900–1963*. Muḥammad Sa'īd Dā'ūd and Ṣāliḥ 'Alī Bā Ṣurra, eds. 'Adan: Maṭba'at Jāmi'at 'Adan.

Dā'ūd, Muḥammad Sa'īd, and Ṣāliḥ 'Alī Bā Ṣurra

1989 *Wathā'iq al-nadwa al-'ilmiyya al-tārīkhiyya ḥawl al-muqāwama al-sha'biyya fī Ḥaḍramawt 1900–1963*. 'Adan: Maṭba'at Jāmi'at 'Adan.

Davies, Douglas

1989 On Mormon History, Identity and Faith Community. In *History and Ethnicity*. E. Tonkin, M. McDonald, and M. Chapman, eds. London: Routledge.

2000 *The Mormon Culture of Salvation*. Aldershot: Ashgate.

Davis, K.

1974 The Migrations of Human Populations. *Scientific American* 231 (3): 92–105.

Ibn al-Dayba', 'Abd al-Raḥmān b. 'Alī

1979 *Bughyat al-mustafīd fī akhbār madīnat Zabīd*. Ṣan'ā': Markaz al-Dirāsāt wa-l-Buḥūth al-Yamanī.

Dodge, Toby

2003 *Inventing Iraq: The Failure of Nation Building and a History Denied*. New York: Columbia University Press.

Donner, Fred

1981 *The Early Islamic Conquests*. Princeton, N.J.: Princeton University Press.

1998 *Narratives of Islamic Origins: The Beginnings of Islamic Historical Writing*. Princeton, N.J.: Darwin Press.

Drakard, Jane

1990 *A Malay Frontier: Unity and Duality in a Sumatran Kingdom*. Ithaca, N.Y.: Southeast Asia Program, Cornell University.

Dresch, Paul

1989 *Tribes, Government, and History in Yemen*. Oxford: Clarendon Press; New York: Oxford University Press.

1990 Imams and Tribes: The Writing and Acting of History in Upper Yemen. In *Tribes and State Formation in the Middle East*. Philip S. Khoury and Joseph Kostiner, eds. Berkeley: University of California Press.

2000 *A History of Modern Yemen*. Cambridge: Cambridge University Press.

Dresch, Paul, and Bernard Haykel

1995 Stereotypes and Political Styles: Islamists and Tribesfolk in Yemen. *International Journal of Middle East Studies* 27 (4): 405–31.

Duri, A. A.
1983 *The Rise of Historical Writing Among the Arabs.* Lawrence I. Conrad, ed. and trans. Princeton, N.J.: Princeton University Press.

Eade, John, and Michael J. Sallnow
1991 *Contesting the Sacred: The Anthropology of Christian Pilgrimage.* London: Routledge.

Eaton, Richard Maxwell
1978 *The Sufis of Bijapur 1300–1700: Social Roles of Sufism in Medieval India.* Princeton, N.J.: Princeton University Press.
1990 *Islamic History as Global History.* Washington, D.C.: American Historical Association.

Eickelman, Dale F., and James Piscatori
1990 *Muslim Travellers: Pilgrimage, Migration, and the Religious Imagination.* Berkeley: University of California Press.
1996 *Muslim Politics.* Princeton, N.J.: Princeton University Press.

van Ess, Josef
1999 Sufism and Its Opponents: Reflections on Topoi, Tribulations, and Transformations. In *Islamic Mysticism Contested: Thirteen Centuries of Controversies and Polemics.* Frederick de Jong and Bernd Radtke, eds. Leiden: Brill.

Evans-Pritchard, E. E.
1949 *The Sanusi of Cyrenaica.* Oxford: Clarendon Press.

Ezrahi, Sidra DeKoven
2000 *Booking Passage: Exile and Homecoming in the Modern Jewish Imagination.* Berkeley: University of California Press.

Bā Faqīh, Muḥammad b. ʿUmar
1999 *Tārīkh al-Shiḥr wa-akhbār al-qarn al-ʿāshir.* ʿAbd Allāh Muḥammad al-Ḥibshī, ed. Ṣanʿāʾ: Maktabat al-Irshād.

Fisher, Michael
1991 *Indirect Rule in India: Residents and the Residency System, 1764–1858.* Delhi: Oxford University Press.

Foucault, Michel
1990 *The History of Sexuality.* London: Penguin.

Franey, Laura E.
2003 *Victorian Travel Writing and Imperial Violence: British Writing on Africa, 1855–1902.* Basingstoke, Eng.: Palgrave Macmillan.

Frank, Andre Gunder
1998 *ReOrient: Global Economy in the Asian Age.* Berkeley: University of California Press.

Freitag, Ulrike
2003 *Indian Ocean Migrants and State Formation in Hadhramaut: Reforming the Homeland.* Leiden: Brill.

Freitag, Ulrike, and William Clarence-Smith, eds.
1997 *Hadrami Traders, Scholars, and Statesmen in the Indian Ocean, 1750s–1960s.* Leiden: Brill.

Gavin, R. J.
1975 *Aden under British Rule.* London: C. Hurst.

Geertz, Clifford
1973 The Integrative Revolution: Primordial Sentiments and Civil Politics in the New States. In *The Interpretation of Cultures.* New York: Basic Books.

Geertz, Hildred
1979 The Meaning of Family Ties. In *Meaning and Order in Moroccan Society.* Clifford Geertz, Hildred Geertz, and Lawrence Rosen, eds. New York: Cambridge University Press.

Gellner, Ernest
1969 *Saints of the Atlas.* Chicago: University of Chicago Press.

al-Ghālibī, Salwā Saʿd Sulaymān
1991 *al-Imām al-mutawakkil ilā Allāh Ismāʿīl ibn al-Qāsim wa-dawruh fī tawḥīd al-Yaman, 1054–1087 H./1644–1676 M.*

al-Ghazzī al-Dimashqī, Najm al-Dīn Muḥammad b. Muḥammad
1981–82 *Luṭf al-samar wa-qaṭf al-thamar: min tarājim aʿyān al-ṭabaqa al-ūlā min al-qarn al-ḥādī ʿashar.* Damascus: Wizārat al-Thaqāfa wa-l-Irshād al-Qawmī.

Ghosh, Amitav
1992 *In an Antique Land.* London: Granta.
2001 *The Glass Palace: A Novel.* New York: Random House.

Gilsenan, Michael
n.d. A Trust in the Family, an Interest in Kinship: English Law, Mahommedan Intentions and Arab Genealogies in Colonial Singapore. Paper presented at the Transnational Middle East Anthropology Workshop, Harvard University, 2004.

Glassman, Jonathan
2000 Sorting Out the Tribes: The Creation of Racial Identities in Colonial Zanzibar's Newspaper Wars. *Journal of African History* 41: 395–428.

Gochenour, David Thomas
1984 The Penetration of Zaydi Islam into Early Medieval Yemen. Ph.D. diss., Harvard University.

Goitein, S. D.
1966 *Studies in Islamic History and Institutions.* Leiden: Brill.
1978 *A Mediterranean Society: The Jewish Communities of the Arab World as Portrayed in the Documents of the Cairo Geniza.* Vol. 2, *The Family.* Berkeley: University of California Press.

Graham, William
1987 *Beyond the Written Word: Oral Aspects of Scripture in the History of Religion.* Cambridge: Cambridge University Press.

Green, Charles

1997 *Globalization and Survival in the Black Diaspora.* Albany: State University of New York Press.

Gruen, Erich S.

2002 *Diaspora: Jews amidst Greeks and Romans.* Cambridge, Mass.: Harvard University Press.

Habib, Irfan

1963 *The Agrarian System of Mughal India.* Bombay: Asia Publishing House.

al-Ḥaddad, ʿAbd Allāh b. ʿAlawī

1876 *Tarjamat ghawth al-ʿibād wa-ghayth al-bilād, wa-fawāʾid tataʿallaq bi-dīwānih, wa-yalīhi dīwān al-Ḥaddād al-madhkūr.* Cairo: al-Maṭbaʿa al-Wahbiyya.

1891 *Risālat al-muʿāwana wa-l-muẓāhara wa-l-muʾāzara li-l-rāghibīn min al-muʾminīn fī sulūk ṭarīq al-ākhira.* Cairo: al-Maṭbaʿa al-ʿĀmira.

1895 *al-Durar al-bahiyya fī-l-akhlāq al-marḍiyya.* Būlāq, Miṣr: al-Maṭbaʿa al-Mīriyya.

1927 *al-Durr al-manẓūm li-dhawī al-ʿuqūl wa-l-fuhūm.* Cairo: Musṭafā al-Bābī al-Ḥalabī.

1981 *Penuntun Hidup Bahagia.* Singapore: Pustaka Nasional.

1991 *The Lives of Man.* London: Quilliam Press.

1992 *Gifts for the Seeker.* London: Quilliam Press.

1995 (1985) *Naṣīḥat Agāma dān Waṣiyyat Īmān.* Singapore: Pustaka Nasional.

2002 *Les vies de l'homme.* Beirut: Albouraq.

2004 *Le livre du rappel mutuel.* Beirut: Albouraq.

al-Ḥaddād, Aḥmad b. Ḥasan b. ʿAbd Allāh b. ʿAlawī

n.d. al-Fawāʾid al-saniyya fī dhikr nubdha min faḍl nisbat man yantasib ilā al-silsila al-nabawiyya wa-aʿnī bi-him al-sāda al-ʿAlawiyya khuṣūṣan minhum al-qāṭinīn bi-l-jiha al-Ḥaḍramiyya wa-dhikr shayʾ min manāqibihim al-ʿulyā wa-dhikr jihatihim wa-mā ikhtaṣṣat bi-hi min al-faḍāʾil wa-l-khuṣūṣiyyāt al-marḍiyya khuṣūṣan minhā baladuhum al-maḥrūsa Tarīm. Manuscript.

al-Ḥaddād, ʿAlawī b. Ṭāhir

n.d.-a *Janā al-shamārīkh, jawāb asʾila fī-l-taʾrīkh.*

n.d.-b *al-Qawl al-faṣl fīmā li-banī Hāshim wa-Quraysh wa-l-ʿArab min al-faḍl.*

n.d.-c *ʿUqūd al-almās bi-manāqib al-imām al-ʿārif billāh al-Ḥabīb Aḥmad b. Ḥasan al-ʿAṭṭās.* Vols. 1 and 2. Cairo: Maṭbaʿat al-Madanī. Printed at the expense of Muʾassasat al-Muḥḍār al-Taḍāmuniyya.

1940 *al-Shāmil fī taʾrīkh Ḥaḍramawt wa-makhālifihā.* Singapore.

1971 *al-Madkhal ilā taʾrīkh al-Islām bi-l-sharq al-aqṣā.* Cairo: Dār al-Fikr al-Ḥadīth.

Haikal, Husain

1987 Indonesia-Arab dalam Pergerakan Kemerdekaan Indonesia (1900–1942). Ph.D. diss., Universitas Indonesia.

Ibn Ḥajar al-ʿAsqalānī, Aḥmad b. ʿAlī

1972–76 *Durar al-kāmina fī aʿyān al-miʾa al-thāmina.* 6 vols. Hyderabad, India: Maṭbaʿat Majlis Dāʾirat al-Maʿārif al-ʿUthmāniyya.

al-Ḥāmid, Ṣāliḥ
1968 *Tārīkh Ḥaḍramawt.* Jeddah: Maktabat al-Irshād.

Hannerz, Ulf
1996 *Transnational Connections: Culture, People, Places.* London: Routledge; New York: Comedia.

Harper, T. N.
1997 Globalism and the Pursuit of Authenticity: The Making of a Diasporic Public Sphere in Singapore. *Sojourn* 12 (2): 261–92.

Hartley, J. G.
1961 The Political Organization of an Arab Tribe of the Hadramaut. Ph.D. diss., University of London.

Harvey, David
1989 *The Condition of Postmodernity: An Enquiry into the Origins of Cultural Change.* Oxford: Blackwell.

bin Hāshim, Muḥammad
1931 *Riḥla ilā al-thagharayn al-Shiḥr wa-l-Mukallā.* Cairo: Maṭbaʿat al-Ḥijāzī. Printed at the expense of the al-Kāf sāda of Tarīm.
1948 *Ta'rīkh al-dawla al-Kathīriyya.* Vol. 1. Printed at the private expense of the sultanate.

Hattox, Ralph S.
1985 *Coffee and Coffeehouses: The Origins of a Social Beverage in the Medieval Near East.* Seattle: University of Washington Press.

Haykel, Bernard
2002 The Salafis in Yemen at a Crossroads: An Obituary of Shaykh Muqbil al-Wādiʿī of Dammāj (d. 1422/2001). *Jemen Report* 33 (1): 28–31.
2003 *Revival and Reform in Islam: The Legacy of Muhammad al-Shawkani.* Cambridge: Cambridge University Press.

Hegel, Georg Wilhelm Friedrich, and Johannes Hoffmeister
1975 *Lectures on the Philosophy of World History: Introduction, Reason in History.* Cambridge: Cambridge University Press.

Helms, Mary W.
1988 *Ulysses' Sail: An Ethnographic Odyssey of Power, Knowledge, and Geographical Distance.* Princeton, N.J.: Princeton University Press.

Hempel, Carl G., and Paul Oppenheim
1965 (1948) Studies in the Logic of Explanation. In *Aspects of Scientific Explanation and Other Essays in the Philosophy of Science.* New York: Free Press.

Herzfeld, Michael
1982 When Exceptions Define the Rules: Greek Baptismal Names and the Negotiation of Identity. *Journal of Anthropological Research* 38: 288–302.
1985 *The Poetics of Manhood: Contest and Identity in a Cretan Mountain Village.* Princeton, N.J.: Princeton University Press.
1997 *Cultural Intimacy: Social Poetics in the Nation-State.* New York: Routledge.

al-Ḥibshī, ʿAbd Allāh Muḥammad

1976 *al-Ṣūfiyya wa-l-fuqahāʾ fī-l-Yaman*. Ṣanʿāʾ: al-Jīl al-Jadīd.

Ibn Hishām, ʿAbd al-Malik

1955 *The Life of Muhammad*. A. Guillaume, trans. London: Oxford University Press.

al-Ḥiyed, ʿAbd Allāh Ḥāmid

1973 Relations between the Yaman and South Arabia during the Zaydi Imamate of Āl al-Qāsim, 1626–1732. D. Phil. diss., University of Edinburgh.

Ho, Engseng

1990 Transformation, Formation and Reformation of Malay Polity and Identity. M.A. thesis, University of Chicago.

1992 Manuscripts in the Collection of the Aḥqāf Manuscripts Library in Tarīm, Ḥaḍramawt, Republic of Yemen. In *al-ʿUṣūr al-Wusṭā, The Bulletin of Middle East Medievalists* 4(1).

1994 La chasse à l'ibex. In *Saba* 3–4, France.

1997 Hadhramis Abroad in Hadhramaut: The Muwalladin. In *Hadrami Traders, Scholars, and Statesmen in the Indian Ocean, 1750s–1960s*. U. Freitag and W. G. Clarence-Smith, eds. Leiden: Brill.

1998 Hunting the Ibex in Hadramawt. *Al-Mahjar* 3 (2): 8–10.

1999 Yemenis on Mars: The End of Diaspora? *Middle East Report*, Summer 1999.

2001 Le don précieux de la généalogie. In *Émirs et présidents. Figures de la parenté et du politique en islam dans le monde arabe*. P. Bonte, É. Conte, and P. Dresch, eds. Paris: CNRS editions 2001.

2002a Before Parochialization: Diasporic Arabs Cast in Creole Waters. In *Transcending Borders: Arabs, Politics, Trade and Islam in Southeast Asia*. Huub de Jonge and Nico Kaptein, eds. Leiden: KITLV Press.

2002b Names Beyond Nations: The Making of Local Cosmopolitans. In *Études Rurales* 163–64, July–December: 215–32.

2004 Empire through Diasporic Eyes: A View from the Other Boat. *Comparative Studies in Society and History* 46 (2): 210–46.

Hodgson, Marshall G. S.

1974 *The Venture of Islam: Conscience and History in a World Civilization*. Vol. 2, *The Expansion of Islam in the Middle Periods*. Chicago: University of Chicago Press.

Hoffman, Valerie J.

1999 Annihilation in the Messenger of God: The Development of Sufi Practice. *International Journal of Middle East Studies* 31 (3): 351–69.

Hogarth, D. G.

1904 *The Penetration of Arabia; A Record of the Development of Western Knowledge Concerning the Arabian Peninsula*. New York: F. A. Stokes.

Hourani, George Fadlo

1951 *Arab Seafaring in the Indian Ocean in Ancient and Early Medieval Times*. Princeton, N.J.: Princeton University Press.

Hume, David

1976 (1757) *The Natural History of Religion*. Oxford: Clarendon Press.

Humphrey, Michael

2000 Globalization and Arab Diasporic Identities. *Bulletin of the Royal Institute for Inter Faith Studies* 2 (1): 141–58.

Hurgronje, C. Snouck

1906 *The Achehnese*. Leyden: Brill.

Al-Husaini, Al-Hamid

1999 *Al-Imam Habib Abdullah bin Alwi Al-Haddad: Riwayat, Pemikiran, Nasihat, dan Tarekatnya*. Bandung, Indonesia: Pustaka Hidayah.

Ibrahim, Safie

1985 Islamic Religious Thought in Malaya, 1930–1940. Ph.D. diss., Columbia University.

Ingrams, Doreen

1949 *A Survey of the Social and Economic Conditions in the Aden Protectorate*. Asmara: The Government Printer, British Administration.

1970 *A Time in Arabia*. London: John Murray.

Ingrams, W. Harold

1936 *A Report on the Social, Economic, and Political Conditions of the Hadhramaut*. Colonial No. 123. London: H.M.S.O.

1940 *Report on a Tour to Malaya, Java and Hyderabad*. Mukalla: Residency.

1942a *Arabia and the Isles*. London: John Murray.

1942b *The Yemen, Imams, Rulers and Revolutions*. London: John Murray.

1966a *Arabia and the Isles*, 3rd ed. London: John Murray.

1966b Author's Introduction to Third Edition, 1966. In *Arabia and the Isles*. New York: Praeger.

Innis, Harold Adams

1950 *Empire and Communications*. Oxford: Clarendon Press.

Isaacs, Harold Robert

1975 *Idols of the Tribe: Group Identity and Political Change*. New York: Harper and Row.

Jain, Ravindra

1998 Indian Diaspora, Globalization and Multiculturalism. *Contributions to Indian Sociology* 32 (2): 337–60.

Jameson, Fredric

1981 *The Political Unconscious: Narrative as a Socially Symbolic Act*. Ithaca, New York: Cornell University Press.

Jamʿiyyat al-Ḥaqq

n.d. Daftar Jamʿiyyat al-Ḥaqq. Manuscript.

Jarman, Robert L., ed.

2002 *Political Diaries of the Arab World: Aden 1899–1967*. Vol. 4, *1928–1934*. London: Archive Editions.

Jāzim, Muḥammad ʿAbd al-Raḥīm, ed.
2003 *Nūr al-maʿārif fī nuẓum wa-qawānīn wa-aʿrāf al-Yaman fī-l-ʿahd al-Muẓaffarī al-wārif.* Ṣanʿāʾ: al-Maʿhad al-Faransī li-l-Āthār wa-l-ʿUlūm al-Ijtimāʿiyya bi-Ṣanʿāʾ.

Jeffrey, Robin, ed.
1978 *People, Princes and Paramount Power.* Delhi: Oxford University Press.

Johnson, Chalmers A.
2000 *Blowback: The Costs and Consequences of American Empire.* New York: Metropolitan Books.

Johnston, Sir Charles Hepburn
1963 *Aden: Valedictory Reflections of Sir Charles Hepburn Johnston, K.C.M.G.* London: Colonial Office.
1964 *The View from Steamer Point.* London: Collins.

de Jong, Frederick
1999 Opposition to Sufism in Twentieth-Century Egypt (1900–1920): A Preliminary Survey. In *Islamic Mysticism Contested: Thirteen Centuries of Controversies and Polemics.* Frederick de Jong and Bernd Radtke, eds. Leiden: Brill.

de Jong, Frederick, and Bernd Radtke, eds.
1999 *Islamic Mysticism Contested: Thirteen Centuries of Controversies and Polemics.* Leiden: Brill.

de Jonge, Huub
1997 Dutch Colonial Policy Pertaining to Hadhrami Immigrants. In *Hadrami Traders, Scholars, and Statesmen in the Indian Ocean, 1750s–1960s.* U. Freitag and W. G. Clarence-Smith, eds. Leiden: Brill.

al-Jufrī, Shaykh b. Muḥammad
n.d. Kanz al-Barāhīn.

al-Junayd, ʿAbd al-Qādir b. ʿAbd al-Raḥmān b. ʿUmar
1994 *al-ʿUqūd al-ʿasjadiyya fī nashr manāqib baʿḍ afrād al-usra al-Junaydiyya.* Singapore: ʿAbd al-Raḥmān and Junayd b. Hārūn b. Ḥasan al-Junayd. Published at the expense of ʿAbd al-Raḥmān and Junayd b. Hārūn b. Ḥasan al-Junayd and distributed *gratis.*

al-Junayd, Aḥmad b. ʿAlī
n.d. Marham al-saqīm fī tartīb ziyārat turbat Tarīm. Manuscript.

Jusdanis, Gregory
1996 Culture, Culture, Everywhere: The Swell of Globalization Theory. *Diaspora* 5 (1): 141–61.

Kearney, M.
1995 The Local and the Global: The Anthropology of Globalization and Transnationalism. *Annual Review of Anthropology* 24 : 547–65.

Keene, Edward
2002 *Beyond the Anarchical Society: Grotius, Colonialism and Order in World Politics.* Cambridge: Cambridge University Press.

Kelly, John

1991 *A Politics of Virtue*. Chicago: University of Chicago Press.

Kenna, Margaret

1976 Houses, Fields and Graves: Property and Ritual Obligation on a Greek Island. *Ethnology* 15: 21–34.

Khalidi, Omar

1997 The Hadhrami Role in the Politics and Society of Colonial India, 1750s–1950s. *In Hadrami Traders, Scholars, and Statesmen in the Indian Ocean, 1750s–1960s*. U. Freitag and W. G. Clarence-Smith, eds. Leiden: Brill.

2004 Sayyids of Hadhramaut in Early Modern India. *Asian Journal of Social Science* 23 (3): 329–52.

al-Khanbashī, Sālim Aḥmad

1989 al-Intifāḍāt al-qabaliyya fī muḥāfaẓat Ḥaḍramawt 1951–1961. In *Wathā'iq al-nadwa al-ʿilmiyya al-tārīkhiyya ḥawl al-muqāwama al-shaʿbiyya fī Ḥaḍramawt 1900–1963*. Muḥammad Saʿīd Dā'ūd and Ṣāliḥ ʿAlī Bā Ṣurra, eds. ʿAdan: Jāmiʿat ʿAdan.

Kharid, Muḥammad b. ʿAlī b. ʿAlawī

1985 *al-Ghurar*. Cairo: Maṭābiʿ al-Maktab al-Miṣrī.

al-Khaṭīb, ʿAbd al-Raḥmān b. Muḥammad b. ʿAbd al-Raḥmān b. ʿAlī

n.d. al-Jawhar al-shaffāf fī karāmāt man fī Tarīm min al-sādāt wa-l-ashrāf. Manuscript.

al-Khazrajī, ʿAlī b. Muḥsin

1914a *al-ʿUqūd al-lu'lu'iyya fī tārīkh al-dawla al-Rasūliyya*. Vol. 5, second half of Arabic text, Gibb Memorial Series, Muḥammad ʿAsal, trans. Leyden: Brill; London: Luzac.

1914b *al-ʿUqūd al-lu'lu'iyya fī tārīkh al-dawla al-Rasūliyya*. Vol. 4, first half of Arabic text, Gibb Memorial Series, Muḥammad ʿAsal, trans. Leyden: Brill; London: Luzac.

al-Khuḍar, Sālim ʿUmar

1989 al-Ṭābiʿ al-iqtiṣādī al-ʿafwī wa-l-intifāḍāt al-qabaliyya fī muḥāfaẓat Ḥaḍramawt 1948m.–1961m. In *Wathā'iq al-nadwa al-ʿilmiyya al-tārīkhiyya ḥawl al-muqāwamāt al-shaʿbiyya fī Ḥaḍramawt 1900–1963*. Ṣāliḥ ʿAlī Bā Ṣurra and Muḥammad Saʿīd Dā'ūd, eds. ʿAdan: Maṭbaʿat Jāmiʿat ʿAdan.

Bā Kathīr al-Kindī, ʿAbd Allāh b. Muḥammad b. Sālim

1985 *Riḥlat al-ʿashwāq al-qawiyya ilā mawāṭin al-sāda al-ʿAlawiyya*. N.p.: Maṭbaʿat Dār Iḥyā' al-Kutub al-ʿArabiyya. Published at the expense of Muḥammad b. ʿAbd al-Raḥmān Bā Shaykh.

al-Kindī, Sālim b. Muḥammad b. Sālim

1991 *Ta'rīkh Ḥaḍramawt al-musammā bi-l-ʿudda al-mufīda*. Vol. 1. ʿAbd Allāh al-Ḥibshī, ed. Ṣanʿā': Maktabat al-Irshād.

King, Anthony D.

1984 *The Bungalow: The Production of a Global Culture*. London: Routledge.

Knysh, Alexander

1997 The Cult of Saints and Religious Reformism in Hadhramaut. In *Hadrami Traders, Scholars, and Statesmen in the Indian Ocean, 1750s–1960s*. U. Freitag and W. G. Clarence-Smith, eds. Leiden: Brill.

1999a The Sāda in History: A Critical Essay on Ḥaḍramī Historiography. *Journal of the Royal Asiatic Society* 9 (2): 215–22.

1999b *Ibn ʿArabi in the Later Islamic Tradition: The Making of a Polemical Image in Medieval Islam*. Albany: State University of New York Press.

2001 The *Tariqa* on a Landcruiser: The Resurgence of Sufism in Yemen. *Middle East Journal* 3 (Summer): 309–414.

Kwee, Tek Hoay

1969 *The Origins of the Modern Chinese Movement in Indonesia*. Lea E. Williams, trans. Ithaca, N.Y.: Southeast Asia Program, Cornell University.

Laffan, Michael

2003 *Islamic Nationhood and Colonial Indonesia: The Umma below the Winds*. London: Routledge; New York: Curzon.

Lambourn, Elizabeth

2003 From Cambay to Samudera-Pasai and Gresik: The Export of Gujarati Grave Memorials to Sumatra and Java in the Fifteenth Century C.E. In *Indonesia and the Malay World* 31 (90): 221–84.

Lane, Frederic C.

1968 Pepper Prices before da Gama. *Journal of Economic History* XXVIII: 590–97.

Lekon, Christian

1997 Impact of Remittances on the Economy of Hadhramaut. In *Hadrami Traders, Scholars, and Statesmen in the Indian Ocean, 1750s–1960s*. U. Freitag and W. G. Clarence-Smith, eds. Leiden: Brill.

Lerner, Daniel

1964 *The Passing of Traditional Society: Modernizing the Middle East*. New York: Free Press.

Lévi-Strauss, Claude

1969 *The Elementary Structures of Kinship*. Boston: Beacon Press.

Lewis, Archibald

1973 Maritime Skills in the Indian Ocean, 1368–1500. *Journal of the Economic and Social History of the Orient* 16 (2–3): 238–64.

Lewis, I. M.

1955 Sufism in Somaliland: A Study in Tribal Islam. Part One. *Bulletin of the School of Oriental and African Studies* 17 : 581–602.

1958 *The Somali Lineage System and the Total Genealogy*. London: Crown Agents.

Liaw, Yock Fang

1976 *Undang-Undang Melaka*. The Hague: Nijhoff.

Lopez, Robert, Harry Miskimin, and Abraham Udovitch

1970 England to Egypt, 1350–1500: Long-term Trends and Long-distance

Trade. In *Studies in the Economic History of the Middle East.* M. A. Cook, ed. London: Oxford University Press.

Low, D. A.

1978 *Laissez-Faire* and Traditional Rulership in Princely India. In *People, Princes and Paramount Power.* Robin Jeffrey, ed. Delhi: Oxford University Press.

Lujnatoen Nashir Watta'lief, Arrabitatoel 'Alaiyah

1931 *Haqa'iq, or A True Explanation Distributed to the Public for a Record in History.* Batavia: Lujnatoen Nashir Watta'lief, Arrabitatoel 'Alaiyah.

al-Maʿbarī, Zayn al-Dīn b. ʿAbd al-ʿAzīz

1987 *Tuḥfat al-mujāhidīn fī baʿḍ akhbār al-Burtughāliyyīn.* Amīn Tawfīq al-Ṭayyibī, ed. Ṭarābulus: Lībiyā: Kuliyyat al-Daʿwa al-Islāmiyya.

Madelung, Wilferd

1997 *The Succession to Muḥammad: A Study of the Early Caliphate.* Cambridge: Cambridge University Press.

Maine, Henry Sumner

1888 *International Law: A Series of Lectures Delivered before the University of Cambridge, 1887.* The Whewell Lectures. London: John Murray.

Bā Makhrama, al-Ṭayyib ʿAbd Allāh b. ʿAbd Allāh b. Aḥmad

1980 *Qilādat al-naḥr fī wafayāt aʿyān al-dahr.* al-Iskandariyya: al-Hayʾa al-ʿĀmma al-Miṣriyya li-l-Kitāb.

1987 *Tārīkh thaghr ʿAdan wa-tarājim ʿulamāʾāhā.* Beirut: Dār al-Jīl.

Maktari, A. M. A.

1971 *Water Rights and Irrigation Practices in Laḥj.* Cambridge: Cambridge University Press.

Malkki, Liisa

1995 *Purity and Exile: Violence, Memory, and National Cosmology among Hutu Refugees in Tanzania.* Chicago: University of Chicago Press.

Mamdani, Mahmood

1996 *Citizen and Subject: Contemporary Africa and the Legacy of Late Colonialism.* Princeton, N.J.: Princeton University Press.

Mandal, Sumit

1994 Finding Their Place: A History of Arabs in Java under Dutch Rule, 1800–1924. Ph.D. diss., Columbia University.

1997 Natural Leaders of Native Muslims: Arab Ethnicity and Politics in Java under Dutch Rule. In *Hadrami Traders, Scholars, and Statesmen in the Indian Ocean, 1750s–1960s.* U. Freitag and W. G. Clarence-Smith, eds. Leiden: Brill.

Manor, James

1978 The Demise of the Princely Order: A Reassessment. In *People, Princes and Paramount Power.* Robin Jeffrey, ed. Delhi: Oxford University Press.

Martin, Bradford G.

1971 Migrations from the Hadramawt to East Africa and Indonesia, c. 1200 to 1900. *Research Bulletin* 7 (December): 1–21.

Marx, Karl

1967 (1867) *Capital: A Critique of Political Economy*. Vol. 1, *The Process of Capitalist Production*. New York: International Publishers.

1978 *The Marx-Engels Reader.* Robert Tucker, ed. New York: Norton.

al-Mashhūr, ʿAbd al-Raḥmān b. Muḥammad b. Ḥusayn

n.d. Minḥat al-ʿazīz al-karīm fī ziyārat awliyāʾ Tarīm. Manuscript.

1911 *Shams al-ẓahīra al-ḍāḥiya al-munīra fī nasab wa-silsilat ahl al-bayt al-nabawī wa-l-sirr al-Muṣṭafawī min banī ʿAlawī furūʿ Fāṭima al-Zahrāʾ wa-Amīr al-Muʾminīn ʿAlī raḍiya Allāh ʿanhu*. Ḥaydar Ābād: al-Maṭbaʿa al-Fayḍiyya. Printed at the expense of al-Sayyid ʿAbd Allāh al-Sayyid Muḥammad al-Hāshimī and distributed *gratis*.

1984 *Shams al-ẓahīra fī nasab ahl al-bayt min Banī ʿAlawī furūʿ Fāṭima al-Zahrāʾ wa-Amīr al-Muʾminīn ʿAlī raḍiya Allāh ʿanhu*. 2 vols. Jeddah: ʿĀlam al-Maʿrifa.

Bā Maṭraf, Muḥammad ʿAbd al-Qādir

1984 *al-Jāmiʿ: Jāmiʿ shaml aʿlām al-muhājirīn al-muntasibīn ilā al-Yaman wa-qabāʾilihā*. 4 vols. ʿAdan: Dār al-Hamdānī.

Mauss, Marcel

1967 *The Gift: Forms and Functions of Exchange in Archaic Societies*. New York: Norton.

McLuhan, Marshall

1964 *Understanding Media: The Extensions of Man*. New York: McGraw-Hill.

McNeill, William Hardy

1963 *The Rise of the West: A History of the Human Community*. New York: New American Library; London: New English Library.

Meloy, John

2003 Imperial Strategy and Political Exigency: The Red Sea Spice Trade and the Mamluk Sultanate in the Fifteenth Century. *Journal of the American Oriental Society* 123 (1): 1–20.

Memon, Muhammad Umar

1976 *Ibn Taimiya's Struggle Against Popular Religion*. The Hague: Mouton.

Messick, Brinkley

1987 Subordinate Discourse: Women, Weaving, and Gender Relations in North Africa. *American Ethnologist* 14 (2): 210–25.

1989 Just Writing: Paradox and Political Economy in Yemeni Legal Documents. *Cultural Anthropology* 4 (1): 26–50.

1993 *The Calligraphic State: Textual Domination and History in a Muslim Society*. Berkeley: University of California Press.

Van der Meulen, D.

1932 *Hadramaut: Some of Its Mysteries Unveiled*. Leyden: Brill.

1961 *Faces in Shem*. London: John Murray.

Mill, John Stuart

1867 Of the Government of Dependencies by a Free State. In *Consideration on Representative Government*. New York: Harper and Brothers.

Milner, A. C.

1992 'Malayness': Confrontation, Innovation and Discourse. In *Looking in Odd Mirrors: The Java Sea.* V. J. H. Houben, H. M. J. Maier, and W. van der Molen, eds. Leiden: Vakgroep Talen en Culturen van Zuidoost-Azie en Oceanie van de Rijksuniversiteit te Leiden.

Misra, S. C.

1982 *The Rise of Muslim Power in Gujarat: A History of Gujarat from 1298 to 1442.* 2nd ed. New Delhi: Munshiram Manoharlal.

Mitchell, Hildi

2003 Postcards from the Edge of History: Narrative and the Sacralisation of Mormon Historical Sites. In *Pilgrim Voices: Narrative and Authorship in Christian Pilgrimage.* Simon Coleman and John Elsner, eds. New York: Berghahn.

Mobini-Kesheh, Natali

1996 The Arab Periodicals of the Netherlands East Indies, 1914–1942. *Bijdragen tot de Taal-, Land-en Volkenkunde* 152 (II): 236–55.

1999 *The Hadrami Awakening: Community and Identity in the Netherlands East Indies 1900–1942.* Ithaca, N.Y.: Southeast Asia Program Publications, Cornell University

Mohammad Redzuan Othman

1997 Hadhramis in the Politics and Administration of the Malay States in the Late Eighteenth and Nineteenth Centuries. In *Hadrami Traders, Scholars, and Statesmen in the Indian Ocean, 1750s–1960s.* U. Freitag and W. G. Clarence-Smith, eds. Leiden: Brill.

Monroe, Elizabeth

1964 *Britain's Moment in the Middle East 1914–1956.* London: Chatto & Windus.

Moreland, W. H.

1998 (1936) Rank *(manṣab)* in the Mogul State Service. In *The Mughal State 1526–1750.* Muzaffar Alam and Sanjay Subrahmahnyam, eds. Delhi: Oxford University Press. Originally published in the *Journal of the Royal Asiatic Society,* 1936, 641–65.

Morris, James

1980 *Farewell the Trumpets: The Decline of an Empire.* New York: Harcourt.

Mortel, Richard

1995 Aspects of Mamluk Relations with Jedda during the Fifteenth Century. *Journal of Islamic Studies* 6 (1): 1–13.

Mottahedeh, Roy P.

1976 The Shuʿūbīyah Controversy and the Social History of Early Islamic Iran. *International Journal of Middle East Studies* 7: 161–82.

1980 *Loyalty and Leadership in an Early Islamic Society.* Princeton, N.J.: Princeton University Press.

al-Muḥḍār, Aḥmad b. Muḥammad

1984 Maqāmat dhamm al-dunyā. In *Maqāmāt min al-adab al-Yamanī.* ʿAbd Allāh Muḥammad al-Ḥibshī, ed. Ṣanʿāʾ: Dār al-Yaman al-Kubrā.

al-Muḥibbī, Muḥammad Amīn b. Faḍl Allāh

1966 *Khulāṣat al-athar fī aʿyān al-qarn al-ḥādī ʿashar.* 4 vols. Beirut: Maktabat Khayyāt.

Mukherjee, Wendy

1995 Representation of the Hadhrami in a Literary Work from West Java. Paper presented at South Arabian Migration Movements in the Indian Ocean: The Hadhrami Case, c. 1750–c. 1967, School of Oriental and African Studies, University of London.

Mulkapuri, ʿAbd al-Jabbar

1912–13 *Tazkira-yi Auliyaʾ-i Dakan.* 2 vols. Hyderabad, India: Hasan Press.

Multatuli

1982 (1876) *Max Havelaar, or, The Coffee Auctions of the Dutch Trading Company.* Amherst: University of Massachusetts Press.

Mundy, Martha

1995 *Domestic Government: Kinship, Community and Polity in North Yemen.* London: I. B. Tauris.

Munn, Nancy D.

1986 *The Fame of Gawa: A Symbolic Study of Value Transformation in a Massim (Papua New Guinea) Society.* Cambridge: Cambridge University Press.

Munson, Henry J.

1984 *The House of Si Abd Allah: The Oral History of a Moroccan Family.* New Haven, Conn.: Yale University Press.

al-Murādī, Muḥammad Khalīl b. ʿAlī

1997 *Silk al-durar fī aʿyān al-qarn al-thānī ʿashar.* 4 vols. Beirut: Dār al-Kutub al-ʿIlmiyya.

al-Muʾtamar al-Iṣlāḥī al-Ḥaḍramī

n.d. al-Muʾtamar al-Iṣlāḥī al-Ḥaḍramī. Singapore. Minutes of the Hadrami Reform Congress in Singapore, 1928. Manuscript.

Myers, Fred R.

1986 *Pintupi Country, Pintupi Self: Sentiment, Place, and Politics among Western Desert Aborigines.* Washington, D.C.: Smithsonian Institution Press; Canberra: Australian Institute of Aboriginal Studies.

Noer, Deliar

1973 *The Modernist Muslim Movement in Indonesia 1900–1942.* Singapore: Oxford University Press.

Nurse, Keith

1999 Globalization and Trinidad Carnival: Diaspora, Hybridity and Identity in Global Culture. *Cultural Studies* 13 (4): 661–90.

O'Fahey, R. S., and Bernd Radtke

1993 Neo-Sufism Reconsidered. *Der Islam* 70 (1): 52–87.

Ong, Aihwa

1993 On the Edge of Empires: Flexible Citizenship among Chinese in Diaspora. *Positions* 1 (3): 745–78.

Ong, Aihwa, and Donald Macon Nonini
1997 *Ungrounded Empires: The Cultural Politics of Modern Chinese Transnationalism*. New York: Routledge.

Ong, Walter J.
1982 *Orality and Literacy: The Technologizing of the Word*. London: Methuen.

Parkin, David, and Stephen C. Headley, eds.
2000 *Islamic Prayer across the Indian Ocean: Inside and Outside the Mosque*. Richmond, Eng.: Curzon.

Patterson, Orlando
1982 *Slavery and Social Death: A Comparative Study*. Cambridge, Mass.: Harvard University Press.

Pearson, M. N.
1976 *Merchants and Rulers in Gujarat: The Response to the Portuguese in the Sixteenth Century*. Berkeley: University of California Press.
1996 *Pilgrimage to Mecca: The Indian Experience, 1600–1800*. Princeton, N.J.: Markus Weiner.

Pease, Theodore Calvin
1915 *The Leveller Movement: A Study in the History and Political Theory of the English Great Civil War*. Washington, D.C.: American Historical Association.

Pelt, Adrian
1970 *Libyan Independence and the United Nations: A Case of Planned Decolonization*. New Haven, Conn.: Yale University Press.

Peskes, Esther
1999 The Wahhābiyya and Sufism. In *Islamic Mysticism Contested: Thirteen Centuries of Controversies and Polemics*. Frederick de Jong and Bernd Radtke, eds. Leiden: Brill.

Phillips, Richard
1997 *Mapping Men and Empire: A Geography of Empire*. London: Routledge.

Philpott, Daniel
2001 *Revolutions in Sovereignty*. Princeton, N.J.: Princeton University Press.

Pires, Tome
1944 *The Suma Oriental of Tome Pires, An Account of the East, From the Red Sea to Japan, Written in Malacca and India in 1512–1515*. London: The Hakluyt Society. Second Series, no. 98–90.

Pomeranz, Kenneth
2000 *The Great Divergence: China, Europe, and the Making of the Modern World Economy*. Princeton, N.J.: Princeton University Press.

Pratt, Mary
1992 *Imperial Eyes: Travel Writing and Transculturation*. London: Routledge.

al-Qadi, Wadad
1988 The Term '*khalīfa*' in Early Exegetical Literature. *Die Welt des Islams* 28: 392–411.

Rae, Heather

2002 *State Identities and the Homogenisation of Peoples*. Cambridge: Cambridge University Press.

Rahman, Fazlur

1979 *Islam*. Chicago: University of Chicago Press.

Raja Ali Haji

1997 *Salasilah Melayu dan Bugis*. Shah Alam, Malaysia: Fajar Bakti.

Raja Ali Haji ibn Ahmad

1982 *The Precious Gift (Tuḥfat al-Nafīs)*. Virginia Matheson and Barbara Watson Andaya, trans. Kuala Lumpur: Oxford University Press.

Raja Haji Ahmad and Raja Ali Haji

1997 *Tuḥfat al-Nafīs*. Virginia Matheson, ed. Shah Alam, Malaysia: Fajar Bakti.

Rawa, Mujahid Haji Yusof

2001 *Permata dari Pulau Mutiara*. Kuala Lumpur: Warathah Haji Yusof Rawa.

Redfield, Robert

1967 The Social Organization of Tradition. In *Peasant Society*. J. Potter, G. Foster, and M. Diaz, eds. Boston: Little, Brown.

Reid, Anthony

1969 *The Contest for North Sumatra: Atjeh, the Netherlands, and Britain, 1858–1898*. Kuala Lumpur: University of Malaya Press.

1993 *Southeast Asia in the Age of Commerce 1450–1680*. Vol. 2, *Expansion and Crisis*. New Haven, Conn.: Yale University Press.

Reynolds, Dwight Fletcher

1995 *Heroic Poets, Poetic Heroes: The Ethnography of Performance in an Arabic Oral Epic Tradition*. Ithaca, N.Y.: Cornell University Press.

Riḍā, Muḥammad Rashīd

1905 Fatāwā al-Manār: Kafā'at al-Zawāj. *al-Manār* 8 (6): 215–17.

Roff, William

1972 *Bibliography of Malay and Arabic Periodicals Published in the Straits Settlements and Peninsular Malay States 1876–1941*. London: Oxford University Press.

1998 Patterns of Islamization in Malaysia, 1890s–1990s: Exemplars, Institutions, and Vectors. *Journal of Islamic Studies* 9 (2): 210–28.

2002 Murder as an Aid to Social History: The Arabs in Singapore in the Early Twentieth Century. In *Transcending Borders: Arabs, Politics, Trade and Islam in Southeast Asia*. Huub de Jonge and Nico Kaptein, eds. Leiden: KITLV Press.

Romero, Patricia

1997 *Lamu: History, Society, and Family in an East African Port City*. Princeton, N.J.: M. Wiener.

Roolvink, Roelof

1970 The Variant Versions of the Malay Annals. In *Sejarah Melayu, or The Malay Annals*. C. C. Brown, trans. Kuala Lumpur: Oxford University Press.

Rosaldo, Renato
1980 *Ilongot Headhunting, 1883–1974: A Study in Society and History*. Stanford, Calif.: Stanford University Press.

Rosenthal, Franz
1952 *A History of Muslim Historiography*. Leiden: Brill.

Rubin, U.
1975 Pre-existence and Light: Aspects of the Concept of Nūr Muḥammad. *Israel Oriental Studies* V: 62–117.

Ruḥayyim Bā Faḍl, ʿAbd Allāh b. Ḥusayn
n.d.-a Riḥla ilā al-Ḥazm wa-Sayʾūn wa-l-Masīla li-l-ḥawl ʿām 1381 H. Manuscript.
n.d.-b Riḥla ilā al-Ḥazm wa-l-Masīla li-l-ḥawl ʿām 1384 H. Manuscript.
n.d.-c Riḥla ilā Tāriba ʿām 1380 H. Manuscript.
n.d.-d Riḥla li-ḥuḍūr mawlid Ḥusayn ʿAydīd. Manuscript.
n.d.-e Riḥlat al-Muḥḍār li-ziyārat Hūd ʿām 1357 H. Manuscript.
n.d.-f Tarjamat Abī Bakr b. Shaykh al-Kāf. Manuscript.

Rush, James
1990 *Opium to Java: Revenue Farming and Chinese Enterprise in Colonial Indonesia, 1860–1910*. Ithaca, N.Y.: Cornell University Press.

Sabbāgh, Layla
1986 *Min aʿlām al-fikr al-ʿArabī fī-l-ʿaṣr al-ʿUthmānī al-awwal: Muḥammad al-Amīn al-Muḥibbī al-muʾarrikh wa-kitābuh Khulāṣat al-athar fī aʿyān al-qarn al-ḥādī ʿashar*. Damascus: al-Sharika al-Mutaḥḥida li-l-Tawzīʿ.

Sahlins, Marshall
1976 *Culture and Practical Reason*. Chicago: University of Chicago Press.
1985 *Islands of History*. Chicago: University of Chicago Press.

al-Sakhāwī, Muḥammad b. ʿAbd al-Raḥmān
1992 *al-Ḍawʾ al-lāmiʿ li-ahl al-qarn al-tāsiʿ*. 12 vols. Beirut: Dār al-Jīl.

al-Sakrān Bā ʿAlawī, "al-Shaykh" ʿAlī b. Abī Bakr
1928 *al-Barqa al-mushīqa fī dhikr libās al-khirqa al-anīqa*. Miṣr: Tubiʿ ʿalā nafaqat ʿAlī b. ʿAbd al-Raḥmān Bā ʿAlawī.

al-Saqqāf, ʿAbd Allāh b. Muḥammad b. Ḥāmid
1984 *Tārīkh al-Shuʿarāʾ al-Ḥaḍramiyyīn*. 5 vols. al-Ṭāʾif: Maktabat al-Maʿārif.

al-Saqqāf, ʿAbd al-Raḥmān b. ʿUbayd Allāh
2002 *Muʿjam buldān Ḥaḍramawt: Idām al-qūt fī dhikr buldān Ḥaḍramūt*. Ṣanʿāʾ: Maktabat al-Irshād.

al-Saqqāf al-ʿAlawī, Aḥmad b. ʿAbd Allāh
1964 *Khidmat al-ʿashīra bi-tartīb wa-talkhīs wa-tadhyīl Shams al-ẓahīra*. Jakarta, Indonesia: al-Maktab al-Dāʾimī li-Iḥṣāʾ wa-Ḍabṭ Ansāb al-Sāda al-ʿAlawiyyīn.

al-Saqqāf, Jaʿfar b. Muḥammad
1993 A Legal Document from Saywūn Relating to Vessels, House and Carriages Owned by a Saqqāf Sayyid in 19th Century Java. *New Arabian Studies* 1: 189–202.

al-Saqqāf, Muḥsin b. ʿAlawī
n.d. Qaṣīdat dhamm Jāwa. Manuscript.

Schiller, Nina Glick, and Georges Eugene Fouron
2001 *Georges Woke up Laughing: Long-distance Nationalism and the Search for Home.* Durham, N.C.: Duke University Press.

Schimmel, Annemarie
1985 *And Muhammad Is His Messenger: The Veneration of the Prophet in Islamic Piety.* Chapel Hill: University of North Carolina Press.

Schivelbusch, Wolfgang
2003 *The Culture of Defeat: On National Trauma, Mourning, and Recovery.* New York: Metropolitan Books.

Schrieke, B.
1960 The Shifts in Political and Economic Power in the Indonesian Archipelago in the Sixteenth and Seventeenth Century. In *Indonesian Sociological Studies,* 1–82. Bandung: Sumur Bandung.

Schulze, R.
1990 Das islamische achtzehnte Jahrhundert. Versuch einer historiographischen Kritik. *Die Welt des Islams* 3: 140–59 .

Scott, Hugh, Kenneth Mason, Mary Marshall, and Great Britain Naval Intelligence Division
1946 *Western Arabia and the Red Sea.* Oxford: Naval Intelligence Division, printed under the authority of His Majesty's Stationery Office at the University Press.

Scott, James C., John Tehranian, and Jeremy Mathias
2002 The Production of Legal Identities Proper to States: The Case of the Permanent Family Surname. *Comparative Studies in Society and History* 44 (1): 4–44.

Serjeant, R. B.
1950a Materials for South Arabian History I. *Bulletin of the School of Oriental and African Studies* XIII (2): 281–307.
1950b Materials for South Arabian History II. *Bulletin of the School of Oriental and African Studies* XIII (3): 581–601.
1957 *The Saiyids of Ḥaḍramawt, An Inaugural Lecture Delivered on 5 June 1956.* London: School of Oriental and African Studies, University of London.
1962 Haram and Hawtah: The Sacred Enclave in Arabia. In *Mélanges Taha Husain.* ʿAbd al-Raḥmān Badawī, ed. Miṣr: Dār al-Maʿarif.
1974 (1963) *The Portuguese off the South Arabian Coast: Hadrami Chronicles.* Beirut: Librairie du Liban.
1981 Historians and Historiography of Hadramawt. In *Studies in Arabian History and Civilisation.* London: Variorum Reprints.

Shain, Yossi
1999 *Marketing the American Creed Abroad: Diasporas in the US and their Homelands.* Cambridge: Cambridge University Press.

Shari'ati, Ali

1980 *On the Sociology of Islam.* Hamid Algar, trans. Berkeley, Calif.: Mizan.

Sharp, Andrew, ed.

1998 *The English Levellers.* Cambridge: Cambridge University Press.

al-Shāṭirī al-ʿAlawī al-Ḥusaynī al-Tarīmī, Aḥmad b.ʿUmar

1949 *al-Yāqūt al-nafīs fī madhhab Ibn Idrīs.* ʿAdan: Maktabat wa-maṭbaʿat Sulaymān Marʿī.

al-Shāṭirī, Muḥammad b. Aḥmad

1973 *Adwār al-taʾrīkh al-Ḥaḍramī.* Vol. 2. al-Mukallā: Maktabat al-Shaʿb.

1983 *Adwār al-taʾrīkh al-Ḥaḍramī.* Vols. 1 and 2. 2nd edition. Jeddah: ʿĀlam al-Maʿrifa.

al-Shawkānī, Muḥammad b. ʿAlī

1947 *Sharḥ al-ṣudūr bi-taḥrīm rafʿ al-qubūr.* Cairo: Maṭbaʿat al-Sunna al-Muḥammadiyya.

al-Shillī, Muḥammad b. Abī Bakr

n.d. al-Sanāʾ al-bāhir bi-takmīl al-Nūr al-sāfir. Manuscript.

1901 *al-Mashraʿ al-rawī fī manāqib al-sāda al-kirām Āl Abī ʿAlawī.* 2 vols. Miṣr: al-Maṭbaʿa al-ʿĀmira al-Sharafiyya.

1982 *al-Mashraʿ al-rawī fī manāqib al-sāda al-kirām Āl Abī ʿAlawī.* 2 vols. With introduction by Muḥammad b. Aḥmad al-Shāṭirī.

2003 *ʿIqd al-jawāhir wa-l-durar fī akhbār al-qarn al-ḥādī ʿashar.* Ṣanʿāʾ: Maktabat Tarīm al-Ḥadītha; Maktabat al-Irshād.

Shryock, Andrew

1997 *Nationalism and the Genealogical Imagination: Oral History and Textual Authority in Tribal Jordan.* Berkeley: University of California Press.

Singer, Milton

1976 Robert Redfield's Development of a Social Anthropology of Civilizations. In *American Anthropology, the Early Years.* John V. Murra, ed. Boston: West Publishing.

Sirriyeh, Elizabeth

1999 *Sufis and Anti-Sufis: The Defense, Rethinking and Rejection of Sufism in the Modern World.* Richmond, Eng.: Curzon.

Skinner, G. William

1996 Creolized Chinese Societies in Southeast Asia. In *Sojourners and Settlers.* Anthony Reid, ed. Australia: Asian Studies Association of Australia/Allen & Unwin.

Smith, Jonathan Z.

1992 *To Take Place.* Chicago: University of Chicago Press.

Smith, Michael

1994 Transnational Migration and the Globalization of Grassroots Movements. *Social Text* 39: 15–34.

Smith, Raymond T.

1988 *Kinship and Class in the West Indies: A Genealogical Study of Jamaica and Guyana.* Cambridge: Cambridge University Press.

Smith, Tony

2000 *Foreign Attachments: The Power of Ethnic Groups in the Making of American Foreign Policy.* Cambridge, Mass.: Harvard University Press.

Stiglitz, Joseph E.

2002 *Globalization and Its Discontents.* New York: Norton.

Stokes, Eric

1959 *The English Utilitarians and India.* Oxford: Clarendon Press.

1978 The Land Revenue Systems of the North-Western Provinces and Bombay Deccan 1830–80: Ideology and the Official Mind. In *The Peasant and the Raj: Studies in Agrarian Society and Peasant Rebellion in Colonial India.* Cambridge: Cambridge University Press.

Stoler, Ann Laura

1989 Rethinking Colonial Categories: European Communities and the Boundaries of Rule. *Comparative Studies in Society and History* 31 (1): 134–61.

Subrahmahnyam, Sanjay, and C. A. Bayly

1990 Portfolio Capitalists and the Political Economy of Early Modern India. In *Merchants, Markets and the State in Early Modern India.* Sanjay Subrahmahnyam, ed. Delhi: Oxford University Press.

Subramanian, Lakshmi

1983 Banias and the British: The Role of Indigenous Credit in the Process of Imperial Expansion in Western India in the Second Half of the Eighteenth Century. *Modern Asian Studies* 21 (3): 473–510.

1996 *Indigenous Capital and Imperial Expansion: Bombay, Surat and the West Coast.* Delhi: Oxford University Press.

Sulaymān, Karāma Mubārak

1994a *al-Tarbiyya wa-l-taʿlīm fī-l-shaṭr al-janūbī. al-Juzʾ al-awwal: 1930–1970 M.* Vol. 1. Ṣanʿāʾ: Markaz al-Dirāsāt wa-l-Buḥūth al-Yamanī.

1994b *al-Tarbiyya wa-l-taʿlīm fī-l-shaṭr al-janūbī. al-Juzʾ al-thānī: 1970–1990 M.* Vol. 2. Ṣanʿāʾ: Markaz al-Dirāsāt wa-l-Buḥūth al-Yamanī.

Suratmin

1984–85 *Abdul Rahman Baswedan: Hasil Karya dan Pengabdiannya.* Jakarta: Departemen Pendidikan dan Kebudayaan, Direktorat Sejarah dan Nilai Tradisional, Proyek Inventarisasi dan Dokumentasi Sejarah Nasional.

Suryadinata, Leo, ed.

2005 *Pemikiran Etnis Tionghua Indonesia 1900–2002.* Jakarta: LP3ES.

Sutton, David

1997 Local Names, Foreign Claims: Family Inheritance and National Heritage on a Greek Island. *American Ethnologist* 24 (2): 415–37.

Svenbro, Jesper

1993 *Phrasikleia: An Anthropology of Reading in Ancient Greece.* Janet Lloyd, trans. Ithaca, N.Y.: Cornell University Press.

al-Ṭabarī, Abū Jaʿfar Muḥammad b. Jarīr

1988 *The History of al-Ṭabarī Volume VI: Muhammad at Mecca*. W. Montgomery Watt and M. V. McDonald, trans. Albany: State University of New York Press.

Tambiah, Stanley J.

1996 *Leveling Crowds: Ethnonationalist Conflicts and Collective Violence in South Asia*. Berkeley: University of California Press.

Taylor, Jean Gelman

1983 *The Social World of Batavia: European and Eurasian in Dutch Asia*. Madison: University of Wisconsin Press.

Ibn Taymiyya, Aḥmad b. ʿAbd al-Ḥalīm b. ʿAbd al-Salām

1998 *Iqtiḍāʾ al-ṣirāṭ al-mustaqīm li-mukhālafat aṣḥāb al-jaḥīm*. Nāṣir b. ʿAbd al-Karīm al-ʿAql, ed. Vol. 2. al-Riyāḍ: Dār al-ʿĀṣima.

Tibbetts, G. R.

1981 *Arab Navigation in the Indian Ocean before the Coming of the Portuguese*. London: Royal Asiatic Society of Great Britain and Ireland.

Tidrick, Kathryn

1989 (1981) *Heart Beguiling Araby: The English Romance with Arabia*. London: I. B. Tauris.

Tilly, Charles

1990 *Coercion, Capital, and European States,* A.D. *990–1992*. Oxford: Basil Blackwell.

de Tocqueville, Alexis

1955 *The Old Regime and the French Revolution*. New York: Doubleday.

Torpey, John

2000 *The Invention of the Passport: Surveillance, Citizenship and the State*. Cambridge: Cambridge University Press

Towle, Philip Anthony

1989 *Pilots and Rebels: The Use of Aircraft in Unconventional Warfare 1918–1988*. London: Brassey's.

Trimingham, J. Spencer

1973 *The Sufi Orders in Islam*. 2nd ed. Oxford: Oxford University Press.

Trocki, Carl

1990 *Opium and Empire: Chinese Society in Colonial Singapore, 1800–1910*. Ithaca, N.Y.: Cornell University Press.

1999 *Opium, Empire, and the Global Political Economy*. London: Routledge.

Tsing, Anna Lowenhaupt

1993 *In the Realm of the Diamond Queen: Marginality in an Out-of-the-Way Place*. Princeton, N.J.: Princeton University Press.

Ulughkhānī, ʿAbd Allāh b. Muḥammad b. ʿUmar al-Makkī al-Āṣafī

1910–28 *Ẓafar al-wālih bi-Muẓaffar wa-ālih*. E. Denison Ross, ed. 3 vols. Arabic text composed circa 1605. London: John Murray (for the Government of India).

Valeri, Valerio

1990 Constitutive History: Genealogy and Narrative in the Legitimation of Hawaiian Kingship. In *Culture Through Time*. Emiko Ohnuki-Tierney, ed. Stanford, Calif.: Stanford University Press.

Varisco, Daniel

1994 *Medieval Agriculture and Islamic Science: The Almanac of a Yemeni Sultan*. Seattle: University of Washington Press.

Voll, John Obert

1982 *Islam, Continuity and Change in the Modern World*. Boulder, Colo.: Westview Press.

Vuldy, C.

1987 *Pekalongan: batik et islam dans une ville du nord de java*. Paris: École des Hautes Études en Sciences Sociales.

Wallerstein, Immanuel

2004 *World-Systems Analysis: An Introduction*. Durham, N.C.: Duke University Press.

Ware, Isaac

1756 *The Complete Body of Architecture*. London: T. Osborne and J. Shipton.

Bā Wazīr, Saʿīd ʿAwaḍ

1954 *Ṣafaḥāt min al-taʾrīkh al-Ḥaḍramī*. ʿAdan: Maktabat al-Thaqāfa.

1961 *al-Fikr wa-l-thaqāfa fī-l-taʾrīkh al-Ḥaḍramī*. Cairo: Dār al-Ṭibāʿa al-Ḥadītha.

Weber, Max

1978 *Economy and Society*. Berkeley: University of California Press.

Werbner, Pnina

1999 Global Pathways: Working Class Cosmopolitans and the Creation of Transnational Ethnic Worlds. *Social Anthropology* 7 (1): 17–35.

Westrate, Bruce

1992 *The Arab Bureau: British Policy in the Middle East, 1916–1920*. University Park, Pa.: Penn State University Press.

Wink, André

1997 *Al-Hind: The Making of the Indo-Islamic World*. Vol. 2., *The Slave Kings and the Islamic Conquest, 11th–13th Centuries*. Leiden: Brill.

Wolf, Eric R.

1982 *Europe and the People Without History*. Berkeley: University of California Press.

Wolters, O. W.

1970 *The Fall of Srivijaya in Malay History*. Ithaca, N.Y.: Cornell University Press.

Wong, Lloyd

1997 Globalization and Transnational Migration. *International Sociology* 12 (3): 329–51.

Yeang, Ken

1992 *The Architecture of Malaysia*. Amsterdam: Pepin Press.

Yegar, Mosher
1979 *Islamic Institutions in British Malaya*. Jerusalem: The Magnes Press, Hebrew University.

Yule, Henry, and A. C. Burnell
1994 (1903) *Hobson-Jobson: A Glossary of Colloquial Anglo-Indian Words and Phrases, and of Kindred Terms, Etymological, Historical, Geographical and Discursive*. New Delhi: Munshiram Manoharlal.

Zabbāl, Salīm
1965 Say'ūn al-bāb al-janūbī li-l-Rub' al-Khālī tarakahā yad al-taṭawwur. *al-'Arabī* (81): 68–89.

Zayd, 'Alī Muḥammad
1981 *Mu'tazilat al-Yaman: dawlat al-Hādī wa-fikruh*. Ṣan'ā': Markaz al-Dirāsāt wa-l-Buḥūth al-Yamanī; Beirut: Dār al-'Awda.

al-Zayn, 'Abd Allāh Yaḥyā
1995 *al-Yaman wa-wasā'iluh al-i'lāmiyya*. Beirut: Dār al-Fikr al-Mu'āṣir.

el Zein, Abdul Hamid M.
1974 *The Sacred Meadows: A Structural Analysis of Religious Symbolism in an East African Town*. Evanston, Ill.: Northwestern University Press.

Zolberg, Aristide
1982 Contemporary Transnational Migrations in Historical Perspective: Patterns and Dilemmas. In *U.S. Immigration and Refugee Policy: Global and Domestic Issues*. Mary M. Kritz, ed. Lexington, Mass.: Lexington Books.
1983 The Formation of New States as a Refugee-Generating Process. *Annals of the American Academy of Social and Political Science* 467 (May): 24–38.

Index

Page references in italics refer to illustrations.

Text:	10/13 Galliard
Display:	Galliard
Compositor:	Integrated Composition Systems
Indexer:	Roberta Engleman
Cartographer:	Bill Nelson
Printer and Binder:	Sheridan Books, Inc.